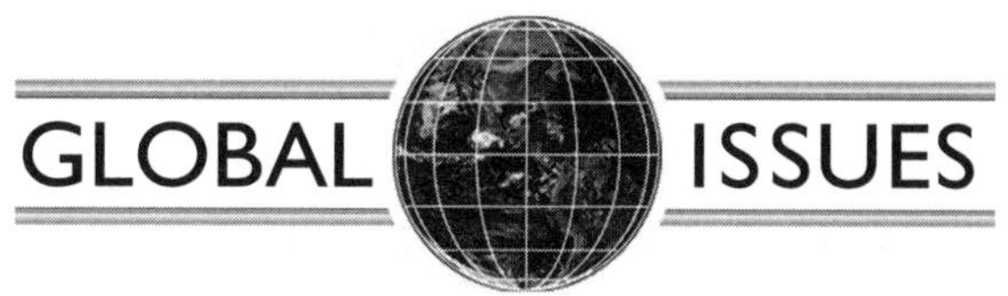

AMERICA'S ROLE IN THE WORLD

Phillip Margulies

Foreword by James M. Goldgeier
George Washington University

GLOBAL ISSUES: AMERICA'S ROLE IN THE WORLD

Facts On File, Inc.
An imprint of Infobase Publishing
132 West 31st Street
New York NY 10001

Library of Congress Cataloging-in-Publication Data
Margulies, Phillip, 1952–
America's role in the world / Phillip Margulies ; foreword by James M. Goldgeier.
p. cm.—(Global issues)
Includes bibliographical references and index.
ISBN: 978-0-8160-7611-6
1. United States—Foreign relations. 2. United States—Foreign public opinion—History. I. Title.

JZ1480.M327 2009
327.73—dc22 2008032102

Facts On File books are available at special discounts when purchased in bulk quantities for businesses, associations, institutions, or sales promotions. Please call our Special Sales Department in New York at (212) 967-8800 or (800) 322-8755.

You can find Facts On File on the World Wide Web at http://www.factsonfile.com

Text design by Erika K. Arroyo
Cover design by Salvatore Luongo
Diagrams by Dale Williams and Melissa Ericksen

Printed in the United States of America

MP MSRF 10 9 8 7 6 5 4 3 2 1

This book is printed on acid-free paper and contains 30 percent postconsumer recycled content.

CONTENTS

PART III: Research Tools

Foreword

"Nearly two decades after the collapse of the Soviet Union," Phillip Margulies reminds us, "there is little agreement about America's role in the world, what it really is, and what it ought to be, and the question seems more urgent than ever."

America knew what its purpose was during the cold war: to contain the threat posed by the Soviet Union. Straddling the Eurasian landmass, the USSR competed with the United States militarily, politically, economically, and ideologically across the globe. For 40 years, the cold war dominated American thinking about foreign policy.

Then communism collapsed. First regimes in eastern Europe crumbled, and then in late 1991, the USSR itself was gone. The United States was now the global superpower, with some analysts comparing its standing to that of Rome 2,000 years earlier. But the United States no longer had a clear direction. America had extraordinary power, but it lacked a sense of purpose. Even when there were tremendous disagreements over Vietnam or Central America during the cold war, Democrats and Republicans alike believed in the need to contain Soviet expansionism. That bipartisan consensus in foreign policy disappeared when the Soviet Union did.

After the attacks of September 11, 2001, many expected bipartisanship to reemerge. But the country remains as divided as ever about how to think about world politics. Why, when, and where should the United States use military force? How should America respond to globalization? Do the institutions created by the United States after World War II—such as the United Nations, the International Monetary Fund, and the World Bank—still work, and if not, what can be done to fix them? These are the types of questions that should be at the heart of our national debate.

To engage in that conversation, students need to be able to put the past 20 years into historical perspective. And by helping students understand the development of more than two centuries of American foreign policy,

Margulies does just that. In particular, he traces the roles of religion and democracy, two powerful factors in America's approach to the world.

From the beginning the United States saw itself as a new kind of country, untainted by the politics of Europe. Most Americans have believed that how other countries are organized politically—in particular, whether they are democratic or not—affects their foreign policy behavior. That does not mean that the United States has always supported democracy elsewhere, but it does mean that its foreign policy was different from the traditional balance-of-power diplomacy of the European great powers.

Once the Soviet Union was gone, the United States emphasized democracy promotion even more, for example, by fostering political and economic freedom in formerly communist parts of Europe. In the 1990s, America used its military for humanitarian purposes, including feeding people in Somalia, protecting Muslim populations in Bosnia and Kosovo, and restoring an elected leader in Haiti.

The emphasis on freedom became a centerpiece of George W. Bush's second term in office. But because of the nation's divisions over the wisdom of the war in Iraq, many Americans are once again debating how active their country should be in promoting democracy elsewhere, and what is the best way to do so. That is a debate as old as the republic itself. In the 19th century, it was a debate that had little impact in the world, since the United States was too weak outside of its own neighborhood. But once the United States became a major world power at the start of the 20th century, the debate had huge practical significance. And so it does today.

The United States may be the world's leading power militarily, economically, diplomatically, and even culturally, but it is not the only major country. How other parts of the world develop affects what America is able to accomplish. And as we gaze out at the world, there are many uncertainties.

Europe has made dramatic strides in forging greater unity in recent decades. A continent torn by war in the first half of the 20th century created a unique institution—known today as the European Union—that stretches from Ireland to Romania, from Portugal to Estonia. In the heart of Europe, one can travel from country to country without having to change currency and old border posts have been dismantled. It is a remarkable development, but one of the great unknowns is whether Europeans will remain America's closest allies or whether growing differences across the Atlantic will overwhelm old ties.

In Asia, two large countries have emerged as economic powerhouses: India and China. In these countries, hundreds of millions have been lifted out of poverty in recent decades. But hundreds of millions remain among the world's poorest people. India is the world's most populous democracy and is often held up as a model for multicultural tolerance. China has combined capitalism with an authoritarian political structure. Each now has a significant impact on world politics, particularly as their middle classes consume more and more, helping to drive up the price of oil and contributing to global warming.

Much of the discussion in U.S. foreign policy circles regarding China centers on whether it will contentedly become more integrated into global institutions or challenge the United States and seek to overturn the post–World War II American-led order. History suggests that countries that increase their economic and military power are not satisfied with the existing order, but many analysts believe China has much at stake in current world structures and will pursue a more peaceful course than rising powers did in previous centuries.

With the collapse of the Soviet Union, Russia's western borders are farther from the center of Europe than they have been for centuries. The country suffered an economic depression of monumental proportions in the 1990s. The population declined dramatically and is projected to continue to fall in the coming decades. With high oil and gas prices, Russia's coffers are now full, and under former president, now premier, Vladimir Putin, the country began to play a more forceful role in world affairs after its decade of decline. The United States sought to promote democracy in Russia in the 1990s, but it learned how hard it is to transform another country's institutions—or at least it should have learned this lesson.

Students will greatly benefit from the document section in part II of the book that points them toward such classic American foreign policy pronouncements as George Washington's Farewell Address, James Monroe's declaration regarding European colonization in the Americas, and General George Marshall's 1947 speech at Harvard University announcing an aid program for a devastated European continent in the aftermath of World War II. The book also includes links to documents from America's friends and adversaries abroad, such as British prime minister Winston Churchill, Soviet premier Nikita Khrushchev, and al-Qaeda leader Osama bin Laden.

Finally, part III of the book includes a useful guide to research. High school is a vitally important time for students to learn how to conduct their own independent projects. Learning how to formulate a question and then how to conduct serious research to find the answers are skills that students must learn in order to succeed in the classroom. It is important not to prejudge the outcomes, but rather to look at different arguments and a range of evidence before drawing conclusions.

AMERICA'S ROLE IN THE WORLD

We live in a globalized world. We are linked electronically to our counterparts across the globe, and more and more people are able to explore disparate cultures. Even as other nations become stronger and more active globally, the United States will remain the world's leader for years to come. It can lead responsibly only if its citizens are well educated and if its foreign policies are well informed.

The future direction of American foreign policy is hotly contested. This book helps students understand those debates so that they can think about how to research topics that interest them and can start becoming more informed citizens who will participate in the national conversation about America's role in the world.

—James M. Goldgeier
George Washington University
Senior Fellow, Council on Foreign Relations

PART I

At Issue

1

Introduction

THE POST–WORLD WAR II WORLD

For around 40 years, most American schoolchildren, if asked who was the leader of the Free World, would have raised their hands and answered, the president. These two phrases described the same reality. Leader of the Free World was the job description of the president of the United States.

By implication, it summed up the role of the United States. It, too, was the leader of the best and luckiest of the three worlds our planet was said to contain. The Free World consisted of the United States and its allies, mostly democracies. It was a realm of vigorous political debate and respect for human rights, not perfect but always improving. It was the necessary opposing force to communism. Fighting communism was the explanation for practically every move the United States made abroad.

Opposed to the Free World was the communist bloc—the Soviet Union, the People's Republic of China, and their allies. It was a vast domain of tyranny and lies, bent on enveloping the globe, an evil empire, as Ronald Reagan described the Soviets in 1982. The people of the communist bloc were fed propaganda in place of news. They were denied freedom of speech. They lived in fear of the secret police. They were poor, while their governments spent a huge proportion of their countries' wealth on weapons.

Finally, there was a Third World consisting mostly of weak countries, many of them former colonies that had recently achieved independence. Third World countries often allied themselves with either the Free World or the communist bloc.

In high school and college, American students would gain a more nuanced understanding of the world, one that would embrace the view that the United States, like other countries, conducts its foreign policy in its own self-interest. Not all of the United States's cold war allies were democracies—some were oppressive dictatorships, which the United States supported because they were anticommunist or because they served American interests that had nothing to do with ideology. When Reagan called the Soviet Union an evil empire, he was turning around a charge that communists frequently made against the United States; the Soviet Union and its allies had always called Americans imperialists. Outside the United States, the accusation looked plausible: The United States dominated much of the world and derived economic advantages from its international power.

Yet, amid this realism, students would hold onto the concept of the three worlds of the cold war, which was a rough description of the international balance of forces. Many realists and idealists—even inhabitants of communist countries—agreed that however one might quarrel with the wisdom or altruism of the small wars the United States conducted in the name of anticommunism, a U.S. victory was preferable to the alternative. The West as a whole was still freer than the communist bloc, where people *were* spied on by their neighbors and signs of liberalization were crushed with guns and tanks, as happened in Hungary in 1956 and Czechoslovakia in 1968. Communism also failed as an economic system. Communist economies grew more slowly than capitalist economies, and attempts to impose communism led to shortages, stagnation, and even mass starvation, as in the Ukraine in the 1930s and China during the 1950s.[1]

In 1991, the United States quietly won the cold war. The Soviet empire's moribund economy, inefficient government, and huge military expenditures had weakened it from within. When its leaders showed signs that they were no longer willing to hold it together by force, it split apart. Countries that had been under its domination took steps to become democracies with free-market economies.

THE POST–COLD WAR WORLD

The end of the Soviet Union was preceded by an opening up of Soviet society and a thaw—an improvement in relations between the Soviet Union and the United States. It may be truer to say that the cold war ended gradually in the late 1980s, rather than overnight in 1991. Still, no one could know, before the collapse, that the thaw would be permanent, and leaders in the West were at first skeptical.

In December 1988, as Ronald Reagan's successor, George H. W. Bush, prepared to take office, Soviet president Mikhail Gorbachev spoke at the United Nations. "Force or the threat of force neither can or should be the instruments of foreign policy," said Gorbachev.[2] With this statement, he rejected the doctrine of his predecessors, who had claimed the right to intervene militarily to keep eastern Europe in the Soviet bloc. To show that he was serious, Gorbachev announced a cut of half a million men from the Soviet Army and a withdrawal of 50,000 men and 5,000 tanks from Soviet forces in eastern Europe.[3]

The United States remained suspicious, as well as uneasy about the change in a balance of power that senior diplomats had lived with most of their lives. In January 1989, U.S. National Security Advisor Brent Scowcroft accused Gorbachev of "making trouble within the Western alliance" by means of "a peace offensive."[4]

In Europe, 1989 would be called the year of miracles, as people and governments in the Soviet orbit—the Soviet satellite states of eastern Europe—took Gorbachev at his word, and it turned out that he had meant what he said. Hungarian troops began removing the barbed wire along the country's frontier with Austria. For the first time since the early 1960s, East Berliners were allowed into West Berlin. The Baltic States, Lithuania, Estonia, and Latvia, parts of the Soviet Union, asserted their sovereignty by declaring that their laws overrode Soviet laws. In Poland free elections were held; the anticommunist Solidarity party won, and no tanks rolled into the country. In November 1989 the Berlin Wall fell. The Romanians overthrew and executed their dictator, Nicolae Ceauşescu, whose rule in the 1980s had become increasingly oppressive and brutal. Free elections were held in Czechoslovakia.

Meanwhile, people in the various republics of the Soviet Union itself—Georgia, Ukraine, Moldova, Byelorussia, and those in Central Asia—began clamoring for independence, wishing to follow the example of the Baltic States. In many cases, local government officials were sympathetic to the nationalist movements; their loyalty to the Soviet Union could no longer be relied on.

By 1990, the West could see a disintegration of the Soviet Union as possible but not necessarily desirable. Some of the post-Soviet states would have nuclear weapons, and their behavior might be unpredictable; perhaps there would be civil wars as newly independent countries fought one another over boundaries. It might be better to face a weakened but stable and intact Soviet Union. Western governments debated the advisability of negotiating a so-called grand bargain under which the Soviet Union would be given financial assistance—around $30 billion a year—to help it restructure its economy. The foreign aid that might have saved the Soviet Union never came, however. This was in part because Gorbachev was struggling to maintain power in his own government and was not in a position to guarantee the concessions that would have been a part of the plan. In part it was because Western countries, including the United States, were in the middle of a recession, and it would have been politically difficult for their governments to devote so much money to preserving the integrity of their historical enemy.[5]

In 1991, with the Soviet economy in crisis, hard-liners in Gorbachev's government attempted a coup, which they hoped would have the support of the Russian people. The coup failed. But the post to which Gorbachev was restored no longer meant very much. He lacked the loyalty of his immediate subordinates as well as the loyalty of the leaders of the various Soviet republics.

In December 1991, Gorbachev gave a speech announcing the formal dissolution of the Soviet Union, which he had tried to prevent. Though a hero in the West, Gorbachev was by this time unpopular in his own country, due to the havoc of the Soviet economy. While acknowledging his mistakes, he asked his people to recognize what he had achieved at the cost of the dictatorial powers that had been his when he assumed office six years earlier.

> *The totalitarian system which deprived the country of an opportunity to become successful and prosperous long ago has been eliminated. A breakthrough has been achieved on the way to democratic changes. Free elections, freedom of the press, religious freedoms, representative organs of power, a multiparty (system) became a reality; human rights are recognized as the supreme principle.*[6]

Earlier, one of Gorbachev's advisers had noted another accomplishment of the Gorbachev years: "We are going to do the worst thing we possibly can to America—we are going to take away their enemy."[7]

AMERICA'S IDENTITY CRISIS

The end of the cold war caused rejoicing but also confusion among U.S. foreign policy experts. America had indeed lost its enemy. Its role as leader of the Free World, as the container of communism, was over. What would its role be now? What was its mission in the world? Certainly, it would have to be different from what it had been since the late 1940s—its purpose would no longer be to contain the Soviet Union. Would another power arise to challenge it, once again creating a bipolar world? Would the United States gradually subside into one of several major powers in a multipolar world such as had existed before World War II? Would the United States remain the sole superpower, using its overwhelming military superiority to spread the principles of democracy, human rights, and free trade, or would it use that power to ensure that its people continued to consume more than their share of the world's resources—or both?

Introduction

The debate about America's post–cold war role intensified after the attacks of September 11, 2001, with President George W. Bush's announcement of a war on terror. In October 2001 the United States invaded Afghanistan, which had been a home base to the leaders of the 9/11 attackers, and installed a new government there. Most governments around the world agreed that the move was justified. The Taliban—Afghanistan's leaders—had provided a safe haven to the terrorists who had plotted to attack the United States and refused to hand over the terrorists' leader, Osama bin Laden. The United States was clearly acting in retaliation and in self-defense.

The United States's next move was more controversial. Warning of the threat to the United States posed by the possibility that a rogue state might give weapons of mass destruction (WMD) to terrorists, Bush asserted a new foreign policy principle, which became known as the Bush doctrine: The United States would reserve the right to make war against emerging threats to its security. It would not wait for a country to attack or even for an attack to be imminent. At the same time Bush announced that the United States would spread democracy around the world so as to "drain the swamps," which were said to breed discontent and terrorism.[8] In the furtherance of these policies, the United States invaded Iraq in 2003, quickly destroying its army but becoming involved in a long, violent, and possibly unsuccessful occupation.

The quick collapse of Iraq's regular armed forces vividly demonstrated America's military strength, and in its wake several books appeared announcing a new age of American imperial dominance. The development was greeted with approval in Niall Ferguson's *Colossus* and Michael Mandelbaum's *The Case for Goliath* and with disapproval in others such as Chalmers Johnson's *The Sorrows of Empire.* These authors often began by emphasizing the power of the United States, but they ended by questioning whether the United States has the staying power to achieve its goals. It seems the authors were responding to late-breaking news; by the time they were in print, the war was going badly. By 2004, many of those who had favored toppling Saddam Hussein's government, including such staunch Republicans as former speaker of the house Newt Gingrich and neoconservative William Kristol, considered that the occupation of Iraq had been badly mismanaged.[9] By 2005, as Iraq descended into civil war, continued U.S. involvement had become deeply unpopular with the American people.

The war was even more unpopular in the Middle East and among America's traditional allies. So was the United States itself. A 2005 poll conducted in Europe by the Pew Global Attitudes Project found that since 2000, positive opinions of the United States and its policies had plummeted in the Muslim world and in western Europe (though not in eastern Europe). "Anti-Americanism in Europe, the Middle East and Asia," had "surged as a result of the U.S. war in Iraq."[10]

Even before the 2003 invasion of Iraq, the 9/11 attacks had evoked a new kind of self-doubt among Americans. The former leaders of the Free World, confident of their good intentions, were asking themselves, "Why do they hate us?" President Bush asked this question in a September 20, 2001, speech to Congress, and answered: "They hate our freedoms—our freedom of religion, our freedom of speech, our freedom to vote and assemble and disagree with each other." He added: "They want to overthrow existing governments in many Muslim countries, such as Egypt, Saudi Arabia, and Jordan."[11] The answer had a familiar sound to American ears, since the preservation of freedom is almost invariably one of the reasons that U.S. presidents give when making a case for war. However, in this instance it did not quite make sense, because the governments the terrorists wished to overthrow were not democracies.

After Bush's speech a great many newspaper and magazine articles appeared with the title "Why Do They Hate Us?" trying to give a better explanation. They have been appearing periodically ever since. The pronoun "they" does not always refer to terrorists or Islamic extremists. Sometimes it refers to other foreigners critical of American policy, including the citizens of western Europe.[12]

Is hostility to the United States simply a function of the fact that it is powerful and its actions are bound to offend some as well as please others? How much of the impact of the United States on the world results from its foreign policy and how much from the sheer size of its economy? And should the world be grateful for or resent America's cultural influences—violent, sex-charged Hollywood movies, rock and hip-hop, fast-food restaurants, Disneyland, the culture of consumption and disposability? Is America a savior or a threat, the world's police force, its secret government, or a power in decline, desperately trying to cover up its internal weaknesses by brandishing its military assets? Nearly two decades after the collapse of the Soviet Union, there is little agreement about America's role in the world, what it really is and what it ought to be, and the question seems more urgent than ever. This book cannot provide a definitive answer, but it can outline the various arguments in the debate.

---

[1] For Ukraine, see "Ukraine Wants Soviet-Era Famine Deemed Genocide." *Boston Globe,* November 25, 2007. Available online. URL: http://www.boston.com/news/world/articles/2007/11/25/ukraine_wants_soviet_era_famine_deemed_ genocide/; for China, see Vaclav Smil, "China's Great Famine: 40 Years Later." *BMJ* 319 (December 18, 1999): 1,619–1,621. *Government and Politics: Introduction to China's Political System—China: A Teaching Work-*

book. Columbia University East Asian Curriculum Project. Available online. URL: http://afe.easia.columbia.edu/china/gov/backgrnd.htm.

[2] Martin Walker. *The Cold War.* New York: Henry Holt and Company, 1993, p. 308.

[3] ———. *The Cold War,* pp. 308–309.

[4] ———. *The Cold War,* p. 310.

[5] "Liberalization and Struggle in Communist Countries." Encyclopaedia Britannica Online. Available online. URL: http://www.britannica.com/eb/article-32994/international-relations. Accessed October 3, 2007.

[6] "Resignation Cites Achievements; Last USSR Leader Recalls a Time of Reforms, Freedoms." *Chicago Tribune,* December 26, 1991, p. 4.

[7] Martin Walker. "The USA This Week." *Manchester Guardian Weekly,* August 2, 1992.

[8] George Cahlink. "Rumsfeld Pledges to 'Drain the Swamps' of Terrorists." Government Executive.com (September 18, 2001). Available online. URL: http://www.govexec.com/dailyfed/0901/091801g2.htm. Accessed October 3, 2007. When U.S. secretary of defense Donald Rumsfeld introduced this phrase in the context of terrorism, it meant a policy of taking action against states (like Afghanistan in 2001) that supported terrorists, but the phrase was later used by commentators and politicians to denote the Bush administration's policy of promoting democracy to combat terrorism.

[9] Kelley Eaucar Vlahos. "Bush Supporters Question Iraq War Tactics." Foxnews.com (September 12, 2005). Accessed October 3, 2007. Available online. URL: http://www.foxnews.com/story/0,2933,169041,00.html.

[10] Pew Global Attitudes Project. "16-Nation Pew Global Attitudes Survey: U.S. Image Up Slightly, but Still Negative." Available online. URL: http://pewglobal.org/reports/display.php?ReportID=247. Accessed October 3, 2007.

[11] "President Declares 'Freedom at War with Fear.'" Address to Joint Session of Congress and the American People, September 20, 2001. Available online. URL: http://www.whitehouse.gov/news/releases/2001/09/20010920-8.html. Accessed October 3, 2007.

[12] Walter Russell Mead. "Why Do They Hate Us? Two Books Take Aim at French Anti-Americanism." *Foreign Affairs* (March/April 2003). Available online. URL: http://www.foreignaffairs.org/20030301fareviewessay10345/walter-russell-mead/why-do-they-hate-us-two-books-take-aim-at-french-anti-americanism.html. Accessed October 4, 2007.

2

Focus on the United States

AMERICA'S IDEA OF ITSELF

A country's ideas about itself affect its actions on the world stage. Even when they do not explain its foreign policy—which always has many causes—a country's ideas are important because they are used to mobilize public support for its policies and justify them before other nations.

America's Sense of Mission

The United States has been a fortunate country since the moment of its founding. Distant from the Eastern Hemisphere and a strong nation relative to its neighbors, the United States grew quickly without the burden of maintaining a large army. It suffered its greatest military losses ever in the war it had with itself between 1860 and 1865. The United States has been the world's leading economy since the early 20th century and the world's leading military power since 1945. Its citizens make up around 5 percent of the world's population but consume far more than their share of the world's resources, including 25 percent of its yearly energy production. They enjoy a great deal of personal and political freedom. While other nations, including the worlds' next most prosperous and powerful—France, Germany, Russia, China, Japan—have endured terrible privation and catastrophic warfare within living memory, the United States since independence has suffered only a handful of skirmishes with foreign antagonists on its own territory. One reason that Pearl Harbor and 9/11 so shocked the nation was that these events were deeply contrary to the experience of the American people. Even in the two world wars, the United States suffered a fraction of the casualties endured by its enemies and allies.

Polls tell us that Americans are a religious people, with nine out of ten of them believing in God. Naturally, they assume that there must be a reason for their country's prominence. Or, as one study of our national mythology puts it

> *[Americans] believe America has a mission and that its destiny is not simply to be rich and powerful and big, but to be so for some God-given purpose. Few believe that America arrived at its present state of wealth and power by accident.*[1]

The commonest idea of America's destiny is easy to glean from the speeches of American politicians, American school textbooks, or the answers American citizens give to man-in-the-street interviews: America's mission is to be an example of freedom, democracy, and equality, and possibly to spread those blessings abroad.

Roots of the American Identity

The United States's self-image as a bastion of freedom has several sources and ingredients; each is linked to a phase in its history. Over the years they have been fused into a powerful myth familiar to anyone who has attended an American elementary school. (A myth, it should be noted, may contain some truth, but it goes beyond the truth. It is a story that helps people make sense of the world and enshrines their values.)

One source of America's myth of itself is the history of the European discovery and conquest of the Americas. Sixteenth-century Europeans, amazed at the existence of two continents unknown to the ancient geographers, called it the New World. Since the North American continent was thinly settled and its native people had a culture of villages, hunting, and small-scale farming, it is part of the myth that America was a virgin land, free of the Old World's burden of history. Treating the Native peoples as if they were part of the landscape—a wild people—made it easier to dismiss their claims to the land. Modern historians and school textbooks acknowledge the flaws in this view. However, after debating the term *discovery* and discussing pre-Columbian cultures, they still use *New World,* which after all contains an emotional truth: It expresses the feelings of Europeans confronting the Americas. The myth of the New World continues to be reinforced by the flow of immigrants to the United States, each of whom is in some sense making a new start in the land of second chances—a new world still no matter how many people already live here.

The colonists' Protestant heritage provided a second ingredient in America's myth. Many of the English settlers were profoundly steeped in the Old Testament. Starting a new life in a frightening environment, they took the ancient

Israelites as a model of a strong-willed people who had stuck together in the face of adversity. The Israelites had made a covenant with God and had been given a promised land—which, though it was a gift, they had to fight for. The settlers saw themselves as another chosen people in a new promised land, who had to hold fast to their own contract with God. As John Winthrop, a leader of the English Puritans' 1630 expedition to the Massachusetts Bay Colony, put it in his sermon aboard the Puritan flagship, the *Arbella:* "Thus stands the cause between God and us. We have entered into a Covenant with Him for this work. We have taken out a commission. . . . For we must consider that we shall be as a city upon a hill. The eyes of all people are upon us."[2]

The mission as envisioned by Winthrop in 1630 had little to do with democracy or equality. He opened his sermon by noting that "God Almighty . . . has so disposed of the condition of mankind, as in all times some must be rich, some poor; some high and eminent in power and dignity; others mean and in submission."[3]

The mission changed—became a mission about democracy, equality, and rights—under the influence of two developments in the Old World. First, there was the long struggle between the British parliament and the monarchy in the 1600s, which led to a new conception of the relationship between government and its citizens, and, second, the European Enlightenment of the 1700s, an intellectual movement that proposed many new ideas about society. When the colonists declared their independence from Great Britain, they did so with a document declaring that "governments are instituted, among men, deriving their just powers from the consent of the governed," that human beings are "created equal" and had "certain inalienable rights" including "life, liberty, and the pursuit of happiness." In the 1776 pamphlet *Common Sense,* written to encourage Americans to fight for independence, Thomas Paine joined the theme of revolution to the idea that America was a virgin land: "We have it in our power to begin the world over again. A situation, similar to the present, hath not happened since the days of Noah until now. The birthday of a new world is at hand."[4]

The principles set forth in the Declaration of Independence were among Europe's most radical ideas. Taking the long view of human history, they remain revolutionary. Human rights and equality have not been the basis of most human societies. The country that emerged saw itself and was seen by other countries as a revolutionary nation based on "equality of condition,"[5] despite the fact that the African-American slaves living in the new country continued to be denied freedom and equal rights and other aspects of the American social order underwent only slow change after independence. The Constitution, the Bill of Rights, and the state governments were vehicles intended to turn the principles set forth in the Declaration of Independence into practical realities. The leaders of the United States justified their behavior based on those principles, and foreigners who criticized the country did so either for its folly of promoting equal rights and self-government or for its failure to live up to those values. Critics usually had it both ways. They emphasized the bad results of democracy and the hypocrisy inherent in America's treatment of African Americans and Native Americans.

Visitors to the Fledgling Democracy

In the first half of the 19th century, a number of foreign tourists wrote books about their travels in the United States, describing what a democratic society looked like. The verdict usually depended upon the political point of view of the traveler. They came with increasing frequency in the 1820s and 1830s, when the right to vote, initially granted only to men of property, was gradually expanded to include all adult males in the United States. Harriet Martineau, an Englishwoman who favored more democracy in England, liked what she saw; noting that by her time the United States had lasted for more than half a century she remarked:

> *The experiment of the particular constitution of the United States may fail; but the great principle which, whether successfully or not, it strives to embody,—the capacity of mankind for self-government,—is established for ever. . . . If a revolution were to take place to-morrow in the United States, it remains an historical fact that, for half a century, a people has been self-governed."*[6]

Frances Trollope, an Englishwoman who favored inherited privilege in her own country, dwelled on the uncouth manners of Americans; they spat tobacco juice on the carpet, they were overfamiliar with strangers, and they considered it beneath their dignity to say thank you. The damage was due to the fact that they believed the words of Thomas Jefferson, the third president of the United States. She cited

> *. . . that phrase of mischievous sophistry, "all men are born free and equal." This false and futile axiom, which has done, is doing, and will do so much harm to this fine country, came from Jefferson; and truly his life was a glorious commentary upon it. I pretend not to criticise his written works, but commonsense enables me to pronounce this, his favourite maxim, false.*[7]

Jefferson, Trollope pointed out, was a slave-owner, and his own children by his female slaves were also "the lawful slaves of their father, and worked in his house and plantations as such . . ." What better proof could there be that all men were not born free and equal?

The United States's idea of itself, as promulgated ever since in Fourth of July speeches, in children's textbooks, and as reasons for courage on battlefields, was by then in place. The United States, to its defenders here and in Europe, was a country carved out of a wilderness, free of the Old World's burden of history—kings, aristocrats, strict social hierarchies—where a constitutional government based on democracy and human rights could grow. Thomas Jefferson called it "the world's best hope." President Abraham Lincoln called it "the last best hope of earth"[8] and maintained, in the Gettysburg Address, that the Civil War was being fought so that "government of the people, by the people and for the people shall not perish from this earth."[9] In an expansive mood, Americans saw themselves as having a mission to spread their values and institutions.

Freedom and America's Wars

American politicians speak as if the United States goes to war only for two reasons: To respond to an attack or to preserve freedom. In practice, they seem to believe that America's wars are always necessary for both these reasons, since only the enemies of freedom would wish to attack us. In a sense this belief reflects the reality of American democracy, since democracies must get their people's consent for war, and consent is more easily obtained if people feel their deepest values are at stake. However, it also distorts reality, since the defense of freedom has been used to justify wars that really had other purposes.

In the early 19th century, when the United States regarded itself as the world's only democracy, practically every conflict the United States engaged in was seen as an effort to protect democracy, while the push westward was viewed as an effort to extend democracy's reach. America *was* democracy. The Mexican-American War (1846–48), which added a large amount of territory, was controversial in the United States: Opponents considered it an act of theft and saw it as a plot to strengthen the South, but advocates defended the war on the grounds that Mexico's least democratic forces had won control of its government. The Spanish-American War (1898), in which the United States evicted Spain from Cuba and the Philippines, looks in retrospect like a shameless land-grab—but at the time it was seen as a war to free Cuba from the despotism of Spain.

On April 2, 1917, President Woodrow Wilson officially brought the United States into World War I, which had been ravaging Europe and its colonial possessions since 1914. The immediate grounds for the declaration of war was the torpedoing of American merchant ships by German submarines. The strategic aim was to prevent a single nation, Germany, from dominating Europe and perhaps becoming the leading sea power as well.[10] Wilson, however, as an American citizen and an American president, felt constrained to make democracy the main issue. Thanks to the Russian Revolution, which had occurred in February, all three of the United States's new allies—France, Britain, and Russia—could now be characterized as democracies. In his address to Congress, Wilson said that the war would help make the world "safe for democracy," and added that the defense of democracy benefited international peace. "A steadfast concert for peace can never be maintained except by a partnership of democratic nations. No autocratic government could be trusted to keep faith within it or observe its covenants."[11]

The proposition that democracies are unwarlike or at least do not make war on each other was originally voiced by the philosopher Immanuel Kant. It is sometimes called the democratic peace theory.[12] It has recently been invoked by U.S. presidents from both parties, and it played a major role in George W. Bush's foreign policy. By linking the humanitarian benefits of spreading democracy to U.S. self-interest in preventing wars, this theory gives powerful support to the idea of a mission to spread democracy.

In World War II, the United States's main adversaries, Japan and Germany, were totalitarian, militarized societies. So Americans viewed this war, too, as a war on behalf of democratic principles. In January 1941, almost a year before the Japanese attack on Pearl Harbor, when the war was already raging in Europe, President Franklin D. Roosevelt told Congress and the nation, "Armed defense of democratic existence is now being gallantly waged in four continents."[13]

The cold war, too, was regarded in the United States as a conflict between freedom and tyranny. When the U.S. government helped to depose democratically elected leaders (as it did in Iran in 1953 and in Chile in 1973) it did so clandestinely, avoiding debate at home. The Vietnam War, which dragged on for more than 10 years, lost support in the United States in part because many Americans began to believe that the South Vietnamese government, which the United States was fighting to preserve, was corrupt and undemocratic.

In post–cold war conflicts such as the U.S. invasion of Panama in 1989 and Iraq in 1991 and 2003, the American people were reminded that the leaders of these countries were tyrants. More recently the invasion of Iraq has been justified as one move in a great plan to make America safe by democratizing the Middle East.

There is an implicit threat in America's sense of mission that is hard for Americans to see. Most countries are not democracies, and the United States cannot have hostile relations with all of them. Yet, many Americans believe that it is all right to wage war on a country that is not democratic, since the people in such a country are not really represented by their government and would only benefit from liberation. This belief is used as a justification virtually whenever the United States goes to war. However, it has not been, and cannot be, a regular basis for America's peacetime foreign policy.

America and Classical Liberalism

The principles of democracy and equality enshrined in the Declaration of Independence are two elements in a three-part system of beliefs often called liberalism. The third element is a belief in free-market principles—a belief that nearly found its way into the Declaration as well, since the phrase "life, liberty and the pursuit of happiness" is an alteration of the phrase "life, liberty and property," which the philosopher John Locke had named as mankind's inalienable rights.

Today it is usual to speak of liberalism as part of the philosophy of the Democratic Party. In TV ads for Republican candidates, the term *liberalism* is usually linked to the phrases "big government" and "tax and spend." However, to historians and political scientists liberalism denotes a program that has been advocated or at least been given lip service to by a broad range of Americans from all parties since the 19th century. Classical liberalism is both a set of ideas and a program for action. It is the real-world version of values enshrined in American myth.

The philosopher Ludwig von Mises, cited by Reagan as an influence on his thinking,[14] described classical liberalism as a political program formulated by the philosophers, sociologists, and economists of the 18th and 19th centuries, one that "served as a guide to social policy first in England and the United States, then on the European continent, and finally in the other parts of the inhabited world as well."[15] Classical liberalism—so-called to distinguish it from modern liberalism, which favors government attempts to redistribute wealth—is a secular political philosophy that values and seeks to ensure human beings' equality before the law and self-government through democratic institutions. It supports individual freedom of thought and action and favors a minimum of government interference in human action.

Focus on the United States

Classical liberalism grew along with the expansion of trade and the growth of modern capitalism. It evolved not only in opposition to earlier ideas such as the divine right of kings and inherited privilege, but also to mercantilism, the economic theory that governments should closely manage their citizens' trade to the benefit of the crown. Adam Smith, whose theories as embodied in his book *The Wealth of Nations* are often citied as a justification for laissez-faire economic policies, is an important liberal philosopher. Classical liberalism sees people as equal before the law, but not in their possessions—indeed, classical liberalism protects the right of property, no matter how unequally distributed. If a millionaire has a dispute with a pauper the law should deal with them impartially—but poverty in and of itself should not concern the government or the law.

Classical liberalism is the dominant political philosophy in the world today, thanks partly to its merits and partly to the success of capitalism and the dominance of the United States. However, it has many competitors and rivals. One is modern liberalism, which views untrammeled economic power (as of big corporations) and sharp, persistent inequalities of wealth as dangers to a free society and seeks to change them through government action. Modern liberalism also emphasizes problems—for example, global warming—whose solution requires restrictions on individual freedom of action (such as a carbon tax or a requirement that cars have a minimum gas mileage). However, modern liberalism shares with classical liberalism a belief that government derives its authority from autonomous rational individuals—the human being with rights, an ability to make decisions, and an ability to join in voluntary associations—and the belief that human rationality and rights are universal. These are ideas most Americans share whether they label themselves liberal or conservative. They are also modern ideas to which most of the world pays lip service, thanks in part to the success of the countries that have espoused liberal values, countries that were victorious in World War I, World War II, and the cold war.

Liberalism competes with views of the world that question whether the individual can be the source of authority. These competing worldviews see authority as coming from somewhere else (from tradition, as conservatives do; or from God, as fundamentalists do), question human equality (as racists do), or believe that liberal values are not universal but are merely an outgrowth of modern economic conditions and justify the privileges of the ruling class (as Marxists do). Psychological theories such as those embodied in behaviorism and Freudianism, which question human beings' ability to make rational independent decisions, also have a potential to undermine liberalism. All these ideas and philosophies have had plenty of adherents in the

United States, of course, and some have provided a strong counterforce to liberalism, but liberalism has been the most persistent and public tradition; it is the one enshrined in the country's institutions and founding documents.

Liberal values are so deeply embedded in American thinking that it is hard for Americans to understand that not everyone shares them. "We hold these truths to be self-evident," wrote Jefferson; yet to Frances Trollope they were nonsense. To an Islamic fundamentalist and to many other devout people, they are immoral, insofar as they make human beings the ultimate source of governmental authority, which, according to their beliefs, must come from God as embodied in scripture and interpreted by the clergy. To conservatives such as the British political philosopher Edmund Burke (1729–97) and the French political philosopher Joseph de Maistre (1753–1821), liberalism is dangerous because it ignores the importance of tradition and religious authority in securing human rights, safety, and order. From time to time, people in American and western European societies have objected to the liberal tradition, in particular its excessively individualistic aspects; they have pointed to the petty selfishness, futility, and loneliness that can follow when people look only to their own pursuit of happiness. Critics have called for an ethos that places a greater emphasis on community and responsibility. The hippie movement of the 1960s expressed both tendencies—extreme individualism (do your own thing) and a hunger for shared responsibility, expressed in the formation of communes. Fundamentalist Christianity and other forms of religious orthodoxy are the products of an even greater desire to temper liberal individualism with discipline and responsibility to a community.

The United States has espoused classical liberalism through most of its history. After the Civil War it freed the slaves in the name of liberal values, including the right of the individual rational human being to sell his labor. Soon afterward, it restricted trade union activity on the classical liberal grounds that unions trespassed on the individual's right to freely sell his labor. While acting in its own interests, the United States has, when possible, justified its international behavior in the name of democracy, freedom, and the right to property and has faced discontent at home when these actions conflicted with liberal values. When it comes to the classical liberal value of free trade the United States has often been inconsistent, opposing tariffs (taxes on imported goods) and subsidies by other countries as an impediment to free trade, yet favoring high tariffs to protect young American industries and helping farmers with agricultural subsidies.

Since the United States has seen liberal values as universal it has usually viewed opposition as the work of the enemies of freedom. Niall Ferguson, who suggests in his book *Colossus* that an American empire would be a good thing, says this is so precisely because the United States would impose a liberal regime upon the world.

> *What is required is a* liberal *empire—that is to say, one that not only underwrites the free international exchange of commodities, labor and capital, but also creates and upholds the conditions without which markets cannot function—peace and order, the rule of law, uncorrupt administration, stable fiscal and monetary policies—as well as provides public goods, such as transport infrastructure, hospitals and schools, which would otherwise not exist.*[16]

Essentially the same point is made in *Global America: Imposing Liberalism on a Recalcitrant World,* written in the 1990s, which maintains that in fact the United States was already doing what Ferguson would later suggest it should do. "Since the end of the cold war, the United States has become progressively more open and aggressive about its pursuit of a liberal world order under which it would dominate."[17] By "a liberal world order," authors David Mosler and Bob Catley did not mean "tax and spend politics." They meant a program that promoted democracy and the elimination of local subsidies and trade barriers.

Is America a Christian Nation?

Since the 1970s, America's evangelical Christians, most of whom are politically conservative, have been demanding a larger voice in the country's affairs; their growing influence on the Republican Party has given rise to a debate about one aspect of America's ideas of itself. Is the United States fundamentally a religious nation or a secular nation, and is it part of America's role to spread Christianity? It is a robust debate because each side has strong arguments to draw on.

The secularists can point out that classical liberalism is a secular political philosophy. It was conceived in opposition to the divine right of kings. It is a product of the European Enlightenment and the Age of Reason. So the ideological foundation of the United States is secular, though not hostile to religion. It would have been divisive to make any particular religion the basis for the constitution of the new republic, since people were of varying faiths. The founders could not appeal to any particular religion as the source of authority for their new government or as a guide to its organization. Such revered heroes of the American Revolution as Thomas Paine and Ethan Allen were freethinkers. Thomas Jefferson, author of the Declaration of Independence, was a Deist, believing in a supreme being but not in miracles or in the divinity of Jesus. As for the great mass of ordinary Americans, only a fraction of them were churchgoers, though in part this was because, in a frontier society, many lived far from any church.

The Declaration of Independence, as befits a document written by a Deist, invokes "the Laws of Nature" and "Nature's God" rather than the Christian savior. The Constitution claims its authority from "the people." The Bill of Rights prohibits the institution of a national state religion (though as it was then interpreted, the constitutions of individual states could have state religions). While school primers in the 1800s contained some Protestant religious instruction and public speakers routinely invoked God and Christianity, the idea that is enshrined in the First Amendment, the separation of church and state, was widely held. Most Americans, even religious Americans, had a strong prejudice against clergymen exerting political power, a tendency that Protestants associated with Roman Catholicism and that Americans associated with Spain and ancien régime France. Early hostility to the Mormons was based in part on their mingling of political and religious leadership.[18]

There is another side to the story, however. Even though the American government is secular, most of the American people are at least nominally Christian and a small but influential minority—perhaps a fifth, swelling at times to a third—has been passionately Christian, making Christian beliefs the center of their lives.

In the mid-1700s, the inhabitants of Britain and its American colonies were swept up by a religious movement that emphasized a deeply emotional experience of salvation; historians call this movement the First Great Awakening. Another and even more widespread religious revival, the Second Great Awakening, occurred in the United States between the 1790s and the 1840s. This second movement was characterized by a change in theology that reflected the individualistic and democratic spirit of that time: It abandoned the Calvinist belief in predestination (whether someone would be saved or damned had already been decided before birth) in favor of a theology that emphasized free will.[19] Some historians believe that the change was also related to changes in the American economy, which was moving from the craft system to the factory system. Under the craft system, workers lived with their employers and were counted as part of the family. In the factory system, workers and employers lived separately. The new organization of labor placed more emphasis on individual self-reliance and self-discipline; men and women had greater responsibility for every aspect of their lives, including their salvation.[20] This change in theology was accompanied by the growth of highly emotional forms of worship meant to encourage people to see their helplessness and sinfulness, open their hearts to God's grace, and be born again.

The second Great Awakening had profound effects on American society. In the North, pious business leaders affected by it engaged in many social reforms that they saw as part of a heavenly plan for the United States—campaigns to distribute Bibles and tracts, fight drunkenness, force steamships not to run on Sunday, rescue prostitutes from a life of shame, stamp out novel-reading and theatergoing, convert Irish immigrants to Protestantism, establish missions in the slums, and abolish slavery. The Emancipation Proclamation, women's suffrage, and Prohibition were among the ultimate fruits of the reforming zeal that began in the 1820s. After the Civil War, these same Christian groups helped to found Negro colleges; some of the leaders of the 20th-century fight against segregation would emerge from those colleges. More recently, as names such as the Southern Christian Leadership Conference and the Reverend Dr. Martin Luther King, Jr., suggest, African-American churches helped provide organization and inspiration for the fight to end segregation. Christian influence on American politics is nothing new.

Among southern whites, the second Great Awakening led to far less social reform (Prohibition excepted) than it did among northern whites and southern blacks. It did, however, encourage the enthusiastic emotional forms of worship that still typify the churches such as those of the Southern Baptists and Pentecostals.

The socially reforming and religiously conservative strains of American evangelical Christianity came together in a midwestern politician named William Jennings Bryan. Bryan, remembered best today for his Cross of Gold speech at the 1896 Democratic National Convention and his involvement in the 1925 Scopes (monkey) trial, was a populist leader of the late 19th and early 20th centuries. Liberals today admire or despise him depending on which part of his career they are examining. In his most famous speech, Bryan used the Christian imagery that came naturally to him and his audience to oppose banking practices that he saw as inimical to the interests of farmers and workers: "You shall not press upon the brow of Labor this crown of thorns; you shall not crucify mankind upon a cross of gold."[21] As secretary of state during Wilson's administration he took a principled opposition to America's entry into World War I; in retirement from politics he spoke out in favor of Prohibition, Florida real estate, and against the teaching of the theory of evolution. No existing political party embraces all these positions, yet to Bryan they were consistent because he believed that democracy was Christianity in practice; he believed that the majority of people—at least the majority of Americans—would also choose the path of righteousness or, as one of his biographers believed, "Never could Bryan entertain any objections to the will of majority. . . . Collective wisdom was superior to individual wisdom."[22] For all his religiosity, Bryan was not really in opposition to America's version of classical liberalism; rather, his ideas were a variant, one which would give more power to the majority will at the expense of elites.

Bryan's religious convictions gave him a great deal of force and optimism; they also made him blind to many realities that other people found obvious. In this he resembled many Americans as seen by Europeans: naïve, pious, energetic, and able—through well-meaning ignorance—to do more damage than a cynic. America has produced many Bryans.

At the end of his life Bryan was a hero to the fundamentalists, as American Christians who opposed the modernizing churches of the northeast were beginning to call themselves. Modernizing churches had made peace with the theory of evolution and with the European scholarship that questioned the divine authorship of the Bible. Churches in the South, convinced that these compromises threatened the very basis of Christianity, reasserted their belief in a core group of fundamentals, which included the literal inerrancy of the Bible. This movement, which has dominated religion in the South ever since, became consciously political in the 1970s as politically conservative leaders from this tradition organized their coreligionists to influence government policies on such issues as abortion, school prayer, creationism, and sexual behavior.

Is the Christian right opposed to classical liberalism? Yes and no. To the degree that Christian fundamentalists believe (as 20 percent of Americans regularly tell pollsters they do) that the Second Coming is imminent, they have abandoned conventional politics. This belief has important practical effects on the Christian right's policy aims, such as its stand on the Palestinian-Israeli conflict. The Christian right favors Israel not on political grounds but because of Bible prophecy concerning a series of tumultuous end-time events that will begin, so fundamentalists believe, any day now.

But belief in the end of the world tends to be a compartmentalized form of belief. Those who say they expect it to happen soon usually do not act as if they do—certainly not when they demand that their children be exposed to less sex on television or that gays not be permitted to marry, demands aimed at a society with a future. And the Christian right, like other political movements, is a continuum that includes both extremists and people with more moderate views. Some evangelical and Christian fundamentalist leaders deny that the Constitution separates church and state—this certainly is a view in opposition to classical liberal tenets. Most of their demands, though, address the balance that American society has made between freedom and discipline and ask that the balance be shifted in favor of discipline. The fundamentalists pursue their agenda through the political process and express a belief in the wisdom of the people—as opposed to the wisdom of highly educated elites—which William Jennings Bryan would have agreed with. Most Christian right activists oppose the place where classical liberalism has led Western culture, but do not oppose its basic tenets. After all, historically, the attempt to spread freedom and democracy has gone hand in hand with the spread of Christianity.

One form of Christian evangelism has a special relationship to America's role in the world—the activity of American missionaries who since the 19th century have gone to every corner of the world to spread their faith. Missionaries have had a varied relationship to American power and the people they have attempted to convert, often failing to distinguish between the value of the Gospel and the value of all things American and falling prey to the racial stereotypes they shared with other Americans of their time. Others came to recognize the values of the cultures in which they spent a large portion of their lives. Christian religious sects with their origins in the United States—such as the Church of Jesus Christ of Latter-day Saints, the Seventh-day Adventists Church, and Jehovah's Witnesses—have sent and continue to send missionaries abroad where they are sometimes welcomed and sometimes resented; they are an important though often overlooked part of the spread of American culture.

A BRIEF HISTORY OF AMERICAN FOREIGN POLICY

America the Island—Early American Foreign Policy

At the outset of its existence the United States was relatively large in territory but small in population. Its greatest military asset was its distance from the well-developed societies of the Eastern Hemisphere. Fortunately for the United States, Spain, France, and England, the three powerful European nations with a significant interest in the Americas, were in competition.

The leaders of the young United States pursued a foreign policy of neutrality typical of small countries that wish to avoid becoming either the client state of a powerful neighbor or a battlefield in a war between two larger countries. It was in the interest of the United States to avoid taking sides in Europe's wars. This course was suggested by the first U.S. president, George Washington, in his 1796 Farewell Address. "Europe has a set of primary interests which to us have none or a very remote relation," he noted. "Why, by interweaving our destiny with that of any part of Europe, entangle our peace and prosperity in the toils of European ambition, rivalship, interest, humor, or caprice? It is our true policy to steer clear of permanent alliances with any portion of the foreign world."[23]

As Thomas Jefferson, the third U.S. president, took office, he promised the nation a foreign policy based on Washington's principles: "Peace, commerce, and honest friendship with all nations: entangling alliances with none."[24]

To stay completely free of Europe's conflicts was not possible, however. The infancy of the United States occurred during the period when France's dictator and self-crowned European emperor Napoléon Bonaparte was consolidating his conquests and Great Britain was attempting to defeat him by means of an Atlantic naval blockade. These events drew the United States into a small, undeclared naval war with France between 1798 and 1800 and later into a much larger declared war with Britain, the War of 1812.

American Claims on the Western Hemisphere—the Monroe Doctrine

The Napoleonic Wars benefited the United States, despite the obstacles they presented to the young republic's neutrality. In 1803, they caused the size of the country to double with the Louisiana Purchase, which a cash-hungry Napoléon offered to the surprised foreign ministers of Thomas Jefferson. A successful slave revolution that took place between 1791 and 1804 in the French colony of St-Domingue (later, Haiti) had already weakened France's hold on the New World. The Napoleonic Wars sped the decline of Spain as a world power, so that large sections of Spain's former colonies on the North American continent became part of the United States, a few by purchase, others by war.

In the wake of the Napoleonic Wars, many of Spain's colonies in South and Central America successfully fought for their independence. This development led to President James Monroe's 1823 speech announcing the policy that became known as the Monroe Doctrine. Most American high school students have heard about this doctrine, which declared that the European powers should not attempt to recolonize the Americas.

It is less well known that the doctrine was originally proposed by Great Britain. After Napoléon's defeat, Great Britain was urged by Russia and by the restored French monarchy to help Spain regain its colonies, as part of a general European effort to undo the effects of the French Revolution. But Britain's government preferred that the new republics remain independent. As independent republics they could be trading partners with Britain, whereas as part of the Spanish Empire they might be required to trade only with Spain. Since this course was obviously in the interest of the United States as well, in 1823 the British foreign minister suggested to the United States that the two nations issue a joint declaration to deter any powers from intervening in Central and South America. Suspicious of British intentions and following established U.S. policy against "entangling alliances," Secretary of State John Quincy Adams opposed a bilateral statement that might limit U.S. expansion in the future. Instead, in a December 2, 1823, address to Congress, President Monroe issued a unilateral statement, letting it be known that while it would not interfere with existing European colonies in the New World, it would resent any attempt to impose new ones.

With its small navy, the United States would have been helpless to enforce the Monroe Doctrine at the time it was pronounced. Instead, the doctrine was enforced—to the degree that it *was* enforced—by Great Britain. Britain throughout the 19th century had the greatest navy in the world, unchallenged by any other, and it used it to supply its existing colonies, to suppress piracy and the slave trade, to enforce free-market principles, and, incidentally, to prevent recolonization of the Americas. Great Britain itself continued to expand its territory north of the United States and claimed several small possessions in South America. Not until the end of the 19th century, when, very quickly, the United States acquired a formidable navy of its own, was it able to enforce its claims on the Americas.

Great Britain, which had defeated Napoléon at the beginning of the 1800s, also led a diplomatic effort that ensured a long period of peace in Europe: Britain would oppose by war or diplomacy any country's attempt to conquer Europe, but, looking outward, would not itself try to conquer Europe. As many historians see it, for nearly a century Britain functioned as Europe's, and increasingly the world's, policeman.

In a lecture given in 1950, U.S. diplomat George F. Kennan (best known for proposing the U.S. policy of containment toward the Soviet Union) pointed out that there is a special relationship between the United States and Great Britain, based on mutual security interests.

> *Today . . . we can see that our security has been dependent throughout much of our history on the position of Britain; that Canada, in particular, has been a hostage to good relations between our country and the British Empire; and that Britain's position, in turn, has depended on the maintenance of a balance of power on the European Continent. Thus it was essential to us, as it was to Britain, that no single Continental land power should come to dominate the entire Eurasian land mass. Our interest has lain rather in the maintenance of some sort of stable balance among the powers of the interior, in order that none of them should effect the subjugation of the others, conquer the seafaring fringes of the land mass, become a great sea power as well as land power, shatter the position of England, and enter—as in those circumstances it certainly would—on an overseas expansion hostile to ourselves and supported by the immense resource of the interior of Europe and Asia.*[25]

Kennan's audience at the time was probably thinking that quite recently Adolf Hitler, like Napoléon, had conquered Europe and planned to invade Britain, and Joseph Stalin's Soviet Union and Mao Zedong's China formed a single Eurasia-dominating communist bloc with a potential to threaten both Europe and the United States. In 1950, the great geostrategic facts seemed obvious.

Earlier in American history, however, this special relationship was not clear. The facts were obscured for Americans by the ideological differences between America and Britain—the latter was a monarchy and an empire—by patriotism, and by the very security that Britain provided. By the late 1800s, said Kennan, Americans "mistook our sheltered position behind the British fleet and British Continental diplomacy for the results of superior American wisdom and virtue in refraining from interfering in the sordid differences of the Old World."[26]

Britain's role as guarantor of peace, together with the Industrial Revolution—which gave Europeans and people of European descent immense military advantages over every potential foe—made possible the century of prosperity during which Europe came to dominate Asia and Africa. It also enabled the United States to expand and flourish without interference from the Old World, while maintaining a small military establishment and fighting relatively small wars with its weak neighbor, Mexico, or with poorly armed and outnumbered Native Americans. The American Civil War, the first modern mechanized war fought with the help of railroads, factories, telegraph lines, and millions of soldiers, showed that the United States was capable of wielding formidable military power, but for most of the 1800s it did not have to, thanks to Great Britain's dominance of the seas.

Today, historians and political scientists like Niall Ferguson and Michael Mandelbaum, who argue that the world, or at least some of the world, benefits from American hegemony, cite the free security that Great Britain provided to the United States in the 1800s as an example of the way the self-interested actions of a great power can provide incidental benefits to small countries. Others such as the historian Arthur Schlesinger Jr. see another moral, that the U.S. faith in its ability to act unilaterally rests in part on the illusion that the United States conducted its own defense in the 1800s. Great Britain, which always conducted its foreign policy through alliances, never had a similar illusion.

Manifest Destiny: Expanding the Empire of Liberty

In the 19th century and after, critics of the U.S. claim to be superior to imperialism have pointed out that the United States from its beginnings has been intensely expansionist. In the 1800s, most of the expansion happened to occur on the North American continent.

Most American students have heard how in the course of the 19th century a country consisting of 13 seaboard states expanded westward by purchase and conquest, until it reached the Pacific. In the 19th century, this rapid overland expansion caused European observers to compare the United States to Russia, which was expanding eastward by conquest at about the same pace. In 1835, the French writer Alexis de Tocqueville predicted that the United States and Russia seemed "marked out by the will of Heaven to sway the destinies of half the globe."[27]

Within the United States the country's expansion was controversial. Empires were bad, weren't they? Hadn't the United States begun by breaking with an empire? Those who favored expansion insisted that the United States was different because it was, in the words of Thomas Jefferson, an "empire of liberty,"[28] by which they meant not merely that the United States was uniquely virtuous, but also that it always incorporated new land as quickly as possible into the main body of the country, turning territories into states and giving their inhabitants (other than African Americans and Native Americans) citizenship and representation. The United States absorbed new territory; it did not find other peoples to rule over. As John Quincy Adams wrote in a letter to his father in 1811:

> *The whole continent of North America appears to be destined by Divine Providence to be peopled by one* nation, *speaking one language, professing one general system of religious and political principles, and accustomed to one general tenor of social usages and customs. For the*

common happiness of them all, for their peace and prosperity, I believe it is indispensable that they should be associated in one federal Union.[29]

In 1845 the annexation of Texas and the dispute between the United States and Great Britain over the boundaries of Oregon led the journalist John L. O'Sullivan to coin the term *manifest destiny,* a higher law that he said entitled the United States to claim the whole of Oregon "by the right of our manifest destiny to overspread and to possess the whole of the continent which Providence has given us for the development of the great experiment of liberty and federated self-government entrusted to us."[30]

The idea of Manifest Destiny joined Americans' desire for cheap land—and the economic opportunities cheap land afforded to farmers, immigrants, real estate speculators, investors, railroad companies, and other enterprising folk—with a patriotic belief in America's great providential mission of liberty. Racism was also a component of Manifest Destiny, for it was usually said to be the destiny of the "Anglo-Saxon race" to inhabit this empire of liberty, nonwhites being either by culture or by ancestry unequipped for it. When some Americans argued for the annexation of the whole of Mexico, Senator John C. Calhoun of South Carolina, who had approved the annexation of Texas, protested that Mexico could not be added to the union because its inhabitants were part "Indian" and "we never dreamt of incorporating into our Union any but the Caucasian race—the free white race."[31]

Since many of the new territories that came into the union were suitable for plantation agriculture, these new additions to the empire of liberty were also, ironically, additions to the empire of slavery. Before he became president, Abraham Lincoln opposed adding to the Union, tending to see each new westward expansion project—in particular those that added territory below the Mason-Dixon line—as a scheme to preserve and extend slavery. Others, like the artist George Catlin, who used his brush to record the Native American way of life, considered expansion unstoppable, but regretted its destructiveness. "I have seen this splendid juggernaut rolling on, and beheld its sweeping desolation."[32]

Within a few decades the coast-to-coast expansion of the United States was complete. The railroad (invented in 1814) and the telegraph (1844) helped to rapidly integrate the newly acquired territories into the nation. The American historian Frederick Jackson Turner took a backward look at the process in his 1893 essay, "The Significance of the Frontier in American History." The frontiers of European countries marked the boundaries between societies that were essentially similar to each other. The frontier in America had been "the outer edge of a wave—the meeting place between savagery and civilization."[33] The existence of this constantly moving frontier, he wrote, had shaped the American character:

> *That coarseness and strength combined with acuteness and inquisitiveness; that practical, inventive turn of mind, quick to find expedients; that masterful grasp of material things, lacking in the artistic but powerful to effect great ends; that restless, nervous energy; that dominant individualism, working for good and for evil, and withal that buoyancy and exuberance which comes with freedom—these are traits of the frontier, or traits called out elsewhere because of the existence of the frontier.*[34]

The frontier helped the United States evade problems that bedeviled Europe, particularly class warfare. Since the discontented could "go west and grow with the country," as the newspaper editor Horace Greeley urged them, there was less danger that they would try to revolutionize society in the East. In fact, the closing of the frontier coincided with a rapid growth of organized labor in the United States, with violent clashes between strikers, strikebreakers, and police, and the appearance of anarchist and socialist parties.

The closing of the frontier also affected U.S. foreign policy: With no places to expand to in the contiguous United States and with no new lands in the Americas that had not already been colonized by European nations, the United States joined the leading nations of Europe in the building of overseas empires.

Manifest Destiny beyond American Shores

The late 1800s and early 1900s were the zenith of European domination of the world, when latecomers such as Belgium and Germany hurried to catch up with Great Britain in a scramble for colonies, especially in Africa. The forces that propelled this trend are worth noting here because they have not ceased to influence America's role in the world.

Manufacturers in the home countries wanted overseas possessions for their raw materials and markets—for example, a place to mine iron ore (the raw material) and a place to sell the steel manufactured from it (the market). Often European governments acquired imperial possessions when their merchants and manufacturers asked them to protect their interests in China, India, or Egypt; to knock down the trade barriers that local governments in China, India, or Egypt had set up against them; and to ensure stability and an uncorrupt local administration that would lower the costs of doing business.[35] European governments helped their merchants and manufacturers because trade strengthened the economy of the home country, kept its workers employed, and provided the funds for a large army and perhaps also government services to keep citizens at home contented. Additionally, governments tended to see their interests as identical with those of the propertied classes, from whose ranks most politicians were drawn.

Imperialism also brought the home country key military assets, especially for the navy of the mother country. At the beginning of the century, Great Britain's naval blockade had helped strangle the vast European empire of Napoléon. In his 1890 book *The Influence of Sea Power upon History,* an American military historian, Alfred Thayer Mahan, predicted that sea power would be even more important to the wars of the 20th century. Leaders in Germany, France, Japan, Russia, and the United States took note and invested in their navies. The buildup was so rapid that naval power soon became a subject for international arms control agreements, with battleships occupying the same place in negotiations that ballistic missiles and nuclear warheads do today. Overseas bases—places for the resupply and refueling of ships and forts from which enemy merchant ships or warships could be bombarded—were critical to sea power, and the need for them fueled imperialism, including America's imperialism.

Another impetus for empire came from finance. By the late 1800s, wealthy and middle-class people in Europe and the United States were no longer deriving most of their income from rents on land; instead, they were investing it, either directly in the stock market or indirectly through banks, thereby making their capital available for profit-making overseas ventures. The availability of capital encouraged economic expansion that was then protected by military expansion.

Racism gave people faith in the imperialist enterprise. Looking at their rapid conquest of the world and new advantages in wealth and scientific knowledge, Europeans and Americans found it easy to believe in their biological superiority; this was not a view of fringe groups but of scientists, jurists, and presidents. Charles Darwin's theories of evolution were said to prove that different races represented different stages of evolution, with whites the most advanced; this idea made white rule look inevitable. Two hundred years earlier, when the global balance of power was more even, Europeans had justified their conquests with religion, not race (and many whites still believed that empires were ordained by God to help spread the gospel). But in this time of overwhelming Western power, belief in white racial superiority was the rule even among clergymen.[36]

Finally, the push for empire was a competition. In the late 1800s, European nations saw themselves in a desperate struggle for survival: Patriotic intellectuals and politicians worried that without empires their countries would become weak, their independence endangered.

The trends that led other industrialized nations to acquire empires motivated the United States to do so as well. The United States was by 1880 an industrial power second only to Great Britain and by 1900 probably the greatest industrial power in the world.[37] It had strength and wealth to spare. Americans began to speak of a Manifest Destiny beyond their shores. In 1881, U.S. secretary of state James G. Blaine pointed out that there might be "openings of assured and profitable enterprise" for American industry "in the mines of South America and the railroads of Mexico . . . While the great powers of Europe are steadily enlarging their colonial domination in Asia and Africa," Blaine argued, the United States should "improve and expand its trade with the nations of America."[38]

In the early 1890s Albert J. Beveridge, a senator from Indiana, went further and used the word "colonies":

> *American factories are making more than the American people can use; American soil is producing more than they can consume. Fate has written our policy for us; the trade of the world must and shall be ours . . . We will establish trading posts throughout the world as distributing points for American products . . . Great colonies governing themselves, flying our flag and trading with us, will grow about our posts of trade. . . . And American law, American order, American civilization, and the American flag will plant themselves on shores hitherto bloody and benighted, but by those agencies of God henceforth to be made beautiful and bright.*[39]

The outlines of America's empire had already been traced. As Blaine had suggested, it would lie to the south in the Americas, which the Monroe Doctrine had claimed as under U.S. protection. There would be another kind of American expansion to the west in the Pacific, where the United States had acquired a handful of small bases—the atoll of Midway in 1867 and Hawaii, where in 1887 the United States had established a naval coaling station. That year, when Congress opposed the annexation of Hawaii, Theodore Roosevelt lamented "the queer lack of imperial instinct that our people show."[40]

Roosevelt and others eager for an American overseas empire got their chance in 1898 with the Spanish-American War. The war began as an outgrowth of a series of insurrections in the Spanish possession of Cuba, a conflict characterized by great brutality on both sides. American public opinion favored the rebels. Many Americans thought that their country was *opposing* imperialism—Spanish imperialism—when, after the sinking of the USS *Maine* (now known to be an accident), the United States fought a quick war, which revealed the weakness of Spain and the newfound strength of the American navy. When the dust cleared, Cuba, Puerto Rico, and the Philippines had come under U.S. control. (As part of the peace treaty with Spain, the United States paid $20 million for the Philippines, but only after the United States had occupied the islands.) Cuba and Puerto Rico were in the Caribbean; the Philippines were closer to Japan and China than to the United States. Those who had expected the United States to liberate these islands soon learned otherwise: The Filipinos, who wanted independence, were subjugated during a bloody three-year campaign more costly in lives than Spain's conflict with the Cuban rebels had been.

President William McKinley justified the U.S. annexation of the Philippines on the grounds that, being backward, "they were unfit for government" and that therefore "there was nothing left for us to do but take them all, and educate the Filipinos, and uplift and civilize and Christianize them, and by God's grace do the very best we could by them as our fellowmen for whom Christ died."[41]

The annexation of the Philippines caused a belated debate on the morality and wisdom of American imperialism. Since the Filipinos were seen as alien and backward, the politician and newspaper editor Whitelaw Reid tried to persuade his fellow Americans to acquire the islands by assuring them that the Philippines would never become a state; the industrialist Andrew Carnegie, who opposed expansion, declared that they would: "You'll have to swallow every last one of them."[42]

Ultimately, the United States did different things with each of the possessions it acquired at the end of the 19th century. Hawaii was annexed in 1898 and in 1959 became a state; George F. Kennan suggests that this outcome resulted from the fact that the United States was able to marginalize its native peoples, treating them as it had the native peoples of North America.[43] Puerto Rico became a self-governing territory whose inhabitants are American citizens but cannot vote in American presidential elections. The Philippines became independent after World War II. Cuba, though its main cash crops were sugar and tobacco, was until its communist revolution in 1959 essentially a banana republic, with a dictatorial government and highly unequal land distribution, permitting American investment on favorable terms, subject by law to invasion by U.S. armed forces whenever American business or strategic interests were threatened. It is also, like the others, the location of an American military base.

History textbooks call the time of the Spanish-American War an era of U.S. imperialism, since during this period the United States annexed territories that it did not put on the road to statehood. To those who define empire narrowly, America's imperialist expansion was brief and limited. With the exception of the Philippines, Puerto Rico, and a few smaller territories, the United States did not rule conquered countries in which local rulers swore allegiance to the mother country, as existed under various arrangements in the empires of England, France, and Germany. (Meanwhile, in the Pacific region, where European powers, as well as Japan, were attempting to carve up separate spheres of influence in China, the United States positioned itself as an anti-imperialist power, promoting an open door policy that would give all foreigners equal access to Chinese commerce and investment and preserve China's sovereignty.)

To those who define imperialism to include an economic, political, and military domination of small countries by a large one and a situation in which the government of the small countries exists by permission of the larger country, America's empire continued long after the era of McKinley and Theodore Roosevelt.

Latin America: Dollar Diplomacy and Gunboat Diplomacy

Cuba before its 1959 revolution was a typical example of the exercise of American power in the Western Hemisphere. Under a 1904 treaty with the United States, Cuba could not enter into a foreign alliance or make any important changes in its internal policy without the agreement of the United States.[44] Yet, in theory, it was an independent country, so the United States did not have to be responsible for the welfare of its people, as it did to some degree for the people of the Philippines, Hawaii, and Puerto Rico, which the United States had annexed. The United States intervened in Cuba only to protect U.S. citizens and their property. The government of Cuba was undemocratic and the people were poor, but Americans did not see this as the fault of the United States.

Nowhere else has the United States intervened so frequently as it has in Latin America, landing the marines to protect American interests, supporting America-friendly dictators, removing the same dictators, fighting trade unionists, suppressing strikes and peasant rebellions, and training national guards that keep authoritarian regimes in power, all in the name of stability, anticommunism, and the protection of U.S. investments. Sometimes a promise of U.S. support for a coup has been sufficient to make one occur. Thus, in order to build the Panama Canal, the United States encouraged local leaders in the Colombian province of Panama to secede from Colombia. U.S. gunboats prevented

Colombia from opposing the secession. Often a hint has been enough. In 1921, to assist the United Fruit Company, U.S. president Calvin Coolidge suggested the overthrow of Guatemalan president Carlos Herrera, and certain Guatemalans obliged him. In other cases, U.S. troops have been sent in for brief periods. There have also been long occupations by American soldiers as in Cuba between 1917 and 1933, Nicaragua between 1912 and 1925, Haiti between 1915 and 1934, and the Dominican Republic between 1916 and 1924.

There was a 15-year hiatus in direct U.S. military intervention in Latin America during the presidency of Franklin Roosevelt with his "Good Neighbor" policy. Intervention resumed in the 1940s, though, and continued through the rest of the 20th century, often covertly through the action of the U.S. Central Intelligence Agency.

The authoritarian pattern of political life in Latin America has many causes. Fidel Castro, a communist who ruled Cuba in the face of U.S. hostility, was as much a dictator as Rafael Trujillo, who ruled the Dominican Republic with U.S. support until 1961. Clearly, the United States has done little for self-government in the region, and, when the United States portrays itself as a beacon of democracy, those who dispute the claim have a large body of contrary evidence available to them in the history of Latin America.

While behaving as an imperial power in the Western Hemisphere, the United States still considered itself a regional power aloof from European quarrels. Two world wars would be necessary to change this view.

World War I and Wilson's Vision of America's Role

World War I (1914–18), pitted the great European powers against each other: the Allies (Russia, Britain, and France) against the Central Powers (Austria-Hungary, Germany, and Italy). In 1917, the United States belatedly entered the fight on the side of the Allies, who won it a year and a half later. The war destroyed a balance of power that had existed since the defeat of Napoléon, a state of equilibrium that had become unstable with the formation of the new states of Germany and Italy and with changing strengths of the other powers. As a result of World War I, France and Britain were wounded and their weaknesses revealed—they had not been able to defeat Germany without America's help. Russia underwent a communist revolution and became ideologically and militarily opposed to the existing European governments. Austria-Hungary was broken up into many small states that lacked the ability to defend themselves. Germany, "smarting from the sting of defeat and plunged into profound social unrest by the breakup of her traditional institutions, was left nevertheless as the only great united state in Central Europe,"[45] a situation that led to the rise of Nazism and another world war. In sum, apart from the immediate horror of the war, with its vast scale and mechanization of death, World War I changed both the world and America's role in the world. The nature of that change and whether it was for the good are still being debated.

To George Kennan, looking back in 1950, the outcome of World War I looked like a strategic disaster for the United States. In Kennan's view, the balance of power in Europe, and Britain's role in maintaining it, had been an unacknowledged basis of American security. It had permitted the United States to remain safe without large military expenditures.[46] The League of Nations, which Woodrow Wilson had pressed on Europe as an idealistic replacement for the cynical old balance of power—a more democratic way of preventing aggression—would turn out to be inadequate to the task. The net result of both the world wars was a more dangerous world in which American citizens were more vulnerable to attack.

There are other ways to look at the events of the two world wars. From a perspective that sees advantages in world leadership, both ended in victories for the United States. They made it the most powerful nation on Earth by hastening the decline of the other great powers. In the wars of the 20th century, industrial manufacturing capacity was the decisive factor, more important than great generals or well-trained soldiers, and the two wars were won by the United States's unmatched industrial might: its ability to turn out battleships, tanks, planes, landing craft, machine guns, and everything else needed for war (by World War II, this would include such unexpected items as Spam,[47] cigarettes, and silk stockings). If U.S. security was no longer guaranteed by Great Britain, the United States had become strong enough to take over Britain's role as guardian of the European balance of power and as master of the seas and to benefit economically from its leading position. In the view of the British historian Paul Kennedy, this transformation had already occurred by the end of World War I. However, the United States refused to recognize its new role—refused to recognize that the United States, not Britain and not the League of Nations, had the job of Europe's guard dog, which may be why there were two world wars instead of one.

Woodrow Wilson, who was president during World War I and the peace settlement that followed, did more than anyone else to shape Americans' perception of the war. At first, Wilson insisted that the quarrels of Europe were no concern of the United States. Later, he began to say that the United States should remain aloof from the conflict so that it could act as a mediator and bring the other powers to a peace settlement. At last, as U.S.

public opinion turned against Germany, the primary reason given by Wilson for entering the war on the side of the Allies was to punish the violation of America's neutrality—a not entirely logical reason since both sides had violated America's neutrality. Wilson gave an additional justification, one drawn from his own personality, from America's founding myth, and from the traditions of American foreign policy, which had always emphasized the country's superiority to the sordid deal-making of European diplomacy. America would intervene in European affairs to make the world "safe for democracy" and to bring about a fair, open peace. The little nations of eastern Europe and the Balkans would have self-determination and self-government and international disputes would be settled by a new international body, the League of Nations, which would prevent international aggression in a very simple way: all signatories of the League covenant would go to war if necessary to preserve "the territorial integrity and existing independence of all Members of the League."[48]

In Wilson's view, this would be a world run by American constitutional methods, which were also enlightened, modern methods, as he pointed out in January 1917: "These are American principles, American policies. We could stand for no other. And they are also the principles and policies of forward-looking men and women everywhere, of every modern nation, of every enlightened community. They are the principles of mankind and must prevail."

Certainly Wilson himself was very American in his confidence that American principles were universal principles and all "forward-looking men and women" would agree to them. Still, his foreign policy represented a departure for the United States, since it required the United States to assume a role of overt global leadership and form alliances, extremely entangling alliances, with all the European nations who would be members of the league. Moreover, there were three problems with Wilson's plan, according to historian Niall Ferguson:

> *The first was that it was richly hypocritical. In 1916 Wilson had drafted a speech that included the characteristically sententious line "It shall not lie with the American people to dictate to another what their government shall be. . . ." His secretary of state, Robert Lansing, wrote succinctly in the margin: "Haiti, S. Domingo, Nicaragua, Panama." The second problem, which a better knowledge of Central Europe's ethnic geography might have helped him avoid, was that the application of self-determination would produce a significantly enlarged German Reich, an outcome unlikely to be congenial to those powers that had fought Germany for three years without American military assistance.*

> *But the fatal flaw of the Wilsonian design was that it simply could not be sold to a skeptical Senate.*[49]

Europeans welcomed Wilson's plan; the United States rejected it. Joining the League of Nations would have meant making an open-ended commitment to send American troops into combat in conflicts that had no direct impact on American security—when no Americans had died or were threatened as a result of enemy action (as had seemed to be the case at the outset of the Spanish-American War and had actually been the case when the United States entered World War I). As Arthur Schlesinger Jr. pointed out, the obstacles to U.S. acceptance of membership in the League of Nations were both political—Americans could not see sending their sons to die for the abstract ideals of international law and collective security—and constitutional—declaring war was supposed to be the prerogative of the U.S. Congress; it could not be relinquished to an international body.[50]

American Isolationism between the Two World Wars

With Congress's rejection of the League of Nations and the electoral victory of Republicans, the people of the United States rejected a leading role in world affairs. The new president, Warren G. Harding, summed up the feeling:

> *America, our America, the America builded on the foundation laid by the inspired fathers, can be a party to no permanent military alliance. It can enter into no political commitments, nor assume any economic obligations which will subject our decisions to any other than our own authority . . . Confident of our ability to work out our own destiny, and jealously guarding our right to do so, we seek no part in directing the destinies of the Old World.*[51]

American isolationism between the two world wars was more than a foreign policy: It was a pervasive mood. Judging by their actions, the majority of Americans regarded the rest of the world as a source of deadly contagion. In 1919, after a series of anarchist bombings, radicals of foreign origin were rounded up all over the United States and deported—sent back to the bad old world which had spawned such alien ideas as anarchism and socialism. In 1921 and 1924, Congress passed bills to reduce immigration, especially from Italy, eastern Europe, and Asia.[52] The Ku Klux Klan gained a membership of 4 million during the 1920s based in part on suspicion of Roman Catholics, whom many Protestant Americans saw as a foreign influence. While remaining a white supremacist organization, the Ku Klux Klan in the 1920s and afterward positioned itself as an ultrapatriotic proponent of "100 percent Americanism." It claimed to defend traditional Protestant American values under threat by immigrants, especially Catholics and Jews, who were said not to share them. It also claimed to be fighting socialism, communism, and anarchism, which many Americans considered to be foreign ideas that would never have naturally arisen under American conditions.[53]

When the 1929 stock market crash was followed by an international economic depression, Congress's response reflected the isolationist temper: In 1930 it passed the Smoot-Hawley Tariff Act, a tax that put up barriers to foreign imports, thereby causing other countries to put up barriers against the United States. The net result was worse for the U.S. economy than for its trading partners.[54] Then, to give a boost to falling exports, the United States devalued its currency in 1933. (This medicine was applied at different times by most of the world's industrialized nations during the depression; it provided short-term benefits but hurt in the long run because it damaged international trade.)

Franklin Roosevelt, who was elected with large majorities twice in the 1930s and had great power thanks to the nation's sense of crisis, was an ardent internationalist and a believer in Wilsonian organizations like the League of Nations. He had served as an assistant secretary of the navy under Wilson. But even Roosevelt could not get the American people to abandon isolationism in the midst of the depression.

It was unfortunate that he could not. It was in the early 1930s that Adolf Hitler was elected chancellor of Germany, subverted its fragile democracy by illegal arrests of opposition leaders, and began a tremendous military buildup in violation of the terms of the Treaty of Versailles. In the view of many historians, Hitler could have been stopped at that time by firm international action. He might even have been stopped without war and without the help of Russia, a totalitarian state with which France and Germany were reluctant to cooperate.

By the late 1930s, the price of standing up to Hitler had risen. War was likely, and Russia would be strengthened by the concessions it would demand. It was a price the leaders of the democracies were unwilling to pay. In 1938, Germany annexed Austria, creating the giant German state that Europe had long feared. It then occupied part of Czechoslovakia, which France had pledged to defend (Britain in turn had pledged to go to war if France did). At Britain's urging, France reneged on its promise, signing the infamous Munich Pact with Hitler. Stalin, concluding that France and England would not fight, signed a non-aggression treaty with Hitler, and it was too late to prevent a war that would take the lives of over 50 million people.[55]

The leaders of France and England have been rightly faulted for their failure of nerve in the late 1930s, but their positions would have been stronger and their decisions different if they had been backed by the United States, the greatest industrial nation in the world. Instead, between 1935 and 1937, Congress passed a series of Neutrality Acts that would prevent it from aiding either side in the coming conflict.

American isolationism gave Hitler a reason to believe that the United States could be ignored until he had consolidated his power in Europe—perhaps even until he had conquered Britain, thereby achieving mastery of land and sea.

The outbreak of war in Europe ushered in a fierce debate about U.S. intervention. Most Americans found the Nazis distasteful and sympathized with the beleaguered British. But it was hard to make the case that American lives must be lost when the United States had not been attacked. The debate ended at the end of 1941. On December 7 of that year, the Japanese attacked Pearl Harbor. Congress declared war on Japan the next day, and on December 11, Hitler, who had already taken the gamble of invading the Soviet Union, declared war on the United States. These actions silenced the isolationists.

By the end of 1945, Japan and Germany, whose conquest of the world had seemed almost unstoppable, had surrendered unconditionally. The United States occupied all of Japan and was thus the greatest power in the Far East. With its weakened ally, Great Britain, the United States occupied half of Germany and was thus the greatest military force in western Europe. The U.S. Navy had undisputed control of the seas. American planes controlled the skies and, with the help of aircraft carriers, could be brought anywhere on Earth. The U.S. land forces, once deployed, were probably unbeatable. With the atomic bombing of Hiroshima and Nagasaki, the United States showed itself to be in possession of a weapon so powerful that one of them could destroy a city. Having suffered the least damage of any party to the conflict, the United States had come out the strongest; it had enough strength to fight World War II all over again if it so chose. Its power was matchless and unprecedented—the Roman Empire, the British Empire, the empire of the Mongols had never wielded comparable military advantages over so wide an area. Yet within a few years the country was gripped by a great fear. Its people felt less safe than they had on the day before Pearl Harbor, perhaps even than they had the day after it.

The United States Assumes International Leadership

As World War II neared its close, members of the Roosevelt administration wondered if the United States would again retreat into isolationism. It seems obvious now that this was unlikely to occur, because changes in the international balance of power were much clearer in 1945 than they had been in 1918. Western Europe was crippled—its cities were in ruins. Though the Soviet Union had suffered greatly in the war as well—as many as 25 million of its people had been killed—its army was still powerful. Its troops were in occupation of eastern Europe, whose nations soon became a collection of Soviet puppets as their native communist parties methodically eliminated opposition parties with the help of the Soviet occupiers. Communists were close to winning a civil war in Greece; in France communists were the largest party; in Italy the Communist Party was close to an electoral victory. In 1949, the victory of Mao Zedong's forces over those of Chiang Kai-shek turned China into a communist ally of the Soviet Union. The same year, much sooner than expected, the Soviet Union tested its own atomic bomb—a development hastened by the activity of Soviet spies in the United States. Today many analysts see postwar Soviet behavior as an outgrowth of traditional Russian diplomatic aims: A country without natural defensive barriers, it had experienced several devastating invasions, and it was surrounding itself with buffer states while attempting to gain access to warm water ports for its navy. That is not how it looked in the late 1940s: Then, it looked like an attempt to conquer the world for communism. Middle-class people in the United States had feared a socialist revolution since the late 1800s, and they had been more afraid since 1917, the year of the Russian Revolution. Greatly enlarged, secretive, mistrustful, and ideologically committed to the overthrow of existing governments in the West, the Soviet Union could not be ignored. Instead of taking stands for and against isolationism, from the late 1940s on Republicans and Democrats would vie with each other to prove who was tougher on communism.

This development was much less clear, however, between 1942 and 1945, when the American people were encouraged to feel warmly toward Joseph Stalin ("A Guy Named Joe," in the words of a *LOOK* magazine profile) and Franklin Roosevelt and his cabinet expected an era of cooperation with the Soviet Union. Roosevelt and many in his administration feared that after victory the country would again retreat from world affairs. Roosevelt's secretary of state, Cordell Hull, stated "The country was going in exactly the same steps it followed in 1918."[56] Roosevelt said, "Anybody who thinks that isolationism is dead in this country is crazy. As soon as this war is over, it may well be stronger than ever."[57]

In the hope of committing the United States to an outward-looking foreign policy after the war, Roosevelt organized a series of conferences, setting up institutions to deal with the problems of peace. Unlike Wilson, who had devised the League of Nations virtually without consulting Congress, Roosevelt involved leading senators and members of the Republican Party in the planning conferences. As Arthur Schlesinger Jr. notes:

> *These conferences, held mostly at American initiative and dominated mostly by American agendas, came up with postwar blueprints for international organization (Dumbarton Oaks); finance, trade and development (Bretton Woods); food and agriculture (Hot Springs); civil aviation (Chicago); relief and reconstruction (Washington).*[58]

The two conferences that historians most often cite for their influence on the world order that followed World War II were Dumbarton Oaks and Bretton Woods.

Beginning on August 21, 1944, representatives of the United States, the United Kingdom, the Soviet Union, and the Republic of China met in Dumbarton Oaks, a mansion in Washington, to devise plans for the United Nations. The United Nations was to be an international body along the lines of the League of Nations, but, it was hoped, more successful. The greatest differences between the League of Nations and the United Nations were, first, the participation of the United States and, second, the existence of the Security Council, a select body within the United Nations that would have the power to recommend action against aggressors. In the agreements hammered out at Dumbarton Oaks and at later conferences at Yalta and San Francisco, the Security Council would include six temporary members and five permanent members; the permanent members would be representatives from the most powerful countries; thus, the institution would reflect the realities of world power. In fact, Security Council membership would be weighted to favor the United States, since for much of the cold war all the permanent members except the Soviet Union would be U.S. allies.

Fatefully, however, each member was given a veto. Since the United States and the Soviet Union virtually never agreed on the use of force, the Security Council authorized the punishment of an aggressor only once during the entire cold war. In 1950, when the Soviet Union was boycotting the institution, the Security Council condemned North Korea's invasion of South Korea.

The Bretton Woods conference was held in the summer of 1944 at the Mount Washington Hotel in Bretton Woods, New Hampshire. In the words of an army information pamphlet published two years later, the conference "considered matters of international money and finance which are important for peace and prosperity."[59] Bretton Woods established the International Bank for Reconstruction and Development (IBRD), which is now one of five institutions of the World Bank Group, and the International Monetary Fund (IMF). (The conference also called for the creation of a World Trade Organization to help govern international trade relations, but this body did not come into being until 1995.) A primary aim of the conference was to set up a system of rules, institutions, and procedures to regulate the international monetary system. During the 1920s, countries had devalued their currency, a policy with short-term benefits for each country, but disastrous to world trade in general. Economists blamed this policy and related failures of regulation for the length and severity of the Great Depression and thus for the political upheavals of the 1930s and for World War II itself. This was a problem that could be effectively addressed by an international body backed by a very powerful country that was willing to assume a leadership role: That country was the United States.

Under the Bretton Woods agreements, countries linked their currencies to the dollar, which in turn was linked to the price of gold. In the 19th century, this kind of international uniformity had been achieved by directly linking each currency to the price of gold. This traditional system (the gold standard) was considered too inflexible for the postwar economy. Experts thought it would act as a brake on development. Instead, under the Bretton Woods system, only the U.S. dollar was linked directly to the price of gold (made convertible to gold at a fixed rate). Other countries would use the dollar as a reserve currency. They would buy and sell dollars in order to raise or lower the value of their own currency to within 1 percent of the internationally agreed-on exchange rates. The U.S. dollar thus became the basic standard for the world exchange rates. This part of the Bretton Woods system came to an end in 1971, when the United States ceased making its currency exchangeable in gold; however, the dollar remained the world's reserve currency.

The central place of the dollar in the world economy was not only a symbol of U.S. strength, it committed the United States to a deep involvement in the economies of every other capitalist country (after the war the Soviets and their allies rejected involvement in the Bretton Woods institutions, including the World Bank and the International Monetary Fund). For Roosevelt and his secretary of state Cordell Hull, Bretton Woods served the double purpose of helping to avoid another international depression and committing the United States to a role of world leadership.

Containment through Alliances and Institutions

While the United States was unquestionably the strongest nation in the world after World War II, the size and rapid growth of the communist bloc convinced its leaders that America could not act alone in the world. The U.S. approach to the cold war was shaped by the philosophy of Franklin D. Roosevelt and his immediate successors (convinced of the value of international institutions) and the military and political realities (the size of the communist bloc, its proximity to western Europe, its eventual acquisition of nuclear weapons).

Politicians in the United States persuaded the American people that their country had to engage the rest of the world in many ways—through international institutions like the United Nations; through regional military alliances like the North Atlantic Treaty Organization (NATO); through comprehensive foreign aid packages like the Marshall Plan; and, more controversially, through the Central Intelligence Agency's efforts to undermine or overthrow governments friendly to the Soviet Union and to put down rebellions in countries whose governments were friendly to the United States. The sheer size of the United States and the Soviet Union meant that their rivalry embraced the whole world. The whole world was asked to choose sides, and the United States had to be involved with every single nation on Earth. Far from shunning entangling alliances, the United States helped to create and joined regional alliances on almost every continent—NATO; South-East Asia Treaty Organization (SEATO); Baghdad Pact, Organization of American States (OAS). The United States got itself involved—sometimes to the point of war—in small, distant countries that most Americans would have had trouble finding on a map, countries of little strategic or economic value to the United States. The basic American strategy in the cold war was outlined in the late 1940s by George F. Kennan. Kennan, who in February 1946 was the second-ranking U.S diplomat at the American embassy in Moscow, made his views known at that time in a dispatch to Washington, famous today as the Long Telegram. Widely circulated in Washington, the Long Telegram warned that the Soviet Union was "impervious to the logic of reason," though "highly sensitive to the logic of force."[60] Kennan expanded on his analysis in an article published under the pseudonym "X" in the July 1947 issue of *Foreign Affairs,* the journal of the Council on Foreign Relations. "Soviet pressure against the free institutions of the Western world is something that can be contained by the adroit and vigorous application of counterforce," Kennan wrote, adding that that force should take the form of diplomacy and covert action, not war.[61] In the telegram and the article Kennan advocated a policy of "containment" of the Soviet Union.

Looking back in another *Foreign Affairs* article, 40 years later, Kennan explained that he was not thinking of the Soviets as a military threat, since he never thought it likely—as many of his colleagues did—that the Red Army would or could overrun Europe. He considered the Soviet threat to be primarily "ideological-political."[62]

> *Great parts of the northern hemisphere—notably Western Europe and Japan—had just then been seriously destabilized, socially, spiritually and politically, by the experiences of the recent war. Their populations were dazed, shell-shocked, uncertain of themselves, fearful of the future, highly vulnerable to the pressures and enticements of communist minorities in their midst. The world communist movement was at that time a unified, disciplined movement, under the total control of the Stalin regime in Moscow. Not only that, but the Soviet Union had emerged from the war with great prestige for its immense and successful war effort. The Kremlin was, for this and for other reasons, in a position to manipulate these foreign communist parties very effectively in its own interests. . . . I felt that if Moscow should be successful in taking over any of those major Western countries, or Japan, by ideological-political intrigue and penetration, this would be a defeat for us, and a blow to our national security, fully as serious as would have been a German victory in the war that had just ended.*[63]

In the hope of weakening the appeal of communism for the West, Kennan helped to formulate a plan to assist in the economic recovery of Europe. The plan was publicly introduced on June 5, 1947, in a speech by Secretary of State George C. Marshall to the graduating class of Harvard University. The Marshall Plan reversed earlier postwar U.S. policy, which had anticipated a deindustrialized Germany and used British weakness and indebtedness to the United States to push commercial arrangements that favored American business.[64] Recognizing that a strong western Europe was more important than short-term commercial advantages, the United States pumped $13 billion in economic and technical assistance into 16 European countries between 1948 and 1952. The Marshall Plan was initially offered to *all* European countries, including Russia itself. It was rejected by Moscow and its allies, a fact that helped the plan obtain approval from an already anticommunist U.S. Congress.[65] The Marshall Plan accelerated the division of Europe into opposing camps, since the Soviets, who saw it as a capitalist plot to buy eastern Europe, were forced to seal off the economies in their sphere of influence from the economies of the West. It also tended to link the western European economies, paving the way for the Common Market and the European Union. The

Soviets later formed an economic plan of their own, the Council for Mutual Economic Assistance, or Comecon, for eastern Europe. The Soviet plan was far less successful than its western counterpart, perhaps because, as Paul Kennedy observes, it was really a plan for "milking" the economies of the eastern European satellite states.[66] It can be argued that it was not in the Soviets' interest for eastern Europe to be prosperous; prosperity would make people more assertive and harder to control. In any event, while the economies of the Soviet Union and eastern Europe did grow in the 1950s, they did not grow as quickly as those in the West.

Economic historians disagree as to how much credit the Marshall Plan deserves for the recovery of western European economies. Despite heavy bombing of its infrastructure, western Europe after World War II remained a well-organized industrial society with a well-educated population; it had the means to recover and nowhere to go but up. The Great Depression, an unprecedented breakdown of the capitalist order, had stymied economic growth all through the 1930s, but it was over now. Perhaps the Dumbarton Oaks Conference did more to help the postwar economies than the Marshall Plan, because it ensured an international economic climate favorable to free trade and investment. This is all said in the comfort of hindsight: In 1947, Europe's prospects did not look good. In any case, the recovery was spectacular. The U.S. economy benefited as well and U.S. assistance generated enormous goodwill in western Europe. There was no postwar depression. Instead, the states of western Europe enjoyed decades of their greatest economic growth ever, even though during this period they lost their remaining colonies. Even Italy, which had always lagged in industrial development, had its economic miracle, and its international image was changed from a nation of decaying palazzos, peasants, and brigands to one of Fiat- and Vespa-driving sophisticates enjoying la dolce vita. Western Europe's prosperity was an advertisement for capitalism (as the Great Depression of the 1930s, which discredited the existing order, had been an advertisement for radical alternatives like communism and fascism). The United States also assisted Japan's economic recovery, which also proved to be astonishing. By 1961 the superiority of life in the West was so obvious—at least to Europeans—that the communists were forced to build a wall to keep the people of East Berlin from emigrating to West Berlin.

From Rebuilding to Development

The U.S.-Soviet military confrontation in Europe spread to other parts of the world; nations or rebel groups supported by the Soviet Union fought nations or rebel groups supported by the United States in Asia, Africa, and South and Central America. The more peaceful sort of competition embodied in the Marshall Plan and Comecon also spread around the globe. The United States and the Soviet Union wooed Third World countries with foreign aid and assistance in development—sometimes with big projects such as Egypt's Aswan Dam, built first with the help of the United States and then with help from the Soviet Union.

Leaders around the globe were convinced that industrial development was the path to prosperity and power. Very neatly, each of the two superpowers offered a contrasting model for economic development—capitalism versus communism. Each had its appeal. Capitalism had made Europe and the United States rich, and perhaps it was what made them democratic. There was something to be said for communism, however. In just three decades, it had turned a backward nation into a superpower. Russia, unlike France or England, had been an underdeveloped country before its revolution. (The reality was more complex, but this was how it looked to many in the Third World.) In their recent experience as colonies, the economic role of the newly independent countries had been to provide the industrial West with raw materials and to purchase manufactured goods, and it was not clear that their role in the new capitalist international system would be any different. Authoritarian leaders in Asia and Africa were attracted to communism because it offered them a way to direct their countries' development, while holding tightly to the reins of government. At the same time, many rebel groups were attracted to communism because it was a revolutionary doctrine, offering a future Utopia in return for their sacrifices and because often the corrupt, oppressive governments they fought were supported by the United States.

The effort to assist underdeveloped economies—and the debate of how best to do it—have survived the demise of the Soviet Union. Today it goes on under the name of globalization. This refers to the rapid integration of countries all over the Earth into a world economy, a process that has been sharply sped up by recent advances in technology and communications. Economists regard the process as inevitable; they disagree as to how best to manage it.

Proxy Wars and U.S. Interventions

The amount given to aid in the economic development of the Third World, though significant, was small in comparison to the amounts spent on the buildup of armaments and the fighting of little wars around the world. Any conflict that took place during the cold war had a way of becoming a U.S.-Soviet conflict, simply from the availability of the two superpowers as potential allies to each side. Through its 1956 invasion of Hungary, the Soviet Union demonstrated that it would not let countries that had become communist return to capitalism—a policy later formally enunciated by

Soviet premier Leonid Brezhnev as the Brezhnev doctrine. Since communism was a one-way street, the United States would allow no country to become communist in the first place—or even to take significant steps in the direction of communism. Though some communist governments, such as Yugoslavia (and China from the 1960s on), were not dominated by the Soviet Union, the United States treated all socialist movements as gains for Soviet totalitarianism and moved to destabilize or overthrow any socialist regime, even ones that were democratically elected. Thus, in the name of defending democracy, the United States limited the choices available to people in other countries, sometimes replacing democratic, socialist-leaning governments with dictatorial anticommunist governments.

The United States viewed governments that nationalized foreign industries as communist-leaning—after all, by nationalizing these industries they had acted against the rights of property, itself a step toward communism. This attitude led to American interventions on behalf of specific American business interests. American leaders were seldom conscious of a conflict between U.S. business interests and general American interests—most were sure that a strong U.S. economy benefited all U.S. citizens. In 1951, Iran's popular prime minister Mohammed Mosaddeq nationalized his country's oil industry, a serious threat to the revenues of the U.S. ally Great Britain. The British government sought U.S. help in overthrowing Mosaddeq, an outspoken supporter of democratic constitutionalism and national sovereignty who had been elected to the Iranian legislature in 1924. At first the United States resisted the idea, but, in 1953, after President Dwight D. Eisenhower took office, the newly formed Central Intelligence Agency worked with Great Britain to topple Mosaddeq's government. The United States installed a monarchical government under Shah Reza Pahlavi. Where there had been an unpredictable independent leader, there was now a staunch ally geographically near to Russia. If, in addition, the Shah was a despot, that was a small price to pay for stopping the advance of international communism. Great Britain, in gratitude, gave American companies a 40 percent interest in Iran's oil business. The strategic interests of the United States and the interests of U.S. oil companies were both served.

The cold war was not merely a pretext for the advancement of short-term economic interests. The superpowers contended with each other in places that had no attraction for them and that were left to their own devices as soon as the cold war was over. The war in Vietnam, which cost millions of lives (nearly 60,000 of them American), damaged U.S. prestige and the U.S. economy, and polarized American politics, was a case in point. It was not fought to gain control over Southeast Asia's rice paddies or to secure a market for U.S. goods, but in the sincere belief that the spread of communism had to be stopped. Similarly, Afghanistan was no plum for the Soviets, yet, beginning in the late 1970s in the name of the Brezhnev Doctrine, the Soviets fought a fruitless war in Afghanistan that helped to hasten the collapse of the Soviet system.

Legacies of the Cold War

The cold war reshaped the United States and the world. As Martin Walker observed in his 1994 history of the conflict, it turned the United States into a "National Security State," with "a vast standing army, a global intelligence network, and a military-industrial economic complex whose booming factories helped spur the post-war growth of California and the Southern states."[67] The U.S. landscape was transformed by a highway system constructed to facilitate the evacuation of its cities in the event of atomic war (the United States got a booming auto industry, an exuberant car culture, and air pollution). The need to appeal to people of color around the world helped tip the balance of forces battling in the United States over segregation and changed white Americans' attitudes toward race. American military spending pumped money into the economies of Europe and the Pacific Rim at a time when investment was badly needed. "For four decades, the United States garrison of 300,000 men in West Germany pumped dollars into the local economy and acted as a bridge which facilitated Europes exports to America."[68] And American GIs stationed around the globe spread the popular culture of the United States.

World War II gave us the atom bomb, but it is to the cold war that we owe the enormous stockpiles of nuclear weapons, ballistic missiles, and weapons systems maintained even today in Russia and the United States. The cold war thwarted efforts to contain the spread of nuclear weapons, and it permanently enlarged the international armaments industry. The automatic weapons wielded by child soldiers in war-ravaged African states today are a legacy of the cold war.

Some of the threats that the United States faces today are blowback from U.S. operations in the cold war. By overthrowing the government of Iran and then intensively assisting in the country's modernization for a decade and a half, the United States created the enemy it faces there today, a country that hates the United States and has advanced nuclear technology it got with U.S. help. The cold war also strengthened al-Qaeda in its formative years. Osama bin Laden's terrorist network had its origins in the fight to get the Soviets out of Afghanistan, a fight that the United States supported through the CIA and the government of neighboring Pakistan. People who the United States once regarded as the enemy of my enemy in the conflict with the Soviet Union are now simply enemies.

Perhaps the greatest legacy of the cold war is the U.S. conception of itself as a dragon-slayer. The United States had to decide what to do with its enormous military establishment. Though the military budget declined in the late 1980s and early 1990s both in absolute numbers and as a percentage of the gross domestic product (GDP), the United States remained in possession of a military force several times greater than that of its nearest competitors.

One reason for the uniqueness of the U.S. military position was that some countries rich enough to support large military establishments had elected not to do so. As Martin Walker points out, it may be the most remarkable legacy of the cold war that "neither Japan nor Europe sought to use its economic prowess to become the military behemoth its wealth could justify."[69] Some analysts maintain that this is because these countries have prospered under the U.S. security umbrella. They do not need to project military power around the world to maintain a stable environment for their investments. The United States does that for them. The question is, with the cold war over, do they still need that protection? Do they want it? What would they do if it were withdrawn?

THE UNITED STATES IN SEARCH OF A NEW ROLE

In the late 1980s it gradually became apparent that the cold war was nearing its end and that, at least for the time being, there existed a unipolar world—a world in which one power, the United States, stood unchallenged by any comparable military and political force.

The U.S. economy was not as supreme as it had been between the 1940s and 1960s. In the 1970s, Americans were shocked to discover that the Japanese had beat them at their own game, producing inexpensive goods of such high quality that American products looked shoddy by comparison. Meanwhile, the U.S. economy was staggering under rising oil prices and inflation caused by the attempt to pay simultaneously for the Vietnam War and the antipoverty programs initiated by President Lyndon Johnson. The United States now had a trade deficit—each year it imported more goods than it exported—as well as a spending deficit—the government did not collect as much in taxes as it spent. But during most of the 1980s (when, under Ronald Reagan, the United States lowered taxes and reduced government regulation, and world oil prices lowered), the U.S. economy once more registered strong growth. In the 1990s the Japanese economy fell into a long slump, the United States balanced its budget, and the growth of new technologies seemed to benefit the United States disproportionately, giving it faster growth rates than those in comparably developed economies such as those of western Europe.

Pax Americana?

Perhaps the United States would impose a Pax Americana—an American peace—on the world, as the Roman Empire had once imposed a Pax Romana on Europe and the countries bordering the Mediterranean Sea. This was the suggestion of a document prepared in 1992 under the supervision of Paul Wolfowitz, an undersecretary of defense, and subsequently leaked to the press. The document, entitled "Defense Planning Guidance for the Fiscal Years 1994–1999," made the case that the United States should retain an overwhelming superiority of power in the world. It would thereby convince "potential competitors that they need not aspire to a greater role or pursue a more aggressive posture to protect their legitimate interests."[70]

The United States, in this view, should act as a sort of world police force. Arguably, Wolfowitz's suggestion was merely a description of the role the United States had recently taken. The United States engaged in conflicts in three foreign states during the George H. W. Bush years. In 1989 in Panama, it ousted the dictator Manuel Noriega. In 1991 in Iraq, it led a coalition in the Gulf that drove Saddam Hussein's armed forces out of Kuwait. In 1992 in Somalia, it led a humanitarian mission that ended badly with a withdrawal of U.S. troops in 1994. They were all, in a sense, police actions. In Panama, as part of the U.S. invasion, Noriega was captured and later convicted of cocaine trafficking, racketeering, and money laundering. In Iraq, the Unitd States stopped the theft of Kuwait and its oil by Saddam Hussein. In Somalia, it had attempted to quell a civil war, and, thus, like a domestic dispute, always one of the most difficult and delicate tasks faced by a police force, and one that often goes awry.

President Bill Clinton, whose campaign team had achieved electoral victory by constantly reminding themselves that "It's the economy, stupid," was much more reluctant to send U.S. troops abroad. During the Somalia intervention, Americans were shocked by images that came to them from a country they had entered with the best of intentions. The mutilated body of a U.S. soldier, who had been killed in a battle with one of Somalia's many warring factions, was dragged through the streets of Mogadishu by Somali civilians as onlookers cheered. Clinton responded by ending U.S. involvement. Clinton was inclined to view the world as a marketplace and to see other countries as business partners, customers, and competitors rather than as security threats or malefactors in need of punishment. In 1994, when the Hutus of Rwanda murdered half a million of their fellow citizens, Clinton refused to call it an act of genocide and even insisted that the UN force sent to Rwanda be kept as small as possible to avoid involving the United States in another Somalia-like conflict with American casualties.[71]

Yet even Clinton found that he could not avoid using American military force in missions that did not directly affect American security. In 1994, he sent American troops to Haiti to depose the dictatorship whose activities had sent thousands of Haitian refugees to the United States.[72] Twice, in 1995 and in 1999, the United States led NATO forces in aerial bombing campaigns waged in conflicts that were outgrowths of the breakup of the former Yugoslavia. In the first case, the bombing was conducted in defense of Bosnian Muslims, who were being subjected to ethnic cleansing (a brutal campaign of rape and murder) by the Bosnian Serbs. The Serbs were also the target of the second campaign, waged in defense of the ethnic Albanians of Kosovo. Both of the Yugoslavian interventions came late in a humanitarian disaster that had dragged on for years. The United States had to overcome a great deal of inertia on the part of its NATO allies to win their cooperation in Kosovo.

Clinton ordered cruise missile strikes on Iraq in 1993, when it was found that Saddam Hussein had sponsored an attempt to assassinate George H. W. Bush by means of a car bomb. He ordered another cruise missile strike in 1996 to punish the Iraqis for violating the northern security zone agreed upon as part of the settlement of the Gulf War. And in December 1998 he ordered another strike when Iraq refused to cooperate with UN weapons inspectors.

Other uses of American force were more directly related to American security. In August 1998, in response to terrorist bombings of U.S. embassies in Tanzania and Kenya, Clinton ordered cruise missile strikes at al-Qaeda training camps in Afghanistan. Yet even these terrorist attacks were not unrelated to America's role as the world's policeman. If Osama bin Laden's pronouncements are to be believed, U.S. military bases and actions abroad are the reasons for al-Qaeda's attacks on the United States.

Meanwhile, U.S. forces remained in place, though in reduced numbers, in Japan and Germany, despite the unlikelihood that either of these countries would face attack in the foreseeable future. Why? Michael Mandelbaum says that America provides a general unacknowledged peacekeeping role.

> *The same American military forces that had once deterred the Soviet Union reassured all Europeans by serving as a buffer between and among countries that, while at peace with one another, harbored suspicions that their neighbors might be tempted to launch dangerous policies if circumstances*

> *changed. The American armed forces reassured one and all that no sudden shifts in Europe's security arrangements would occur.*[73]

George W. Bush, who became president in 2000, brought into office with him a group of thinkers who looked forward to an opportunity to assert America's role as policeman around the world, a role that would include the undermining or overthrowing of regimes the United States considered a threat to world peace.

According to the political scientist Francis Fukuyama, the Bush administration was influenced by the theories of intellectuals like William Kristol and Robert Kagan, who had been arguing for a more aggressive U.S. foreign policy in the pages of the magazine *The Weekly Standard*[74], arguments they summed up in a book entitled *Present Dangers*, published in 2000. Kristol and Kagan called for the United States to assert "benevolent hegemony" over the world, a policy that entailed "resisting, and where possible undermining, rising dictators and hostile ideologies; . . . supporting American interests and liberal democratic principles; and . . . providing assistance to those struggling against the more extreme manisfestations of human evil."[75] Fukuyama calls this policy "Wilsonianism minus international institutions."[76] That is, Kristol and Kagan, as well as other neoconservatives, wanted an outward-looking foreign policy, but had little confidence in the United Nations. According to Fukuyama:

> *In place of international institutions, Kristol and Kagan emphasized three tools for projecting U.S. influence: overwhelming military superiority; a renewed dedication to U.S. alliances; and missile defense as a means of protecting the American homeland from counterattack.*

Kristol and Kagan argued explicitly for regime change as a central component of their new-Reaganite policy. They asserted that getting tyrannical regimes to play by civilized rules through agreements, international law, or norms was ultimately unworkable, and that in the long run only democratization could ensure compliance and converging interests.

Kristol and Kagan represent a recent evolution of the neoconservative political tradition, which had a relatively minor voice in the administration of George H. W. Bush and a much greater voice in the administration of George W. Bush, whose major speeches were drafted by neoconservatives like David Frum. On domestic policy, neoconservatives are similar to regular conservatives in their criticism of large government programs intended to help the disadvantaged (which, it is argued, only perpetuate the social problems the programs aim to solve). On foreign policy, neoconservatives share with traditional conservatives a deep suspicion of the Soviet Union and an impatience with the United Nations. However, their concerns with the internal affairs of foreign governments separate them from traditional American conservatives, who are usually either isolationists or realists in the mode of George F. Kennan and Henry Kissinger. Realists believe that foreign policy should concern itself with the outward behavior of states. They are willing to deal with dictators if dictators have pro-American policies. By contrast, neoconservatives share with liberals the view that the United States should promote democracy and human rights. They differ with liberals as to the means they would use. Liberals favor international institutions; neoconservatives tend to favor unilateral or narrower multilateral agreements.

As Fukuyama points out, there is much that is subtle and perceptive in neoconservative thinking, and a great deal was evidently lost in translation when theory became policy during the Bush administration. Still, George W. Bush's insistence, in the lead-up to the war in Iraq, that Saddam Hussein must be stopped as Hitler should have been stopped and that the United States should fight terrorism by helping to spread democracy was consistent with both the agenda and the analysis of neoconservatives like Kristol and Kagan.

The second Bush administration, in contrast to the first one, showed an impatience for working with international institutions like the United Nations. This impatience was motivated not merely by a philosophical position but by experience. The United Nations's most ardent defenders admit that it is a flawed institution. Most of the member states of the United Nations are not democracies. Many, within their own borders, are abusers of human rights; thus, the United Nations has a dismal record of protecting those rights despite the lip service all its members routinely give to them. The UN charter stresses the sovereignty of its members, and so the United Nations is helpless to act in cases of civil war, a major form of conflict in the world today, which often threatens international peace. Thanks to the Security Council veto, the United Nations also has done little to punish aggression. It has been more successful as a peacekeeper and inspector after war has resolved conflict (as after the first Gulf War)—but even here its effectiveness has been limited by member states' reluctance to risk casualties in conflicts that do not directly affect their national interest. The United Nations's apparent inability to prevent Saddam Hussein from rebuilding his weapons program made conservatives and neoconservatives doubtful of its efficacy.

An even deeper problem with the United Nations, for neoconservatives, is inherent in the imbalance of U.S. military might. Why should the United States give up its freedom of action to an international body whose members are weaker than the United States and whose collective will and collective interests are bound to be different from those of the United States? Would the U.S. government be serving the American people well if it did so? It is one thing to give up some freedom of maneuver in order to participate in a coalition that makes you stronger—countries do that all the time. The case for working with the United Nations would have to rest on other grounds. The United States does not need the United Nations to repel a conventional attack or topple a regime it dislikes.

Possibly the U.S. failure to stabilize Iraq after defeating it and the many billions of dollars that have been spent in the effort provide an argument for more international involvement, but those lessons lay in the future as the new century began and a new president took office. General Wesley Clark, the former Supreme Allied Commander Europe of NATO who wrote about his experiences leading the intervention in Kosovo, reports meeting a senior member of the Bush administration soon after the 2000 election. The official told him: "We read your book—no one is going to tell us where we can or can't bomb."[77]

The idea that the United States should be—or already is—a sort of global police has recently been promoted by many voices in many ways. Neoconservatives promote it, but it rests on a reality that would be recognized by such a realist as George Kennan (who, late in his 10th decade, nevertheless opposed the 2003 invasion of Iraq). The U.S. military is many times stronger than any competitor, it has a global reach, and its existence has to be considered by anyone who has ambitions to be a regional big shot. Great Britain used to function as the watchdog of Europe, determined to prevent any one continental power from conquering its neighbors and thus becoming strong enough to challenge Great Britain. Great Britain did not perform this function out of altruism, nor for the advantage of Spain, France, or Germany, when each in its turn attempted to achieve hegemony on the continent. Most European countries benefited, and their sovereignty was maintained. Furthermore, as both the conservative George Kennan and the liberal Arthur Schlesinger Jr. have suggested, the United States itself may owe its long history of prosperity and freedom to Britain's protection (during the period when it was a matter of routine for American politicians to decry British imperialism).[78]

Those who favor the police role for the United States, whether they use the phrase "benevolent hegemony" as Kristol and Kagan do, or call the United States the "world's government" as Michael Mandelbaum does, believe the United States naturally fills this role, or ought to, for the world as a whole. They can point to the very small military establishments of western Europe and the nonexistence of Japan's army as signs that the best-developed economies of the world already rely on the protection of U.S. armed might. People in those countries, particularly in western Europe, might be inclined to say that their armed forces are small because they have at last entered an era of regional peace. They are surrounded by democracies, and as neoconservatives like to point out, democracies do not make war on one another. Why would they need U.S. protection?

U.S. Relative Economic Decline in a Multipolar World?

Others doubt that the United States could sustain a world police role. Instead, they expect to see a decline in U.S. power as was predicted by Paul Kennedy in his 1987 book, *The Rise and Fall of the Great Powers.*

In Kennedy's view, the military strength of powerful nations is based ultimately on the health and strength of their economies compared with the economies of other great powers. Relative economic decline leads to military decline and a loss of international influence. This effect is not immediately obvious, however, because it occurs after a delay. Great powers that are losing ground still possess the military forces and strategic assets (such as alliances, colonies, and military bases) that they have built up at the height of their prosperity, and they at first respond to economic decline by spending a larger percentage of their revenues on their armed forces.

In his book, which was widely read by U.S. policy makers in the late 1980s, Kennedy argued that the U.S. economy was in relative decline. It had enjoyed unmatched economic superiority for most of the 20th century. Although it continued to grow, other countries were catching up. While the cold war lasted, the United States was caught in the classic dilemma of a great power in its late stages. Its military obligations (to defend the Free World) were unchanged, while its economy was on the downturn. From this perspective (which probably enjoyed more favor in the Clinton administration than in the Bush adminstration) the end of the cold war was an opportunity for the United States to reduce its security obligations so as to bring "into balance . . . the nation's commitments and the nation's power."[79]

Kennedy's advice was given before the collapse of the Soviet Union and before the Internet-driven, information age resurgence of the U.S. economy in the 1990s, which made him amend his forecast.[80] The annual growth rate of the U.S. GDP between 1995 and 2001, according to the Organization for Economic Cooperation and Development (OECD), was 3.6 percent.[81] This is an impressive rate for a country that is already so well developed. (It is easier for a developing country, starting from a very low point, to show fast growth rates.)

Kennedy's thesis was given an update in a recent book, *After the Empire: The Breakdown of the American Order,* by the French political scientist Emmanuel Todd. Todd has an impressive credential: In a 1976 book, *La Chute finale* (published in English in 1979 as *The Final Fall*), he predicted the collapse of the Soviet Union. Todd believes, as Kennedy formerly did, that U.S. military power must inevitably diminish since its share of the world economy is diminishing. He further believes that much of the U.S. economic resurgence in the 1990s was illusory and rests on a bubble that is bound to burst, forcing a shrinking of U.S. commitments abroad. Since the early 1970s, the United States has had a trade deficit with the rest of the world—it has been importing more than it exports. This trade deficit has grown as manufacturing has moved to the economies of Asia where labor is cheaper. Yet the United States remains outwardly prosperous, and its people enjoy cheap consumer goods, thanks to the strength of the dollar (prior to 2007) and the constant inflow of foreign investment into the United States, especially foreign purchases of U.S. bonds. The dollar's strength is in large part artificial: Foreign central banks do not want the dollar to collapse, fearing its collapse would lower U.S. demand for their own exports and reduce the value of their own investments in dollars, bonds, and the U.S. infrastructure. They fear the collapse of the dollar would cause an international economic crisis. Therefore they buy dollars to help keep the value of the dollar high relative to other currencies. Consumers in the United States benefit because, as a result, their money buys more goods internationally. Advocates for American power, like Michael Mandelbaum in *The Case for Goliath,* make a virtue of this U.S. necessity: The American consumer performs a valuable service to the world economy by serving as a reliable source of demand and priming the pump of international trade and production according to the principles outlined by John Maynard Keynes. (Keynes, who argued for government intervention in the economy, is not otherwise admired by the free traders who usually favor this argument.)

In Todd's view, this situation is bound to be temporary. If the dollar collapses in value despite efforts to support it, if the U.S. economy is perceived as weak, foreign investors will move their money to other places. They would have to absorb a loss to do so, but they might do it during the next international financial crisis. Foreigners invest in the United States because they think it is a safe place to put their money, says Todd. "But if we agree that the American economy is weak when it comes to real, physical productivity, as the massive and still growing levels of imports of consumer goods would suggest, then one has to conclude that the capitalization of the American stock and bond markets is a fiction and therefore the money that is traveling to the United States is literally traveling to a mirage and not the true oasis that many take it for."[82] Europe's new currency, the euro, could soon come to replace or rival the dollar.

The dollar did decline in value in late 2007 and remains depressed as this book is being written; it remains to be seen what the long-term effect will be on the United States and its place in the world economy.

The United States has other weaknesses besides its trade deficit. With an aging population, the United States faces enormous shortfalls in anticipated payments to Social Security and Medicare programs. Economists disagree about the causes and seriousness of these deficits. Some lay the blame on demographic trends and say that only a cutback in promised services will solve the problem. Others, like the Princeton University professor and Nobel laureate James Paul Krugman, say that the problem arises from the rise of health care costs and therefore must be solved by a universal health care program that would lower costs. So far, nothing has been done except put off the solution to another day.

Emmanuel Todd sees U.S. foreign policy in the late 1990s and 2000s as a great bluff, intended to maintain a central role for the United States in a world that no longer needs it. In contrast to some critics of the United States, he regards America's international role during the cold war as positive. For half a century, the United States was "the guarantor of political freedom and economic order," but now (as of 2002) "the United States appears more and more to be contributing to international disorder. . . ."[83]

> *America has become a sort of black hole—absorbing merchandise and capital but incapable of furnishing the same goods in return. To assure its hold over the world that nourishes it, the country has to define a new role for itself other than the one it has lately fallen into, namely that of being the world's ultimate Keynesian consumer. This is not easy. Its redefinition as a hegemonic power has to be a political and military imposition—it must put itself forward as* the *state of the entire planet and acquire a global monopoly on legitmate domination. However, America does not have the necessary resources for this sort of recasting of itself. . . .*[84]

Todd maintained in 2002 that the United States exaggerated the threat posed by Iraq, Iran, terrorism, and Islamic fundamentalism in order to justify its quest for hegemony. Iran, though strong enough to merit serious consideration, was "a nation clearly on its road to becoming a normal democracy," while North Korea, Cuba, and Iraq were "outdated remains of a bygone era," whose regimes were bound to disappear without outside intervention. By building up these tiny threats, the United States "works to maintain the illusory fiction of the world as a dangerous place in need of American protection."[85]

But the world does not need the United States the way it needed it during the cold war, according to Todd. Worldwide demographic trends, such as the general increase in literacy and a resulting decline in birthrates, will lead to a more democratic and peaceful world without the need of a world police to depose dictators. The disorders seen in much of the Islamic world today are simply a symptom of transition to the modern condition of high literacy and low birthrates. Such transitions are often accompanied by reactionary movements that wish to restore traditional values, but which ultimately fail.

Nor does the world need to fear the United States. Due to the hidden weaknesses of the U.S. economy and the lack of commitment of the American people, the United States will not be able to pull off its imperial bluff. Todd predicts that after a coming economic collapse—not so drastic as that of the Soviet Union—the United States will simply have to get its economy in order, fix its trade deficit at the cost of a somewhat lower standard of living for its people, and return to world citizenship as a power existing on terms of equality with Russia, China, Japan, and the European Union.

From Leader of the Free World to Leader of Western Civilization?

Another objection to a U.S. role as world policeman was voiced by the political scientist Samuel P. Huntington in a 1993 *Foreign Affairs* article, "The Clash of Civilizations." America cannot be a world police force because the rules it might attempt to enforce are only a product of its own culture, and other cultures will not accept them.

Huntington's thinking was influenced by the rise of Islamic fundamentalism, which rejects core tenets of classical liberalism in favor of a belief that laws derive their authority directly from God, and the rise of China, which increased its economic power and transitioned to a free-market economy without becoming democratic. He suggested that in the coming era the world would be divided between civilizations rather than nations; he defined a civilization as a "cultural grouping." It might consist of one nation (Japan) or several "as is the case with Western, Latin American, and Arab civilizations."

Huntington suggested that it might be unwise for one civilization to attempt to impose its values on others.

> *Western ideas of individualism, liberalism, constitutionalism, human rights, equality, liberty, the rule of law, democracy, free markets, the separation of church and state, often have little resonance in Islamic, Confucian, Japanese, Hindu, Buddhist or Orthodox cultures. Western efforts to propagate each [sic] ideas produce instead a reaction against*

"human rights imperialism" and a reaffirmation of indigenous values, as can be seen in the support for religious fundamentalism by the younger generation in non-Western cultures.[86]

Though Huntington warned *against* attempts to impose American values on the rest of the world, many evangelical Christians in the United States would come to see it as supporting the view that the United States should assume a role as leader of a Christian world—a crusade in opposition to the Islamic world's jihad. This view became especially popular after the terrorist attacks of 9/11, which were perpetrated by Arabs in the name of Islam.

End of the Nation-State?

It has also been suggested that discussion of America's role in the world misses the point because the nation-state has played itself out as a leading factor in history. The nation-state evolved in western Europe, beginning in the 16th century. It assumed its fully modern form with the French Revolution, thanks to revolutionary France's military success. In the 20th century it became the basic model for national organization around the world. A nation-state has a strong central government and a strong sense of identity. Its people are united, not as a collection of a monarch's personal possessions, but by common beliefs and culture that are actively promoted by their governments and most educated people.

The nation-state has always had competition. Citizens of nation-states have always had other loyalties that may run counter to their loyalty to the nation-state—loyalties to class, ideology, ethnicity, or religion. In the 21st century, the economy has become intensely international. The economy's central economic unit—the multinational corporation—ultimately has no preference for one nation-state over another but instead exerts its influence to raise profits with a basic indifference to geography.

Even small, local companies and individuals are linked to a global economic network as never before. Goods, money, and information travel faster and in higher volume across national boundaries than ever before. An American who dials a number to get technical support for a laptop computer is likely to be helped by someone in India. The parts of the laptop are made in Korea; the programs it runs were perhaps designed in Japan. The venture capital to support the company that made the computer may come from anywhere.

Globalization's threat to the nation-state is all the greater in a world that is committed to the principle of free trade. At the beginning of the 21st century, there is a broad consensus among economists that global prosperity can be best ensured by the reduction or elimination of tariffs (taxes on imported goods) and subsidies that support home products or attempt to protect the jobs of people in a particular country. While free trade has its critics, who argue that it depresses wages and intensifies class divisions, economists favoring free trade greatly outnumber opponents. Free traders believe that the Great Depression of the 1930s was greatly worsened, if not caused, by the tariff barriers that were erected in Europe and the United States in reaction to economic declines. They advise politicians against actions that would seem, in the short term, to protect home industries and jobs. Thus, free trade principles restrict governments' ability to interfere with the global economy on behalf of their citizens, thereby reducing governments' role and the power of the nation-state. The United States is a nation-state, so it seems likely that if the nation-state's role in the world diminishes, so will the United States's role. This has clearly not happened yet.

If globalization does lead to the end of the nation-state, the United States will have done more than any other country to make it happen. The economists and politicians of the United States are the world's most enthusiastic promoters of globalization. Globalization American-style is also a major cause of anti-American feeling in many parts of the world.

America's Role in Global Economic Liberalization

Free trade is the third pillar of classical liberal ideology (along with democracy and human rights), and, since the late 1980s, the United States, both through its own actions and through its influence on international institutions such as the World Bank and the International Monetary Fund, has aggressively promoted economic liberalization. The 1980s not only saw the collapse of communism in the USSR and eastern Europe, it was also a time when central planning in democracies was discredited and the United States led a worldwide movement from left to right in economic policy.

For most of the cold war, the governments of the Free World embraced social democratic policies intended to guarantee workers a great deal of security. Though communism was anathema in the West, government intervention to reduce inequalities created by capitalism was viewed as inevitable and positive. The most influential economist of the time, John Maynard Keynes, had in the 1930s recommended heavy government spending during recessions to maintain high employment and prime the pump of national economies during business downturns. Economists like Keynes and John Kenneth Galbraith considered unequal income distribution to have been a cause of the Great Depression and looked with favor on government efforts to reduce that inequality. These efforts included a progressive, redistributive tax system (one that taxed high incomes more heavily than lower incomes), laws that favored union organization so that workers would be able to obtain higher wages and better benefits, large government programs like Social Security and Medicare, and relatively heavy regulation of industry. Thus, prevailing economic theory, the need to counter the appeal of communism, and the success of government regulation during World War II all inclined the leaders of the West to create a welfare state. The economist Paul Krugman notes that the welfare state, embodied in programs like Social Security, unemployment insurance, Medicare, the progressive tax code, and the encouragement of union growth expanded the middle class in the United States and western Europe. It created a degree of economic equality that had never before existed in the United States—and which Krugman maintains no longer exists.[87] The robust growth of Western economies during the 1950s and 1960s showed that regulation, strong unions, and redistributive tax programs could coexist with economic growth.

In the 1970s, however, a slowdown in the world economy made this bargain look much less workable. At the same time, in academia, laissez-faire capitalism was being reestablished as economic orthodoxy, as it had been in the late 19th century.

This change toward neoliberal economic theory, as it is often called, is associated with economist Milton Friedman. Its opponents deride it as free-market fundamentalism. When applied to international relations it is also called the Washington consensus, in recognition of its widespread acceptance among policy makers and the role of the United States in promulgating its principles.[88] Adherents of the Washington Consensus believe strongly in the self-regulation of free markets. The market, left to itself, will ensure full employment and an efficient functioning of the economy that, ultimately, will bring a better standard of living to everyone. If, for a while, there are hard times for some people, as there were for so many in the United States before the 1940s, those are merely the costs a society pays during its transition to a mature capitalist economy. It is to the natural life cycle of capitalism—not to welfare programs—that the economies of the West owe their high standard of living and relatively fair distribution of wealth. Government interference, however well meant, makes that transition take longer or may prevent it and at best merely takes credit for the achievements of capitalism.

Neoliberal economics is not a mere expression of ideology. It is sophisticated. Even opponents like Joseph E. Stiglitz and Paul Krugman praise the scientific rigor of academic neoliberals while criticizing the real-life consequences of their theories. However, neoliberalism's basic line of argument is identical to those used in the late 19th century by foes of laws to set a minimum wage, abolish child labor, and regulate food and drugs.

In the 1980s, Margaret Thatcher in Great Britain and Ronald Reagan in the United States came to office, each determined to apply Friedman's theories in their country. Though some of Friedman's prescriptions backfired and forced their governments to beat a hasty retreat, the 1980s nevertheless accelerated a worldwide trend away from state planning and regulation and toward free-market principles, a trend begun in the late 1970s with the deregulation of the telephone company and the airline industries. Taxes were lowered and the tax code became less redistributive; government-run industries were privatized; government regulations on industry were reduced; union membership fell (whether primarily because of global economic trends or less favorable treatment by governments is a matter of dispute); and subsidies and tariffs that protected home industries and acted as a barrier to trade were reduced. While applying these principles at home, the United States made strenuous efforts to promulgate them abroad. Those who favor these policies have been able to point to overall positive economic trends—stagflation has been licked—and the rapid growth of East Asian economies, which they attribute to the international application of free-market, Friedmanite principles.

Opponents point to the growing inequality and class divisions wherever free-market fundamentalism has been applied, including the United States. They maintain that government investment and regulation played a large role in East Asian growth and even in such lauded free-market triumphs as the Internet (ultimately based on government-funded research).

The example of Chile is frequently cited by experts on both sides of the argument. In 1970, the people of Chile elected a Marxist president, Salvador Allende, who moved to nationalize much of Chile's foreign-owned industry. In 1973, with assistance from the CIA, right-wingers in Chile staged a military coup. For the next 16 years, the country was ruled by a dictator, Augusto Pinochet. Pinochet stifled all political opposition by means of arbitrary arrests and secret executions. Meanwhile, starting in 1975, he turned the reform of the Chilean economy over to a group of Chilean economists who had been trained at the University of Chicago under the influence of Milton Friedman. Pinochet gave his Chicago-trained economists a free hand, even when their prescriptions ran counter to the wishes of the elites that had put him in power. Thus, from 1975 to 1989, Chile became a laboratory for the application of Friedmanism (much as Russia had become a laboratory for communism after 1917). Milton Friedman himself, though he said he deplored the military junta, praised its wisdom in applying his principles.

The interpretation of the effects of Friedmanism in Chile is an intellectual battleground for liberals and neoliberals, Keynesians and Friedmanists.

Friedman's advocates point out that Chile's economy grew at a rate of 6.6 percent between 1978 and 1981 (1982 was the year of a worldwide recession during which the Chilean economy suffered more than most). The economy was booming again in 1988, enough for Pinochet to risk an election. Expecting to win, he permitted himself to be voted out of office. Friedman's opponents point out that during the period when Pinochet was in power income was redistributed from the poor to the rich, wages fell sharply, and unemployment grew to massive proportions (40 percent). They also dispute Friedmanism's contribution to Chile's overall growth. Consequently, they argue, the economic policies had a negative effect on Chilean society, increasing inequality, making workers less secure, and giving Chile one of the worst pollution problems in the world, thanks to decisions to relieve the country's foreign-owned mining industry from regulation.[89]

The experience of Chile is especially important because Friedman's economic "shock therapy" has since been applied to many economies around the world. The collapse of the Soviet Union provided an opportunity for free-market fundamentalists in the United States to apply their policies in eastern Europe and the Russian Federation. Former communist republics sought help in remaking themselves into modern capitalist economies. Leaders of developing countries accepted the idea that communism had failed and took the advice to fully embrace the forces of the market.

The system has been adopted partly through the initiatives of governments persuaded by free-market theories, partly with the influence of the United States, and especially through the three Bretton Woods economic organizations: the World Bank, the International Monetary Fund, and the World Trade Organization. Often governments of developing countries had no choice but to take the advice of these organizations, since they were applying for assistance that was conditional on their applying neoliberal policies within their countries. Since the 1980s these bodies have been staffed by experts who believe in the Washington Consensus, and the policies that they have recommended to, and in many cases forced on, developing nations have been policies hostile to labor unions and government regulation. According to Joseph E. Stiglitz, former chief economist for the World Bank and a critic of the "shock therapy," the existing Bretton Woods institutions underwent a dramatic change in the 1980s, becoming

> *. . . the new missionary institutions through which [free market] ideas were pushed on the reluctant poor countries that often badly needed their loans and grants. The ministers of finance in poor countries were willing to become converts, if necessary, to obtain the funds, though the*

vast majority of government officials, and, more to the point, people in these countries, often remained skeptical.[90]

Stiglitz is highly critical of IMF performance in particular, observing that a blinkered, ideologically driven imposition of antigovernment and antiregulatory principles has resulted in disaster in Africa, Latin America, and the former Soviet republics. Economic shock therapy in countries with underdeveloped economic and political institutions has destroyed jobs, raised unemployment levels, destroyed infant industries, benefited a small elite, and increased poverty among many. It has done this even when it has led to overall growth for the country—and often it has led to crashes rather than growth. Paul Krugman notes:

> *A decade ago it was common to cite the success of the Chilean economy, where Augusto Pinochet's Chicago-educated advisers turned to free-market policies after Pinochet seized power in 1973, as proof that Friedman-inspired policies showed the path to successful economic development. But although other Latin nations, from Mexico to Argentina, have followed Chile's lead in freeing up trade, privatizing industries, and deregulating, Chile's success story has not been replicated.*

On the contrary, Krugman points out most Latin Americans view neoliberal policies as a failure. The promised takeoff in economic growth never came, while income inequality has worsened.[91]

Rise and Fall of the Bush Doctrine

The debate about America's post–cold war role gained new momentum after the attacks of September 11, 2001, with President George W. Bush's announcement of a War on Terror. In 2002, warning of the threat to the United States that would be posed by terrorists armed with weapons, Bush asserted a new foreign policy principle: The United States would reserve the right to respond unilaterally—without assistance or sanction from allies—to *emerging* threats to its security.

The Bush doctrine was first enunciated in a June 1, 2002, speech at the United States Military Academy at West Point, New York. "We must take the battle to the enemy . . . and confront the worst threats before they emerge. In the world we have entered, the only path to safety is the path of action. And this nation will act."[92] In another speech a month later, Bush said, "America must act against these terrible threats before they're fully formed."[93] In other words, the United States could wage preventive war. This doctrine was later confirmed in *The National Security Strategy of the United States of America,* released by the White House in September 2002. According to Arthur M. Schlesinger Jr., preventive war was a departure from the United States's traditional doctrine of justification for war. It "replaced a policy aimed at peace through the prevention of war by a policy aimed at peace through preventive war."[94] Schlesinger believed that the Bush administration hard-liners like Paul Wolfowitz were responsible for this change in view and that their ulterior motive in asserting the Bush Doctrine was to achieve American "global hegemony."[95]

> *Where did Mr. Bush get the revolutionary idea of preventive war as the basis of U.S. foreign policy? His conviction apparently is that the unique position of the United States as the planet's supreme military, economic, and cultural power creates an unprecedented opportunity for America to impose its values on other countries and thereby save them from themselves. Our supremacy, rendered permanent, will enable us to promote democracy, free markets, private enterprise, and godliness, and thereby control the future.*[96]

When weapons inspectors failed to find the expected WMDs in Iraq (the supposed justification for the war), the creation of democracy in Iraq was cited as the new justification for the war. By bringing democracy to Iraq, the United States would help to spread democracy throughout the Middle East. A democratic Middle East, the theory went, would not spawn terrorists, since its people would have a nonviolent means of expressing their political will. It would not practice violence on its neighbors or on the West, since, historically, democracies never made war on one another.

By 2004, many of those who had favored the war in Iraq considered that it had been badly mismanaged. By 2005, as Iraq descended into civil war, continued U.S. involvement became unpopular among the American people.

The Iraq War was even more unpopular in the Middle East and among America's traditional allies. A 2005 poll conducted in Europe by the Pew Global Attitudes Project found that since 2000 opinion of the United States and its policies had plummeted in the Muslim world and in western Europe (though not in eastern Europe). "Anti-Americanism in Europe, the Middle East and Asia," had "surged as a result of the U.S. war in Iraq."[97]

CONCLUSION

With an unusually conservative president in office, his party in control of both houses of Congress, and a people united by the attacks of 9/11, neoconservatives gained a unique opportunity to put into action the policies they were sure would save the world. They were able to perform a historical experiment. As of 2008, the majority of Americans seem to believe that these policies have failed. At present, there is little enthusiasm in the United States for the Bush Doctrine.

On the contrary, throughout 2008 U.S. public opinion polls consistently showed a majority of Americans disapproving of George Bush's performance as president, opposing the war in Iraq, and favoring a timetable for withdrawal from Iraq. Though it seemed that Iraq was becoming more stable thanks to a recent influx of American troops, Americans were apparently unwilling to sustain those levels, and it was far from clear that the Iraqi government could stand on its own. Afghanistan seemed to require a still greater American commitment if it was not to return to the hands of the Taliban, the radical Islamic fundamentalists who sheltered Osama bin Laden while he planned the 9/11 attacks. Looking elsewhere abroad, Americans were wary when the Russian military rolled into South Ossetia in response to shelling by Georgian forces, displaying an aggressiveness not seen since the end of the cold war.

Adding to the administration's unpopularity was an economic crisis. The United States was in recession, and at the same time battling inflation, a situation that had not occurred since the 1970s. The dollar had lowered in value relative to other currencies, immediately reducing the purchasing power of American consumers. Americans were made effectively poorer by high food and gas prices, both linked to a permanent rise in international demand.

It is common during U.S. recessions for some commentators to call them cyclical and predict a speedy recovery and for others to call them structural and predict that the suffering will go on for years. In the past, the gloomier commentators have usually been proven wrong. If, this time, they are correct, then Emmanuel Todd (who foretold the collapse of the Soviet Union) will have been a prophet a second time. The United States, though still formidable, would no longer be the unquestioned leader of the world. Still rich, but less so relative to rising Asian economies, it would be one of several major international powers. It would have to further its interests with less military might and more diplomacy.

---

[1] James Oliver Robertson. *American Myth, American Reality.* New York: Hill & Wang, 1980, p. 25.

[2] John Winthrop. "A Model of Christian Charity." Available online. URL: http://religiousfreedom.lib.virginia.edu/sacred/charity.html. Accessed October 11, 2007.

[3] ———. "A Model of Christian Charity."

[4] Thomas Paine. *Common Sense.* Available online. URL: http://www.earlyamerica.com/early america/milestones/commonsense/text.html. Accessed October 11, 2007.

[5] Alexis de Tocqueville. *Democracy in America.* Author's Introduction. Available online. URL: http://xroads.virgiedu/~HYPEDETOC/toc_html. Accessed November 20, 2008.

[6] Harriet Martineau, *Society in America,* Part I, Politics. London: Saunders & Ottey, 1837, p. 2.

[7] Trollope, Frances. *Domestic Manners of the Americans.* Available online. URL: http://www.gutenberg.org/etext10345. Accessed August 12, 2008.

[8] Abraham Lincoln. State of the Union Address, December 1, 1862. Available online. URL: http://www.infoplease.com/t/hist/state-of-the-union/74.html. Accessed November 20, 2008.

[9] ———. The Gettysburg Address. Available online. URL: http://www.yale.edu/lawweb/avalon/gettyb.htm. Accessed November 20, 2008.

[10] Arthur M. Schlesinger Jr. *War and the American Presidency.* New York: W. W. Norton & Company, 2004, pp. 4–5.

[11] Wilson's War Message to Congress, April 2, 1917—Woodrow Wilson. *War Messages.* 65th Cong., 1st Sess., Senate Doc. No. 5, Serial No. 7264, Washington, D.C., 1917, pp. 3–8, *passim.* Available online. URL: http://www.lib.byu.edu/index.php/Wilson%27s_War_Message_to_Congress. Accessed August 7, 2008.

[12] Michael E. Brown, Sean M. Lynn-Jones, and Steven E. Miller. *Debating the Democratic Peace.* Cambridge, Mass.: MIT Press, 1996.

[13] Franklin Roosevelt. The Four Freedoms, December 6, 1941. Available online. URL: http://www.americanrhetoric.com/speeches/fdrthefourfreedoms.htm. Accessed November 20, 2008.

[14] Greg Kaza. "Going to School on Reaganomics." *National Review Online,* June 15, 2004. Available online. URL: http://www.nationalreview.com/nrof_comment/kaza200406151029.asp. Accessed November 20, 2008.

[15] Ludwig von Mises. *Liberalism.* Available online. URL: http://www.mises.org/liberal/isec1.asp. Accessed December 11, 2007.

[16] Niall Ferguson. *Colossus: The Price of America's Empire.* New York: Penguin, 2004, p. 2.

[17] David Mosler and Bob Catley. *Global America: Imposing Liberalism on a Recalcitrant World.* Westport, Conn.: Praeger, 2000, p. xiii.

[18] Fawn M. Brodie. *No Man Knows My History: The Life of Joseph Smith.* New York: Vintage, 1995.

[19] Curtis D. Johnson. *Islands of Holiness: Rural Religion in Upstate New York 1790–1860.* Ithaca, N.Y.: Cornell University Press, 1989, p. 42.

[20] Paul E. Johnson. *A Shopkeeper's Millennium: Society and Revivals in Rochester, New York, 1815–1837.* New York: Hill & Wang, 2004, pp. 136–141.

[21] "Bryan's 'Cross of Gold' Speech: Mesmerizing the Masses." *History Matters: US Survey Course on the Web.* Available online. URL: http://historymatters.gmu.edu/d/5354/. Accessed December 11, 2007.

[22] Lawrence W. Levine. *Defender of the Faith: William Jennings Bryan: The Last Decade, 1915–1925.* Cambridge, Mass.: Harvard University Press, 1987, p. 359.

[23] George Washington. *The Farewell Address, 1796.* Available online. URL: http://www.yale.edu/lawweb/avalon/washing.htm. Accessed August 12, 2008.

[24] Jefferson, Thomas. *First Inaugural Address, March 4, 1801.* Available online at http://avalon.law.yale.edu/19th_century/jefinau1.asp. Retrieved January 30, 2009.

[25] George F. Kennan. *American Diplomacy 1900–1950.* Chicago: The University of Chicago Press, 1951, pp. 4–5.

[26] Kennan. *American Diplomacy,* p. 5.

[27] Paul Kennedy. *The Rise and Fall of the Great Powers.* New York: Random House, 1987, p. 95.

[28] "We shall divert through our own Country a branch of commerce which the European States have thought worthy of the most important struggles and sacrifices, and in the event of peace on terms which have been contemplated by some powers we shall form to the American union a barrier against the dangerous extension of the British Province of Canada and add to the Empire of liberty an extensive and fertile Country thereby converting dangerous Enemies into valuable friends." Jefferson to George Rogers Clark, December 25, 1780. Boyd, Julian P., ed. Papers of Thomas Jefferson, vol. 4, Princeton, N.J.: Princeton University Press, 1951, pp. 237–238.

[29] Walter A. McDougall. *Promised Land, Crusader State: The American Encounter with the World Since 1776.* New York: Houghton Mifflin, 1997, p. 78.

[30] Sam W. Haynes and Christopher Morris, eds. *Manifest Destiny and Empire: American Antebellum Expansionism.* Arlington: Texas A&M University Press, 1997, p. 9. O'Sullivan is quoted in the introduction by Robert W. Johannsen.

[31] John Nieto-Phillips. "Citizenship and Empire: Race, Language, and Self-Government in New Mexico and Puerto Rico." *Centro Journal* 11, p. 53.

[32] Quoted in Haynes. *Manifest Destiny and Empire,* p. 49.

[33] Frederick Jackson Turner. *The Significance of the Frontier in American History.* Available online. URL: http://xroads.virginia.edu/~Hyper/TURNER. Accessed October 11, 2007.

[34] ———. *The Significance of the Frontier.*

[35] Scott Nearing and Joseph Freeman. *Dollar Diplomacy: A Study in American Imperialism.* 1925. Reprint, New York: Arno Press, 1970, p. xiii.

[36] Bays, Daniel H., "The Foreign Missionary Movement in the 19th and early 20th Centuries." National Humanities Center. Available online. URL: http://nationalhumanitiescenter.org/tserve/nineteen/nkeyinfo/fmmovement.htm. Retrieved February 1, 2009; and Gossett, Thomas F. *Race, the History of an Idea in America.* New York: Oxford University Press, 1997, pp. 176–197.

[37] Kennedy. *The Rise and Fall,* p. 201.

[38] Ferguson. *Colossus,* p. 43.

[39] Quoted in Frederick Merk. *Manifest Destiny and the Mission in American History: A Reinterpretation.* New York: Knopf, 1963, p. 232; quoted in Niall Ferguson. *Colossus,* p. 44.

[40] Ferguson. *Colossus,* p. 46.

[41] ——. *Colossus*, p. 49.

[42] Kennan. *American Diplomacy*, p. 15; R. Cortissoz. *Life of Whitelaw Reid.* New York: Charles Scribner's Sons, 1921, Part II, p. 266, from a letter of January 22, 1900, to Senator William R. Chandler.

[43] Kennan. *American Diplomacy*, p. 18.

[44] Nearing and Freeman. *Dollar Diplomacy*, p. 121.

[45] Kennan. *American Diplomacy*, p. 68.

[46] ——. *American Diplomacy*, p. 71.

[47] Spam, a canned precooked meat, is a product of Hormel Foods. Standard fare for American G.I.s during World War II, it was also supplied to the Red Army of the Soviet Union.

[48] Ferguson. *Colossus*, p. 64.

[49] ——. *Colossus*, pp. 63–64.

[50] Schlesinger. *War and the American Presidency*, p. 7.

[51] Warren G. Harding. Inaugural Address, March 4, 1921. Available online. URL: http://www.yale.edu/lawweb/avalon/presiden/inaug/harding.htm. Accessed August 26, 2008.

[52] Thomas F. Gossett. *Race: The History of an Idea in America.* New York: Schocken Books, 1965, p. 406.

[53] David J. Goldberg. "The Rapid Rise and the Swift Decline of the Ku Klux Klan." In *Discontented America: The United States in the 1920s.* Baltimore: Johns Hopkins University Press, 1999. Excerpted in Phillip Margulies, ed. *The Roaring Twenties.* San Diego, Calif.: Greenhaven Press, 2004, pp. 172–174.

[54] Kennedy, *The Rise and Fall*, pp. 282–283.

[55] Winston S. Churchill. *The Gathering Storm.* Boston: Houghton Mifflin Company, 1953, pp. 259–321, 392–395.

[56] Schlesinger. *War and the American Presidency*, p. 11.

[57] ——. *War and the American Presidency*, p. 12.

[58] ——. *War and the American Presidency*, p. 13.

[59] "Conference at Bretton Woods: United Nations Monetary and Financial Conference at Bretton Woods. Summary of Agreements. July 22, 1944. Source: Pamphlet No. 4, PILLARS OF PEACE." Available online. URL: http://www.ibiblio.org/pha/policy/1944/440722a.html. Accessed November 20, 2008.

[60] George Kennan. The Long Telegram, February 22, 1946. Available online. URL: http://www.ntanet.net/KENNAN.html. Accessed August 26, 2008.

[61] ——. The Long Telegram.

[62] ——. "Containment: 40 Years Later: Containment Then and Now." *Foreign Affairs* (Spring 1987). Available online. URL: http://www.foreignaffairs.org/19870301faessay7847/george-f-kennan/containment-40-years-later-co ntainment-then-and-now.html. Accessed October 24, 2007.

[63] ——. "Containment."

64 Martin Walker. *The Cold War: A History.* New York: Henry Holt & Company, 1994, pp. 22–23.

65 USINFO.STATE.GOV. "The Marshall Plan: Rebuilding Europe," International Information Programs. Available online. URL: http://usinfo.state.gov/products/pubs/marshallplan/. Accessed October 25, 2007.

66 Kennedy. *The Rise and Fall,* p. 425.

67 Walker. *The Cold War.* Walker attributes the phrase "National Security State" to Daniel Patrick Moynihan.

68 ———. *The Cold War,* p. 2.

69 ———. *The Cold War,* p. xii.

70 Atif A. Kubursi. "Oil and the Gulf War: An 'American Century' or a 'New World Order.'" *Arab Studies Quarterly* Fall 1993, p. 11. Available online. URL: http://findarticles.com/p/articles/mi_m2501/is_n4_v15/ai_16075106/.pg_1?tag=artBody;col1. Accessed August 26, 2008.

71 Ferguson. *Colossus,* pp. 148–149.

72 Michael Mandelbaum. *The Case for Goliath.* New York: PublicAffairs, 2005, p. 66.

73 Mandelbaum. *The Case for Goliath,* p. 34.

74 Francis Fukuyama. *America at the Crossroads: Democracy, Power, and the Neoconservative Legacy.* New Haven, Conn.: Yale University Press, 2006, p. 40.

75 William Kristol and Robert Kagan. *Present Dangers: Crisis and Opportunity in American Foreign and Defense Policy.* New York: Encounter Books, 2000, p. 12. Quotes in Fukuyama, *America at the Crossroads.* p. 41.

76 Fukuyama. *America at the Crossroads,* p. 41.

77 Wesley K. Clark. *Waging Modern War: Bosnia, Kosovo, and the Future of Combat.* New York: Public Affairs, 2002, pp. xxvi–xxvii.

78 Schlesinger. *War and the American Presidency,* p. 5. Schlesinger quotes the American historian C. Vann Woodward as suggesting that in the 19th century the United States enjoyed "free security."

79 Paul Kennedy. *The Rise and Fall,* p. 534. Kennedy is quoting the midcentury newspaper columnist Walter Lippmann. Kennedy discusses U.S. relative decline on pp. 514–535.

80 ———. "What Hasn't Changed since September 11." *Los Angeles Times,* September 11, 2002.

81 Ferguson. *Colossus,* p. 240.

82 Emmanuel Todd. *After the Empire: The Breakdown of the American Order.* New York: Columbia University Press, 2002 (translation 2003), p. 97.

83 ———. *After the Empire,* p. 1.

84 ———. *After the Empire,* p. 123.

85 ———. *After the Empire,* p. 133.

86 Samuel P. Huntington. "The Clash of Civilizations?" *Foreign Affairs.* New York: Summer 1993, vol. 22, is. 3, p. 22.

[87] Paul Krugman. *The Conscience of a Liberal.* New York: W. W. Norton & Company, 2007, pp. 3–9.

[88] Joseph E. Stiglitz. *Globalization and Its Discontents.* New York: W. W. Norton & Company, 2003, p. 22.

[89] "Chile Air Pollution," *TED Case Studies.* Available online. URL: http://www.american.edu/TED/chileair.htm. Retrieved January 30, 2009.

[90] Stiglitz. *Globalization,* p. 15.

[91] "Chile Air Pollution." *TED Case Studies.* Available online. URL: http://www.american.edu/ted/chileair.htm. Accessed August 26, 2008.

[92] Office of the Press Secretary. "President Bush Delivers Graduation Speech at West Point," June 1, 2002. Available online. URL: http://www.whitehouse.gov/news/releases/2002/06/20020601-3.html. Accessed October 3, 2007.

[93] ———. "President Salutes Troops of the 10th Mountain Division," July 19, 2002. Available online. URL: http://www.whitehouse.gov/news/releases/2002/07/20020719.html. Accessed October 3, 2007.

[94] Schlesinger. *War and the American Presidency,* p. 21.

[95] ———. *War and the American Presidency,* p. 25.

[96] ———. *War and the American Presidency,* p. 25.

[97] "Pew Global Attitudes Project. "16-Nation Pew Global Attitudes Survey: U.S. Image Up Slightly, but Still Negative." Available online. URL: http://pewglobal.org/reports/display.php?ReportID=247. Accessed March 15, 2008.

3

Global Perspectives

America seeks its new global role in a world that is itself in flux, a place of shifting alliances and identities. The United States has, by now, a long history and a different, complex relationship with each international region. Europe is the continent with which the United States has the deepest historical and cultural links. It was America's closest cold war ally, and after such closeness perhaps it is inevitable that the most prominent trend is a gradual drift apart in ideology and policy. Latin America has been dominated by the United States for more than a century. Impoverished and politically backward for most of that time, Latin America has shown a trend toward greater democracy and, at the same time, greater independence from its powerful neighbor to the north. The several regions that are lumped together, for purposes of discussion, as "the Muslim world" have been in a state of political turmoil for many years. Thanks to Middle Eastern oil resources and the 9/11 attacks, they have been the principal focus of American foreign policy for almost a decade. In Asia, the United States confronts the rising economies, which may, before the middle of the 21st century, displace the United States as global economic, military, and political leaders. As China and India grow, they will demand more and more of the world's resources, and the United States will have to find a way to compete and live peacefully with them: Some analysts believe that in the long run, this may be the greatest U.S. foreign policy challenge today. Meanwhile, the United States faces a surprise in the Russian Federation—the old enemy it had thought was vanquished and rehabilitated has lately retreated from democracy and shown its old aggressiveness, and it is still armed with nuclear weapons.

All these trends take place in a world linked more closely than ever by the technology and the economics of global trade, where terrorists post pictures of their latest murders on the Internet, and computer users in Houston, Texas, are not surprised to have their tech-support questions answered by a woman in New Delhi.

EUROPE

Introduction

Leaders in the United States tend to think Europeans and Americans ought to cooperate on foreign policy. When the United States invades Iraq to depose Saddam Hussein, Europe should provide funds and soldiers. If the United States regards Iran's quest for nuclear weapons as a threat to world peace, Europeans should be equally concerned. Europe should help, because Europe is strong: Taken as a whole, it is the world's largest or second largest economy (depending on which countries are included). It contains two nuclear weapons states and holds two permanent seats on the UN Security Council. Europe should also help because the United States and Europe have so much in common. They have a shared history and culture, similar forms of government, similarly mature economies, and for nearly 40 years during the cold war the United States was western Europe's protector against Soviet communism. Yet even during the 1950s, 1960s, 1970s, and 1980s, with Soviet tanks and intermediate range nuclear missiles staring them in the face, western Europeans often irked the United States with a desire to go their own way and to make deals with the enemy.

The past has a way of seeming simpler than it was. Both Americans and Europeans tend to forget the quarrels that marked the cold war alliance of the United States and western Europe. The cold war's end, which turned several eastern European nations from Soviet satellites into pro-American democracies and shrank support for left-leaning policies in western Europe, was the high-water mark of European approval of the United States. Since then, the politics of Americans and Europeans have been drifting apart in many ways. In the view of many Europeans, it is America that has changed.

Anatomy of the Region

Europe embraces 47 countries, including the Vatican but not Russia, which for the purposes of this discussion is Europe's eastern neighbor. The region's many natural geographical barriers have given it a history of fragmentation into numerous separate, sovereign countries. Modern European history can be viewed as a series of efforts to put its pieces together by conquest. Spain, France, Germany, and arguably the Soviet Union have each in turn attempted to dominate the continent.

What these states could not do by force may now be occurring by mutual consent. Aware that they must unite to continue to exert global influence, Europeans have begun to create a federal system that will preserve national languages and cultures while enabling Europeans to act as one. The first big formal step toward integration came in 1957, when the Treaty of Rome established the European Economic Community (EEC). Though the EEC's immediate purpose was simply to unify European economic policy and reduce trade barriers within Europe, some supporters hoped that it would lead eventually toward political unification. In 1993, after the collapse of the Soviet Union, the European Union (EU) was established, with a European parliament, a European court, a central bank, and a pan-European currency, the euro. The euro is now the regular national currency of 13 EU member states and is a potential rival of the dollar as a worldwide reserve currency. Membership in the European Union has steadily expanded, with former communist states gradually being accepted. Turkey has long sought membership, but must overcome the resistance other Europeans feel toward inclusion of a Muslim country. Opponents also object to Turkish restrictions on free speech—in particular to Article 301 of the Turkish penal code, which makes it illegal to "insult" Turkish government institutions.

European integration faces many obstacles, chief among them the member states' reluctance to surrender their independence. The reluctance is reflected in the EU's main political institutions, which give equal weight to each country regardless of size.

As of 2005, Europe, exclusive of Russia but including Ukraine, was home to 587 million people. It has a high population density, and the lowest birthrate of any region of comparable size in the world: The average European woman gives birth to 1.52 children—less than the two needed for a natural replacement by birth of the population. Europe's population is growing slightly, nevertheless, thanks to immigration.

Political Culture

Most of Europe's 587 million people inhabit genuine parliamentary democracies whose leaders can be voted out of office in popular elections. The jury is still out on a few of the countries of the former Soviet Union.

When it comes to politics, Europeans differ among themselves, as Americans do, but in general European voters are to the left of the United States.[1] On a host of issues, European opinions—especially in western Europe—correspond to those of the liberal wing of the Democratic Party in the United States. Europeans tend to be against the death penalty; they take global warming seriously and did so much earlier than most people in the United States; they believe that they derive benefits from higher taxes; and higher prices for gasoline seem like a necessary evil to raise revenue and encourage conservation.[2] They tend to favor international law and multilateral institutions like the United Nations; most of them are dubious about the value of ballistic missile defense systems; most opposed the 2003 Iraq War; they tend to be sympathetic to the plight of Palestinians and critical of Israel; and while they worry about Iran's quest for nuclear weapons, most do not believe it was helpful to list it with Iraq and North Korea as part of an axis of evil and don't care for talk of preventive war; and they deplore human rights abuses associated with the United States–led war on terror.

In the 1500s and 1600s, European Protestants and Catholics burned each other at the stake over religion, but today polls consistently show Europe overall to be a more secular society than the United States.[3] Few Europeans believe that religion should influence government, and they tend to disapprove of the power that fundamentalist Christians exert on U.S. policy (many American fundamentalists return the compliment by identifying the European Union with the beast of Revelation). Europeans are not particularly suspicious of the state, and European politicians do not obtain votes by promising to "get the government off the backs" of the people. With some exceptions, most notably England under Prime Minister Margaret Thatcher in the 1980s, European voters have not supported efforts to eliminate the welfare state, and even in England the social safety net is more complete than in America (including as it does national health insurance). In part because the government pays for health care, European agencies impose stricter regulations on food and drugs than does the United States Food and Drug Administration.

The formerly communist countries of eastern Europe, which were under Soviet domination during the cold war, have political characteristics of their own deriving from their common historical experience. This Europe, thanks to memories of the cold war and proximity to Russia, tends to be more pro-American and anti-Russian than western Europe. It is economically less mature, with lower per capita incomes but faster growth. In the 1990s, the economy of Poland underwent a sudden and drastic liberalization of its market on advice from economists in the United States.[4]

Europe and the United States

In *Of Paradise and Power,* the American neoconservative Robert Kagan finds deep differences in U.S. and European approaches to foreign policy.

> *When it comes to setting national priorities, determining threats, defining challenges, and fashioning and implementing foreign and defense policies, the United States and Europe have parted ways. . . . The European caricature at its most extreme depicts an America dominated by a "culture of death," its warlike temperament the natural product of a violent society where every man has a gun and the death penalty reigns.*[5]

Kagan wrote this long essay in 2002 and was reacting in part to European reluctance to support the U.S. invasion of Iraq (so angry did this reluctance make some American politicians that U.S. politicians wanted to rename French fries "freedom fries"). Though Europeans were not unanimous on the subject, they had tended to see Iraq as less of an immediate threat than the Bush administration claimed it to be. The United States invaded Iraq on the grounds that this was the best way, perhaps the only way, to keep Iraq's dictator, Saddam Hussein, from using weapons of mass destruction (chemical weapons and nuclear weapons) and giving them to terrorists. Shortly before the invasion, United Nations weapons inspectors in Iraq had asked for more time to look for Iraq's weapons of mass destruction. The United States insisted that Saddam Hussein would only continue to mislead and trick the weapons inspectors as he had in the past. Europeans were inclined to let the weapons inspectors finish their work. As of 2008, the European view regarding Iraq looks prudent, since, ultimately, no WMDs were found in Iraq after the U.S. invasion. However, as Kagan points out, European reluctance to use force goes beyond the Middle East. For several years, Europeans did little to stop a brutal civil war going on nearby in the former Yugoslavia.

For Kagan, one key to understanding European and American foreign policy differences is the weakness of Europe's military forces. Europe's forces are small not only in comparison to those wielded by the United States, but also in proportion to its economy. According to Kagan, it is only natural that Europeans prefer that the United States clear its military actions with quasi-governmental international bodies like the United Nations: Europeans have a standing in international bodies that is out of proportion to European military power. The United Kingdom and France each have seats on the UN Security Council, reflecting international power roles that were outdated even in 1945 when France and the United Kingdom obtained their seats. Europeans do not have the military strength to enforce the decisions they insist should be made through international bodies. If the Security Council votes to chastise an errant state, the United States must do the chastising.

But why have Europeans permitted their military forces to become weak? Europeans might say because history has brought them to a point where they do not face large security threats. They no longer have the Soviet Union to fear and no longer fear each other. If the democratic peace theory is true, they face few threats because they live on a continent full of democracies.

Kagan maintains that the logic of this argument is backward. Europeans face fewer threats because their global role has changed. Since the United States functions as a guarantor of international security, the Europeans do not need to take on this task. The United States faces greater security threats, because it is the enforcer of the rule of law in the world. Putting a new spin on the European charge that Americans act like cowboys, Kagan points out that actually America has the role of "international sheriff, self-appointed perhaps but widely welcomed nevertheless, trying to enforce some peace and justice in what Americans see as a lawless world where outlaws need to be deterred or destroyed, often through the muzzle of a gun. Europe, by this Wild West analogy, is more like the saloonkeeper. Outlaws shoot sheriffs, not saloonkeepers."[6] If Europeans do not find Islamic fundamentalist terrorism as threatening as the United States does, it is because the United States, not Europe, is the principal target.

There is undoubtedly some truth in Kagan's argument. The United States is more of a target than Europe due to the different role it plays in the world. If we can believe Osama bin Laden's statements, he attacked the United States in part because American soldiers were on Saudi Arabian soil, where they had been invited to fend off a threat from Iraq. According to bin Laden, al-Qaeda also targeted the United States in Somalia in 1993 when the United States was engaged in a mission to feed starving people. Using its power, whether in its own interests or in other people's interests, does make the United States a target.

Four years after the 2003 invasion of Iraq, it may seem to some that there is also truth in the European claim to greater wisdom about the limits of military force. This point is made by two international relations professors Robert J. Jackson and Philip Towle in direct response to Kagan in *Temptations of Power: The United States in Global Politics after 9/11,* a disapproving analysis of America's post–9/11 role published in 2006, when civil war raged in Iraq and U.S. forces were committed to a long war with a doubtful outcome.

> *In the light of the Iraqi experience, it is questionable whether Washington has proved to be better than European capitals at judging military policy. Kagan attacks Europeans both for being too idealistic about the Third World and for being introverted and ignoring it. In fact, Europeans are often more realistic. They have learned from their colonial experience that permanent settlements cannot be imposed from the outside and will last only if they are accepted by the masses of the people concerned.*[7]

Europe as a Rival and Counterweight to the United States

Neoconservatives see Europe as a spoiled dependent of America, indulging in a safe pseudo-rebellion: Europeans do not really mean it. If they were really afraid of the United States (as suggested by recent polls in which Europeans call the United States a greater threat to peace than China or Iran),[8] they would build up their own armed forces.

Others see a changing balance of power. In a few years, perhaps, a new, stronger unified Europe might act either by itself or with other large power blocs—Russia, China, Japan, India—as a counterweight to the United States, especially if they come to see the United States as a greater threat to world peace than these other four nations that at least recently have shown little inclination to make war. Europeans like Emmanuel Todd see a shifting balance of power they attribute to hidden weaknesses in the American economy. Others see a unified Europe by itself capable of challenging American domination even if the U.S. economy does not suffer serious setbacks. Even if Europe does not change course and build up its military, it may use its economic might and diplomatic skill to influence events. Former French president Jacques Chirac was said by one of his advisers to call for "a multipolar world in which Europe is the counterweight to American political power."[9] Former German chancellor Helmut Schmidt said that Germany and France "share a common interest in not delivering ourselves into the hegemony of our mighty ally, the United States."[10]

Some American analysts also believe that Europe has the potential to chart a more independent course in foreign policy. The Harvard political scientist Samuel Huntington is best known for the thesis suggested in a 1999 *Foreign Affairs* article, "The Clash of Civilizations" that European integration would lead away from the unipolar world of the post–cold war period toward a "truly multipolar world."[11] In 2002, Charles Kupchan, professor of international relations at the School of Foreign Service and Government of Georgetown University and senior fellow and director of Europe studies at the Council on Foreign Relations, made a similar prediction in *The End of the American Era: U.S. Foreign Policy and Geopolitics of the Twenty-first Century* that "Europe will soon catch up with America . . . because it is coming together, amassing the impressive resources and intellectual capital already possessed by its constituent states. Europe's political union is in the midst of altering the global landscape." Kupchan draws a historical analogy with events in the ancient world, when the Roman Empire split into a western empire with a capital in Rome and an eastern empire with a capital in Constantinople. The two empires, though having much in common, eventually drifted apart. Similarly, Kupchan sees Europe's resurgence "dividing the West into American and European halves."[12]

> *Washington today, like Rome then, enjoys primacy, but is beginning to tire of the burdens of hegemony as it witnesses the gradual diffusions of power and influence away from the imperial core. And Europe today, like Byzantium then, is emerging as an independent center of power, dividing a unitary realm in two.*[13]

European Weaknesses

Analysts dubious about Europe's prospects see economic obstacles preventing Europe from becoming a power to rival the United States. For two and a half decades, the economy of Europe, with its Keynesian, welfare state policies, has grown more slowly than the U.S. economy, with its relatively laissez-faire style of capitalism. Europeans—in particular the citizens of western Europe—are famous for short hours, long vacations, guaranteed pensions, and protections against unemployment. Free-market proponents think Americans are better off in the long run, since they have a larger income on average, and Europe has a much higher rate of unemployment than the United States. Critics blame much of the gap in growth and employment levels on Europe's leisure preference. In addition, Europe faces a demographic crisis due to its low birthrate and a divisive political issue in foreign immgration. For 200 years, Europeans, whenever they are in an anti-American mood, have pointed to the hypocrisy inherent in the fact that the United States preaches equality while discriminating against minority groups, in particular against African Americans. Yet Europeans (whose past treatment of their own minorities was far from enlightened) face a new minority problem in the large numbers of immigrants that have come to live in Europe since the end of World War II. Many of the immigrants are Muslims, raising the specter of Islamic fundamentalism and complicating the problem of their integration into European society. Turning immigrants into patriotic citizens is an American specialty: Europeans have far less experience in the matter, and such experience as they do have is not promising—the modern, racist anti-Semitism that culminated in the Nazi movement grew up in Austria and Germany in response to Jewish immigration from Russia and Poland. A 2002 "World Economic Outlook Study" by the International Monetary Fund (IMF) decided that what the European economy needs is Americanization: Europe should bring more of the population into the labor force, reduce employee benefits, reduce job security, lower taxes, weaken trade unions, and decentralize wage bargaining (make deals on wages EU–wide rather than regional or national). An IMF table definitively demonstrates—on paper—that these policies would reduce overall European unemployment by 1.65 percent after three years and 3.29 in the long term.[14]

The neoliberalism that drives the IMF policy has its proponents in Europe, where people do desire lower unemployment and faster growth. But can we expect its principles to be applied there as the IMF recommends? The answer probably depends on the accuracy and effectiveness of neoliberal principles and their benefits to the people of each country as a whole. European intellectuals (and many Americans) claim that neoliberalism is flawed—it brings faster growth, but only the rich benefit from that growth and in the long run it is neither fair nor sustainable. Applied as shock therapy to underdeveloped economies it does more harm than good. Proponents of neoliberalism say that it is the welfare state that is unsustainable, especially in Europe, where fewer and fewer workers are paying for the benefits of a larger unproductive part of the population, a situation made worse by Europe's low birthrate. In 2002, Germany was expected to have had one worker for every pensioner.[15]

Although from a military standpoint, the United States is still Europe's protector rather than its foe, the U.S. way of life and the European way of life are being tested against each other much as the capitalist and communist systems were tested against each other during the cold war. There are those who say the American economy is headed for disaster and there are those who say the European economy is headed for disaster. It seems safe to say that whichever economy comes to grief first will change.

LATIN AMERICA

Introduction

Americans are used to ignoring Latin America or seeing it as a backwater, a place of corrupt governments and people who lack American know-how: They do not know how to have an honest police force, how to have a stable government, how to have a large middle class, how to resist communist subversion, or how to make a living without producing illegal drugs.

Critics of U.S. policy toward Latin America believe the United States is responsible for many of the region's problems. Latin America has been dominated by the United States since the end of the 19th century, if not earlier. The United States has caused the overthrow of many Latin American governments and has trained elite Latin American military units that have gone on to torture and kill their own people. It has used its influence on international economic institutions to force economic shock therapy on Latin America's debt-ridden economies. In the view of Greg Grandin, author of *Empire's Workshop: Latin America, the United States, and the Rise of the New Imperialism,* Latin America is a place where the methods of U.S. hegemony have been tested.[16] It is the place, he argues, where hegemony's long-term effects can be seen. According to Grandin, we can look at Latin America and ask whether being a part of an American empire brings prosperity, human rights, and democracy. Though Latin America certainly has its own internal handicaps, the region's chronic poverty, inequality, and long history of human rights abuses make it a poor advertisement for the benefits of U.S. hegemony.

Defenders of American policy attribute Latin America's political backwardness to its history of colonization by Spain and Portugal, which imposed a semifeudal order on the region. While the United States and Canada inherited British institutions of self-government and liberal values, Latin America became a society of rich landowners and downtrodden peasants. Then, the argument goes, Latin America's political backwardness made it ripe for communist revolution, and U.S. support for anticommunist dictators is justified because it has saved Latin America from something worse. American conservatives distinguish between authoritarian regimes (like those the United States supported in Latin America) and totalitarian regimes (like that of the communist USSR). Authoritarian regimes restrict political freedom but do not try to control every area of life, as totalitarian regimes do; and authoritarian regimes are less bloodthirsty than totalitarian regimes. According to *National Review* editor at large John O'Sullivan, we can see this distinction in the different legacy of "two Latin American dictators, authoritarian Pinochet [Augusto Pinochet, 1915–2006, dictator of Chile from 1973 to 1990, supported by the United States] and totalitarian Castro [Fidel Castro, 1926– , dictator of Cuba 1959–2008, opposed by United States] . . . Castro murdered three times as many people as Pinochet in executions, prison, informal murders, etc."[17]

Anatomy of the Region

For the purposes of this book, Latin America refers to the nations and territories in the Americas south of the United States. It embraces 20 independent countries and a handful of small dependencies, including Puerto Rico, a U.S. territory. Around 560 million people live in Latin America. The majority of them are Spanish speaking; the next most common language is Portuguese, spoken by the 190 million inhabitants of Brazil, Latin America's largest country both in area and population. French is spoken in Haiti and a few other Caribbean countries. The majority of the population of Latin America is Roman Catholic, but membership in the Roman Catholic Church is declining while membership in Protestant churches is increasing.[18]

Political Culture

Latin American governments are more democratic today than at any point in history. From Mexico to Chile, presidents who can actually be voted out of office are the norm, where once it was common to find presidents who ruled for decades by means of force. Latin American democracy is volatile and still often works outside the electoral process. Between 1998 and 2001, the presidents of Ecuador, Peru, and Argentina were forced to resign in the face of angry street demonstrations. By 2004, three more elected heads of state had been ousted. Yet, as Moisés Naím noted in an April 2002 *Financial Times* article, the outcome of these events was a refreshing novelty for Latin America:

> *In contrast to what, for decades, was the usual practice throughout Latin America, the fall of a democratically elected president in Ecuador, Peru and Argentina did not lead to repression by a ruthless military junta and the disappearance of thousands of political opponents. . . . Moreover, in all three cases, civil society and not the military was the main agent of change.*[19]

According to Naím, the majority of people in Latin America prefer democracy, and, from the evidence, Latin American elites are now willing to give democracy a chance. But another survey, conducted by the United Nations in 2004, was less encouraging, showing that a majority of Latin Americans in 18 countries would prefer a dictatorship if it produced economic benefits.[20] They also do not trust their governments. As Roger Noriega, the former assistant secretary of state for Western Hemisphere affairs in the Bush administration, noted in 2005, "polls show . . . that Latin Americans by and large don't trust their governments and their institutions. The survey numbers suggest that overwhelming majorities in virtually all countries of the region have 'little' or 'no' confidence in their executive, judiciary, legislature, political parties, armed forces or police."[21] Noriega attributed this lack of trust to the perceived aloofness of Latin America's political elites, their legal and political immunity from the consequences of their mistakes, and electoral systems that favor the party in power, which invariably represents vested interests. "Poverty and the inequality of income and wealth which characterize much of the region make it difficult for democracy to thrive."

Economy

According to the World Bank, nearly 25 percent of Latin America's population lives on less than $2 U.S. a day.[22] According to the United Nations Economic Commission for Latin America and the Caribbean (ECLAC), Latin America is the region of the world where income inequality is most severe.[23] Throughout much of the 20th century, Latin American governments, whenever left to themselves, practiced protectionist economic policies—setting up barriers to foreign imports—and tended to print too much money, causing inflation. During the 1970s, Latin America borrowed a great deal from international banks and fell into debt when interest rates rose and demand for Latin American exports fell in the early 1980s. This financial crisis occurred just as neoliberalism was becoming the economic orthodoxy of the U.S. government and the IMF. In the 1980s and early 1990s, when Latin American countries sought debt relief through the IMF and the United States, the assistance was given on the condition that the debtor countries reduce import restrictions, downsize the state, and encourage the growth of the private sector. Latin America was rewarded not only with debt relief but with a great deal of investment by American corporations that now saw Latin America as a safer place to invest.

In the early 1990s the North American Free Trade Agreement (NAFTA), embracing the United States, Canada, and Mexico, boosted trade. Proponents of neoliberalism hailed its successes in Latin America. Yet, the vast majority of Latin America's people have yet to benefit. The historian Thomas F. O'Brien, author of *Making the Americas: The United States and Latin America from the Age of Revolution to the Era of Globalization,* observes, "Unemployment rates in Latin America rose during the 1990s, real wages fell, and income distribution worsened. As a result, during that decade, 35 percent of the region's people remained trapped in abject poverty—just as they were a decade ago."[24]

America's Role in Latin America

The United States has surely done more to affect Latin America than Latin America has done to affect the United States, yet when Americans look south, they think defensively. During the cold war, many viewed Latin America as a backdoor through which communism might enter the Western Hemisphere. From the 1980s to the present, Americans criticized the region as a source of illegal drugs, especially the cocaine that was smuggled into the United States causing crime and health problems. And while free traders see Latin America as a place of opportunity for U.S. businesses, American workers see it as a threat to their jobs. There is more immigration to the United States from Latin America than from anywhere else, and the number of immigrants continues to increase. About half of the immigrants enter the country illegally—bypassing American immigration rules and quotas.[25] The fear of immigration from Latin America centers on not just jobs but culture. Americans sense—and demographers predict—that in the coming century people of Hispanic descent will make up a larger and larger proportion of the American population, and many Americans fear the changes that this will bring to the country. They fear that Spanish will have to be given equal treatment with English, that a flood of semiliterate immigrants will lower standards at American schools, that poor Hispanic immigrants will be a drain on American social services and on better-off American taxpayers, and that people of Hispanic descent from the authoritarian regimes of Latin America will fail to absorb the United States's civic values and the political culture will be changed for the worse. While the United States has managed to preserve its political culture (not without change) in the face of large waves of immigration before, Hispanic immigration has one thing different about it—its unprecedented size and speed. A 2008 U.S. census report predicted that people whose ancestors came to the United States from Latin America will make up 30 percent of the population by 2050.[26] Samuel P. Huntington voiced the concerns of those who see Latin American immigration as a threat to U.S. identity. In a 2004 book *Who Are We?* Huntington wrote that Hispanic immigrants are failing to assimilate to American culture and to its Anglo-Saxon values. The charge is very familiar to readers of American history: It is exactly the same as that leveled against the Irish, the Italians, the Jews, and Asians in their time. There is no denying that the United States would be a very different place had these immigrants not come here, but these groups have all learned to speak English and to maintain and defend the institutions they were once thought to threaten.

Since the end of the cold war, drugs, the economy, and immigration—issues that are not completely unrelated—have motivated the largest U.S. initiatives in Latin America. During the 1990s, the United States spent billions of dollars on the eradication of cocaine in Colombia and Bolivia, spraying coca fields with herbicides while attempting to interest local farmers in alternative crops.[27] In Colombia, where rebels fund their insurgency by taxing the drug trade,[28] the eradication program led to intensified warfare between insurgents and militias, and in Bolivia, it contributed to the toppling of President Gonzalo Sánchez de Lozada Sánchez Bustamente through the efforts of angry, well-organized crop growers in 2003. Latin American leaders complain that eradication programs have led to human rights abuses by the military and that, after short-term gains, the drug growing merely spreads to new areas.[29] Echoing these charges that the war on drugs strengthens antidemocratic forces in Latin America, many pundits in the United States insist that expanded drug treatment programs in the United States would be a better way of dealing with the problem. In 2001, *Time* columnist Tony Karon noted, "Any Economics 101 student can tell you that if supply falls faster than demand, the price of the commodity rises—and with it the incentive of the supplier to take the risks involved in bringing it to market." As daunting a problem as it may seem, lowering the American consumer's appetite for cocaine may be easier than suppressing the criminal enterprise of drug smuggling.[30]

Government military forces in Latin America are often responsible for human rights abuses, which tend to increase when the United States gives them money to hire more troops and buy more military hardware. After 2001, the war on terror led to an increase in military aid of this sort, despite the scarcity of Islamic extremists in Latin America.

> *In March 2004, General James Hill, the head of the U.S. Southern Command that oversees U.S. military interests in the southern half of the Western Hemisphere, told a congressional committee that the United States faced a real threat from terrorism in Latin America and must therefore take assertive actions, including strengthening other militaries in the region. . . . Hill painted a picture of an area stalked by thousands of terrorists. Hill's definitions of terrorists included drug traffickers, criminal gangs, and even populist politicians.*[31]

Later that year, U.S. defense secretary Donald Rumsfeld met with Latin American defense ministers to stress the need to wage a battle against drugs and terrorism, urging them to create closer links between the military and the police. The Latin American defense ministers were cool to the idea, according to Thomas O'Brien. They were unconvinced that terrorism was a serious threat to their societies and, having just recovered from a century of military dictatorship, they were also unconvinced that what they needed was more military involvement in civilian affairs.[32]

In the economic sphere, the United States continues to promote neoliberalism—free trade, a downsized state, and increased foreign investment—in Latin America. It has done so consistently through changes of administration in Washington, from Ronald Reagan and George H. W. Bush to Bill Clinton and George W. Bush. The result of neoliberal policy in Latin America is mixed. It has brought a great deal of foreign investment into Latin America and increased its links to the global economy, but it has also led to increased inequality, poverty, and unemployment as segments of society suffer from the swings of the international export market. Industrialization in the United States in the 19th century ultimately led to the demise of small farms and the movement of displaced farmers into other places and other sectors of the economy. It is doing so in Latin America today, at great human cost. In societies without strong legal and democratic institutions, neoliberalism has effects not seen in economics classrooms: A 2001 lawsuit filed in the United States on behalf of Coca-Cola workers in Colombia charged the corporation and its subsidiaries and affiliates with murdering, torturing, kidnapping, and threatening union leaders at Coke's bottling plants in Colombia.[33]

The benefits and costs of these policies remain matters of intense debate in Latin America. Today, when most American citizens consider the U.S. relationship to Latin America, they think of the flow of immigrants north to the United States. It is an issue that strongly resembles the immigration controversies in Europe, complicated by the United States's image of itself as a land of opportunity. As in Europe, workers from countries where wages are low come to the high-wage United States to do jobs most Americans don't want to do. Those favoring immigration point out that the workers do jobs Americans are reluctant to do, but it is more complicated than that. One reason Americans are reluctant to do these jobs is that they pay relatively little, and, since labor obeys the economic law of supply and demand, these jobs would pay more if there were not foreign workers available to do them. However, higher wages in turn would lead to higher prices, which American workers would pay in their capacity as consumers. The same free trade logic that supports opening borders to commodities supports opening borders to labor. There is another reason why so many foreign workers and permanent immigrants to the United

States today are from Latin America, and this reason is similar to the why's of European immigration. Countries tend to experience especially heavy immigration from their former colonies: South Asians come to England, North Africans to France, and Latin Americans to the United States. Such immigration is, as one writer puts it, the "harvest of empire."[34]

Immigration, legal and illegal, is a wedge issue for both major U.S. political parties. Democrats have traditionally appealed both to immigrants and to low-wage workers who compete with them. Republicans have traditionally appealed both to social conservatives who feel threatened by immigration and to employers who benefit by low-wage labor. The last time immigration was seriously restricted in the United States, in the 1920s, the country was in a highly conservative mood and the Republican Party was in power. Ultimately, however, according to Paul Krugman, it was liberals who benefited. By the 1940s, labor was scarce, a situation that helped to give labor more clout; and American workers and unions became a powerful force in American politics.

Latin American Views of the United States

When Latin Americans look north at the United States, they focus on many of the same issues that preoccupy Americans looking south—immigration, free trade, the war on drugs, democracy, and human rights; but naturally things look different from their end of the telescope. Concern with the war on drugs in Latin America is restricted to the few countries that are major sources of cocaine and recipients of U.S. aid in the war on drugs. The issue of immigration to the United States looms nearly as large in Latin America as in the United States, but Latin American governments tend to see it as a fair exchange. Latin America has an abundance of unskilled workers who would benefit from jobs that Americans consider low wage. The United States has more low-wage jobs than workers willing to do them. Why should the United States object to the exchange?

About free trade, opinion in Latin America is divided. Most Latin American governments favor the creation of a Free Trade Area of the Americas (FTAA), which would do for the whole of Latin America what the North American Free Trade Agreement (NAFTA) did for the United States, Canada, and Mexico—sharply reduce trade barriers and thereby stimulate the economy. Many of the people ruled by these governments, however, are hostile to the agreements, unconvinced of neoliberal economic theory and certain that in any case the burden of the transition will fall on the poor. Peter Hukim, president of the Inter-American Dialogue, noted in a 2006 *Foreign Affairs* article that even Latin American governments eager for regional free trade agreements view U.S. trade demands as unfair and protectionist when it comes to U.S. agricultural products. They resent Washington's unwillingness to compromise on issues "such as the trade-distorting support payments the U.S. government makes to U.S. farmers, harsh U.S. antidumping rules, and Washington's demands for new standards of intellectual property protection. Sky-high tariffs and quota limitations on sugar, orange juice, cotton, and many other high-volume Latin American exports make the United States seem ungenerous and breed cynicism about Washington's advocacy of free trade."[35] That is, Latin American governments tend to see America as preaching free trade, but practicing protectionism when it comes to American farmers. (In this respect the United States resembles Europe and Japan, which also subsidize their own farmers to the disadvantage of farmers in underdeveloped countries.)

The war on terror, which made Latin America a low priority for U.S. foreign policy in the decade following 2001, also reminded Latin Americans that when it comes to human rights, the United States does not always practice what it preaches. Here, as in other parts of the world, the revelations of the systematic mistreatment of Iraqi prisoners by U.S. guards in Abu Ghraib and the torture of suspected terrorists in Guantánamo Bay undermined U.S. prestige, according to Hakim."[36]

Latin America Charts a More Independent Course

In recent years three trends have combined to make Latin America less dependent on the United States economically and less subservient to it politically. First, the occupations of Afghanistan and Iraq turned U.S. diplomatic and military attention to the Old World and away from Latin America. At the same time, international prices for raw materials and food—two major Latin America exports—buoyed Latin American economies. Though growth in the region was still sluggish compared with the growth of Asian economies, and its people remain desperately poor, the upward trends helped Latin American countries climb out of debt and made them less dependent on the international financial institutions that are strongly influenced by the United States. High oil prices gave Venezuela's president Hugo Chávez the freedom to thumb his nose at the United States. Chávez befriended the Cuban government, and he derided the FTAA as an "annexation plan"[37] (that is, a plan for the U.S. corporations to dominate, even take over, Latin America). In a third, related trend, globalization made Latin America—its raw materials and food—an object of interest to the burgeoning Chinese economy, promising to free Latin America from its economic dependence on the United States.

As a sign of Latin America's political independence from the United States, some of the United States's closest allies in the region opposed the 2003 U.S. invasion of Iraq. Of the 34 Latin American and Caribbean countries, only seven supported the war.[38] In 2006, Nicaraguans elected Daniel Ortega, a leftist and an old foe of the United States, as its president; the following year Ortega visited Iran, where the Nicaraguan president (who is both a Marxist and a Roman Catholic, two things usually unpalatable to Iranian leaders) found common ground with Ali Khamenei and Mahmoud Ahmadinejad. All agreed on the menace of U.S. imperialism.

Meanwhile, Latin America's trade with China has steadily increased. China's rapidly growing industrial economy and the rising living standards of its people are driving that country to look outward for new economic ties, much as the United States looked outward at the beginning of the 20th century. One of the places China seems to be looking right now is Latin America. China's trade with the region—though still small compared to U.S. trade—has been expanding very rapidly. According to the Council on Hemispheric Affairs, China's trade with Brazil and Mexico—the United States's largest trading partners in Latin America—amounted to $44.6 billion in 2007, and the amount is bound to increase as long as China continues to hunger for foreign raw materials and food.[39]

From time to time, the U.S. Congress expresses alarm over China's growing interest and expected influence in the region, but so far this feeling has been relatively mild. At present, the United States is far more interested in China's trade with the United States than China's trade with Latin America. Above all, the United States is preoccupied with the Middle East.

THE ISLAMIC WORLD

Introduction

Islam is a religion, not a place, but it is a religion whose adherents are concentrated in just a few parts of the world, which are clustered near each other and linked by a common history and culture. Today, they are also linked by an international Islamic fundamentalist movement some of whose members consider terrorism a legitimate form of warfare in defense of Islam. The regions in which Islam is the majority religion are the Middle East, the southern Asian countries of Afghanistan and Pakistan, the former Soviet republics of Central Asia, and the nations of Indonesia and Malaysia.

Thirty years ago, a book on America's role in the world would probably have dealt with these regions separately. That this one considers them as part of the Islamic world is a result of the rise of Islamic fundamentalism as a factor in international politics. To discuss these regions as a bloc runs the risk of prejudicing the discussion, hiding the problems and goals that Malaysia and Indonesia, for example, do not share with the Middle East, but to minimize the importance of Islamic fundamentalism would be even more of a distortion. Culture and religion matter greatly when it comes to U.S. relations with all countries that have Muslim majorities.

The Islamic world is the location of two wars currently being waged by U.S. troops, in Iraq and in Afghanistan. It is the place from which the 9/11 hijackers hailed. It is constantly in the news in connection with small-scale wars, nuclear proliferation, suicide bombings, and as a critical source of petroleum, the natural resource vital to the industrial economies. It is the location of the bitter, 60-year-long Israeli-Palestinian conflict. It is a region in which the United States maintains key alliances, but also the one most associated with fierce anti-American feelings. To analyze the cause of these feelings is to state one's political ideology. A liberal, a leftist, a conservative realist, and a neoconservative will each arrange the same facts to present a distinctly different picture of America's role in the Islamic world.

Anatomy of the Region

Before World War II, almost the entire Islamic world was under the domination of European colonial powers—Indonesia was Dutch, Malaysia and South Asia were under British control, and the French and British controlled much of the Middle East and North Africa (Italy, in a last-minute scramble for empire, conquered some of North Africa as well). Saudi Arabia and Iran were independent but greatly under British influence. The only state that was truly independent was Turkey, the rump state of the defunct Ottoman Empire, but it looked to Europe as a model for modernization. The Central Asian republics, conquered by czarist Russia in the 19th century, were part of the Soviet Union. Except for the Central Asian republics, independence came to most of these countries in the decades after World War II. As British, French, and Dutch influence waned, U.S. and Soviet influence grew. Both superpowers sought the friendship and allegiance of the new independent nations and at times attempted to exert control over them.

The world's billion and a half Muslims belong to many ethnic groups and speak many languages. Although Arabic is the language of the Koran, only about 15 percent of Muslims speak it as their native language. As Americans have learned in recent years, there is an important division in the Muslim world between the Shii and Sunni sects. About 10 to 15 percent of Muslims belong to the minority Shii sect and the remainder are Sunnis (although there are other sectarian divisions within Sunni and Shii Islam).[40] The vast majority of Iranians are Shiis; Shiis are also a majority in Iraq, where until the U.S. invasion Sunnis held power in a secular government under the dictatorship of Saddam Hussein. Shiis are also a majority of the Muslims in Lebanon.

The Islamic world contains relatively wealthy countries like Iran, Turkey, Saudi Arabia, and Indonesia, with gross domestic products (GDP) of $610 billion, $708 billion, $408 billion, and $350 billion, respectively. Some of the world's wealthiest individuals live in the Islamic world, as do some of the world's poorest. According to the CIA World Factbook, the per capita gross domestic products of the United Arab Emirates (which has a population of 2,445,989) was $55,200 in 2007. (Per capita GDP roughly corresponds to income level.) The per capita gross domestic products of the Gaza Strip and West Bank was $1,100 in 2006 and probably lower in the Gaza Strip alone, where more than 80 percent of the inhabitants live below the poverty line.[41] Except for Turkey, Egypt, and Israel, the economies of the wealthiest Middle Eastern countries are heavily dependent on the sale of oil. Indonesia, while it also benefits from fossil fuel resources, has an expanding manufacturing sector that has given it fast growth rates in recent years.

Oil has also had a fateful influence on the politics and economies of the Islamic world—in particular the Middle East. Oil has brought both foreign investment and foreign military intervention to the Middle East. It has changed the balance of power within the region. The higher price of oil since the 1970s has lessened the regional importance of Egypt, which has no oil reserves, and increased the power of Iran, Iraq, and Saudi Arabia, which have abundant oil resources. Oil affects the internal politics of a country like Iraq, where struggles between ethnic and religious groups are also a struggle for control of territory containing the country's oil reserves. Oil has turned the once poor and politically backward country of Saudi Arabia—a monarchy whose main other claim to importance is control of Islam's holiest places—into an important player on the world's economic and political scene. Oil has drawn the United States to intervene repeatedly in the Islamic world.

Governments of countries like Iran and Saudi Arabia find their power and popularity waxing and waning with the price of oil. Critics of the regimes often charge those in power with failing to diversify the economies to prepare for the day when oil reserves run out or their customers find an alternative fuel.

Political Culture

The Islamic world is famed for its despotic and backward political culture—for the brutality of regimes like that of Saddam Hussein (1937–2006) of Iraq and Hafez al-Assad (1930–2000) of Syria. The governments include constitutional monarchies, hereditary monarchies, absolute monarchies, democracies, dictatorships with the trappings of republics, and one mixture of revolutionary Islamic theocracy and democracy. The number of democracies has increased recently. Turkey and Israel are usually considered genuine democracies. Lebanon has a freely elected government, but its democracy is considered very fragile. Israel's democracy is seriously compromised by its de facto rule over 2.4 million Palestinian Arabs in the occupied territory of the West Bank, who cannot vote in Israeli elections. Indonesia, for many years a dictatorship with a strong military role for the government written into its constitution, transformed itself into a democracy between 1998 and 2004. Iran is sometimes considered a mixed case, since its elections have limited force, but ultimate authority rests with a group of Muslim clerics. Of the two South Asian countries considered here, Pakistan has been fluctuating between periods of flawed democracy and outright military dictatorship since 1958. Afghanistan is a fragmented democracy that only a few years ago was ruled by the Taliban, a revolutionary Islamic group that is still fighting to regain control. Iraq is a sputtering democracy, thanks to an American invasion, but as of this writing terrorism and civil war prevent its government from functioning, and no one knows whether it could stay in power without U.S. troops.

Governments in the Islamic world suffer from a chronic scarcity of legitimacy—acceptance by the people of the government's right to rule. A country's legitimacy may be sound even if this acceptance is grudging. A government does not have to be a democracy to be legitimate, but frequent resort to force against one's own people is obviously a sign of illegitimacy. Legitimacy was less of a concern for governments hundreds of years ago when most people were illiterate peasant farmers who had little knowledge of the world and little interest in national politics. People today are in touch with events and considerably more demanding, so the Islamic world's lack of legitimacy is a serious source of instability.[42]

Some of the governments of the Islamic world lack legitimacy because their boundaries are arbitrary—drawn by imperial powers in very recent history. This is true, for example, of Iraq. Some lack legitimacy because they have existed only briefly as modern independent nations and their ruling families owe their current positions to clever maneuvering at the end of the imperial era (Jordan, Saudi Arabia). Some lack legitimacy because—as in Pakistan—the military is the country's most respected institution and has repeatedly dislodged civilian governments on the grounds that they are corrupt. Some lack legitimacy because they are corrupt. Some lack legitimacy because their security depends on the military backing of the United States (Saudi Arabia, Kuwait, other Gulf states, Afghanistan, Iraq). Some lack legitimacy because the rulers and the ruled belong to different tribes or ethnic groups, to different sects of Islam, or to some combination of these differences. Since the 1970s, many have lacked legitimacy because they are seen as too secular for many of their citizens who are demanding an Islamic government. Western observers call the Muslims who make these demands Islamic fundamentalists.

Islamic fundamentalism is a political movement of Muslims who insist that government and law should be closely guided by the Koran, Islam's holy book said to have been divinely revealed by the prophet Mohammed. This movement draws its strength from a reinterpretation of ancient traditions. It contrasts the supposed spiritual emptiness and lawlessness of the West with the faith and discipline of the Islamic world. Although it is a revolutionary doctrine, it casts itself as a return to origins.

Islamic fundamentalism rejects the separation of church and state, which many nations see as an essential aspect of modernity. The historian Bernard Lewis accounts for this rejection by pointing to basic characteristics of Islam. He notes that, unlike Jesus, Islam's founder and prophet Mohammed was both a military and a spiritual leader. Mohammed never said, "Render under Caesar that which is Caesar's and unto God that which is God's," as Jesus did. So church-state separation makes a worse fit with Islam than with Christianity.[43] Muslim clerics are also jurists—from their reading of the Koran and other authoritative Islamic scripture, they reach judgments that to many Muslims have the force of law. It happens that for most of history, most Muslims have lived under two legal systems, the law of the rulers—as during the time of the Ottoman Empire—and the law of the Muslim clerics. The rulers have usually been Muslims themselves. Only in modern times did a large part of the Islamic world come under the rule of people with a different religion. Thus, the liberal tradition of church-state separation is not only alien to the spirit of Islam; it is seen as a legacy of imperialism.

With that said, it should be remembered that many legacies of imperialism, secularism included, were eagerly embraced in newly independent states, as a means of acquiring the former conquerors' strengths. Turkey, the rump state of the former Ottoman Empire, modernized its institutions in the 1920s, abolishing the age-old office of the caliph (in theory the leader of all Muslims as Mohammed was) and becoming officially a secular state. In other nations with Muslim majorities, both elites in power and dissident intellectuals were attracted to Marxism, an anti-religious ideology. The Baath Party, which took power in Syria and Iraq, had an ideology with similarities to fascism, also secular. This is not to deny that religion was a greater political factor in the Islamic world than in the modern West. Pakistan was formed as a state for Muslims who feared becoming a minority in postcolonial India. The Saudi family's claims to legitimacy rested on their role in preserving Islam's holiest sites in Mecca and on their adherence to Wahhabism, a puritanical strain of Islam. Secretive Islamic political groups such as the Muslim Brotherhood were centers of political agitation in the Middle East and South Asia. But Islamic fundamentalism was one ideology among many, and the future seemed to lie with secular leaders like Gamal Abdel Nasser of Egypt, whom many Arabs looked toward to unite them and restore their pride wounded by colonialism.

Probably no event did more to change this situation than Israel's victory in 1967 over the combined armies of Egypt, Syria, and Jordan (which was assisted by troops from Iraq, Saudi Arabia, Kuwait, and Algeria). The outcome of this war was shocking in many ways. In terms of men and material, Egypt and its allies seemed to have a big advantage just before the war. Many Arabs had been anticipating a final defeat of Israel, whose continued existence was a demonstration of the weakness of the Middle East, since its countries had been officially at war with Israel since 1948. Instead, Israel dealt its foes a devastating defeat. Israel emerged from the 1967 war occupying large swathes of Arab territory—including much of the Sinai, territory not very valuable but impressive looking on the map, the Gaza Strip, formerly Egyptian territory where many Arab refugees from the 1948 Israeli-Arab War resided; the territory between Israel and the Jordan River (the West Bank); a piece of Syria called the Golan Heights; and the city of Jerusalem, regarded as holy by Jews, Christians, and Muslims.

The Israeli victory discredited existing Arab regimes and the ideologies that they had embraced. It gave ammunition to Islamic fundamentalists who had been saying for years that Muslims were losing because they had abandoned God. Some Arab intellectuals even said that Israel had won because its citizens were faithful to their own religion.[44] Israeli conquest of Jerusalem promoted the Arab-Israeli conflict from a territorial dispute into a religious conflict for all Muslims, since Jerusalem is the third of the three holiest cities of Islam. Islamic fundamentalists view any rule over Muslim territory by non-Muslims as an outrage, but Jerusalem is considered an especially urgent matter on religious grounds.

Islamic fundamentalism gained further prestige with the 1979 Iranian revolution, led by Ayatollah Ruhollah Khomeini (1902–89), who quickly announced that he was instituting the government of God. Muslim clerics have been in power in Iran ever since, proving that an Islamic fundamentalist regime is viable and can defy the United States with impunity. The government that Khomeini overthrew was that of Shah Reza Pahlavi, who had been installed and sustained by the United States since 1953.

Iran's Muslims, who are Shiis, represent a minority sect in the Islamic world and are not natural allies for Islamic fundamentalists of the Sunni variety. Thus, in the 1990s, Iran was hostile to Afghanistan when it was under the control of the Taliban, who were Sunni Islamic fundamentalists. Even so, the victory and continued existence of an Islamic fundamentalist government in Iran has inspired all Islamic fundamentalists. Iran has also provided funds to Islamic terrorist groups—or as most Muslims see it, resistance fighters—of both the Shii variety (Hezbollah in Lebanon) and the Sunni variety (Hamas in the Gaza Strip and the West Bank).

Islamic fundamentalism has often been encouraged by the autocratic governments in the Islamic world as a way of playing different antigovernmental forces against each other, of deflecting criticism from themselves, or even as an extremely dangerous and unpredictable tool of foreign policy. Thus, in the 1970s, Egyptian president Anwar Sadat permitted large demonstrations organized by the Muslim Brotherhood to take place, while suppressing demonstrations by the Egyptian left. Saudi Arabia is often accused of a cowardly bargain—supporting jihadists abroad in exchange for immunity from attacks at home. Pakistan's secret intelligence forces have for many years nurtured Islamic militants as a weapon in Pakistan's disputes with India and to influence the situation in neighboring Afghanistan.

The United States, too, has supported Islamic fundamentalists, giving arms and money to them through Pakistan to support the fight against the Soviets in Afghanistan. Even Israel has supported Islamic fundamentalism. Israel initially encouraged the growth of Hamas (an Islamic fundamentalist Palestinian group) as a counterforce to the Palestine Liberation Organization (PLO) when the PLO was seen as the major threat to Israel. As all these instances show, trying to control Islamic fundamentalism is a dangerous game. Sadat was eventually assassinated by Islamic fundamentalists; Saudi Arabia has experienced attacks by Islamic terrorists (usually aimed at foreign nationals) in 1995, 1996, 2003, 2004, 2005, 2006, and 2007) Israel finds in Hamas a more implacable foe than in the PLO; the United States confronts al-Qaeda; and Pakistan, which under Pervez Musharraf became officially a U.S. ally in the war on terror, finds that it cannot control the Islamic militants it has helped nurture.

Islamic fundamentalism is a threat to most current governments in the Islamic world. The failure to eradicate it, when governments have so much to lose by its victory, is itself a testimony to the movement's wide appeal. Even Saudi Arabia, which is officially an Islamic state and uses some of its oil profits to fund religious schools (madrassas) that promote its highly puritanical, conservative sect of Islam, is a target for al-Qaeda. Muslim fundamentalists see the Saudi leaders as hypocritical and despise them for their military alliances with the United States. They were especially angered by the stationing of U.S. soldiers in Saudi Arabia after the first Gulf War. Saudi Arabia, the country that contains the two holy cities of Mecca and Medina, should be off-limits to non-Muslims entirely, according to some interpretations of Muslim tradition (though, in fact, Saudi Arabia contains more than 1 million non-Muslim foreign workers). American troops were withdrawn from Saudi Arabia in 2003.[45]

America's Role in the Islamic World

The United States has been deeply involved in the Islamic world, particularly in the Middle East, since the end of World War II. The reasons for U.S. concern with the Middle East are well known. How much weight should be given to each of them is a matter of hot debate, but no one would dispute that the following are included:

- Both the U.S. government and U.S.–based oil companies have an intense interest in the region's oil resources. Saudi Arabia alone is believed to possess one-fifth of the world's oil reserves.[46] U.S. oil companies have profited directly from the oil business in partnership with local owners and rulers. The U.S. government considers access to oil a strategic military necessity. Since the 1970s, when high oil prices made the U.S. economy stagnate, the United States has considered it vital to keep oil prices down. The Islamic world's oil producers are key players in the Organization of Petroleum Exporting Countries (OPEC), the international oil cartel that has the power to control oil prices by raising or lowering the amount they produce. Presidents George H. W. Bush, George W. Bush, and Vice President Dick Cheney were all former oil company executives, a fact that no doubt struck people in the Middle East as very significant.
- The Middle East and South Asia were important theaters of competition in the cold war. The Soviet Union had a strategic interest in Middle Eastern oil and warm-water ports. It also considered Afghanistan, a country situated between Soviet Turkmenistan and Iran (a U.S. ally until 1979), a buffer state.
- American Jews have a special interest in Israel and so do many Christian fundamentalists who expect the Middle East to fulfill end-time prophecies in the near future.
- Some countries in and near the region have sought to become nuclear weapons states, arousing fears of a threat to world peace emanating from the region. Pakistan and Israel have nuclear weapons, and Pakistan has spread its nuclear weapons know-how to other countries, including Libya, which eventually abandoned its nuclear program. Iran is suspected of attempting to acquire the ability to make nuclear weapons. Iraq had a nuclear weapons program, which it abandoned in the 1990s and was suspected of attempting to restart. In 2003, the United States, claiming that Iraq had not abandoned its nuclear program, invaded Iraq.
- Finally the United States must care about the Middle East because the region is the seedbed of the worldwide Islamic fundamentalist movement, some of whose adherents have systematically targeted American soldiers and civilians, perpetrating the 9/11 attacks and threatening bigger ones in the future.

Relations between the United States and the Islamic world run in two directions, and the Islamic world also has its own interests in the United States.

- Leaders in the oil-producing countries have a special concern with the U.S. economy; many of them have invested their oil profits in the United States. When the U.S. economy falters, their investments suffer. They also fear that disaster for the U.S. economy might lead to an international depression. All over the world, factories would fire workers, people would use their cars less, and there would be less demand for oil. This is why the cartel of oil-producing countries does not work to keep the price of oil as high as it can but seeks to strike a balance. Since the early 1970s, when the Arab oil producers lowered production to protest U.S. support for Israel, the oil producers have not used control of oil for political purposes, probably because the results are too costly for their own economies. This does not prevent an oil-producing nation like Iran from being hostile to the United States—but Iran has very little investment in the United States. Saudi Arabia, Kuwait, and other Gulf states have a great deal.
- The United States is the world's chief supporter of Israel. Muslims sympathize with the Palestinians in the Israeli-Palestinian conflict. Millions of them believe that either the United States controls Israel or Israel controls the United States. In the past some of the region's leaders have wanted the United States to help broker a settlement of this long-standing conflict that arouses anger in the Arab street and makes existing governments look helpless.[47] Today, very few Muslims see the United States as an impartial referee in the conflict.
- The United States is the chief supplier of weapons in the Islamic world. It once supplied weapons to Saddam Hussein's Iraq, and it supplies billions of dollars worth of weapons to Egypt, Israel, Pakistan, Saudi Arabia, and the United Arab Emirates.[48]
- The United States is seen by some countries in the Islamic world as a threat and by others as a guarantor of security. Kuwait, Saudi Arabia, and other oil-rich Gulf states have in the past relied on help from the United States to retain their sovereignty. In 1990, when Iraq invaded Kuwait and attempted to annex it, the United States led the coalition that drove Iraq out. The United States created bases in Saudi Arabia.
- Millions of Muslims believe that the United States conducts its policies not merely in search of profit or power but as part of a deliberate war against Muslims and against their religion. This is the view promulgated in the speeches of Osama bin Laden. Polls do not tell us how widespread this belief is, but, in the judgment of former CIA analyst Michael Scheuer, it is not a fringe view but very widespread and quite beyond the reach of change by Arabic-language TV commercials or leaflets. "Thus," says Scheuer, "as bin Laden and his ilk defend the things they love . . .

they are themselves loved not just for defending the faith but as symbols of hope. . . ."[49]

Sources of Islamic Anti-Americanism

Probably no part of the world is more spectacularly anti-American than the Islamic world. The government of Iran refers to the United States as the great Satan. In Saudi Arabia, whose security has been greatly enhanced by the United States, Muslim clerics regularly excoriate the United States for its hedonistic culture and hypocritical politics.

This is the part of the world where the question Why do they hate us? seems acutely in need of an explanation. Some analysts, looking at the Islamic world almost as if it were a child from a broken home or a troubled adolescent, see a region torn by pathological violence, some of which has happened to turn outward. "Muslims worldwide confront a multidimensional crisis," notes Professor Alan Richards of the University of California at Santa Cruz in a 2004 article. It is a crisis linked to modernization, a process which, Richards maintains, has always been violent, wherever it has occurred.

> *The transition from a society of illiterate farmers, ruled by a literate, urban elite, into an urban, mass-educated society with an economy based on industry and services has been deeply traumatic. Worse, such change has always and everywhere spawned grotesque violence. The modern history of both Europe and East Asia, the only places in the world where this transition has been more or less successfully accomplished, often reads like a horror novel: World Wars I and II, Stalin's Gulag, Hitler's Holocaust, Japanese fascism, the Chinese revolution, the "Great Leap Forward" and its attendant famine, and the Cultural Revolution. The American experience has also been bloody: the extermination of Native Americans, the racial violence of slavery and Jim Crow, and the more than half-million casualties of its own Civil War. . . .*
>
> *Much of the violence during this transition has been perpetrated by utopian fanatics, a category that includes fascists, Nazis, Leninists, and Maoists, and the followers of al-Qa'ida.*[50]

Emmanuel Todd, author of *After the Empire: The Breakdown of the American Order,* also attributes the political upheaval of the Islamic world to modernization, but is more optimistic. He sees the Muslim countries as too weak to pose a serious threat to Europe or the United States and believes they will ultimately become democratic as a result of their own internal developments. In Todd's view, the key factors in the transition to modernity are literacy and birthrate, which are linked to each other. High rates of literacy, extending to women, lead to lower birthrates, because educated women can control the number of children they have. Literacy also makes citizens demand a greater say in their government, leading to political upheaval until democratic regimes have been established that give people a peaceful way to influence government. Literacy is high and birthrates are declining throughout the Islamic world. Todd believes that without outside interference these developments will lead to a new stability and that the United States has been playing up the threat by Islamic extremists as a way to justify America's continued world hegemony.

Others who agree that the Islamic world's turmoil results from such impersonal forces as modernization and globalization and not from U.S. policy think that nevertheless Islamic fundamentalism represents a serious threat to the United States and to world peace. This is the view of neoconservatives like Robert Kagan, David Frum, and Richard Perle, assistant secretary of defense for international security policy under President Reagan.

Still other analysts link anti-Americanism squarely to American policy. Political science professor Timothy Mitchell, while denying that anti-Americanism is as extensive as claimed—"The most surprising thing about anti-Americanism in the Middle East is that there is so little of it"[51]—thinks that people in the Islamic world have very good grounds for hating the United States. Further, he argues that the turmoil—which observers like Richards and Todd link to internal conditions in the Islamic world—is really a product of a deliberate U.S. policy since the 1970s, "to prolong, intensify and prevent the resolution of armed conflict. There were three major instances of this policy, in Iran and Iraq, in Afghanistan, and Israel and Palestine."[52]

To support this theory of a consistent, secret American policy of prolonging conflicts, Mitchell points out that during the Iran-Iraq War, the United States supplied arms overtly to Iraq and covertly to Iran. He believes the imposition of economic sanctions on Iraq during the 1990s (which the United Nations imposed with strong U.S. support to force Iraq to disclose information about its weapons of mass destruction program and which further devastated an economy already in shambles after a desperate eight-year war with Iran) were intended to "keep the country financially crippled and to prevent its economic recovery."[53] Then there is Afghanistan. Mitchell, taking note of the land reform policies of Afghanistan's Marxist government, which seized power in 1978, seems convinced that the Marxist government would have survived had the United States not interfered. He attributes the problems the Soviets experienced there largely to a U.S.–initiated rebellion against Soviet rule. (This is debatable—no one disputes that the United States supported the rebellion, but most would reject the idea that they created it.) "The third major conflict that the United States helped prolong was that between Israel and the Palestinians." Like many in the Islamic world itself,

Mitchell does not believe the United States has sincerely attempted to resolve the conflict, but has instead worked to help Israel colonize the territories it took over after the 1967 war, "while reserving pockets of territory for the occupied population." Meanwhile, the United States has supplied Israel with "the financial and military support necessary to maintain the occupation and suppress Palestinian resistance to it."[54]

In an interesting twist, Mitchell denies the usual liberal interpretation of Islamic anti-Americanism:

> *The argument that anti-Americanism might arise in the Middle East because of the role of the United States in sustaining unpopular governments misunderstands the main character of U.S. power in the region. What shaped that power was its relative weakness, its frequent inability to place client regimes in control, and the long-term failure of many of its efforts to do so.*[55]

Whether anti-Americanism is caused by cultural differences, by American support for unpopular regimes, by the endless Arab-Israeli conflict, by civilian casualties in American-led wars, or by the erroneous belief that the United States hates Islam, it is certainly accurate to say that the United States has often failed to impose its will on the region. The United States installed a pro–U.S. regime in Iran in 1953 and in 1979 it was overthrown. It supported an autocratic government in Lebanon in the 1950s and 1960s but has little control over Lebanon today. It overthrew the Taliban in Afghanistan in 2002 and Saddam Hussein in Iraq in 2003 and is embroiled in wars in both those countries. Osama bin Laden, the leader of al-Qaeda (which Mitchell calls "the group held responsible by the United States for the September 11 attacks,"), is believed to be in Pakistan. Pakistan's president Pervez Musharraf pledged himself America's ally but did not dare go after Osama bin Laden for fear his government would fall, which it eventually did in 2007 and 2008 when he lost control of the army and parliament. As of August 2008, Pakistan ruling parties say they are beginning impeachment proceedings against him.

How the U.S. Response to the 9/11 Attacks Has Affected the Islamic World

The timing of the terrorist attacks of 9/11 has maximized their effects on world history. George W. Bush, the president of the United States in 2001, had come under the influence of a group of neoconservative thinkers who strongly believed in the exercise of military power to achieve ambitious foreign policy goals, especially in the Islamic world. Bush and his advisers believed in the democratic peace theory and were sure that behind every terrorist group was a nation-state pulling the strings. They responded to the attacks by putting into place long-meditated plans for remaking the Middle East. With scant attention to local stresses within each country, they installed friendly regimes in Afghanistan and Iraq. These two states happen, perhaps not coincidentally, to lie on either side of Iran, the most anti-American state remaining in the region. If these wars had gone well, it is possible that Iran would have been next. At least Iran would have found itself isolated and surrounded and would have found it in its best interest to be more cooperative with the United States. So far, however, these wars have not gone well. At least one of them—the Iraq invasion—was ill advised to start with, and both were executed badly because, as Michael Scheuer says, the United States did not "do the checkables."[56] Scheuer believes that those charged with planning the invasions and occupations did not inform themselves about Afghanistan and Iraq or the resources that would be needed to stabilize them once their armies were defeated.

The ultimate outcome of these actions remains unknown, but, as this book is written, they seem to have played into the hands of Osama bin Laden and others who wish to weaken the United States. They have drawn many new recruits to al-Qaeda and been a shot in the arm to Islamic fundamentalism, a movement that analysts such as Oliver Roy and Gilles Kepel were writing off as moribund in the 1990s. The number of people who loathe the United States across the Islamic world and who believe the United States is conducting a war on Islam has greatly increased. Instead of being cowed and surrounded, America-hating Iran finds itself the greatest beneficiary of the two invasions. Afghanistan, its feared neighbor to the northeast, has been neutralized. Iraq, its feared neighbor to the west, formerly dominated by its Sunni minority, is now dominated by its Shii majority, members of the same sect as the clerics who rule Iran. Iran's great enemy, the United States, faces nothing but unpalatable choices: It can continue to bleed, losing soldiers and dollars in long occupations of these two countries; it can suffer a serious loss of credibility by abandoning these countries and the governments it put in place; or it can go hat in hand to the other countries in the region—Iran in particular—as the Iraq Study Group (an expert panel appointed by Congress to study the Iraq situation) recommended in 2006.[57]

ASIA

Introduction

"When China wakes up, it will shake the world." This remark has been attributed to Napoléon Bonaparte, and, whether or not he really said it, many analysts of the world scene today expect to see the truth of this prophecy in the not-too-distant future.

From the point of view of the United States, the key fact about the region that contains China, India, Japan, and the two Koreas is that it has achieved a successful industrial takeoff and will likely dominate the world economy in the 21st century. Asia, which the West once feared would choose communism, has instead embraced capitalism and made it work, and the United States finds the consequences are not all positive. U.S. links to the region are complex. America's consumers find in Asia a source of inexpensive manufactured goods; America's citizens and corporations find in Asia a competitor for natural resources, including oil and gas; the U.S. government sees in Asia, especially China, a rival for world hegemony and a potential military threat. Recognizing that China's rise cannot be stopped, American diplomats see their goal as giving China reasons to defend the status quo. According to U.S. secretary of state Condoleezza Rice: "It is crucial for the U.S. to help integrate China into an international, rules-based economy." In 2005, former deputy secretary of state Robert Zoelick said, "We need to urge China to become a responsible stakeholder in [the] system."[58]

Anatomy of the Region

The countries discussed here as part of Asia are India, China, Taiwan, North Korea, South Korea, Japan, Malaysia, and Indonesia. The last two have already been considered as part of the Islamic world, since the majority of their people are Muslims, but geographically they are part of Asia and have strong economic ties to the economies of Japan and China. Australia is in the neighborhood, too, and is often discussed with Japan, China, the two Koreas, and the United States as part of the Pacific Rim.

Three of four countries with the world's largest populations are located in Asia: China (1.3 billion), India (1 billion), and Indonesia (235 million). The United States, with 300 million, is number three. Asia is culturally and ethnically diverse, both from country to country and within each country. India is the world's largest Hindu country, Indonesia the world's largest Muslim country. China, since it is still technically communist, is the world's largest officially atheist country.

Political Culture

Forms of government are diverse as well. India and Indonesia are the largest and third largest democracies in the world; Japan, South Korea, and Taiwan are also democracies; China is ruled by a communist party that no longer practices communism but exerts authoritarian control over its people; North Korea's government is one of the world's most repressive, featuring a sort of hereditary dictatorship under which the leader is revered almost as a god.

Though the countries of Asia experienced colonial domination, as did the countries of the Middle East, and their boundaries and forms of state have changed, most of their people live under governments with strong national identities, without the endemic problems of legitimacy that plague countries in the Middle East and Africa. In particular, China, Japan, and Korea have histories as nations with a unity that roughly corresponds to the Western idea of a nation-state: China was ruled as a single nation for thousands of years; Japan and Korea go back deep into history. India, though a highly complex society whose boundaries are a legacy of imperialism, is also a stable state despite occasional violent clashes between different religious and ethnic groups. Other Asian states, like Indonesia, Malaysia, and the Philippines, do contend with violent separatist movements and terrorism, but even these seem less of a threat to the state than similar movements in the Middle East. In general, Asia's many ethnic divisions and minorities are less of a preoccupation for government, which does not have to resort to frequent violence to impose its will (as in Iraq under Saddam Hussein) or to find itself a government in name only over large portions of its territory (as Pakistan and Afghanistan do).

For much of its history, Asian political culture—particularly that of Japan, Korea, and China—has struck observers in the West as less individualistic than our own; less respectful of human rights, and less attentive to the interests of small groups. To historians in the West, Asia signifies the mobilization of vast numbers of people—at one time for projects like the irrigation of the Yellow River or the building of the Great Wall of China; in modern times for rapid industrialization with strong encouragement, sometimes coercion, from the government.

Nationalism has caused a great deal of trouble in the last two centuries, but the rise of Asia is a reminder that nationalism can be useful. With their well-developed sense of nationhood and strong political organization, Asian countries have been more successful than other formerly colonized peoples in achieving economic strength and regaining control of their own destinies.

Economy

There are many reasons for thinking the 21st century may be dominated by Asia, and almost all of them are rooted in the economic takeoff of the region.

The first Asian—indeed, the first non-Western—country to achieve industrialization was Japan. Isolated by its own decision for more than 200 years, Japan was forced open by American gunboats in 1853. Japan at the time was a military dictatorship (under a shogun) with a preindustrial economy. Viewing the situation with remarkable calmness and accuracy, Japan's elite reformed their government and their economy. By 1905 they were able to win a war with Russia. By 1941 they felt bold enough to simultaneously attack the United States and Great Britain in a bid to carve out an empire in Asia. Though as a result the Japanese suffered a devastating defeat in a war that culminated in the use of nuclear weapons on two of their cities, with subsequent U.S. help they rebounded sufficiently to become, by the 1970s, the United States's most formidable economic competitor.

In the 1930s and 1940s, when Japan attempted to establish an empire by conquest in Korea, Southeast Asia, Indonesia, and parts of China, it called its proposed sphere of influence the Greater East Asia Co-Prosperity Sphere, making the claim that its domination would be to the ultimate benefit of all the conquered peoples (some, like Indonesian nationalist leader Sukarno [1901–70], were in fact pleased to trade European domination for Japanese, but others found the Japanese yoke more unpleasant). Though the United States undid Japan's military victories, since the 1970s Japan's economic system has stretched out to embrace much of the empire it tried to acquire by force. These countries—although some are still suspicious of Japan and resentful of its refusal to acknowledge the Japanese war crimes of the 1930s and 1940s—have industrialized as low-cost suppliers of manufactured components to the Japanese. This trend accelerated in the 1980s, when a higher Japanese standard of living began to make Japanese labor too expensive.

The long expansion of Japanese trade and influence occurred during a period of unusual weakness for their great neighbor, China. Through most of Asian history China has dominated the region, obliging its neighbors, especially those to the northeast (Korea) and south (Southeast Asia), to declare their allegiance to the Chinese emperor and pay him tribute. But in the 1800s, with an ossified government and an economy based on land ownership rather than on commerce, China was weak relative to industrialized Europe. European countries forced unequal trade agreements on China. In two emblematic and bitterly resented episodes of European domination, the Opium Wars (1839–42 and 1856–60), the British forced the Chinese government to permit the importation of opium grown in British India. By weakening Japan's old enemy, European domination of China gave Japan the breathing room it needed to industrialize and eventually to challenge Western dominance in Asia. The communist regime of Mao Zedong, from the late 1940s to the early 1970s, unified and stabilized China, but excessive state planning and ill-advised government initiatives like the Great Leap Forward and the Cultural Revolution kept China poor.

After Mao's death, China embarked on a new course, essentially abandoning communism as an economic system while retaining the Communist Party's control of government. Local entrepreneurs were encouraged to build factories, trade abroad, and get rich. Three decades later, China has transformed itself economically. As of 2007, it was the world's third largest trading nation, after the United States and Japan. Its economy grows at the very high rate of 10 percent annually.[59] The streets of the capital city, Beijing, full of bicycle traffic 15 years ago, are now clogged with automobiles. China's size and rate of growth seems to ensure that its GDP will overtake that of the United States, perhaps before 2050.

Taking the long view, China's growth may be more significant than Japan's. Perhaps it has taken China's economy longer to grow than Japan's because it is has more than 10 times the population of Japan and could not be expected to change course as quickly.

China's rapid development—though it brings problems like environmental pollution, inequality, and political corruption—is a boon to its people. Along with capitalism, China is developing a consumer culture that will keep its people demanding more and more of the world's resources in years to come. This development is also a challenge for the rest of the world, since China is now a formidable competitor for trade and resources and will only become more so as the size of its economy doubles and triples.

Some analysts, like political economy professor Zhiqun Zhu, author of *United States-China Relations in the 21st Century: Power Transition and Peace,* consider it inevitable that China will eventually replace the United States as the most powerful nation, certainly in Asia, and perhaps in the world:

> *The United States assumed global leadership at the end of World War II: If history repeats itself again, it is likely that some time in the twenty-first century the United States may relinquish, either willingly or unwillingly, its global and regional leadership. China is one of the few potential contenders that might accept the new leadership role, especially in Asia.*[60]

Though China is the big story, the industrial expansion extends to the rest of Asia as well, and sheer size is a significant factor as well in India with its billion people. Already, Japan, China, and South Korea are three of the top 10 economies in the world. India is the 11th, and its large population and rapid growth in recent years are likely to propel it to the top 10 eventually.

America's Role in Asia

The Mexican-American War (1846–48), which gave California to the United States, made the United States part of the Pacific Rim, and the United States promptly began to extend its trade and influence eastward. U.S. gunboats opened Japan to Western trade in 1851. Over the next half-century, the United States acquired a series of naval stepping-stones toward Asia in the form of Midway Island, Hawaii, and the Philippines. Unable to enjoy a monopoly of influence in Asia as it did in Latin America, in the late 19th and early 20th centuries the United States pursued what it called the Open Door policy in the region—insisting that everyone should have equal rights to trade in Asia. U.S. diplomats considered the open door policy a model of fairness and idealism. Asians, and particularly the Chinese, were inclined to think of it as merely America's mode of imperialism in Asia. In the early 20th century, Cambodia, Laos, and Vietnam were French, Indonesia was Dutch, and Myanmar (then called Burma), Malaysia (then called Malaya, and the Malayan city of Singapore, today an independent country), Hong Kong, and Australia were British. The Philippines were American.

World War II increased U.S. involvement and influence in Asia. The United States was drawn into the war in the Pacific when Japan attacked not only the U.S. naval base at Pearl Harbor but also the Philippines. From the Japanese point of view it was a military necessity to eliminate the U.S. presence in the South Pacific to make it possible for the Japanese to take over the Dutch, British, and French colonies in Asia. Japanese planners hoped that by the time the U.S. Navy recovered Japan's position would be unassailable. The Japanese gamble failed, and subsequent events worked to increase the U.S. military presence in the region. Victory in World War II returned the United States to the Philippines as the United States continued to maintain a major military base there after the Philippines became independent in 1946. The United States (with help from its World War II allies) occupied Japan until 1952, imposing a democratic, pacifist constitution on the country and putting a permanent U.S. military base on the Japanese island of Okinawa. World War II also led to the split of Korea into a communist, Soviet-allied North Korea and a U.S.-allied South Korea. In the early 1950s, the United States helped South Korea repel an invasion from North Korea. This conflict was fought to a stalemate by 1953 and left yet another set of U.S. army camps and military bases in Asia, this time in South Korea.

Meanwhile, a civil war between the Communist forces of Mao Zedong and the Nationalist forces of Chiang Kai-shek led to the establishment of two rival Chinese governments, one in China proper, the other on the island of Taiwan (previously called Formosa). Each laid claim to the other's territory and to being the sole legitimate China, although the population of Taiwan was miniscule by comparison to the population of mainland China. The United States, which had supported Chiang Kai-shek, made itself the protector of Taiwan. Later, the United States became involved in several anticommunist battles in Southeast Asia, the best remembered of which is the Vietnam War.

Thus, as the Netherlands, France, and Britain willingly or after tough fighting surrendered their colonial possessions in Asia, the United States became Asia's chief military power, with large permanent bases in the region to back up commitments to protect Japan, South Korea, and Taiwan. During the cold war, as the nuclear arms race between the United States and the Soviet Union accelerated, these countries were often said to be sheltered under the U.S. nuclear umbrella. As thankless as the Korean and Vietnam Wars were for the United States, they did show that the United States would fight to defend its allies in the region and perhaps one outcome was that Japan could remain a pacifist nation. The Japanese, who had been intensely militaristic up until 1945, cultivated an image of themselves as peace-loving victims of the nuclear bomb. Japan's unwillingness to acknowledge its own war crimes is still an obstacle in its relations with its neighbors, particularly China and South Korea.

Changing U.S. Relationship with China

When Mao's forces won China's civil war in 1949 and China became communist, the United States classed it as a part of the communist bloc and assumed that China had become a puppet of the Soviet Union. The national interests of China and the Soviet Union, large countries with long borders, began to conflict, however. In the 1970s, U.S. president Richard Nixon and his secretary of state Henry Kissinger decided to exploit the division between the two communist giants and began to cultivate China as an ally. This diplomatic initiative was well timed. Mao Zedong was ill—he died in 1976—and losing power, and the emerging Chinese leadership would prove eager to experiment with a more liberal economy.

The new relationship with China came at some sacrifice to the U.S. reputation as a reliable friend. Ever since 1949, the United States had assisted Taiwan in occupying China's permanent seat on the UN Security Council, despite Taiwan's small size and power. An October 1971 UN General Assembly resolution simultaneously gave the permanent UN Security Council seat to communist China and expelled Taiwan from the United Nations. U.S. presidents Richard Nixon and Jimmy Carter made large concessions to China on the subject of Taiwan, essentially supporting China's position that Taiwan belonged to mainland China. These concessions were contradicted by the U.S. Congress, and the Taiwan issue remains a headache for the U.S. government and perhaps for mainland China as well.

Trade between the United States and China began to grow, a development that did much to transform the economies of both nations. Today the economies of China and the United States are deeply interdependent. The

United States has a huge trade deficit with the world—it imports far more than it exports; this deficit reached $711 billion in 2007 after rising for five years in a row and than decreasing slightly in 2007. China accounted for $256 billion of that deficit. To finance its trade gap, the United States must borrow $2 billion dollars each day—it does so through foreign sales of U.S. treasury securities, for which Japan and China are the biggest customers. Thus, these countries with which the United States has a trade imbalance lend the United States money to buy their goods.

Both because of this interdependency and as a legacy of the China strategy during the cold war, U.S. protests over China's authoritarian government and its human rights abuses are relatively muted. According to Human Rights Watch, China leads the world in executions, aggressively censors the Internet, bans independent trade unions, and represses minorities such as Tibetans, Uighurs, and Mongolians.[61] China is a major trading partner of the Sudan, which is conducting a brutal campaign of removal, rapes, kidnapping, and mass murder against its citizens in Darfur. Western countries have boycotted Sudan, but China, in its desire for Sudanese oil, continues this trade. The United States sometimes protests this behavior, but does little else to try to stop it.

Some observers, like Dana R. Dillon, author of *The China Challenge: Standing Strong Against the Military, Economic, and Political Threats That Imperil America,* think that the United States has been too timid in confronting China in many instances in which China bullies its neighbors, flouts international law, or pushes the law to its limits in order to expand its power. For example, based on dubious reading of international rules intended to protect the interests of nations whose territories are scattered on groups of islands or which have highly indented coastlines, China claims the entire South China Sea as its territorial waters. These claims conflict with those of Taiwan, Vietnam, Malaysia, the Philippines, and Brunei. The issue has huge economic consequences since the South China Sea is an important zone of maritime trade and a major source of fossil fuels, especially natural gas. In some of these disputes, veiled military threats have prompted China's neighbors to back down. The United States has remained neutral in these disputes, a position Dillon considers a mistake. One reason the United States has not done much to intervene, Dillon points out, is that the United States has not ratified the Law of the Sea Treaty: It is difficult to insist that China adhere to a treaty to which the United States is not a party.

Dillon and many other observers are also concerned about China's military buildup. In 2008, China increased its defense spending for the 26th straight year, giving China the largest defense budget in Asia and the third largest in the world. China's defense spending is rising faster than its economic growth, but no country is making claims to Chinese territory or threatening China's interests. According to Dillon, one can only assume that it is China that intends to upset the current world order.[62]

Actually, as Dillon himself notes elsewhere, China is a party to regional territorial disputes and its military buildup may partly be intended to intimidate its neighbors. But some Chinese military developments seem to anticipate a future conflict with the United States: In January 2007, Americans were alarmed to learn that China had successfully carried out an experiment with an antisatellite missile, the first such test by any power in more than 20 years. Since the United States makes extensive use of satellites for both civilian and military purposes, some consider the Chinese test a threat to the United States. (The United States protested China's experiment. In February of the following year, the United States tested the same technology, shooting down one of their main satellites.)

Even if the Chinese military buildup is aimed primarily at gaining power in its own backyard, this may be a threat to U.S. interests, because the United States itself is the leading military power in Asia. If there is war in Asia, the United States might find itself involved.

Other common complaints against China concern its trade practices, which are viewed in the United States as one-sided and relatively protectionist. Many of China's industries are supported by the government and American books, films, movies, and computer software are routinely pirated by Chinese firms. The Chinese government gives lip service to international copyright laws but does little to enforce them.

Complaints over China's unfair trading practices are voiced both by critics who are enthusiastic supporters of free trade and by critics who lament the loss of U.S. manufacturing jobs to Asia and are more dubious about free trade's benefits. If the United States does not act very strongly in trade disputes with China, one reason may be this disunity among China's critics. In any case, U.S. policy on free trade is inconsistent, China can point to U.S. subsidies and antidumping laws as evidence of America's double standard on this issue.

U.S-India Relations

India, like China, is poised to be a more important player on the world scene in the 21st century than it was in the 20th. It is the world's largest democracy, has the world's second-largest population, and in recent years has had the world's second-fastest growing economy, waxing about 8 percent annually before the global recession that began in 2008. Since 1998, when it conducted tests of nuclear and thermonuclear weapons, India has been a member of the nuclear club. Yet India has received far less diplomatic attention from the United States than China has.

There are several reasons for the relative coolness of U.S.-Indian relations. In part it is a legacy of the cold war. Prior to the breakup of the Soviet Union, India was the leader of the Non-Aligned movement of nations that were careful to wed themselves neither to the United States nor the Soviet Union. Though its democracy was authentic, India's economy was heavily regulated and seemed to be veering toward socialism. Furthermore, U.S. policy makers viewed India as far too friendly to the Soviets—in fact, as Soviet-leaning, rather than genuinely nonaligned. Ironically, the dictatorial and officially communist nation of China was wooed strenuously by the United States, in the hope of exploiting the tensions between the Soviets and the Chinese, and this campaign led to close economic ties between the United States and China. India, though ideologically closer to the United States, did not seem to offer the United States a similar foreign policy bonanza. In the great game of the cold war, the United States played the China card; there was no India card to play. In fact, since India feared its neighbor China, closer relations between the United States and China added to the chill in U.S.-Indian relations.

Another cold war necessity—U.S. support for the Afghan rebellion against Soviet occupation in the 1980s—caused the United States to seek closer ties with India's old enemy, Pakistan, whose security forces helped the United States to provide assistance to the rebels. Appealing to Pakistan has often meant alienating India. In 2001, when Afghanistan became a front in the U.S. war against Islamic extremism, Pakistan again became militarily important to the United States. Once again the United States had alienated India, the thriving multicultural democracy, in order to win the cooperation of Pakistan, the Islamic military dictatorship and nuclear proliferator. In 2003, the U.S. government was miffed when India refused to send troops to Iraq to help depose Saddam Hussein.

India has not signed the Nuclear Nonproliferation Treaty, and ever since 1974, when India announced the explosion of what it described as a peaceful nuclear device, nuclear nonproliferation has been the primary focus of the United States's diplomatic efforts with respect to India. The United States aimed first to keep India from becoming an official member of the nuclear club—which it did in 1998—and thereafter to prevent or slow a nuclear arms race between India and Pakistan. However, due to U.S. support for China and Pakistan, the United States has relatively little influence on India. Without much other leverage, the United States's main tool in slowing the progress of India's nuclear-weapons program has been to impose economic sanctions—further restricting the growth of U.S. trade with India, already much smaller than U.S. trade with China—and to block the sale of nuclear technology to India.

In December 2006, India and the United States signed a comprehensive Civilian Nuclear Agreement, under which the United States would provide

India with civilian nuclear technology, which the United States had previously withheld as part of nonproliferation efforts. Some critics in the United States regarded the deal as a final admission of failure in the U.S. effort to contain India's nuclear ambitions.

Though India's leaders may not be happy with the closer ties to Pakistan that the war in Afghanistan has brought, they do not want the Taliban to return to Afghanistan, and they have given the Afghan government more than half a billion dollars in aid. The way seems to be open for more U.S.-India trade and more cooperation on security issues. Perhaps, at last, U.S. foreign policy will give India a place commensurate with its size, population, and power.

Balance of Power and International Law

The security and economic problems the United States faces in Asia seem to highlight the flaws in any foreign policy based primarily on overwhelming U.S. military superiority and a foreign policy of American exceptionalism that regards international institutions with suspicions. Military strength is based on economic strength, and American economic strength, relative to the rest of the world and relative to particular rising nations, such as China, will inevitably decline. Short of an unjustifiable preventive war that would kill millions of people and make the United States anathema to the whole world, the United States cannot stop the continuing growth of the Chinese economy, nor can military threats prevent China from spending as much of its new wealth as it chooses on its armed forces. If China is a threat to U.S. interests, the threat will have to be managed by diplomacy and by the cultivation of relationships with China itself and with other Asian nations with their own interests that might stand up to China if they act together and have the backing of the United States. At the same time, as Condoleezza Rice and other American diplomats have suggested, the United States needs to encourage China to respect international law and act through international institutions. That is going to be difficult to do as long as the United States's own commitment to international institutions is weak.

RUSSIA AND THE FORMER SOVIET SPHERE

Introduction

For nearly half a century the Soviet Union was America's most feared enemy. Then, over the course of the late 1980s and early 1990s, the Soviet Union collapsed and disintegrated. It did so with astonishingly little violence, and most of its pieces, including the largest one, Russia, turned from implacable foe to friend and supplicant, newly democratic and eager to learn about free-market capitalism, which had worked so well for America. The biggest security threats presented by the former Soviet republics were loose nukes, the possibility that, in the chaos following the Soviet collapse, terrorists or hostile countries might get their hands on some of the weapons or fissile materials the Soviet Union had amassed during the cold war (this problem has not gone away). There was little else to fear from Russia. Not only was Russia weak, but Russia had become a democracy, and democracies do not make war on each other.

But Russia's transition to free-market capitalism proved more difficult than anticipated and much less popular with its people, who were not pleased with Russia's loss of prestige and their decline in security and living standards. The genial and hotheaded Boris Yeltsin, Russia's first president following the breakup of the Soviet Union, was replaced at the end of 1999 by Vladimir Putin, a former official of the KGB, the Soviet Union's espionage and secret police apparatus, and its successor, the FSB. Putin, benefiting from Russian nationalism and from rising oil prices that helped bring prosperity during his tenure in office, has systematically tightened the reins of government control, making Russia less democratic and more authoritarian. He has accomplished this by legal, and, it is widely suspected, extra-legal means. His political opponents and hostile journalists have been assassinated. Though no one has proven that Putin himself was behind these acts, the benefit he derived from them and his KGB background provide grounds for suspicion. Even without the assassinations, the growing centralization of power in Russia and the state's growing control over the media—refreshingly free during Yelstin's time—make it possible to question whether Russia's experiment with democracy is over.

Russia's rapid changes under Putin and his handpicked successor, Dmitry Medvedev, have taken the United States by surprise. While the United States has been distracted by al-Qaeda and Iraq, announcing its intention to cure the Middle East of terrorism by spreading democracy, democracy has been rolled back in one of the world's most powerful nations. It is by no means certain what U.S. leaders can or should do about it.

Anatomy of the Region

The 15 separate countries that were once part of the Soviet Union had a population of about 295 million in 2007. The largest in population is Russia, with 141.4 million; the next largest is Ukraine, with 46.1 million; and the third largest is Uzbekistan, with 27.8 million. Aside from Russia itself, the former Soviet states fall into four groups, with countries within each group sharing regional proximity and common cultural similarities: The Baltic States—Estonia, Latvia, and Lithuania—were late additions to the USSR and the United States never recognized them as being part of the USSR. Most people in the Central Asian republics—Kazakhstan, Kyrgyzstan, Tajikistan, Turkmenistan, and Uzbekistan—are Muslim (some of these republics have substantial fossil fuel resources and are contending with Islamic extremism). The Caucasian republics—Armenia, Azerbaijan, and Georgia—have historical ties to the Ottoman Empire and considerable oil and gas resources. The remaining three countries, Belarus, Moldova, and Ukraine, are sometimes called the eastern European states.

Political Culture

While all the former Soviet republics are officially parliamentary democracies and most of them are freer than they were during the cold war, the health of their democracies varies considerably, and their ultimate outcome is very uncertain. As previously noted, Russia's government has become more centralized and authoritarian and opposition leaders and journalists hostile to the government have been assassinated. Several former Soviet republics have had the same leaders since independence in 1991. The CIA World Factbook notes Turkmenistan as having "authoritarian presidential rule, with little power outside the executive" while the 2006 report of the U.S.-based independent NGO Freedom House lists it as one of the eight most repressive regimes in the world.[63] Freedom House also lists Russia, Belarus, Azerbaijan, Uzbekistan, Turkmenistan, Tajikistan, and Kazakhstan as "not free."

Economy

After independence most of the former Soviet republics turned from communism to free-market capitalism; in most cases this transition was very badly managed. In Russia, assets that had belonged to the government—in theory to the people—were auctioned off in ways that gave big advantages to government bureaucrats with good political connections. These individuals were able, in effect, to steal natural resources and industrial infrastructure that had been built up at enormous human cost through decades of brutal forced labor and five-year plans, and they became instant capitalist plutocrats, deeply resented by ordinary Russians. The new order was at least as corrupt as the old one, less secure, less equal, and for a long time less successful in generating economic growth. By 2004 only a handful of the former Soviet republics had achieved a higher gross domestic product (GDP) than they had had in 1991. The Baltic States, all relatively small, have managed to remake themselves into stable and successful free-market economies. Russia, after returning to greater state intervention in the economy, has benefited from the global rise in oil prices.

Russia's major export is oil and, like China and oil-exporting countries such as Saudi Arabia, Russia has invested its earnings in foreign reserves—in 2007, Russia's foreign reserves had grown to $470 billion, the third largest in the world. Despite this prosperity, according to the CIA World Factbook, the majority of Russia's trade with the rest of the world consists primarily of raw materials and agricultural products, which are a key source of government revenue. In 2006 Russia signed a bilateral market access agreement with the United States. This agreement, which requires Russia to open up its markets to American goods and services and abide by international intellectual property rules, is a prerequisite for Russia's membership in the World Trade Organization. The U.S. Congress will decide whether to ratify Permanent Normal Trade Relations (PNTR) with Russia. If it does, undoubtedly the U.S. trade with Russia will increase.

America and the Former Soviet Republics

As the Brookings Institution's president, Strobe Talbott, noted in testimony to the House Committee on Foreign Affairs in October 2007, America has "an enduring interest in Russia's evolution . . . because how Russia conducts itself beyond its borders has always depended in large measure on how it is governed internally."

Russian behavior during the Putin years has provided fresh evidence for this theory. In the 1990s the United States had the experience of confronting a Russia that was weakened, democratic, and cooperative. In the 2000s, it faces a Russia that is both more authoritarian and more aggressive. Thanks to high oil and natural gas prices, the new Russia is "a resurgent nation-state with a chip on its shoulder, a bundle of petrodollars in its pockets, and the whip hand of being a major gas supplier. The Russians are trying to leverage their oil and gas wealth into both economic and political power."[64]

In 2004, Russia began selling gas at a very low price to Ukraine in order to assist the election of a Russia-friendly candidate in Ukraine's elections. Later, when the candidate the Russians preferred lost, the Russians insisted on renegotiating the deal and at one point, in early 2005, stopped the flow of gas to Ukraine. In November 2006, Alexander Litvinenko, a former senior Russian intelligence (FSB) officer and the author of books critizing Vladimir Putin and calling his rise to power a coup d'état organized by the FSB, died after ingesting polonium. Since polonium is a radioactive substance that could be produced only in a sophisticated nuclear lab, it is widely believed that Putin was behind the assassination. In May 2007, in a dispute with Estonia, Russia launched what has been called a cyber-war against its former member state, attacking Estonia's government Web sites and the Web sites of its news organizations.

Talbott considers the backlash against the chaos of the Yeltsin years "natural and perhaps inevitable." Thanks to Vladimir Putin's ruthlessness, the swing away from democracy has been more extreme than it would otherwise have been. However, Talbott insists, the United States must be careful to see Russia for what it is right now: Neither a democracy nor a dictatorship, but rather a "quasi-democracy . . . supported by a recentralized government bureaucracy . . . Russia's rulers today want public opinion on their side. . . . but they also want to control public opinion through the media and to control the electoral process . . ."[65]

Russia showed its willingness to use force in foreign affairs in a brief shooting war it conducted in August 2008 with the former Soviet republic of Georgia. Since the early 1990s, Georgia and Russia have been in dispute over South Ossetia and Abkhazia, two regions that sought independence from Georgia during the breakup of the Soviet Union. For almost two decades, the Soviet Union had supported both regions' bids for independence.[66] American and European leaders tend to see Russia's policy toward these regions as a possible bid to annex them to Russia and certainly a means of weakening Georgia and its president, Mikhael Saakashvili, who has angered Putin by seeking closer ties with the West and wants Georgia to join NATO.

Separatist militia have been clashing with Georgian troops for years, and Russia and Georgia have each gradually escalated the conflict—which is far from equal, however, because of Russia's enormous advantages in size and military strength. When, in August 2008, the Georgian government launched an assault on the separatists, Russian tanks moved into Ossetia on the grounds that the move was necessary to defend Russian peacekeepers in the region.[67]

Richard C. Holbrooke, the former American ambassador to the United Nations, suggested that Russia has "Two goals—to do a creeping annexation of South Ossetia and Abkhazia and, secondly, to overthrow Saakashvili. . . ."[68] U.S. secretary of state Condoleezza Rice compared the incursion to the 1968 Soviet invasion of Czechoslovakia, and President Bush said that Russia was trying to act like a cold war superpower.[69]

Though pictures of Russian tanks advancing on a neighboring country do conjure up images of 1968, the comparison is not exact. In Czechoslovakia, the Soviet Union used brute force to keep a country within the Soviet bloc. In this case, Russia has been conducting an ongoing campaign intending to strip Georgia of the separatist territories, making it gradually more and more difficult for Georgia to hold them. Georgia's president Saakashvili seems to have taken a gamble by launching an attack against the separatists, and Putin seems to have welcomed it as an opportunity to flex Russian military muscle.

Episodes like Russia's recent Georgian adventure play better in Russia than they do in Europe. Another way Russian leaders today court Russian public opinion is by criticizing the foreign policy of the United States. The Russian media is full of stories that blame Russian problems on the outside world, and many Russians were probably pleased when Vladimir Putin lambasted U.S. policies in a speech reported around the world at a February 2007 international security conference in Munich. Accusing the United States of attempting to establish a "uni-polar world," the Russian president asked rhetorically

> *What is a uni-polar world? No matter how we beautify this term, it means one single center of power, one single center of force and one single master . . . The United States has overstepped its borders in all spheres—economic, political and humanitarian, and has imposed itself on other states . . . Local and regional wars did not get fewer, the number of people who died did not get less but increased. We see no kind of restraint—a hyper-inflated use of force.*[70]

Nor had it brought a more secure world, Putin was able to point out, because the United States has only gone "from one conflict to another without achieving a fully-fledged solution to any of them."[71] Putin's own antidemocratic behavior at home and aggressive posturing abroad were well known to his listeners. Their responses criticized his statements as unhelpful. However, they could hardly quarrel with the analysis itself, since by 2007 it represented an international consensus of foreign policy experts around the world.

As Talbott and many others have pointed out, it is not only the Russians who are upset about U.S. foreign policy in the 2000s. Europeans, too, object to a U.S. policy that emphasizes American exceptionalism and preventive war. Russia, even as it bullies its neighboring countries whose sovereignty it does not fully recognize, can present itself as less belligerent and less dangerous than the United States.

CONCLUSION

As this conclusion is written, there are still analysts who maintain that the United States, thanks to its robust economy and unmatched military strength, is poised to become the undisputed world hegemon lauded only a few years ago in books like Michael Mandelbaum's *The Case for Goliath.* As of 2008, it is safe to say that the number of these analysts have been thinned by a U.S. business recession and years of setbacks in the war on terror.

Whatever else may be debated about America's relationship with the regions discussed in this chapter, that relationship is sure to be different by 2050, because the regions themselves are changing so quickly. They are changing faster than the United States is changing. It is easy to forget, when the headlines are full of war, that most of this change is for the better. The economies of most formerly colonized, impoverished countries are growing. For the most part, their people are becoming more literate, more well-informed, and more prosperous. While poverty remains an enormous problem and the strain on the world's resources is also growing, it is hard to argue with the fact that this growth is bringing a better life to billions of people around the world. Certainly, the United States cannot oppose the world's increasing prosperity, and Americans would not want to oppose it.

But this growth also brings greater power to the governments of the countries in which it is taking place. If there is truth to the theory—proposed by Paul Kennedy and others—that relative economic strength is the foundation of military strength, it seems inevitable that there will be an end to the unparalleled dominance that the United States was able to exercise during the second half of the 20th century and first few years of the 21st. It seems likely that we will soon again see a multipolar world, with several centers of power, such as existed prior to World War II. And since prosperity does not always bring peace and countries will be competing for resources, it may continue to be a dangerous world. It may be a world bristling with nuclear weapons, intractable small-scale conflicts, and terrorism.

The job of America's foreign policy makers now is to prepare for that near-future world, in which, like it or not, the United States will undoubtedly place greater reliance on allies and international institutions than it has in recent years.

---

[1] On European v. American attitudes, see Tony Judt. "Europe vs. America," *New York Review of Books,* February 10, 2005, vol. 2, no. 2; on the death penalty, see John R. Schmidt. "The EU Campaign against the Death Penalty." *Survival.* London: Winter 2007/2008, vol. 49, Iss. 4, p. 123; on global warming, "U.S. attacked as EU ratifies Kyoto," CNNA.com/WORLD, June 1, 2002. Available online. URL: http://archives.cnn.com/2002/WORLD/europe/06/0l/kyoto.eu/. Accessed September 2, 2008; on gas taxes, see Guy Chazan and Marcus Walker. "World News: Europeans Protest Fuel Taxes but Accept High Prices; Rising Cost of Gas Ignites Little Ire; 'Dumb Acceptance,'" *Wall Street Journal* (eastern edition), May 28, 2008, p. A.8; on multilateral institutions, Joachim Krause. "Multilateralism: Behind European Views." Available online. URL: http://www.twq.com/04spring/docs/04spring_krause.pdf. Accessed September 2, 2008; on opposition to Iraq war, "Survey Says European Support for U.S. Falling." Available online. URL: http://www.washingtonpost.com/wp-dyn/articles/A57913-2003Jan28.html. Accessed September 2, 2008, and Anne Applebaum. "Here Comes the New Europe" Washingtonpost.com; on Israeli-Arab conflict, Anti-Defamation League. "European Attitudes toward Jews, Israel and the Palestinian-Israeli Conflict," June 27, 2002. Available online URL: http://ww.adl.org/anti_semitism/european_attitudes.pdf. Accessed September 2, 2008.

[2] Peter Ford. "Gas Prices Too High? Try Europe." *Christian Science Monitor,* August 26, 2005. Available online. URL: http://www.csmonitor.com/2005/0826/p01s03-woeu.html. Accessed February 12, 2008.

[3] ———. "What Place for God in Europe?" *Christian Science Monitor,* February 21, 2005. Available online. URL: http://www.usatoday.com/news/world/2005-02-21-god-europe_x.htm.

Accessed August 11, 2008. "Secular Europe confirmed by poll." *International Herald Tribune,* June 7, 2005. Available online. URL: http://www.iht.com/articles/2005/06/06/news/religion.php. Accessed August 11, 2008.

[4] "Up for Debate: Shock Therapy: Bolivia, Poland, Russia. Same Policies—Different Results." *Commanding Heights on PBS.* Available online. URL: http://www.pbs.org/wgbh/commanding heights/shared/minitextlo/ufd_shocktherapy.html. Accessed February 12, 2008.

[5] Robert Kagan. *Of Paradise and Power.* New York: Knopf, 2003, p. 4.

[6] ———. *Of Paradise and Power,* pp. 35–36.

[7] Robert J. Jackson and Philip Towle. *Temptations of Power: The United States in Global Politics after 9/11.* New York: Palgrave MacMillan, 2006, p. 32.

[8] Daniel Dombey and Stanley Pignal. "Europeans See US as Threat to Peace." *Financial Times* (July 1, 2007), Available online. URL: http://www.ft.com/cms/s/0/70046760-27f0-11dc-80da-000b5df10621.html. Accessed September 1, 2008. "A survey carried out in June by Harris Research for the *Financial Times* shows that 32 percent of respondents in five European countries regard the US a a bigger threat than any other state." "US 'biggest global peace threat." BBC News (6/14/2006). Available online. URL: http://news.bbc.co.uk/2/hi/americas/5077984.stm. Accessed September 1, 2008. "People in European and Muslim countries see US policy in Iraq as a bigger threat to world peace than Iran's nuclear programme. . . ."

[9] Niall Ferguson. *Colossus: The Price of America's Empire.* New York: Penguin, 2004, p. 227.

[10] ———. *Colossus,* p. 227.

[11] Samuel Huntington. "The Lonely Superpower." *Foreign Affairs* 78 (March–April 1999), p. 2.

[12] Charles A. Kupchan. *The End of the American Era: U.S. Foreign Policy and the Geopolitics of the Twenty-first Century.* New York: Knopf, 2002, pp. 119, 132.

[13] ———. *End of the American Era,* p. 153.

[14] Ferguson. *Colossus,* pp. 241–242.

[15] Kupchan. *End of the American Era,* p. 145.

[16] Greg Grandin. *Empire's Workshop: Latin America, the United States, and the Rise of the New Imperialism.* New York: Henry Holt, 2006, pp. 1–9.

[17] John O'Sullivan. "She was right: Jeane Kirkpatrick, statesman and intellectual." *National Review,* December 31, 2006. Available online. URL: http://findarticles.com/p/articles/mi_m1282/is_24_58/ai_n26711633. Accessed September 3, 2008.

[18] Diego Cevallos. "Religion—Latin America: Catholic Church Losing Followers in Droves." *IPS,* October 21, 2004. Available online. URL: http://ipsnews.net/news.asp?idnews=25966. Accessed February 12, 2008.

[19] Moises Naim. "Democracy Dictates Latin America's Future." *Financial Times* (April 26, 2002). Available online. URL: http://vcrisis.com/index.php?content=analysis/moises1002. Accessed September 7, 2008.

[20] Juan Forero. "Latin America Graft and Poverty Trying Patience with Democracy." *New York Times,* June 24, 2004. Available online. URL: http://query.nytimes.com/gst/fullpage.html?res=9C00E3DE1E39F937A15755C0A9629C8B63. Accessed February 12, 2008.

[21] Robert F. Noriega. "State of Democracy in Latin America," statement before the U.S. House of Representatives Committee on International Relations, Subcommittee on the

Western Hemisphere, Washington, D.C., March 9, 2005. Available online. URL: http://www.state.gov/p/wha/rls/rm/2005/ql/43221.htm. Accessed September 7, 2008.

22 The International Bank for Reconstruction and Development/The World Bank. "Annual Report 2006: Latin America and the Caribbean." Available online. URL: http://web.worldbank.org/WBSITE/EXTERNAL/EXTABOUTUnitedStates/EXTANNREP/EXTANNREP2K6/0,,contentMDK:21046814~menuPK:2915 694~pagePK:64168445~piPK:64168309~theSitePK:2838572,00.html. Accessed February 12, 2008.

23 Samuel Morley. "The Income Distribution Problem in Latin America and the Caribbean." Economic Commission for Latin America and the Caribbean. Available online. URL: http://www.eclac.org/cgi-bin/getProd.asp?xml=/publicaciones/xml/3/7213/P7213.xml&xsl=/de/tpl-i/p9f.xsl&base=/de/tpl/top-bottom.xsl. Accessed February 12, 2008.

24 Thomas F. O'Brien. *Making the Americas: The United States and Latin America from the Age of Revolutions to the Era of Globalization.* Albuquerque: University of New Mexico Press, 2007, p. 299.

25 International Affairs Journal at UC Davis. Available online. URL: http://davisiaj.com/content/view/192/86/. Accessed February 12, 2008. "Regional Spotlight: Latin America." *International Affairs Journal at UC Davis* (May 23, 2006). Available online. URL: http://davisiaj.com/content/view/192/86/. Accessed February 12, 2008.

26 Olivia Winslow. "Census Report Sees Minorities Becoming Majority by 2042." Newsday.com (August 14, 2008). Available online. URL: http://www.newsday.com/news/printedition/longisland/ny-licens145800578aug14,0,2712431.story. Accessed September 3, 2008.

27 O'Brien. *Making the Americas,* p. 291.

28 Globalsecurity.org. "Revolutionary Armed Forces of Colombia—Fuerzas Armadas Revolucionarias de Colombia—FARC." Available online. URL: http://www.globalsecurity.org/military/world/para/farc.htm. Accessed February 12, 2008.

29 O'Brien. *Making the Americas,* p. 291.

30 Tony Karon. "Peru Plane Tragedy Highlights a Troubled War on Drugs." *Time,* April 24, 2001. Available online. URL: http://www.time/com/time/columnist/karon/article/0,9565,107559,00.html. Accessed September 1, 2008.

31 ———. *Making the Americas,* pp. 291–292.

32 ———. *Making the Americas,* p. 292.

33 ———. *Making the Americas,* p. 302.

34 Juan Gonzalez. *Harvest of Empire: A History of Latinos in America.* New York: Viking, 2000, pp. 138–139.

35 Peter Hukim. "Is Washington Losing Latin America?" *Foreign Affairs* (January/February 2006). Available online. URL: http://www.foreignaffairs.org/20060101faessay85105/peter hakim/iewashington-losing-latin-am erica.html. Accessed September 5, 2008.

36 ———. "Is Washington Losing Latin America?"

37 John Hughes. "Chavez Is Troublemaker to Be Watched." *Deseret News,* November 9, 2005. Available online. URL: http://findarticles.com/p/articles/mi_qn4188/is_20051109/ai_n158420. Accessed September 5, 2008.

[38] Hakim, "Is Washington Losing Latin America?"

[39] "China's Claim in Latin America: So Far, a Partner Not a Threat." Council on Hemispheric Affairs (July 25, 2008). Available online. URL: http://www.coha.org/2008/07/china%E2%80%99s-claim-in-latin-america-so-far-a-partner-not-a-threat/. Accessed September 5, 2008.

[40] Febe Armanios. "Islam: Sunnis and Shiis." Congressional Research Service Report for Congress, February 23, 2004. Available online. URL: http://www.fas.org/irp/crs/RS21745.pdf. Accessed February 12, 2008.

[41] CIA World Factbook. "Gaza Strip." Available online. URL: http://www.cia.gov/library/publications/the-world-factbook/geos/gz.html. Accessed February 13, 2008.

[42] Michael C. Hudson. *Arab Politics: The Search for Legitimacy.* New Haven: Yale University Press, 1977, pp. 1–16. Though Hudson wrote his book in the 1970s, the problems he discussed clearly persist today, as events in Iraq, Lebanon, and farther afield in the Islamic states Pakistan and Afghanistan illustrate.

[43] Bernard Lewis. "The Roots of Muslim Rage." *Atlantic Monthly,* September 1990. Available online. URL: http://www.theatlantic.com/doc/199009/muslim-rage. Accessed February 12, 2008.

[44] Fouad Ajami. *The Arab Predicament: Arab Political Thought and Practice since 1967.* Cambridge: Cambridge University Press, 1981, pp. 68–71. "The Israeli capture of Jerusalem and its significance for the Israelis gave Muslim believers ammunition in their debate with Arab secularists."

[45] Stephen J. Hedges. "U.S. Military to leave Saudi Arabia amid strained relations." *Chicago Tribune,* April 30, 2003. Available online. URL: http://www.globalsecurity.org/org/news/2003/030430-psab01.htm. Accessed February 14, 2008.

[46] *EIA, Energy Information Administration, Official Energy Statistics from the United States Government.* "Saudi Arabia." February 2007. Available online. URL: http://www.eia.doe.gov/cabs/Saudi_Arabia/Background.html. Accessed February 14, 2008.

[47] Serge Schemann. "Quickly, a Saudi Peace Idea Gains Momentum in Mideast." *New York Times,* February 14, 2008. Available online. URL: http://query.nytimes.com/gst/fullpage.html?res=9E03EED61E31F930A35750C0A9649C8B63 &sec=&spon=&pagewanted=1. Accessed February 14, 2008.

[48] Warren P. Strobel. "U.S. to Sell Advanced Weapons to Saudi Arabia and Others." *McClatchy Newspapers,* July 27, 2007. Available online. URL: http://www.mcclatchydc.com/homepage/story/18457.html. Accessed February 14, 2008.

[49] Michael Scheuer (published as Anonymous). *Imperial Hubris: Why the West Is Losing the War on Terror.* Washington, D.C.: Potomac Books, 2004.

[50] Alan Richards. "At War with Utopian Fanatics." *Middle East Policy* 8 (4), December 2001, pp. 5–9. Available online. URL: http://www.blackwell-synergy.com/doi/abs/10.1111/j.1475-4967.2001.tb00002.x?cookieSet=1 &journalCode=mepo. Accessed February 14, 2008.

[51] Timothy Mitchell. "American Power and Anti-Americanism in the Middle East." In Andrew Ross and Kristan Ross, editors. *Anti-Americanism.* New York: New York University Press, 2004, p. 87.

[52] Mitchell. *Anti-Americanism,* pp. 91–92.

53 ———. *Anti-Americanism,* p. 92.

54 ———. *Anti-Americanism,* p. 95.

55 ———. *Anti-Americanism,* p. 95.

56 Scheuer. *Imperial Hubris,* p. 2.

57 James A. Baker III and Lee H. Hamilton, co-chairs. "The Iraq Study Group Report." Available online. URL: http://www.usip.org/isg/iraq_study_group_report/report/1206/iraq_study_group_report.pdf. Accessed February 14, 2008.

58 Dana R. Dillon. *The China Challenge: Standing Strong against the Military, Economic, and Political Threats That Imperil America.* New York: Rowman & Littlefield Publishers, 2007, p. 2.

59 ———. *The China Challenge,* p. 102.

60 Zhiqun Zhu. *United States-China Relations in the 21st Century: Power Transition and Peace.* New York: Routledge, 2006, p. 8.

61 Human Rights Watch. "Essential Background: Overview of Human Rights Issues in China." December 12, 2005. Available online. URL: http://www.hrw.org/english/docs/2006/01/18/china12270.htm. Accessed February 14, 2008.

62 Dillon. *The China Challenge,* p. 8.

63 Clear Bigg. "World: Freedom House Ranks Most Repressive Countries." Radio Free Europe/Radio Liberty, September 7, 2006. Available online. URL: http://www.rferl.org/features article/2006/09/4553e9de-78a6-444c-82ff-001c91bd71b4.htm. Accessed February 13, 2008.

64 Strobe Talbott. Building a Constructive U.S.-Russian Relationship, speech to the House Committee on Foreign Affairs, October 30, 2007. Available online. URL: http://www.brookings .edu/testimony/20O7/1030_russia_ta lbott.aspx. Accessed September 7, 2008.

65 Talbott. Building a Constructive U.S.-Russian Relationship.

66 Michael Schwirtz, Anne Bernard and C. J. Chivers. "Russia and Georgia Clash over Separatist Region." *New York Times,* August 8, 2008. Available online. http://www.nytimes.com/2008/08/09/world/europe/O9georgia.html. Accessed September 7, 2008.

67 "Russian Tanks Enter South Ossetia." *BBC News,* August 8, 2008. Available online. URL: http://news.bbc.co.uk/2/hi/europe/7548715.stm. Accessed September 7, 2008.

68 Schwirtz, et al. "Russia and Georgia Clash over Separatist Region."

69 Borzou Daraghi and Maura Reynolds. "Harsh Words Beat up Georgia Crisis." *Los Angeles Times,* August 16, 2008. Available online. URL: http://www.latimes.com/news/nationworld/world/la-fgossetial6-2008aug16,O,4516389.story. Accessed September 7, 2008.

70 Rob Watson. "Putin Speech: Back to Cold War?" BBC News, February 10, 2007. Available online. URL: http://news.bbc.co.uk/2/hi/europe/6350847.stm. Accessed February 15, 2008.

71 Watson. "Putin Speed." BBC News, February 10, 2007.

PART II

Primary Sources

4

United States Documents

America's changing picture of itself and its role in the world, from a tiny British colony to a superpower, can be traced in the following 20 documents. They include excerpts from a speech given to the passengers of a ship of Puritan immigrants, several presidential addresses, a congressional bill, a government pamphlet, a famous "long telegram" from a U.S. diplomat in Russia, and testimony before a Senate subcommittee. They are presented in chronological order and divided into three sections. The first, "U.S. Expansion and Imperialism," takes the story from its legendary beginnings, with John Winthrop proposing that the new Puritan colony be like a "city on a hill," to Albert J. Beveridge's unashamed arguments in favor of an American empire. The second section, "From Diplomacy to Neutrality," depicts the nation's rejection of Woodrow Wilson's internationalism. In the third, "World War and Cold War Strategy," we see an America thrust into a leadership role. The fourth, "America as a World Superpower," shows American foreign policy in the age of the Bush doctrine.

U.S. EXPANSION AND IMPERIALISM

John Winthrop: A Model of Christian Charity (City upon a Hill) (1630) (excerpt)

The Puritans began as a religious faction within the Church of England. Following the doctrines of the Protestant theologian John Calvin, Puritans believed in close adherence to biblical teachings and the importance of a personal relationship with God. During the reign of the Stuart kings James I and Charles I, the Puritans, a strong influence in Parliament, came into conflict with the Crown. This conflict would eventually lead to a civil war.

In 1629, John Winthrop, a devout Puritan, learned about the Massachusetts Bay Company, a new trading venture that had received rights to a plot of land in North America and authority from the king to establish a settlement there. The charter was an unusual one that would allow the colony to be self-governing, its chief officers located on the spot in New England. In 1630, the company departed for North America. Winthrop, who led the company and would be the governor of the colony, preached the lay sermon excerpted below aboard the expedition's flagship, the Arbella *(so tradition holds: Some recent scholarship suggests the speech may have been given in England before the Puritans left for America). Winthrop's full sermon is a mixture of passion and careful reasoning. It is an early statement of a comparison that would often be made between America and the biblical promised land. Winthrop's plea that the members of his expedition remain true to each other and to their ideals would be transmuted into a lasting sense of America's political mission.*

Thus stands the cause between God and us. We are entered into covenant with Him for this work. We have taken out a commission. The Lord hath given us leave to draw our own articles. We have professed to enterprise these and those accounts, upon these and those ends. We have hereupon besought Him of favor and blessing. Now if the Lord shall please to hear us, and bring us in peace to the place we desire, then hath He ratified this covenant and sealed our commission, and will expect a strict performance of the articles contained in it; but if we shall neglect the observation of these articles which are the ends we have propounded, and, dissembling with our God, shall fall to embrace this present world and prosecute our carnal intentions, seeking great things for ourselves and our posterity, the Lord will surely break out in wrath against us, and be revenged of such a people, and make us know the price of the breach of such a covenant.

Now the only way to avoid this shipwreck, and to provide for our posterity, is to follow the counsel of Micah, to do justly, to love mercy, to walk humbly with our God. For this end, we must be knit together, in this work, as one man. We must entertain each other in brotherly affection. We must be willing to abridge ourselves of our superfluities, for the supply of others' necessities. We must uphold a familiar commerce together in all meekness, gentleness, patience and liberality. We must delight in each other; make others' conditions our own; rejoice together, mourn together, labor and suffer together, always having before our eyes our commission and community in the work, as members of the same body. So shall we keep the unity of the spirit in the bond of peace. The Lord will be our God, and delight to dwell among us, as His own people, and will command a blessing upon us in all our ways, so that we shall see much more of His wisdom, power, goodness and truth, than formerly we have been acquainted with. We shall find that the God of Israel is among us, when ten of us shall be able to resist a thousand of our enemies; when He shall make us a praise and glory that men shall say of succeeding plantations, "may the Lord make it like that of New England." For we must consider that we shall be as a city upon a hill. The eyes of all people are upon us. So that if we shall deal falsely with our God in this work we have undertaken, and so cause Him to withdraw His present help from us, we shall be made a story and a by-word through the world. We shall open the mouths of enemies to speak evil of the ways of God, and all professors for God's sake. We shall shame the faces of many of God's worthy servants, and cause their prayers to be turned into curses upon us till we be consumed out of the good land whither we are going.

And to shut this discourse with that exhortation of Moses, that faithful servant of the Lord, in his last farewell to Israel, Deut. 30. "Beloved, there is now set before us life and death, good and evil," in that we are commanded this day to love the Lord our God, and to love one another, to walk in his ways and to keep his Commandments and his ordinance and his laws, and the articles of our Covenant with Him, that we may live and be multiplied, and that the Lord our God may bless us in the land whither we go to possess it. But if our hearts shall turn away, so that we will not obey, but shall be seduced, and worship other Gods, our pleasure and profits, and serve them; it is propounded unto us this day, we shall surely perish out of the good land whither we pass over this vast sea to possess it.

Therefore let us choose life,
that we and our seed may live,
by obeying His voice and cleaving to Him,
for He is our life and our prosperity.

Source: Available online. URL: http://religiousfreedom.lib.virginia.edu/sacred/charity.html

George Washington's Farewell Address (1796) (excerpt)

George Washington delivered the first presidential farewell address in 1796 before the start of the next presidential election. The speech is a comprehensive survey, in very general terms, of the young nation's problems and prospects. The tone is fatherly, and the counsel is one of moderation, warning against excessive factionalism, regionalism, government expense and miserliness, and constitutional innovation. When it comes to America's foreign relations, Washington recommends that the United States avoid a "habitual" preference for one over another, but act with fairness to all.

. . . Observe good faith and justice towards all nations; cultivate peace and harmony with all. Religion and morality enjoin this conduct; and can it be, that good policy does not equally enjoin it? It will be worthy of a free, enlightened, and, at no distant period, a great nation, to give to mankind the magnanimous and too novel example of a people always guided by an exalted justice and benevolence. Who can doubt, that, in the course of time and things, the fruits of such a plan would richly repay any temporary advantages, which might be lost by a steady adherence to it? Can it be, that Providence has not connected the permanent felicity of a Nation with its virtue? The experiment, at least, is recommended by every sentiment which ennobles human nature. Alas! is it rendered impossible by its vices?

In the execution of such a plan, nothing is more essential than that permanent, inveterate antipathies against particular Nations, and passionate attachments for others, should be excluded; and that, in place of them, just and amicable feelings towards all should be cultivated. The Nation, which indulges towards another an habitual hatred, or an habitual fondness, is in some degree a slave. It is a slave to its animosity or to its affection, either of which is sufficient to lead it astray from its duty and its interest. Antipathy in one nation against another disposes each more readily to offer insult and injury, to lay hold of slight causes of umbrage, and to be haughty and intractable, when accidental or trifling occasions of dispute occur. Hence frequent collisions, obstinate, envenomed, and bloody contests. The Nation, prompted by ill-will and resentment, sometimes impels to war the Government, contrary to the best calculations of policy. The Government sometimes participates in the national propensity, and adopts through passion what reason would reject; at other times, it makes the animosity of the nation subservient to projects of hostility instigated by pride, ambition, and other sinister and pernicious motives. The peace often, sometimes perhaps the liberty, of Nations has been the victim.

So likewise, a passionate attachment of one Nation for another produces a variety of evils. Sympathy for the favorite Nation, facilitating the illusion of an imaginary common interest, in cases where no real common interest exists, and infusing into one the enmities of the other, betrays the former into a participation in the quarrels and wars of the latter, without adequate inducement or justification. It leads also to concessions to the favorite Nation of privileges denied to others which is apt doubly to injure the Nation making the concessions; by unnecessarily parting with what ought to have been retained, and by exciting jealousy, ill-will, and a disposition to retaliate, in the parties from whom equal privileges are withheld. . . .

The great rule of conduct for us, in regard to foreign nations, is, in extending our commercial relations, to have with them as little engagements, let them be fulfilled with perfect good faith. Here let us stop. Europe has a set of primary interests, which to us have none, or a very remote relation. Hence she must be engaged in frequent controversies, the causes of which are essentially foreign to our concerns. Hence, therefore, it must be unwise in us to implicate ourselves, by artificial ties, in the ordinary vicissitudes of her politics, or the ordinary combinations and collisions of her friendships or enmities.

Our detached and distant situation invites and enables us to pursue a different course. If we remain one people, under an efficient government. the period is not far off, when we may defy material injury from external annoyance; when we may take such an attitude as will cause the neutrality, we may at any time resolve upon, to be scrupulously respected; when belligerent nations, under the impossibility of making acquisitions upon us, will not lightly hazard the giving us provocation; when we may choose peace or war, as our interest, guided by justice, shall counsel.

Why forego the advantages of so peculiar a situation? Why quit our own to stand upon foreign ground? Why, by interweaving our destiny with that of any part of Europe, entangle our peace and prosperity in the toils of European ambition, rivalship, interest, humor, or caprice?

It is our true policy to steer clear of permanent alliances with any portion of the foreign world; so far, I mean, as we are now at liberty to do it; for let me not be understood as capable of patronizing infidelity to existing engagements. I hold the maxim no less applicable to public than to private affairs, that honesty is always the best policy. I repeat it, therefore, let those engagements be observed in their genuine sense. But, in my opinion, it is unnecessary and would be unwise to extend them.

Taking care always to keep ourselves, by suitable establishments, on a respectable defensive posture, we may safely trust to temporary alliances for extraordinary emergencies. . . .

Source: The Avalon Project at Yale Law School. Available online. URL: http://www.yale.edu/lawweb/avalon/washing.htm. Accessed March 20, 2009.

The Monroe Doctrine (December 2, 1823) (excerpt)

In the early 1800s, during the Napoleonic Wars, Spain's American colonies revolted and declared their independence. After Napoléon's defeat, an effort was made to restore the international balance of power that had existed before the French Revolution. Spain, together with Russia and France (once again a monarchy) wanted this restoration to include the return to Spain of her American colonies. Britain, however, expected to reap economic benefits from the continued independence of the former colonies and suggested that the United States join it in declaring their intention to oppose recolonization. U.S. secretary of state John Quincy Adams pointed out that such a joint declaration might hinder U.S. expansion into former Spanish territory. So, to declare U.S. opposition to European colonization in a way that did not limit the United States's own interests in the Americas, the statement that become known as the Monroe Doctrine was instead written into President James Monroe's seventh annual message to Congress, December 2, 1823.

The citizens of the United States cherish sentiments the most friendly in favor of the liberty and happiness of their fellow-men on that side of the Atlantic. In the wars of the European powers in matters relating to themselves we have never taken any part, nor does it comport with our policy to do so. It is only when our rights are invaded or seriously menaced that we resent injuries or make preparation for our defense. With the movements in this hemisphere we are of necessity more immediately connected, and by causes which must be obvious to all enlightened and impartial observers. The political system of the allied powers is essentially different in this respect from that of America. This difference proceeds from that which exists in their respective Governments; and to the defense of our own, which has been achieved by the loss of so much blood and treasure, and matured by the wisdom of their most enlightened citizens, and under which we have enjoyed unexampled felicity, this whole nation is devoted. We owe it, therefore, to candor and to the amicable relations existing between the United States and those powers to declare that we should consider any attempt on their part to extend their system to any portion of this hemisphere as dangerous to our peace and safety. With the existing colonies or dependencies of any European power we have not interfered and shall not interfere. But with the Governments who have declared their independence and maintain it, and whose independence we have, on great consideration and on just principles, acknowledged, we could not view any interposition for the purpose of oppressing them, or controlling in any other manner their destiny, by any European power in any other light than as the manifestation of an unfriendly disposition toward the United States. In the war between those new Governments and Spain we declared our neutrality at the time of their recognition, and to this we have adhered, and shall continue to adhere, provided no change shall occur which, in the judgement of the competent authorities of this Government, shall make a corresponding change on the part of the United States indispensable to their security.

The late events in Spain and Portugal shew that Europe is still unsettled. . . . Our policy in regard to Europe, which was adopted at an early stage of the wars which have so long agitated that quarter of the globe, nevertheless remains the same, which is, not to interfere in the internal concerns of any of its powers; to consider the government de facto as the legitimate government for us; to cultivate friendly relations with it, and to preserve those relations by a frank, firm, and manly policy, meeting in all instances the just claims of every power, submitting to injuries from none. But in regard to those continents circumstances are eminently and conspicuously different.

It is impossible that the allied powers should extend their political system to any portion of either continent without endangering our peace and happiness; nor can anyone believe that our southern brethren, if left to themselves, would adopt it of their own accord. It is equally impossible, therefore, that we should behold such interposition in any form with indifference. If we look to the comparative strength and resources of Spain and those new Governments, and their distance from each other, it must be obvious that she can never subdue them. It is still the true policy of the United States to leave the parties to themselves, in hope that other powers will pursue the same course. . . .

Source: The Art Bin Origo. Available online. URL: http://art-bin.com/art/omonroe.html.

Manifest Destiny (1845) (excerpt)

Americans of the 19th century believed they inhabited a revolutionary nation based on higher principles than those of Europe. Not only were Europeans autocratic where the United States was democratic, but Europeans were imperialistic and the United States was not. Yet paradoxically, the United States was expanding and most of its citizens expected it to continue to expand westward all the way to the Pacific Ocean. Americans resolved this contradiction by believing that North America was essentially a virgin land whose original inhabitants—Native Americans—were really a part of the landscape, like its plants and animals. Besides, if the United States did not spread across North America, making it a part of what Jefferson had called "the empire of liberty," some other nations would. A United States that stretched from one ocean to the other was inevitable and good. The poplar catchphrase that summed up this belief was Manifest Destiny, first introduced by the political journalist John L. O'Sullivan, who used it in more than one essay advocating U.S. expansion.

The American people having derived their origin from many other nations, and the Declaration of National Independence being entirely based on the great principle of human equality, these facts demonstrate at once our disconnected position as regards any other nation; that we have, in reality, but little connection with the past history of any of them, and still less with all antiquity, its glories, or its crimes. On the contrary, our national birth was the beginning of a new history, the formation and progress of an untried political system, which separates us from the past and connects us with the future only; and so far as regards the entire development of the natural rights of man, in moral, political, and national life, we may confidently assume that our country is destined to be the great nation of futurity. . . .

We have no interest in the scenes of antiquity, only as lessons of avoidance of nearly all their examples. The expansive future is our arena, and for our history. We are entering on its untrodden space, with the truths of God in our minds, beneficent objects in our hearts, and with a clear conscience unsullied by the past. We are the nation of human progress, and who will, what can, set limits to our onward march? Providence is with us, and no earthly power can. We point to the everlasting truth on the first page of our national declaration, and we proclaim to the millions of other lands, that "the gates of hell"—the powers of aristocracy and monarchy—"shall not prevail against it."

The far-reaching, the boundless future will be the era of American greatness. In its magnificent domain of space and time, the nation of many nations is destined to manifest to mankind the excellence of divine principles; to establish on earth the noblest temple ever dedicated to the worship of the Most High—the Sacred and the True. Its floor shall be a hemisphere—its roof the firmament of the star-studded heavens, and its congregation an Union of many Republics, comprising hundreds of happy millions, calling, owning no man master, but governed by God's natural and moral law of equality, the law of brotherhood—of "peace and good will amongst men." . . .

Yes, we are the nation of progress, of individual freedom, of universal enfranchisement. Equality of rights is the cynosure of our union of States, the grand exemplar of the correlative equality of individuals; and while truth sheds its effulgence, we cannot retrograde, without dissolving the one and subverting the other. We must onward to the fulfilment of our mission—to the entire development of the principle of our organization—freedom of conscience, freedom of person, freedom of trade and business pursuits, universality of freedom and equality. This is our high destiny, and in nature's eternal, inevitable decree of cause and effect we must accomplish it. All this will be our future history, to establish on earth the moral dignity and salvation of man—the immutable truth and beneficence of God. For this blessed mission to the nations of the world, which are shut out from the life-giving light of truth, has America been chosen; and her high example shall smite unto death the tyranny of kings, hierarchs, and oligarchs, and carry the glad tidings of peace and good will where myriads now endure an existence scarcely more enviable than that of beasts of the field. Who, then, can doubt that our country is destined to be *the great nation* of futurity?

Source: "The Great Nation of Futurity," *The United States Democratic Review,* vol. 6, # 23, pp. 426–430. The complete article can be found in *The Making of America series* at Cornell University. Available online. URL: http://www.mtholyoke.edu/acad/intrel/osulliva.htm.

William McKinley on the Philippines "Rebellion" (March 4, 1901) (excerpt)

Encouraged by American newspaper reports of Spain's brutality toward Cuban rebels and by the belief that the explosion of the USS Maine *was a dastardly act of Spanish aggression, in 1898 the United States went to war with Spain—or, to be specific, with Spain's overseas colonies. The United States won a quick victory and took over Spain's choicest possessions in the Caribbean and the Pacific, including the Philippine Islands, which gave the United States an instant empire in the Far East. U.S. marines were dispatched to suppress an insurgency by Filipino patriots who did not want to exchange one master for another. To reconcile U.S. actions in this matter with U.S. ideals was no easy matter in this case, but President McKinley attempted to do so in his second inaugural speech. Not long afterward McKinley was assassinated, and his vice president, the unapologetic imperialist Theodore Roosevelt, became president.*

Four years ago we stood on the brink of war without the people knowing it and without any preparation or effort at preparation for the impending peril. I did all that in honor could be done to avert the war, but without avail. It became inevitable; and the Congress at its first regular session, without party division, provided money in anticipation of the crisis and in preparation to meet it. It came. The result was signally favorable to American arms and in the highest degree honorable to the Government. It imposed upon us obligations from which we cannot escape and from which it would be dishonorable to seek escape. We are now at peace with the world, and it is my fervent prayer that if differences arise between us and other powers they may be settled by peaceful arbitration and that hereafter we may be spared the horrors of war. . . .

The American people, entrenched in freedom at home, take their love for it with them wherever they go, and they reject as mistaken and unworthy the doctrine that we lose our own liberties by securing the enduring foundations of liberty to others. Our institutions will not deteriorate by extension, and our sense of justice will not abate under tropic suns in distant seas. As heretofore, so hereafter will the nation demonstrate its fitness to administer any new estate which events devolve upon it, and in the fear of God will "take occasion by the hand and make the bounds of freedom wider yet." If there are those among us who would make our way more difficult, we must not be disheartened, but the more earnestly dedicate ourselves to the task upon which we have rightly entered. The path of progress is seldom smooth. New things are often found hard to do. Our fathers found them so. We find them so. They are inconvenient. They cost us something. But are we not made better for the effort and sacrifice, and are not those we serve lifted up and blessed?

We will be consoled, too, with the fact that opposition has confronted every onward movement of the Republic from its opening hour until now, but without success. The Republic has marched on and on, and its step has exalted freedom and humanity. We are undergoing the same ordeal as did our predecessors nearly a century ago. We are following the course they blazed. They triumphed. Will their successors falter and plead organic impotency in the nation? Surely after 125 years of achievement for mankind we will not now surrender our equality with other powers on matters fundamental and essential to nationality. With no such purpose was the nation created. In no such spirit has it developed its full and independent sovereignty. We adhere to the principle of equality among ourselves, and by no act of ours will we assign to ourselves a subordinate rank in the family of nations. . . .

While the treaty of peace with Spain was ratified on the 6th of February, 1899, and ratifications were exchanged nearly two years ago, the Congress has indicated no form of government for the Philippine Islands. It has, however, provided an army to enable the Executive to suppress insurrection, restore peace, give security to the inhabitants, and establish the authority of the United States throughout the archipelago. It has authorized the organization of native troops as auxiliary to the regular force. It has been advised from time to time of the acts of the military and naval officers in the islands, of my action in appointing civil commissions, of the instructions with which they were charged, of their duties and powers, of their recommendations, and of their several acts under executive commission, together with the very complete general information they have submitted. These reports fully set forth the conditions, past and present, in the islands, and the instructions clearly show the principles which will guide the Executive until the Congress shall, as it is required to do by the treaty, determine "the civil rights and political status of the native inhabitants." The Congress having added the sanction of its authority to the powers already possessed and exercised by the Executive under the Constitution, thereby leaving with the Executive the responsibility for the government of the Philippines, I shall continue the efforts already begun until order shall be restored throughout the islands, and as fast as conditions permit will establish local governments, in the formation of which the full co-operation of the people has been already invited, and when established will encourage the people to administer them. The settled purpose, long ago proclaimed, to afford the inhabitants of the islands self-government as fast as they were ready for it will be pursued with earnestness and fidelity. Already something has been accomplished in this direction. The Government's representatives, civil and military, are doing faithful and noble work in their mission of emancipation and merit the approval and support of their countrymen. The most liberal terms of amnesty have already been communicated to the insurgents, and the way is still open for those who have raised their arms against the Government for honorable submission to its authority. Our countrymen should not be deceived. We are not waging war against the inhabitants of the Philippine Islands. A portion of them are making war against the United States. By far the greater part of the inhabitants recognize American sovereignty and welcome it as a guaranty of order and of security for life, property, liberty, freedom of conscience, and the pursuit of happiness. To them full protection will be given. They shall not be abandoned. We will not leave the destiny of the loyal millions to the disloyal thousands who are in rebellion against the United States. Order under civil institutions will come as soon as those who now break the peace shall keep it. Force will not be needed or used when those who make war against us shall make it no more. May it end without further bloodshed, and there be ushered in the reign of peace to be made permanent by a government of liberty under law!

Source: Inaugural Addresses of the Presidents of the United States. Available online. URL: http://www.bartleby.com/124/pres41.html.

Albert J. Beveridge on American Empire (January 9, 1900) (excerpt)

Albert J. Beveridge (1862–1927) was an American historian and U.S. senator from Indiana. Politically, he was both an ardent progressive along the lines of Theodore Roosevelt—a believer in breaking up monopolies and regulating food and drugs—and, like Roosevelt, an ardent imperialist. Elected to the Senate as a Republican in 1899, at the beginning of the new century he gave the speech excerpted here, stating the case for annexation of the Philippines in frankly imperialist terms.

MR. PRESIDENT, the times call for candor. The Philippines are ours forever, "territory belonging to the United States," as the Constitution calls them. And just beyond the Philippines are China's illimitable markets. We will not retreat from either. We will not repudiate our duty in the archipelago. We will not abandon our opportunity in the Orient. We will not renounce our part in the mission of our race, trustee, under God, of the civilization of the world. And we will move forward to our work, not howling out regrets like slaves whipped to their burdens but with gratitude for a task worthy of our strength and thanksgiving to Almighty God that He has marked us as His chosen people, henceforth to lead in the regeneration of the world.

This island empire is the last land left in all the oceans. If it should prove a mistake to abandon it, the blunder once made would be irretrievable. If it proves a mistake to hold it, the error can be corrected when we will. Every other progressive nation stands ready to relieve us.

But to hold it will be no mistake. Our largest trade henceforth must be with Asia. The Pacific is our ocean. More and more Europe will manufacture the most it needs, secure from its colonies the most it consumes. Where shall we turn for consumers of our surplus? Geography answers the question. China is our natural customer. She is nearer to us than to England, Germany, or Russia, the commercial powers of the present and the future. They have moved nearer to China by securing permanent bases on her borders. The Philippines give us a base at the door of all the East.

Lines of navigation from our ports to the Orient and Australia, from the Isthmian Canal to Asia, from all Oriental ports to Australia converge at and separate from the Philippines. They are a self-supporting, dividend-paying fleet, permanently anchored at a spot selected by the strategy of Providence, commanding the Pacific. And the Pacific is the ocean of the commerce of the future. Most future wars will be conflicts for commerce. The power that rules the Pacific, therefore, is the power that rules the world. And, with the Philippines, that power is and will forever be the American Republic. . . .

But if they did not command China, India, the Orient, the whole Pacific for purposes of offense, defense, and trade, the Philippines are so valuable in themselves that we should hold them. I have cruised more than 2,000 miles through the archipelago, every moment a surprise at its loveliness and wealth. I have ridden hundreds of miles on the islands, every foot of the way a revelation of vegetable and mineral riches. . .

Here, then, senators, is the situation. Two years ago there was no land in all the world which we could occupy for any purpose. Our commerce was daily turning toward the Orient, and geography and trade developments made necessary our commercial empire over the Pacific. And in that ocean we had no commercial, naval, or military base. Today, we have one of the three great ocean possessions of the globe, located at the most commanding commercial, naval, and military points in the Eastern seas, within hail of India, shoulder to shoulder with China, richer in its own resources than any equal body of land on the entire globe, and peopled by a race which civilization demands shall be improved. Shall we abandon it?

That man little knows the common people of the republic, little understands the instincts of our race who thinks we will not hold it fast and hold it forever, administering just government by simplest methods. We may trick up devices to shift our burden and lessen our opportunity; they will avail us nothing but delay. We may tangle conditions by applying academic arrangements of self-government to a crude situation; their failure will drive us to our duty in the end.

The military situation, past, present, and prospective, is no reason for abandonment. Our campaign has been as perfect as possible with the force at hand. We have been delayed, first, by a failure to comprehend the immensity of our acquisition; and, second, by insufficient force; and, third, by our efforts for peace. In February, after the treaty of peace, General Otis had only 3,722 officers and men whom he had a legal right to order into battle. The terms of enlistment of the rest of his troops had expired, and they fought voluntarily and not on legal military compulsion. It was one of the noblest examples of patriotic devotion to duty in the history of the world.

Those who complain do so in ignorance of the real situation. We attempted a great task with insufficient means; we became impatient that it was not finished before it could fairly be commenced; and I pray we may not add that other element of disaster, pausing in the work before it is thoroughly and forever done. That is the gravest mistake we could possibly make, and that is the only danger before us. Our Indian wars would have been shortened, the lives of soldiers and settlers saved, and the Indians themselves benefited had we made continuous and decisive war; and any other kind of war is criminal because ineffective. We acted toward the Indians as though we feared them, loved them, hated them—a mingling of foolish sentiment, inaccurate thought, and paralytic purpose. . . .

Mr. President, that must not be our plan. This war is like all other wars. It needs to be finished before it is stopped. I am prepared to vote either to make our work thorough or even now to abandon it. A lasting peace can be secured only by overwhelming forces in ceaseless action until universal and absolutely final defeat is inflicted on the enemy. To halt before every armed force, every guerrilla band opposing us is dispersed or exterminated will prolong hostilities and leave alive the seeds of perpetual insurrection.

Even then we should not treat. To treat at all is to admit that we are wrong. . . .

Source: Record, 56 Cong., I Sess., pp. 704–712. Available online. URL: http://www.mtholyoke.edu/acad/intrel/ajb72.htm.

FROM DIPLOMACY TO NEUTRALITY

The Fourteen Points (January 18, 1918) (excerpt)

World War I began in 1914, two years after a high-minded former Princeton University president named Woodrow Wilson was elected president of the United States. Wilson opposed U.S. involvement in the European war, which seemed to him a cynical conflict between imperialist nations. Most Americans supported Wilson's stance of neutrality, and he was reelected in 1916 on the slogan, "He kept us out of war." The German naval strategy—submarine warfare against all maritime trade, including that of neutral countries—finally drew the United States into war on the side of the Allies. Wilson, wedded to the idea of the United States as a country above cynical balance-of-power diplomacy, strove to give the war a higher meaning that would advance the cause of democracy and self-determination. His vision was embodied in his Fourteen Points program, laid out in his January 18, 1918, speech to Congress. From a diplomatic point of view, the flaw in Wilson's program was that it failed to address the upset to the European balance of power that had been created by the very existence of a united Germany. Had Wilson's principle of self-determination—Serbs ruling Serbs, Italians ruling Italians, Germans ruling Germans—been followed to the letter, Germany would have included Austria as well as parts of Poland and Czechoslovakia—as indeed it did for a while during Hitler's Third Reich.

It will be our wish and purpose that the processes of peace, when they are begun, shall be absolutely open and that they shall involve and permit henceforth no secret understandings of any kind. The day of conquest and aggrandizement is gone by; so is also the day of secret covenants entered into in the interest of particular governments and likely at some unlooked-for moment to upset the peace of the world. It is this happy fact, now clear to the view of every public man whose thoughts do not still linger in an age that is dead and gone, which makes it possible for every nation whose purposes are consistent with justice and the peace of the world to avow nor or at any other time the objects it has in view.

We entered this war because violations of right had occurred which touched us to the quick and made the life of our own people impossible unless they were corrected and the world secure once for all against their recurrence. What we demand in this war, therefore, is nothing peculiar to ourselves. It is that the world be made fit and safe to live in; and particularly that it be made safe for every peace-loving nation which, like our own, wishes to live its own life, determine its own institutions, be assured of justice and fair dealing by the other peoples of the world as against force and selfish aggression. All the peoples of the world are in effect partners in this interest, and for our own part we see very clearly that unless justice be done to others it will not be done to us. The programme of the world's peace, therefore, is our programme; and that programme, the only possible programme, as we see it, is this:

I. Open covenants of peace, openly arrived at, after which there shall be no private international understandings of any kind but diplomacy shall proceed always frankly and in the public view.

II. Absolute freedom of navigation upon the seas, outside territorial waters, alike in peace and in war, except as the seas may be closed in whole or in part by international action for the enforcement of international covenants.

III. The removal, so far as possible, of all economic barriers and the establishment of an equality of trade conditions among all the nations consenting to the peace and associating themselves for its maintenance.

IV. Adequate guarantees given and taken that national armaments will be reduced to the lowest point consistent with domestic safety.

V. A free, open-minded, and absolutely impartial adjustment of all colonial claims, based upon a strict observance of the principle that in determining all such questions of sovereignty the interests of the populations concerned must have equal weight with the equitable claims of the government whose title is to be determined.

VI. The evacuation of all Russian territory and such a settlement of all questions affecting Russia as will secure the best and freest cooperation of the other nations of the world in obtaining for her an unhampered and unembarrassed opportunity for the independent determination of her own political development and national policy and assure her of a sincere welcome into the society of free nations under institutions of her own choosing. . . .

VIII. All French territory should be freed and the invaded portions restored, and the wrong done to France by Prussia in 1871 in the matter of Alsace-Lorraine, which has unsettled the peace of the world for nearly fifty years, should be righted, in order that peace may once more be made secure in the interest of all.

IX. A readjustment of the frontiers of Italy should be effected along clearly recognizable lines of nationality.

X. The peoples of Austria-Hungary, whose place among the nations we wish to see safeguarded and assured, should be accorded the freest opportunity to autonomous development. . . .

XI. Rumania, Serbia, and Montenegro should be evacuated; occupied territories restored; Serbia accorded free and secure access to the sea; and the relations of the several Balkan states to one another determined by friendly counsel along historically established lines of allegiance and nationality; and international guarantees of the political and economic independence and territorial integrity of the several Balkan states should be entered into.

XII. The turkish portion of the present Ottoman Empire should be assured a secure sovereignty, but the other nationalities which are now under Turkish rule should be assured an undoubted security of life and an absolutely unmolested opportunity of autonomous development, and the Dardanelles should be permanently opened as a free passage to the ships and commerce of all nations under international guarantees.

XIII. An independent Polish state should be erected which should include the territories inhabited by indisputably Polish populations, which should be assured a free and secure access to the sea, and whose political and economic independence and territorial integrity should be guaranteed by international covenant.

XIV. A general association of nations must be formed under specific covenants for the purpose of affording mutual guarantees of political independence and territorial integrity to great and small states alike.

In regard to these essential rectifications of wrong and assertions of right we feel ourselves to be intimate partners of all the governments and peoples associated together against the Imperialists. We cannot be separated in interest or divided in purpose. We stand together until the end.

For such arrangements and covenants we are willing to fight and to continue to fight until they are achieved; but only because we wish the right to prevail and desire a just and stable peace such as can be secured only by removing the chief provocations to war, which this programme does remove. We have no jealousy of German greatness, and there is nothing in this programme that impairs it. We grudge her no achievement or distinction of learning or of pacific enterprise such as have made her record very

> bright and very enviable. We do not wish to injure her or to block in any way her legitimate influence or power. We do not wish to fight her either with arms or with hostile arrangements of trade if she is willing to associate herself with us and the other peace- loving nations of the world in covenants of justice and law and fair dealing. We wish her only to accept a place of equality among the peoples of the world,—the new world in which we now live,—instead of a place of mastery.

Source: The Avalon Project at Yale Law School. Available online. URL: http://www.yale.edu/lawweb/avalon/wilson14.htm.

Isolationism and the Return to Normalcy (March 4, 1921) (excerpt)

Warren G. Harding, a handsome but not especially clever or talented politician, was chosen as the Republican candidate for president in a backroom deal by the Republican Party bosses. This meant that that year the party bosses chose the president, for it was a year the Republicans could not lose. The U.S. electorate had recently seen more change than they could stomach. After a century of avoiding foreign entanglements, the country had been a major player in a world war. U.S. participation in the League of Nations had been rejected after a fractious battle in Congress. New constitutional amendments had given women the vote and outlawed alcoholic beverages. Middle-class Americans had been shocked by a wave of nationwide strikes and anarchist bombings, and much of the country was eager for a return to the prewar America, a return to business as usual, or as Harding would put it in his speech, to "normalcy." In Harding's view, and in the view of most Americans, normalcy included a rejection of ambitious foreign policy commitments such as those represented by the League of Nations. His speech heralded an era of American isolationism, which was to continue until World War II.

> The recorded progress of our Republic, materially and spiritually, in itself proves the wisdom of the inherited policy of noninvolvement in Old World affairs. Confident of our ability to work out our own destiny, and jealously guarding our right to do so, we seek no part in directing the destinies of the Old World. We do not mean to be entangled. We will accept no responsibility except as our own conscience and judgment, in each instance, may determine.
>
> Our eyes never will be blind to a developing menace, our ears never deaf to the call of civilization. We recognize the new order in the world, with the closer contacts which progress has wrought. We sense the call of the

human heart for fellowship, fraternity, and cooperation. We crave friendship and harbor no hate. But America, our America, the America builded on the foundation laid by the inspired fathers, can be a party to no permanent military alliance. It can enter into no political commitments, nor assume any economic obligations which will subject our decisions to any other than our own authority.

I am sure our own people will not misunderstand, nor will the world misconstrue. We have no thought to impede the paths to closer relationship. We wish to promote understanding. We want to do our part in making offensive warfare so hateful that Governments and peoples who resort to it must prove the righteousness of their cause or stand as outlaws before the bar of civilization.

We are ready to associate ourselves with the nations of the world, great and small, for conference, for counsel; to seek the expressed views of world opinion; to recommend a way to approximate disarmament and relieve the crushing burdens of military and naval establishments. We elect to participate in suggesting plans for mediation, conciliation, and arbitration, and would gladly join in that expressed conscience of progress, which seeks to clarify and write the laws of international relationship, and establish a world court for the disposition of such justiciable questions as nations are agreed to submit thereto. In expressing aspirations, in seeking practical plans, in translating humanity's new concept of righteousness and justice and its hatred of war into recommended action we are ready most heartily to unite, but every commitment must be made in the exercise of our national sovereignty. Since freedom impelled, and independence inspired, and nationality exalted, a world supergovernment is contrary to everything we cherish and can have no sanction by our Republic. . . .

Source: Inaugural Address of Warren G. Harding, Friday, March 4, 1921. The Avalon Project at the Yale Law School. Available online. URL: http://www.yale.edu/lawweb/avalon/presiden/inaug/harding.htm.

"War Is Just a Racket"—Smedley Darlington Butler on Imperialism (1933) (excerpt)

Smedley Darlington Butler (1881–1940) was a major general in the U.S. Marine Corps who was on active duty during the period of open imperialism that followed the Spanish-American War. At the time of his death he was the most decorated marine in U.S. history. He received the Medal of Honor twice. Following his retirement, he was a highly vocal opponent of the sort of military intervention in which he had engaged throughout his career. He put his views into a book entitled War Is a Racket *and was a frequent speaker at meetings organized by veterans, pacifists, and church groups in the 1930s. The following is an excerpt from a speech Butler gave in 1933.*

War is just a racket. A racket is best described, I believe, as something that is not what it seems to the majority of people. Only a small inside group knows what it is about. It is conducted for the benefit of the very few at the expense of the masses.

I believe in adequate defense at the coastline and nothing else. If a nation comes over here to fight, then we'll fight. The trouble with America is that when the dollar only earns 6 percent over here, then it gets restless and goes overseas to get 100 percent. Then the flag follows the dollar and the soldiers follow the flag.

I wouldn't go to war again as I have done to protect some lousy investment of the bankers. There are only two things we should fight for. One is the defense of our homes and the other is the Bill of Rights. War for any other reason is simply a racket.

There isn't a trick in the racketeering bag that the military gang is blind to. It has its "finger men" to point out enemies, its "muscle men" to destroy enemies, its "brain men" to plan war preparations, and a "Big Boss" Super-Nationalistic-Capitalism.

It may seem odd for me, a military man to adopt such a comparison. Truthfulness compels me to. I spent thirty-three years and four months in active military service as a member of this country's most agile military force, the Marine Corps. I served in all commissioned ranks from Second Lieutenant to Major-General. And during that period, I spent most of my time being a high class muscle-man for Big Business, for Wall Street and for the Bankers. In short, I was a racketeer, a gangster for capitalism.

I suspected I was just part of a racket at the time. Now I am sure of it. Like all the members of the military profession, I never had a thought of my own until I left the service. My mental faculties remained in suspended animation while I obeyed the orders of higher-ups. This is typical with everyone in the military service.

I helped make Mexico, especially Tampico, safe for American oil interests in 1914. I helped make Haiti and Cuba a decent place for the National City Bank boys to collect revenues in. I helped in the raping of half a dozen Central American republics for the benefits of Wall Street. The record of racketeering is long. I helped purify Nicaragua for the international banking house of Brown Brothers in 1909–1912 (where have I heard that name before?). I brought light to the Dominican Republic for American sugar interests in 1916. In China I helped to see to it that Standard Oil went its way unmolested.

During those years, I had, as the boys in the back room would say, a swell racket. Looking back on it, I feel that I could have given Al Capone a few hints. The best he could do was to operate his racket in three districts. I operated on three continents.

Source: Record, 56 Cong., I Sess., pp. 704–712. Available online. URL: http://www.mtholyoke.edu/acad/intrel/ajb72.htm.

Neutrality Act (1939) (excerpt)

American isolationism between the wars had a fateful effect on world history since it permitted the German dictator Adolf Hitler to leave the United States out of his calculations as he made his bid for the domination of the European continent. Just as fatefully, it left the United States out of the calculations of Hitler's opponents. It is likely that had the United States, by then the world's leading industrial power, made it clear it would go to war to prevent the realization of Hitler's ambitions, the leaders of France and Britain would have stood up to him earlier and the USSR would not have made its pact with Germany, a diplomatic coup for Hitler that was essential to his later moves. But the American people in the 1920s and 1930s had a bitter memory of World War I (1914–18) and its outcome, which they regarded as a cynical repudiation of the high-minded sounds with which Wilson had led the country into war. The Great Depression only reinforced most Americans' rejection of the outside world. The act excerpted here was one of a series of neutrality acts passed in the 1930s.

November 4, 1939
76th Congress, 2nd Session, Public Resolution No. 54

JOINT RESOLUTION

To preserve the neutrality and the peace of the United States and to secure the safety of its citizens and their interests. . . .

PROCLAMATION OF A STATE OF WAR BETWEEN FOREIGN STATES

Section 1. (a) That whenever the President, or the Congress by concurrent resolution, shall find that there exists a state of war between foreign states, and that it is necessary to promote the security or preserve the peace of the United States or to protect the lives of citizens of the United States, the President shall issue a proclamation naming the states involved; and he shall, from time to time, by proclamation, name other states as and when they may become involved in the war.

(b) Whenever the state of war which shall have caused the President to issue any proclamation under the authority of this section shall have ceased to exist with respect to any state named in such proclamation, he shall revoke such proclamation with respect to such state.

COMMERCE WITH STATES ENGAGED IN ARMED CONFLICT

Sec. 2. (a) Whenever the President shall have issued a proclamation under the authority of section 1 (a) it shall thereafter be unlawful for any American vessel to carry any passengers or any articles or materials to any state named in such proclamation.

(b) Whoever shall violate any of the provisions of subsection (a) of this section or of any regulations issued thereunder shall, upon conviction thereof, be fined not more than $50,000 or imprisoned for not more than five years, or both. Should the violation be by a corporation, organization, or association, each officer or director thereof participating in the violation shall be liable to the penalty herein prescribed.

(c) Whenever the President shall have issued a proclamation under the authority of section 1 (a) it shall thereafter be unlawful to export or transport, or attempt to export or transport, or cause to be exported or transported, from the Untied States to any state named in such proclamation, any articles or materials (except copyrighted articles or materials) until all right, title, and interest therein shall have been transferred to some foreign government, agency, institution, association, partnership, corporation, or national. . . .

COMBAT AREAS

Sec. 3. (a) Whenever the President shall have issued a proclamation under the authority of section 1 (a), and he shall thereafter find that the protection of citizens of the United States so requires, he shall, by proclamation, define combat areas, and thereafter it shall be unlawful, except under such rules and regulations as may be prescribed, for any citizen of the United States or any American vessel to proceed into or through any such combat area. The combat areas so defined may be made to apply to surface vessels or aircraft, or both. . . .

TRAVEL ON VESSELS OF BELLIGERENT STATES

Sec. 5. (a) Whenever the President shall have issued a proclamation under the authority of section 1 (a) it shall thereafter be unlawful for any citizen of the United States to travel on any vessel of any state named in such proclamation, except in accordance with such rules and regulation as may be prescribed. . . .

ARMING OF AMERICAN MERCHANT VESSELS PROHIBITED

Sec.6. Whenever the President shall have issued a proclamation under the authority of section 1 (a), it shall thereafter be unlawful until such proclamation is revoked, for any American vessel, engaged in commerce with any foreign state to be armed, except with small arms and ammunition therefor, which the President may deem necessary and shall publicly designate for the preservation of discipline aboard any such vessel. . . .

Source: 76th Congress, 2nd Session, Public Resolution No. 54. Available online. URL: http://xroads.virginia.edu/~1930s2/Time/1939/1939ne.html.

WORLD WAR II AND COLD WAR STRATEGY

America, Arsenal of Democracy: President Franklin D. Roosevelt (March 15, 1941) (excerpt)

Franklin Delano Roosevelt, elected in 1932 as the Great Depression neared its deepest point, was an internationalist, but he led a country that was deeply isolationist. Americans were desperate enough during Roosevelt's first two terms to agree to experiments in many economic and social matters but not in foreign affairs. By late 1940, the Germans had conquered Paris, occupied part of France and negotiated a peace treaty with the remainder of it, and Great Britain stood alone against the Nazi war machine. Roosevelt had been elected for an unprecedented third presidential term of office—a fact that in itself implied a recognition by American citizens that events in Europe amounted to an emergency for the United States. The United States was still not ready to declare war but was already supplying Great Britain with arms. Roosevelt was trying to find an easier way—one the Congress would approve—to supply Britain with the means to defend itself. The answer to this problem became known as lend-lease, whose principles Roosevelt explained at a speech to the White House Correspondents' Association dinner on March 15, 1941.

Nazi forces are not seeking mere modifications in colonial maps or in minor European boundaries. They openly seek the destruction of all elective systems of government on every continent including our own; they seek to establish systems of government based on the regimentation of all human beings by a handful of individual rulers who have seized power by force.

Yes, these men and their hypnotized followers call this a new order. It is not new and it is not order. For order among Nations presupposes something enduring some system of justice under which individuals, over a long peiod of time, are willing to live. Humanity will never permanently accept a system imposed by conquest and based on slavery.

These modern tyrants find it necessary to. their plans to eliminate all democracies—eliminate them one by one. The Nations of Europe, and indeed we ourselves, did not appreciate that purpose. We do now. The process of the elimination of the European Nations proceeded according to plan through 1939 and well into 1940, until the schedule was shot to pieces by the unbeatable defenders of Britain. . . .

We believe firmly that when our production output is in full swing, the democracies of the world will be able to prove that dictatorships cannot win.

But, now, now, the time element is of supreme importance. Every plane, every other instrument of war, old and new, every instrument that we can spare now, we will send overseas because that is the common sense of strategy.

The great task of this day, the deep duty that rests upon each and every one of us is to move products from the assembly lines of our factories to the battle lines of democracy Now! . . .

I must tell you tonight in plain language what this undertaking means to you—to you in your daily life.

Whether you are in the armed services; whether you are a steel worker or a stevedore; a machinist or a housewife; a farmer or a banker; a storekeeper or a manufacturer—to all of you it will mean sacrifice in behalf of your country and your liberties. Yes, you will feel the impact of this gigantic effort in your daily lives. You will feel it in a way that will cause, to you, many inconveniences.

You will have to be content with lower profits, lower profits from business because obviously your taxes will be higher.

You will have to work longer at your bench, or your plow, or your machine, or your desk.

Let me make it clear that the Nation is calling for the sacrifice of some privileges, not for the sacrifice of fundamental rights. And most of us will do it willingly. That kind of sacrifice is for the common national protection and welfare; for our defense against the most ruthless brutality in all history; for the ultimate victory of a way of life now so violently menaced. . . .

A few weeks ago I spoke of four freedoms: freedom of speech and expression, freedom of every person to woship God in his own way, freedom from want, freedom from fear. They are the ultimate stake. They may not be immediately attainable throughout the world but humanity does move toward those glorious ideals through democratic processes. And if we fail—if democracy is superseded by slavery—then those four freedoms, or even the mention of them, will become forbidden things. Centuries will pass before they can be revived.

By winning now, we strengthen the meaning of those freedoms, we increase the stature of mankind, we establish the dignity of human life. . . .

The British people and their Grecian allies need ships. From America, they will get ships.

They need planes. From America, they will get planes.

From America they need food. From America, they will get food.

They need tanks and guns and ammunition and supplies of all kinds. From America, they will get tanks and guns and ammunition and supplies of all kinds.

China likewise expresses the magnificent will of millions of plain people to resist the dismemberment of their historic Nation. China, through the Generalissimo, Chiang Kai-shek, asks our help. America has said that China shall have our help.

And so our country is going to be what our people have proclaimed it must be the arsenal of democracy.

Our country is going to play its full part.

And when no, I didn't say if, I said when dictatorships disintegrate—and pray God that will be sooner than any of us now dares to hope—then our country must continue to play its great part in the peiod of world reconstruction for the good of humanity.

We believe that the rallying cry of the dictators, their boasting about a master-race, will prove to be pure stuff and nonsense. There never has been, there isn't now, and there never will be, any race of people on the earth fit to serve as masters over their fellow men.

Source: Available online. URL: http://history.sandiego.edu/GEN/text/us/fdr1941b.html.

Conference at Bretton Woods (July 1944) (excerpt)

In the first three weeks of July 1944, when it was clear that the United States and its allies would win World War II, 730 delegates from 44 nations gathered at the United Nations Monetary and Financial Conference in Bretton Woods,

New Hampshire. The delegates met to discuss the postwar recovery of Europe as well as a number of monetary issues, such as unstable exchange rates and protectionist trade policies. The members hoped to avoid the instability of world currency exchange rates that had worsened the depression of the 1930s. As one outcome of the conference, the U.S. dollar became the world's reserve currency, with economic advantages to the United States. The Bretton Woods system also served the global economy well. Though the dollar was allowed to float starting in the early 1970s, bringing an end to the Bretton Woods system, the U.S. dollar remains the world's unofficial reserve currency.

This Conference at Bretton Woods, representing nearly all the peoples of the world, has considered matters of international money and finance which are important for peace and prosperity. The Conference has agreed on the problems needing attention, the measures which should be taken, and the forms of international cooperation or organization which are required. The agreements reached on these large and complex matters are without precedent in the history of international economic relations.

I. THE INTERNATIONAL MONETARY FUND

Since foreign trade affects the standard of life of every people, all countries have a vital interest in the system of exchange of national currencies and the regulations and conditions which govern its working. Because these monetary transactions are international exchanges, the nations must agree on the basic rules which govern the exchanges if the system is to work smoothly. When they do not agree, and when single nations and small groups of nations attempt by special and different regulations of the foreign exchanges to gain trade advantages, the result is instability, a reduced volume of foreign trade, and damage to national economies. This course of action is likely to lead to economic warfare and to endanger the world's peace.

The Conference has therefore agreed that broad international action is necessary to maintain an international monetary system which will promote foreign trade. The nations should consult and agree on international monetary changes which affect each other. They should outlaw practices which are agreed to be harmful to world prosperity, and they should assist each other to overcome short-term exchange difficulties.

The Conference has agreed that the nations here represented should establish for these purposes a permanent international body, *The International Monetary Fund,* with powers and resources adequate to perform the tasks assigned to it. Agreement has been reached concerning these powers and resources and the additional obligations which the member countries should undertake. Draft Articles of Agreement on these points have been prepared.

II. THE INTERNATIONAL BANK FOR RECONSTRUCTION AND DEVELOPMENT

It is in the interest of all nations that post-war reconstruction should be rapid. Likewise, the development of the resources of particular regions is in the general economic interest. Programs of reconstruction and development will speed economic progress everywhere, will aid political stability and foster peace.

The Conference has agreed that expanded international investment is essential to provide a portion of the capital necessary for reconstruction and development.

The Conference has further agreed that the nations should cooperate to increase the volume of foreign investment for these purposes, made through normal business channels. It is especially important that the nations should cooperate to share the risks of such foreign investment, since the benefits are general.

The Conference has agreed that the nations should establish a permanent international body to perform these functions, to be called The International Bank for Reconstruction and Development. It has been agreed that the Bank should assist in providing capital through normal channels at reasonable rates of interest and for long periods for projects which will raise the productivity of the borrowing country. There is agreement that the Bank should guarantee loans made by others and that through their subscriptions of capital in all countries should share with the borrowing country in guaranteeing such loans. The Conference has agreed on the powers and resources which the Bank must have and on the obligations which the member countries must assume, and has prepared draft Articles of Agreement accordingly.

The Conference has recommended that in carrying out the policies of the institutions here proposed special consideration should be given to the needs of countries which have suffered from enemy occupation and hostilities.

The proposals formulated at the Conference for the establishment of the Fund and the Bank are now submitted, in accordance with the terms of the invitation, for consideration of the governments and people of the countries represented.

Source: Pamphlet No. 4, *PILLARS OF PEACE,* Documents Pertaining to American Interest in Establishing a Lasting World Peace: January 1941–February 1946. Published by the Book Department, Army Information School, Carlisle Barracks, Pa., May 1946. Available online. URL: http://www.ibiblio.org/pha/policy/1944/440722a.html.

George Kennan's "Long Telegram" (February 22, 1946) (excerpt)

George F. Kennan, an American diplomat, served as deputy head of the U.S. mission in Moscow from July 1944 to April 1946. Near the end of that term, Kennan sent his famous "Long Telegram" from Moscow to Secretary of State James Byrnes. In this message, Kennan outlined the threat he believed the Soviet Union posed to the United States and the essence of a strategy to deal with it—essentially the strategy of containment that the United States did follow throughout the cold war. A revised version of the Long Telegram was published the following year in the magazine Foreign Affairs *under the title "The Sources of Soviet Conduct." It is one of the most influential pieces of political analysis every printed.*

Kennan later maintained that he would have rather had the United States put less emphasis on the military side of containment and that the crude application of the containment strategy unnecessarily prolonged and intensified the cold war.

Part 5: [Practical Deductions from Standpoint of U.S. Policy]

In summary, we have here a political force committed fanatically to the belief that with US there can be no permanent *modus vivendi* that it is desirable and necessary that the internal harmony of our society be disrupted, our traditional way of life be destroyed, the international authority of our state be broken, if Soviet power is to be secure. This political force has complete power of disposition over energies of one of world's greatest peoples and resources of world's richest national territory, and is borne along by deep and powerful currents of Russian nationalism. In addition, it has an elaborate and far flung apparatus for exertion of its influence in other countries, an apparatus of amazing flexibility and versatility, managed by people whose experience and skill in underground methods are presumably without parallel in history. Finally, it is seemingly inaccessible to considerations of reality in its basic reactions. For it, the vast fund of objective fact about human society is not, as with us, the measure against which outlook is constantly being tested and re-formed, but a grab bag from which individual items are selected arbitrarily and tendenciously to bolster an outlook already preconceived. This is admittedly not a pleasant picture. Problem of how to cope with this force in [is] undoubtedly greatest task our diplomacy has ever faced and probably greatest it will ever have to face. It should be point of departure from which our political general staff work at present juncture should proceed. It should be approached with same thoroughness and care as solution of major strategic problem in war, and if necessary, with no smaller outlay in planning effort. I cannot attempt to suggest all answers here. But I would like to record my conviction that problem is within our power to solve—and that without recourse to any general military conflict. And in support of this conviction there are certain observations of a more encouraging nature I should like to make:

(1) Soviet power, unlike that of Hitlerite Germany, is neither schematic nor adventuristic. It does not work by fixed plans. It does not take unnecessary risks. Impervious to logic of reason, and it is highly sensitive to logic of force. For this reason it can easily withdraw—and usually does when strong resistance is encountered at any point. Thus, if the adversary has sufficient force and makes clear his readiness to use it, he rarely has to do so. If situations are properly handled there need be no prestige-engaging showdowns.

(2) Gauged against Western World as a whole, Soviets are still by far the weaker force. Thus, their success will really depend on degree of cohesion, firmness and vigor which Western World can muster. And this is factor which it is within our power to influence.

(3) Success of Soviet system, as form of internal power, is not yet finally proven. It has yet to be demonstrated that it can survive supreme test of successive transfer of power from one individual or group to another. Lenin's death was first such transfer, and its effects wracked Soviet state for 15 years. After Stalin's death or retirement will be second. But even this will not be final test. Soviet internal system will now be subjected, by virtue of recent territorial expansions, to series of additional strains which once proved severe tax on Tsardom. We here are convinced that never since termination of civil war have mass of Russian people been emotionally farther removed from doctrines of Communist Party than they are today. In Russia, party has now become a great and—for the moment—highly successful apparatus of dictatorial administration, but it has ceased to be a source of emotional inspiration. Thus, internal soundness and permanence of movement need not yet be regarded as assured.

(4) All Soviet propaganda beyond Soviet security sphere is basically negative and destructive. It should therefore be relatively easy to combat it by any intelligent and really constructive program.

For those reasons I think we may approach calmly and with good heart problem of how to deal with Russia. As to how this approach should be made, I only wish to advance, by way of conclusion, following comments:

(1) Our first step must be to apprehend, and recognize for what it is, the nature of the movement with which we are dealing. We must study it with same courage, detachment, objectivity, and same determination not to be emotionally provoked or unseated by it, with which doctor studies unruly and unreasonable individual.

(2) We must see that our public is educated to realities of Russian situation. I cannot over-emphasize importance of this. Press cannot do this alone. It must be done mainly by Government, which is necessarily more experienced and better informed on practical problems involved. In this we need not be deterred by [ugliness?] of picture. I am convinced that there would be far less hysterical anti-Sovietism in our country today if realities of this situation were better understood by our people. There is nothing as dangerous or as terrifying as the unknown. It may also be argued that to reveal more information on our difficulties with Russia would reflect unfavorably on Russian-American relations. I feel that if there is any real risk here involved, it is one which we should have courage to face, and sooner the better. But I cannot see what we would be risking. Our stake in this country, even coming on heels of tremendous demonstrations of our friendship for Russian people, is remarkably small. We have here no investments to guard, no actual trade to lose, virtually no citizens to protect, few cultural contacts to preserve. Our only stake lies in what we hope rather than what we have; and I am convinced we have better chance of realizing those hopes if our public is enlightened and if our dealings with Russians are placed entirely on realistic and matter-of-fact basis.

(3) Much depends on health and vigor of our own society. World communism is like malignant parasite which feeds only on diseased tissue. This is point at which domestic and foreign policies meets Every courageous and incisive measure to solve internal problems of our own society, to improve self-confidence, discipline, morale and community spirit of our own people, is a diplomatic victory over Moscow worth a thousand diplomatic notes and joint communiqués. If we cannot abandon fatalism and indifference in face of deficiencies of our own society, Moscow will profit—Moscow cannot help profiting by them in its foreign policies.

(4) We must formulate and put forward for other nations a much more positive and constructive picture of sort of world we would like to see than we have put forward in past. It is not enough to urge people to develop political processes similar to our own. Many foreign peoples, in Europe at least, are tired and frightened by experiences of past, and are less interested in abstract freedom than in security. They are seeking guidance rather than responsibilities. We should be better able than Russians to give them this. And unless we do, Russians certainly will.

(5) Finally we must have courage and self-confidence to cling to our own methods and conceptions of human society. After All, the greatest danger that can befall us in coping with this problem of Soviet communism, is that we shall allow ourselves to become like those with whom we are coping.

Source: Available online. URL: http://www.gwu.edu/~nsarchiv/coldwar/documents/episode-1/kennan.htm.

The Truman Doctrine, 1947 (excerpt)

Civil wars and rebellions raged all over the world after World War II, as armed local groups struggled with each other in the power vaccuum left by the collapse of western European powers. In the countries that had experienced German and Japanese occupation during the war, matters were complicated by the fact that the most effective resistance groups had been led by communists, who had been in opposition to their own governments before the takeover by the Nazis or the Japanese and refused to lay down their arms when fascists were defeated. Now, with Soviet support, or the support of the Soviet Union's other communist allies, these movements were fighting for control of their countries. In 1947, one these communist-led insurrections led U.S. president Harry Truman to ask Congress to enact legislation to assist Greece in its battle against communism. Truman simultaneously asked for aid to strengthen Turkey, which faced a bullying Soviet demand to share control of the Dardanelle Straits (a Russian strategic goal since czarist times). Congress responded by granting $300 million to Greece and $100 million to Turkey in military and economic aid.

Historians look back on Truman's speech as the start of the application of the United States's cold war strategy that ended 45 years later with the collapse of the Soviet Union. However, it should be remembered that Truman and his advisers did not know the future and were not committed to a single policy toward the Soviet Union. They were committed not merely to the abstract idea of not letting communism spread, but to denying to the

Soviets the specific strategic advantages of allies in Greece and Turkey. Turkey later jointed NATO and became a base for nuclear missiles that targeted the Soviet Union.

The gravity of the situation which confronts the world today necessitates my appearance before a joint session of the Congress. The foreign policy and the national security of this country are involved. One aspect of the present situation, which I present to you at this time for your consideration and decision, concerns Greece and Turkey. The United States has received from the Greek Government an urgent appeal for financial and economic assistance. Preliminary reports from the American Economic Mission now in Greece and reports from the American Ambassador in Greece corroborate the statement of the Greek Government that assistance is imperative if Greece is to survive as a free nation. . . .

The very existence of the Greek state is today threatened by the terrorist activities of several thousand armed men, led by Communists, who defy the government's authority at a number of points, particularly along the northern boundaries. A Commission appointed by the United Nations Security Council is at present investigating disturbed conditions in northern Greece and alleged border violations along the frontier between Greece on the one hand and Albania, Bulgaria, and Yugoslavia on the other.

Meanwhile, the Greek Government is unable to cope with the situation. The Greek army is small and poorly equipped. It needs supplies and equipment if it is to restore the authority of the government throughout Greek territory. Greece must have assistance if it is to become a self-supporting and self-respecting democracy. . . .

No government is perfect. One of the chief virtues of a democracy, however, is that its defects are always visible and under democratic processes can be pointed out and corrected. The Government of Greece is not perfect. Nevertheless it represents eighty-five per cent of the members of the Greek Parliament who were chosen in an election last year. Foreign observers, including 692 Americans, considered this election to be a fair expression of the views of the Greek people.

The Greek Government has been operating in an atmosphere of chaos and extremism. It has made mistakes. The extension of aid by this country does not mean that the United States condones everything that the Greek Government has done or will do. We have condemned in the past, and we condemn now, extremist measures of the right or the left. We have in the past advised tolerance, and we advise tolerance now.

Greek's [sic] neighbor, Turkey, also deserves our attention. The future of Turkey as an independent and economically sound state is clearly no less important to the freedom-loving peoples of the world than the future of Greece. The circumstances in which Turkey finds itself today are considerably different from those of Greece. Turkey has been spared the disasters that have beset Greece. And during the war, the United States and Great Britain furnished Turkey with material aid.

Nevertheless, Turkey now needs our support. Since the war Turkey has sought additional financial assistance from Great Britain and the United States for the purpose of effecting that modernization necessary for the maintenance of its national integrity. That integrity is essential to the preservation of order in the Middle East. The British government has informed us that, owing to its own difficulties can no longer extend financial or economic aid to Turkey. As in the case of Greece, if Turkey is to have the assistance it needs, the United States must supply it. We are the only country able to provide that help. . . .

At the present moment in world history nearly every nation must choose between alternative ways of life. The choice is too often not a free one. One way of life is based upon the will of the majority, and is distinguished by free institutions, representative government, free elections, guarantees of individual liberty, freedom of speech and religion, and freedom from political oppression. The second way of life is based upon the will of a minority forcibly imposed upon the majority. It relies upon terror and oppression, a controlled press and radio; fixed elections, and the suppression of personal freedoms.

I believe that it must be the policy of the United States to support free peoples who are resisting attempted subjugation by armed minorities or by outside pressures.

I believe that we must assist free peoples to work out their own destinies in their own way.

I believe that our help should be primarily through economic and financial aid which is essential to economic stability and orderly political processes.

The world is not static, and the status quo is not sacred. But we cannot allow changes in the status quo in violation of the Charter of the United Nations by such methods as coercion, or by such subterfuges as political infiltration. In helping free and independent nations to maintain their freedom, the United States will be giving effect to the principles of the Charter of the United Nations. . . .

The free peoples of the world look to us for support in maintaining their freedoms. If we falter in our leadership, we may endanger the peace of the world. And we shall surely endanger the welfare of our own nation.

Great responsibilities have been placed upon us by the swift movement of events. . . .

Source: The Avalon Project. Available online. URL: http://www.yale.edu/lawweb/avalon/trudoc.htm.

The Marshall Plan: Secretary of State George Marshall's Speech at Harvard University (June 5, 1947) (excerpt)

When World War II was over the United States was the strongest economy in the world, while the economies of Europe had been devastated. From the U.S. point of view, the situation was both a humanitarian crisis and a political threat. The Soviet Union was consolidating its hold on eastern Europe, where the Soviet's occupying armies had cooperated with homegrown communist parties to destroy opposition. Political analysts like George Kennan (author of the Long Telegram, quoted earlier) feared that economic turmoil in western Europe would make communism attractive to the people of western Europe and they, too, would fall into the Soviet orbit. The Truman administration addressed this problem with a plan for the economic recovery of Europe, introduced by U.S. secretary of state George C. Marshall in this speech at Harvard University.

I need not tell you, gentlemen, that the world situation is very serious. That must be apparent to all intelligent people. I think one difficulty is that the problem is one of such enormous complexity that the very mass of facts presented to the public by press and radio make it exceedingly difficult for the man in the street to reach a clear appraisement of the situation. Furthermore, the people of this country are distant from the troubled areas of the earth and it is hard for them to comprehend the plight and consequent reactions of the long-suffering peoples, and the effect of those reactions on their governments in connection with our efforts to promote peace in the world.

In considering the requirements for the rehabilitation of Europe, the physical loss of life, the visible destruction of cities, factories, mines and railroads was correctly estimated but it has become obvious during recent months that this visible destruction was probably less serious than the dislocation of the entire fabric of European economy. For the past 10 years conditions have been highly abnormal. The feverish preparation for war and the more feverish maintenance of the war effort engulfed all aspects of national economies. Machinery has fallen into disrepair or is entirely obsolete. Under the arbitrary and destructive Nazi rule, virtually every possible enterprise was geared into the German war machine. Long-standing commercial ties, private institutions, banks, insurance companies, and shipping companies disappeared, through loss of capital, absorption through nationalization, or by simple destruction. In many countries, confidence in the local currency has been severely shaken. The breakdown of the business structure of Europe during the war was complete. Recovery has been seriously retarded by the fact that two years after the close of hostilities a peace settlement with Germany and Austria has not been agreed upon. But even given a more prompt solution of these difficult problems the rehabilitation of the economic structure of Europe quite evidently will require a much longer time and greater effort than had been foreseen.

There is a phase of this matter which is both interesting and serious. The farmer has always produced the foodstuffs to exchange with the city dweller for the other necessities of life. This division of labor is the basis of modern civilization. At the present time it is threatened with breakdown. The town and city industries are not producing adequate goods to exchange with the food producing farmer. Raw materials and fuel are in short supply. Machinery is lacking or worn out. The farmer or the peasant cannot find the goods for sale which he desires to purchase. So the sale of his farm produce for money which he cannot use seems to him an unprofitable transaction. He, therefore, has withdrawn many fields from crop cultivation and is using them for grazing. He feeds more grain to stock and finds for himself and his family an ample supply of food, however short he may be on clothing and the other ordinary gadgets of civilization. Meanwhile people in the cities are short of food and fuel. So the governments are forced to use their foreign money and credits to procure these necessities abroad. This process exhausts funds which are urgently needed for reconstruction. Thus a very serious situation is rapidly developing which bodes no good for the world. The modern system of the division of labor upon which the exchange of products is based is in danger of breaking down.

The truth of the matter is that Europe's requirements for the next three or four years of foreign food and other essential products—principally from America—are so much greater than her present ability to pay that she must have substantial additional help or face economic, social, and political deterioration of a very grave character.

The remedy lies in breaking the vicious circle and restoring the confidence of the European people in the economic future of their own countries and of Europe as a whole. The manufacturer and the farmer throughout wide areas must be able and willing to exchange their products for currencies, the continuing value of which is not open to question.

Aside from the demoralizing effect on the world at large and the possibilities of disturbances arising as a result of the desperation of the people concerned, the consequences to the economy of the United States should be apparent to all. It is logical that the United States should do whatever it is able to do to assist in the return of normal economic health in the world, without which there can be no political stability and no assured peace. Our policy is directed not against any country or doctrine but against hunger, poverty, desperation and chaos. Its purpose should be the revival of a working economy in the world so as to permit the emergence of political and social conditions in which free institutions can exist. Such assistance, I am convinced, must not be on a piecemeal basis as various crises develop. Any assistance that this Government may render in the future should provide a cure rather than a mere palliative. Any government that is willing to assist in the task of recovery will find full co-operation I am sure, on the part of the United States Government. Any government which maneuvers to block the recovery of other countries cannot expect help from us. Furthermore, governments, political parties, or groups which seek to perpetuate human misery in order to profit therefrom politically or otherwise will encounter the opposition of the United States. . . .

Source: Primary Sources: Workshops in American History. Available online. URL: http://www.learner.org/channel/workshops/primarysources/coldwar/docs/marshall.html.

Vietnam Veterans Against the War Statement by John Kerry to the Senate Committee on Foreign Relations (April 23, 1971) (excerpt)

Anticommunism led the United States to support dubious allies in places where the United States had few economic or strategic interests. In the early 1950s, it backed French efforts to retain hold of Vietnam in the face of a communist-led insurgency. When the French pulled out in 1954 an international conference at Geneva temporarily divided Vietnam into two parts—North Vietnam, controlled by the insurgents, and South Vietnam, controlled by people who had collaborated with the French—with the expectation that elections would soon be held to determine who would govern the whole country. Judging that communists would win, the United States encouraged South Vietnam to maintain itself as a separate, U.S.-aligned country. Forces from the North began infiltrating South Vietnam using guerrilla and terrorist tactics. The South Vietnamese government was corrupt, inept, and unpopular, and the United States was forced to make increasing military commitments to prop up the regime. U.S. leaders portrayed this effort as the support of a freedom-loving people against communist-led outsiders. However, its actions damaged its reputation in Europe, and eventually many in the United States, too, were horrified by the brutality of this war whose end was not in sight and whose purpose was so hard to explain.

AMERICA'S ROLE IN THE WORLD

John Kerry, who had won a Purple Heart during his tour of duty in Vietnam, delivered this statement to the Senate Committee on Foreign Relations on April 23, 1971. Kerry later became a U.S. senator and was the Democratic presidential candidate in 2004.

I would like to talk on behalf of all those veterans and say that several months ago in Detroit we had an investigation at which over 150 honorably discharged, and many very highly decorated, veterans testified to war crimes committed in Southeast Asia. These were not isolated incidents but crimes committed on a day-to-day basis with the full awareness of officers at all levels of command. It is impossible to describe to you exactly what did happen in Detroit—the emotions in the room and the feelings of the men who were reliving their experiences in Vietnam. They relived the absolute horror of what this country, in a sense, made them do.

They told stories that at times they had personally raped, cut off ears, cut off heads, taped wires from portable telephones to human genitals and turned up the power, cut off limbs, blown up bodies, randomly shot at civilians, razed villages in fashion reminiscent of Ghengis Khan, shot cattle and dogs for fun, poisoned food stocks, and generally ravaged the countryside of South Vietnam in addition to the normal ravage of war and the normal and very particular ravaging which is done by the applied bombing power of this country. . . .

In our opinion and from our experience, there is nothing in South Vietnam which could happen that realistically threatens the United States of America. And to attempt to justify the loss of one American life in Vietnam, Cambodia or Laos by linking such loss to the preservation of freedom, which those misfits supposedly abuse, is to us the height of criminal hypocrisy, and it is that kind of hypocrisy which we feel has torn this country apart.

We found that not only was it a civil war, an effort by a people who had for years been seeking their liberation from any colonial influence whatsoever, but also we found that the Vietnamese whom we had enthusiastically molded after our own image were hard put to take up the fight against the threat we were supposedly saving them from.

We found most people didn't even know the difference between communism and democracy. They only wanted to work in rice paddies without helicopters strafing them and bombs with napalm burning their villages and tearing their country apart. They wanted everything to do with the war, particularly with this foreign presence of the United States of America, to leave them alone in peace, and they practiced the art of survival by siding with whichever military force was present at a particular time, be it Viet Cong, North Vietnamese or American.

We found also that all too often American men were dying in those rice paddies for want of support from their allies. We saw first hand how monies from American taxes were used for a corrupt dictatorial regime. We saw that many people in this country had a one-sided idea of who was kept free by the flag, and blacks provided the highest percentage of casualties. We saw Vietnam ravaged equally by American bombs and search and destroy missions, as well as by Viet Cong terrorism—and yet we listened while this country tried to blame all of the havoc on the Viet Cong.

We rationalized destroying villages in order to save them. We saw America lose her sense of morality as she accepted very coolly a My Lai and refused to give up the image of American soldiers who hand out chocolate bars and chewing gum.

We learned the meaning of free fire zones, shooting anything that moves, and we watched while America placed a cheapness on the lives of orientals.

We watched the United States falsification of body counts, in fact the glorification of body counts. We listened while month after month we were told the back of the enemy was about to break. We fought using weapons against "oriental human beings." We fought using weapons against those people which I do not believe this country would dream of using were we fighting in the European theater. We watched while men charged up hills because a general said that hill has to be taken, and after losing one platoon or two platoons they marched away to leave the hill for reoccupation by the North Vietnamese. We watched pride allow the most unimportant battles to be blown into extravaganzas, because we couldn't lose, and we couldn't retreat, and because it didn't matter how many American bodies were lost to prove that point, and so there were Hamburger Hills and Khe Sanhs and Hill 81s and Fire Base 6s, and so many others.

Now we are told that the men who fought there must watch quietly while American lives are lost so that we can exercise the incredible arrogance of Vietnamizing the Vietnamese.

Each day to facilitate the process by which the United States washes her hands of Vietnam someone has to give up his life so that the United States doesn't have to admit something that the entire world already knows, so that we can't say that we have made a mistake. Someone has to die so that President Nixon won't be, and these are his words, "the first President to lose a war."

We are asking Americans to think about that because how do you ask a man to be the last man to die in Vietnam? How do you ask a man to be the last man to die for a mistake? . . .

Source: Modern History Sourcebook. Available online. URL: http://www.fordham.edu/halsall/mod/1972VVAW.html.

Ronald Reagan Speech to the British House of Commons (June 8, 1982) (excerpt)

The 1970s were a dispiriting time for many Americans. After 25 years of post-war growth the economy had stalled, with chronic inflation, high unemployment, and high gas prices; Japanese cars had become superior to American cars; President Richard Nixon resigned to escape being impeached for serious abuses of executive power. After nearly 60,000 American deaths and at least 1.3 million Vietnamese deaths, the war in Vietnam had ended with America's first defeat. America's prestige was damaged, and the Soviets were encouraging communists in Africa and the Americas with a new confidence. The United States was suffering from Vietnam syndrome, a reluctance to be involved in similar foreign adventures. There was something almost European about the United States during this period—it had experienced failure and it saw things in a rueful, complex way.

This turned out to be an intolerable state of mind for most Americans. In 1980 they elected as president a former movie actor who evoked the stark certainties of the early 1950s. Ronald Reagan combined excellent communication skills with a firm, consistent, and blinkered conservative ideology. In his view, all communists were totalitarian and all anticommunists were freedom fighters. He called the contras, a U.S.–supported group of Nicaraguan rebels who raped and mutilated civilians "the moral equivalent of the founding fathers." This surely was not true and is really a terrible thing to say. Yet Reagan's speech, excerpted here, was essentially accurate. The Soviet system was indeed rotten from within.

We're approaching the end of a bloody century plagued by a terrible political invention—totalitarianism. Optimism comes less easily today, not because democracy is less vigorous, but because democracy's enemies have refined their instruments of repression. Yet optimism is in order because day by day democracy is proving itself to be a not at all fragile flower. From Stettin on the Baltic to Varna on the Black Sea, the regimes planted by totalitarianism have had more than thirty years to establish their legitimacy. But none—not one regime—has yet been able to risk free elections. Regimes planted by bayonets do not take root.

The strength of the Solidarity movement in Poland demonstrates the truth told in an underground joke in the Soviet Union. It is that the Soviet Union would remain a one-party nation even if an opposition party were permitted because everyone would join the opposition party. . . .

Historians looking back at our time will note the consistent restraint and peaceful intentions of the West. They will note that it was the democracies who refused to use the threat of their nuclear monopoly in the forties and early fifties for territorial or imperial gain. Had that nuclear monopoly been in the hands of the Communist world, the map of Europe—indeed, the world—would look very different today. And certainly they will note it was not the democracies that invaded Afghanistan or suppressed Polish Solidarity or used chemical and toxin warfare in Afghanistan and Southeast Asia.

If history teaches anything, it teaches self-delusion in the face of unpleasant facts is folly. We see around us today the marks of our terrible dilemma—predictions of doomsday, antinuclear demonstrations, an arms race in which the West must, for its own protection, be an unwilling participant. At the same time we see totalitarian forces in the world who seek subversion and conflict around the globe to further their barbarous assault on the human spirit. What, then, is our course? Must civilization perish in a hail of fiery atoms? Must freedom wither in a quiet, deadening accommodation with totalitarian evil?

Sir Winston Churchill refused to accept the inevitability of war or even that it was imminent. He said, "I do not believe that Soviet Russia desires war. What they desire is the fruits of war and the indefinite expansion of their power and doctrines. But what we have to consider here today while time remains is the permanent prevention of war and the establishment of conditions of freedom and democracy as rapidly as possible in all countries."

Well, this is precisely our mission today: to preserve freedom as well as peace. It may not be easy to see; but I believe we live now at a turning point.

In an ironic sense Karl Marx was right. We are witnessing today a great revolutionary crisis, a crisis where the demands of the economic order are conflicting directly with those of the political order. But the crisis is happening not in the free, non-Marxist West but in the home of Marxism-Leninism, the Soviet Union. It is the Soviet Union that runs against the tide of history by denying human freedom and human dignity to its citizens. It also is in deep economic difficulty. The rate of growth in the national product has been steadily declining since the fifties and is less than half of what it was then.

The dimensions of this failure are astounding: a country which employs one-fifth of its population in agriculture is unable to feed its own people. Were it not for the private sector, the tiny private sector tolerated in Soviet agriculture, the country might be on the brink of famine. These private plots occupy a bare 3 percent of the arable land but account for nearly one-quarter of Soviet farm output and nearly one-third of meat products and vegetables. Overcentralized, with little or no incentives, year after year the Soviet system pours its best resources into the making of instruments of destruction. The constant shrinkage of economic growth combined with the growth of military production is putting a heavy strain on the Soviet people. What we see here is a political structure that no longer corresponds to its economic base, a society where productive forced are hampered by political ones.

The decay of the Soviet experiment should come as no surprise to us. Wherever the comparisons have been made between free and closed societies—West Germany and East Germany, Austria and Czechoslovakia, Malaysia and Vietnam—it is the democratic countries that are prosperous and responsive to the needs of their people. And one of the simple but overwhelming facts of our time is this: of all the millions of refugees we've seen in the modern world, their flight is always away from, not toward the Communist world. Today on the NATO line, our military forces face east to prevent a possible invasion. On the other side of the line, the Soviet forces also face east to prevent their people from leaving.

The hard evidence of totalitarian rule has caused in mankind an uprising of the intellect and will. Whether it is the growth of the new schools of economics in America or England or the appearance of the so-called new philosophers in France, there is one unifying thread running through the intellectual work of these groups—rejection of the arbitrary power of the state, the refusal to subordinate the rights of the individual to the superstate, the realization that collectivism stifles all the best human impulses. . . .

Source: Modern History Sourcebook. Available online. URL: http://www.fordham.edu/halsall/mod/1982reagan1.html.

AMERICA AS A WORLD SUPERPOWER

U.S. Strategy Plan Calls for Insuring No Rivals Develop—A One-Superpower World (1992) (excerpt)

By 1992 the Soviet Union had broken apart. The United States, the sole superpower, had successfully conducted its first major post–cold war military operation, easily smashing Saddam Hussein's military forces in a demonstration of America's overwhelming military superiority. Many thinkers around the world were contemplating America's future role following the defeat of its main foe, which it had always maintained was the foe of freedom. Within the U.S. Defense Department a group of neoconservatives suggested that the United States should take advantage of this moment in history to solidify its position as the sole superpower, retaining a permanent military superiority so great that no one would dare challenge it. Clearly a situation like this would enormously simplify American diplomacy. The authors of this plan became major influences when George W. Bush came to office in 2001.

WASHINGTON, March 7—In a broad new policy statement that is in its final drafting stage, the Defense Department asserts that America's political and military mission in the post-cold-war era will be to ensure that no rival superpower is allowed to emerge in Western Europe, Asia or the territories of the former Soviet Union.

A 46-page document that has been circulating at the highest levels of the Pentagon for weeks, and which Defense Secretary Dick Cheney expects to release later this month, states that part of the American mission will be "convincing potential competitors that they need not aspire to a greater role or pursue a more aggressive posture to protect their legitimate interests."

The classified document makes the case for a world dominated by one superpower whose position can be perpetuated by constructive behavior and sufficient military might to deter any nation or group of nations from challenging American primacy.

Rejecting Collective Approach

To perpetuate this role, the United States "must sufficiently account for the interests of the advanced industrial nations to discourage them from challenging our leadership or seeking to overturn the established political and economic order," the document states.

With its focus on this concept of benevolent domination by one power, the Pentagon document articulates the clearest rejection to date of collective internationalism, the strategy that emerged from World War II when the five victorious powers sought to form a United Nations that could mediate disputes and police outbreaks of violence.

Though the document is internal to the Pentagon and is not provided to Congress, its policy statements are developed in conjunction with the National Security Council and in consultation with the President or his senior national security advisers. Its drafting has been supervised by Paul D. Wolfowitz, the Pentagon's Under Secretary for Policy. Mr. Wolfowitz often represents the Pentagon on the Deputies Committee, which formulates policy in an interagency process dominated by the State and Defense Departments.

The document was provided to The New York Times by an official who believes this post-cold-war strategy debate should be carried out in the public domain. It seems likely to provoke further debate in Congress and among America's allies about Washington's willingness to tolerate greater aspirations for regional leadership from a united Europe or from a more assertive Japan.

Together with its attachments on force levels required to insure America's predominant role, the policy draft is a detailed justification for the Bush Administration's "base force" proposal to support a 1.6-million member military over the next five years, at a cost of about $1.2 trillion. Many Democrats in Congress have criticized the proposal as unnecessarily expensive.

Implicitly, the document foresees building a world security arrangement that pre-empts Germany and Japan from pursuing a course of substantial rearmament, especially nuclear armament, in the future.

In its opening paragraph, the policy document heralds the "less visible" victory at the end of the cold war, which it defines as "the integration of Germany and Japan into a U.S.-led system of collective security and the creation of a democratic 'zone of peace.'"

The continuation of this strategic goal explains the strong emphasis elsewhere in the document and in other Pentagon planning on using military force, if necessary, to prevent the proliferation of nuclear weapons and other weapons of mass destruction in such countries as North Korea, Iraq, some of the successor republics to the Soviet Union and in Europe.

Nuclear proliferation, if unchecked by superpower action, could tempt Germany, Japan and other industrial powers to acquire nuclear weapons to deter attack from regional foes. This could start them down the road to global competition with the United States and, in a crisis over national interests, military rivalry.

The policy draft appears to be adjusting the role of the American nuclear arsenal in the new era, saying, "Our nuclear forces also provide an important deterrent hedge against the possibility of a revitalized or unforeseen global threat, while at the same time helping to deter third party use of weapons of mass destruction through the threat of retaliation."

U.N. Action Ignored. The document is conspicuously devoid of references to collective action through the United Nations, which provided the mandate for the allied assault on Iraqi forces in Kuwait and which may soon be asked to provide a new mandate to force President Saddam Hussein to comply with his cease-fire obligations. . . .

Bush Administration officials have been saying publicly for some time that they were willing to work within the framework of the United Nations, but that they reserve the option to act unilaterally or through selective coalitions, if necessary, to protect vital American interests.

But this publicly stated strategy did not rule out an eventual leveling of American power as world security stabilizes and as other nations place greater emphasis on collective international action through the United Nations.

In contrast, the new draft sketches a world in which there is one dominant military power whose leaders "must maintain the mechanisms for deterring potential competitors from even aspiring to a larger regional or global role."

Source: Patrick E. Tyler. "U.S. Strategy Plan Calls for Insuring No Rivals Develop." *New York Times,* March 8, 1992. Available online. URL: http://query.nytimes.com/gst/fullpage.html?res=9E0CE5D61E38F93BA35750C0A964958260. Accessed August 12, 2008.

The Axis of Evil (January 29, 2002) (excerpt)

In his 2002 State of the Union address, George W. Bush again enunciated the principles of the Bush doctrine, justifying preventive war in the name of U.S. national security. Bush named Iraq, Iran, and North Korea as belonging to an axis of evil, evoking the triple alliance of Italy, Germany, and Japan during World War II (1939–45). Since there is no alliance joining Iran, Iraq, and North Korea, but they are all hostile in different ways to the United States, to many people both inside and outside the United States the speech seemed merely to enunciate a hit list. In 2003 the United States invaded and occupied the first country on the list.

THE PRESIDENT: Thank you very much. Mr. Speaker, Vice President Cheney, members of Congress, distinguished guests, fellow citizens: As we gather tonight, our nation is at war, our economy is in recession, and the civilized world faces unprecedented dangers. Yet the state of our Union has never been stronger. (Applause.)

We last met in an hour of shock and suffering. In four short months, our nation has comforted the victims, begun to rebuild New York and the Pentagon, rallied a great coalition, captured, arrested, and rid the world of thousands of terrorists, destroyed Afghanistan's terrorist training camps, saved a people from starvation, and freed a country from brutal oppression. (Applause.)

The American flag flies again over our embassy in Kabul. Terrorists who once occupied Afghanistan now occupy cells at Guantanamo Bay. (Applause.) And terrorist leaders who urged followers to sacrifice their lives are running for their own. (Applause.)

America and Afghanistan are now allies against terror. We'll be partners in rebuilding that country. And this evening we welcome the distinguished interim leader of a liberated Afghanistan: Chairman Hamid Karzai. (Applause.)

The last time we met in this chamber, the mothers and daughters of Afghanistan were captives in their own homes, forbidden from working or going to school. Today women are free, and are part of Afghanistan's new government. And we welcome the new Minister of Women's Affairs, Doctor Sima Samar. (Applause.)

Our progress is a tribute to the spirit of the Afghan people, to the resolve of our coalition, and to the might of the United States military. (Applause.) When I called our troops into action, I did so with complete confidence in their courage and skill. And tonight, thanks to them, we are winning the war on terror. (Applause.) The men and women of our Armed Forces have delivered a message now clear to every enemy of the United States: Even 7,000 miles away, across oceans and continents, on mountaintops and in caves—you will not escape the justice of this nation. (Applause.)

For many Americans, these four months have brought sorrow, and pain that will never completely go away. Every day a retired firefighter returns to Ground Zero, to feel closer to his two sons who died there. At a memorial in New York, a little boy left his football with a note for his lost father: Dear Daddy, please take this to heaven. I don't want to play football until I can play with you again some day.

Last month, at the grave of her husband, Michael, a CIA officer and Marine who died in Mazur-e-Sharif, Shannon Spann said these words of farewell: "Semper Fi, my love." Shannon is with us tonight. (Applause.)

Shannon, I assure you and all who have lost a loved one that our cause is just, and our country will never forget the debt we owe Michael and all who gave their lives for freedom.

Our cause is just, and it continues . . .

Our second goal is to prevent regimes that sponsor terror from threatening America or our friends and allies with weapons of mass destruction. Some of these regimes have been pretty quiet since September the 11th. But we know their true nature. North Korea is a regime arming with missiles and weapons of mass destruction, while starving its citizens.

Iran aggressively pursues these weapons and exports terror, while an unelected few repress the Iranian people's hope for freedom.

Iraq continues to flaunt its hostility toward America and to support terror. The Iraqi regime has plotted to develop anthrax, and nerve gas, and nuclear weapons for over a decade. This is a regime that has already used poison gas to murder thousands of its own citizens—leaving the bodies of mothers huddled over their dead children. This is a regime that agreed to international inspections—then kicked out the inspectors. This is a regime that has something to hide from the civilized world.

States like these, and their terrorist allies, constitute an axis of evil, arming to threaten the peace of the world. By seeking weapons of mass destruction, these regimes pose a grave and growing danger. They could provide these arms to terrorists, giving them the means to match their hatred. They could attack our allies or attempt to blackmail the United States. In any of these cases, the price of indifference would be catastrophic.

We will work closely with our coalition to deny terrorists and their state sponsors the materials, technology, and expertise to make and deliver weapons of mass destruction. We will develop and deploy effective missile defenses to protect America and our allies from sudden attack. (Applause.) And all nations should know: America will do what is necessary to ensure our nation's security.

We'll be deliberate, yet time is not on our side. I will not wait on events, while dangers gather. I will not stand by, as peril draws closer and closer. The United States of America will not permit the world's most dangerous regimes to threaten us with the world's most destructive weapons. (Applause.)

Source: The White House. "President Delivers State of the Union Address." January 29, 2002. Available online. URL: http://www.whitehouse.gov/news/releases/2002/01/20020129-11.html. Accessed August 12, 2008.

The Bush Doctrine (June 1, 2002) (excerpt)

Within a year of the 9/11 attacks and the toppling of the Taliban regime in Afghanistan, the Bush administration began to promulgate the military policy that is known as the Bush doctrine. It was set forth in speeches and government documents like the National Security Strategy of the United States. It asserted that the cold war policy of containment was outdated. The United States could not afford to sit by idly while rogue states acquired weapons of mass destruction. Mere deterrence—enemies' fear of overwhelming retaliation by the United States—could no longer be relied on since it had not deterred the Taliban regime of Afghanistan from helping al-Qaeda. It made the case for preventive war, which has generally been condemned by international law. In this excerpt, Bush makes his case to a West Point graduating class.

In defending the peace, we face a threat with no precedent. Enemies in the past needed great armies and great industrial capabilities to endanger the American people and our nation. The attacks of September the 11th required a few hundred thousand dollars in the hands of a few dozen evil and deluded men. All of the chaos and suffering they caused came at much less than the cost of a single tank. The dangers have not passed. This government and the American people are on watch, we are ready, because we know the terrorists have more money and more men and more plans.

The gravest danger to freedom lies at the perilous crossroads of radicalism and technology. When the spread of chemical and biological and nuclear weapons, along with ballistic missile technology—when that occurs, even weak states and small groups could attain a catastrophic power to strike great nations. Our enemies have declared this very intention, and have been caught seeking these terrible weapons. They want the capability to blackmail us, or to harm us, or to harm our friends—and we will oppose them with all our power. (Applause.)

For much of the last century, America's defense relied on the Cold War doctrines of deterrence and containment. In some cases, those strategies still apply. But new threats also require new thinking. Deterrence—the promise of massive retaliation against nations—means nothing against shadowy terrorist networks with no nation or citizens to defend. Containment is not possible when unbalanced dictators with weapons of mass destruction can deliver those weapons on missiles or secretly provide them to terrorist allies.

We cannot defend America and our friends by hoping for the best. We cannot put our faith in the word of tyrants, who solemnly sign non-proliferation treaties, and then systemically break them. If we wait for threats to fully materialize, we will have waited too long. (Applause.)

Homeland defense and missile defense are part of stronger security, and they're essential priorities for America. Yet the war on terror will not be won on the defensive. We must take the battle to the enemy, disrupt his plans, and confront the worst threats before they emerge. (Applause.) In the world we have entered, the only path to safety is the path of action. And this nation will act. (Applause.)

Our security will require the best intelligence, to reveal threats hidden in caves and growing in laboratories. Our security will require modernizing domestic agencies such as the FBI, so they're prepared to act, and act quickly, against danger. Our security will require transforming the military you will lead—a military that must be ready to strike at a moment's notice in any dark corner of the world. And our security will require all Americans to be forward-looking and resolute, to be ready for preemptive action when necessary to defend our liberty and to defend our lives. (Applause.)

The work ahead is difficult. The choices we will face are complex. We must uncover terror cells in 60 or more countries, using every tool of finance, intelligence and law enforcement. Along with our friends and allies, we must oppose proliferation and confront regimes that sponsor terror, as each case requires. Some nations need military training to fight terror, and we'll provide it. Other nations oppose terror, but tolerate the hatred that leads to terror—and that must change. (Applause.) We will send diplomats where they are needed, and we will send you, our soldiers, where you're needed. (Applause.)

All nations that decide for aggression and terror will pay a price. We will not leave the safety of America and the peace of the planet at the mercy of a few mad terrorists and tyrants. (Applause.) We will lift this dark threat from our country and from the world.

Because the war on terror will require resolve and patience, it will also require firm moral purpose. In this way our struggle is similar to the Cold War. Now, as then, our enemies are totalitarians, holding a creed of power with no place for human dignity. Now, as then, they seek to impose a joyless conformity, to control every life and all of life.

America confronted imperial communism in many different ways—diplomatic, economic, and military. Yet moral clarity was essential to our victory in the Cold War. When leaders like John F. Kennedy and Ronald Reagan refused to gloss over the brutality of tyrants, they gave hope to prisoners and dissidents and exiles, and rallied free nations to a great cause.

Some worry that it is somehow undiplomatic or impolite to speak the language of right and wrong. I disagree. (Applause.) Different circumstances require different methods, but not different moralities. (Applause.) Moral truth is the same in every culture, in every time, and in every place. Targeting innocent civilians for murder is always and everywhere wrong. (Applause.) Brutality against women is always and everywhere wrong. (Applause.) There can be no neutrality between justice and cruelty, between the innocent and the guilty. We are in a conflict between good and evil, and America will call evil by its name. (Applause.) By confronting evil and lawless regimes, we do not create a problem, we reveal a problem. And we will lead the world in opposing it. (Applause.)

As we defend the peace, we also have an historic opportunity to preserve the peace. We have our best chance since the rise of the nation state in the 17th century to build a world where the great powers compete in peace instead of prepare for war. The history of the last century, in particular, was dominated by a series of destructive national rivalries that left battlefields and graveyards across the Earth. Germany fought France, the Axis fought the Allies, and then the East fought the West, in proxy wars and tense standoffs, against a backdrop of nuclear Armageddon.

Competition between great nations is inevitable, but armed conflict in our world is not. More and more, civilized nations find ourselves on the same side—united by common dangers of terrorist violence and chaos. America has, and intends to keep, military strengths beyond challenge—(applause)—thereby, making the destabilizing arms races of other eras pointless, and limiting rivalries to trade and other pursuits of peace. . . .

Source: The White House. "President Bush Delivers Graduation Speech at West Point." Available online. URL: http://www.whitehouse.gov/news/releases/2002/06/20020601-3.html. Accessed August 12, 2008.

5

International Documents

As America's role in the world has changed, so have the world's views of America, and not surprisingly they are often a good deal less flattering than America's view of itself. The 16 excerpts that follow, organized by region—"Europe," "Latin America," "The Islamic World," "Asia," "Russia and the Former Soviet Union"—depict the international developments that have affected the United States, and give us glimpses of America in the eyes of people in other countries—people who have loved it, despised it, feared it.

EUROPE

Frances Trollope Hates the United States (1832) (excerpt)

Francis Trollope, an English lady of refined background but limited means, visited the United States in the 1820s at a period when voting rights were being extended to an ever-widening proportion of the white male population and the country was becoming more democratic in spirit and in fact. While in the United States, she attempted to start a series of small business enterprises, which failed, and was constantly annoyed by the rough manners and naïve boasting of the young country's inhabitants. On her return to England she poured out her irritation in a book entitled Domestic Manners of the Americans, *which became a best seller and spawned so many imitators that writers criticizing America were said to be "Trollopizing." Though Mrs. Trollope is prejudiced, she is a good writer, and her unusual attention to everyday details makes her book valuable to anyone who wants to know what life was like in the United States in the 1820s. Many of her criticisms are a reminder that in the 1820s Europeans considered the United States a social and political experiment.*

I had not been three days at Mohawk-cottage before a pair of ragged children came to ask for medicine for a sick mother; and when it was given to them, the eldest produced a handful of cents, and desired to know what he was to pay. The superfluous milk of our cow was sought after eagerly, but every new comer always proposed to pay for it. When they found out that "the English old woman" did not sell anything, I am persuaded they by no means liked her the better for it; but they seemed to think, that if she were a fool it was no reason they should be so too, and accordingly the borrowing, as they called it, became very constant, but always in a form that shewed their dignity and freedom. One woman sent to borrow a pound of cheese; another half a pound of coffee; and more than once an intimation accompanied the milk-jug, that the milk must be fresh, and unskimmed: on one occasion the messenger refused milk, and said, "Mother only wanted a little cream for her coffee."

I could never teach them to believe, during above a year that I lived at this house, that I would not sell the old clothes of the family; and so pertinacious were they in bargain-making, that often, when I had given them the articles which they wanted to purchase, they would say, "Well, I expect I shall have to do a turn of work for this; you may send for me when you want me." But as I never did ask for the turn of work, and as this formula was constantly repeated, I began to suspect that it was spoken solely to avoid uttering the most un-American phrase "I thank you." . . .

Jefferson's posthumous works were very generally circulated whilst I was in America. They are a mighty mass of mischief. He wrote with more perspicuity than he thought, and his hot-headed democracy has done a fearful injury to his country. Hollow and unsound as his doctrines are, they are but too palatable to a people, each individual of whom would rather derive his importance from believing that none are above him, than from the consciousness that in his station he makes part of a noble whole. The social system of Mr. Jefferson, if carried into effect, would make of mankind an unamalgamated mass of grating atoms, where the darling "I'm as good as you," would soon take place of the law and the Gospel. As it is, his principles, though happily not fully put in action, have yet produced most lamentable results. The assumption of equality, however empty, is sufficient to tincture the manners of the poor with brutal insolence, and subjects the rich to the paltry expediency of sanctioning the falsehood, however deep their conviction that it is such. It cannot, I think, be denied that the great men of America attain to power and to fame, by eternally uttering what they know to be untrue. American citizens are not equal. Did Washington feel them to be so, when his word outweighed (so happily for them) the votes of thousands? Did Franklin think that all were equal when he shouldered his way from the printing press to the cabinet? True, he looked back in high good humour, and with his kindest smile told the poor devils whom he left behind, that they were all his equals; but Franklin did not speak the truth, and he knew it. The great, the immortal Jefferson himself, he who when past the three score years and ten, still taught young females to obey his nod, and so became the father of unnumbered generations of groaning slaves, what was his matin and his vesper hymn? "All men are born free and equal." Did the venerable father of the gang believe it? Or did he too purchase his immortality by a lie?

Source: Project Gutenberg's Domestic Manners of the Americans, by Fanny Trollope. Available online. URL: http://www.gutenberg.org/dirs/1/0/3/4/10345/10345.txt. Accessed September 8, 2008.

Alexis de Tocqueville on the Future Prospects of the United States and Russia (1835) (excerpt)

The French historian Alexis de Tocqueville is best known for Democracy in America, *his two-volume study of the young United States, which he toured for nine months from May 1831 to February 1832. Unlike Frances Trollope, he did not try to start a business or tend to sick family members while he was in the United States and for this reason as well as reasons of style and temperament his portrait is not as intimate as hers. His book is written on a level of high abstraction; much of the time it seems as if he might just as well have reached his conclusions if he had stayed in France reading newspapers. Yet he is uncannily perceptive, and the American characteristics that most interested him would prove to be essential and persistent. This prophetic passage in which he suggests that the United States and Russia may one day contend for world domination ends part I of* Democracy in America.

There are, at the present time, two great nations in the world which seem to tend towards the same end, although they started from different points: I allude to the Russians and the Americans. Both of them have grown up unnoticed; and whilst the attention of mankind was directed elsewhere, they have suddenly assumed a most prominent place amongst the nations; and the world learned their existence and their greatness at almost the same time.

All other nations seem to have nearly reached their natural limits, and only to be charged with the maintenance of their power; but these are still in the act of growth; all the others are stopped, or continue to advance with extreme difficulty; these are proceeding with ease and with celerity along a path to which the human eye can assign no term. The American struggles against the natural obstacles which oppose him; the adversaries of the Russian are men; the former combats the wilderness and savage life; the latter, civilization with all its weapons and its arts: the conquests of the one are therefore gained by the ploughshare; those of the other by the sword. The Anglo-American relies upon personal interest to accomplish his ends, and gives free scope

> to the unguided exertions and common-sense of the citizens; the Russian centres all the authority of society in a single arm: the principal instrument of the former is freedom; of the latter servitude. Their starting-point is different, and their courses are not the same; yet each of them seems to be marked out by the will of Heaven to sway the destinies of half the globe.

Source: Alexis de Tocqueville. *Democracy in America* New York: Vintage, 1959, p. 452.

Harriet Martineau on American Democracy (1837) (excerpt)

Harriet Martineau was the daughter of a British textile manufacturer. Thanks to the advanced views of her Unitarian parents, she received an education unusual for a woman in her time, and thanks to her own talents and drive became a working journalist. In the 1830s, she toured the United States and on her return to England published Society in America. *Like Frances Trollope, Martineau found many things to criticize in the United States, but she was more sympathetic to the aims of democracy. The excerpt here from her book's first chapter shows how literally Europeans and Americans took the idea that the United States was an experiment in a new form of government.*

> MR. MADISON remarked to me, that the United States had been "useful in proving things before held impossible." Of such proofs, he adduced several. Others, which he did not mention, have since occurred to me; and, among them, the pursuit of the *a priori* method in forming a constitution:—the *a priori* method, as it is styled by its enemies, though its advocates, with more reason, call it the inductive method. Till the formation of the government of the United States, it had been generally supposed, and it is so still by the majority of the old world, that a sound theory of government can be constructed only out of the experience of man in governments; the experience mankind has had of despotisms, oligarchies, and the mixtures of these with small portions of democracy. But the essential condition of the fidelity of the inductive method is, that all the elements of experience should be included. If, in this particular problem, of the true theory of government, we take all experience of government, and leave out all experience of man, except in his hitherto governing or governed state, we shall never reach a philosophical conclusion. The true application of the inductive method here is to test a theory of government deduced from the principles of human nature, by the results of all governments of which mankind has had experience. No narrower basis will serve for such an induction. Such a method of finding a good theory of government was considered impossible, till the United States "proved" it.

This proof can never be invalidated by anything that can now happen in the United States. It is common to say "Wait; these are early days. The experiment will fail yet." The experiment of the particular constitution of the United States may fail; but the great principle which, whether successfully or not, it strives to embody,—the capacity of mankind for self-government,—is established for ever. It has, as Mr. Madison said, proved a thing previously held impossible. If a revolution were to take place to-morrow in the United States, it remains an historical fact that, for half a century, a people has been self-governed; and, till it can be proved that the self-government is the cause of the instability, no revolution, or series of revolutions, can tarnish the lustre, any more than they can impair the soundness of the principle that mankind are capable of self-government. The United States have indeed been useful in proving these two things, before held impossible; the finding a true theory of government, by reasoning from the principles of human nature, as well as from the experience of governments; and the capacity of mankind for self-government.

Source: Harriet Martineau. *Society in America.* London: Saunders and Otley, 1837. Available online. URL: http://www.bolender.com/Sociological%20Theory/Martineau,%20Harriet/Society%20in%20A merica%201837.htm#INTRODUCTION. Accessed September 8, 2008.

Joseph Goebbels's New Year's Address (1940) (excerpt)

American isolationism in the 1920s and 1930s made it possible for Hitler's Germany to rearm in violation of the Versailles Treaty, to bully Britain and France into accepting its annexation of Austria and Czechoslovakia, and finally to take the fatal gamble of invading Poland, at which point Britain and France declared war on Germany. By June 1940, the Germans had defeated France. Nazi plans for Europe included the murder of millions of Jews as a final solution to the Jewish question and the murder of millions of Poles and Czechs to make room for German colonization. Thanks to American inaction, the United States and Britain faced the choice of accepting Nazi rule of Europe or engaging in the most destructive war in history. In his address to the German people, The New Year 1940–41, the Reich minister of public enlightenment and propoganda, Joseph Goebbels, crows over a string of Nazi victories.

One of the most significant years in German history ends today. Not only the Reich, but Europe as a whole changed greatly during its course. States, nations and peoples have been transformed, and changes in the balance of power occurred that one would not have thought possible in decades, much less one short year. People would have thought me a fool and a dreamer, certainly not a politician to be taken seriously, had I prophesied in my New Year address last year that we would now have a front reaching from Kirkenes to Biskaya, that German soldiers would be standing watch along this 5000 kilometer long front, that Norway would be under German protection up to the Arctic Circle, that France would be militarily destroyed, that England would be suffering under the German counter blockade, that it would be receiving attacks by day and night on its centers as revenge from the German Luftwaffe, that it would be reeling from the blows of our army and struggling for its very existence, and that London would be begging for help from the rest of the world to survive even a few months longer. . . .

Our opponents have always talked more than we do. Before something happens they talk a lot, only to grow suddenly silent when it actually happens. When things did not seem to be happening, they made the grandest threats against us. It has always been their fate to make the same mistake our enemies did during our struggle for power—they failed to take the Führer seriously. They ignored his warnings and when he was silent concluded that he did not know what to say or do. Three weeks before Hitler became chancellor, the then chancellor said that Hitler's day was over. Schuschnigg railed against the Reich two hours before he was driven in shame from the chancellor's palace in Vienna. Benesch had already packed his bags when he maintained that he had a plan to deal with the apparently hopeless situation. Polish statesmen dreamed of a victory at the gates of Berlin as German guns were already shelling Warsaw. Two months before France's collapse Monsieur Reynaud innocently showed diplomats a map of how Germany would be divided into separate parts. Is Mr. Churchill doing any different today? In his speeches and in the newspapers he explains the peace conditions for Germany once the war is over, while the British Isles in fact are bleeding heavily and gasping for breath. From our beginnings to the present, National Socialism's enemies seem determined to prove the accuracy of the old proverb: "The Lord makes blind those whom he wishes to punish."

Might I ask what Monsieur Reynaud would have done a year ago had he known what 1940 would bring France, or what Mr. Churchill would do now if he knew England's fate in 1941? We National Socialists seldom make prophecies, but never false ones. Had one believed the Führer back then, the world would have been spared much misery. Things probably had to happen as they did, however, since a new order of the coming proportions can be born only with pain, and the historical sins of the western democracies must find their historical recompense. . . .

I greet the entire German people at the end of this great and eventful year. I greet the men at home whose hard work supports the war, the workers at the wharves and munitions factories. I greet the women who accept all the difficulties and challenges the war brings, who have jumped in everywhere to replace the men who have gone to the front, who in the midst of it all still give birth. I greet the children, the countless German children who are touched by the hard facts of war, who often have left their parents' homes in regions threatened by air attacks. I greet our workers, our farmers, our professionals, who together are a people who have proven worthy of the time in which we live.

Are warmest and most grateful greetings go to our soldiers. I express the wishes and greetings of the homeland. From the depths of our heart to think of our brave army, our glorious Luftwaffe, and our victorious German navy.

The homeland and the front form a big family as we bid farewell to a year that was full of challenges, but also of big historical victories. The German people bows in praise before the Almighty, who has so clearly blessed us in the past year by standing by us in battle and crowning our weapons with victory. He knows that we are waging this war for a better peace, that we are fighting for the happiness of people who have so often been oppressed by their governments.

The entire German nation, at home and at the front, joins in a warm thanks to the Führer. 90 million glowing hearts greet him. It is with him both in good times and bad, just as it knows that the Führer is always with his people. We Germans wish him happiness and blessing for the new year, a strong, firm and sure hand, health and strength in all his efforts. Long may he life, long may he protect the people as the first fighter for a true and real peace and for the happiness, honor and fame of his people. The world admires him, but we may love him. We all extend our hands to him and hold firmly and inseparably to him.

The old year is over. A new one comes. May it be no less full of happiness, blessing and proud victory than the last!

Source: Available online. URL: http://xroads.virginia.edu/~1930s2/Time/1940/goebb.html. Accessed August 12, 2008.

Three-Power Pact between Germany, Italy, and Japan (1940) (excerpt)

The term axis for the German-allied side in World War II originally referred to the Rome-Berlin axis, an alliance between the regimes of fascist Italy and Nazi Germany. When Japan joined the alliance, with the treaty excerpted here, the two wars that had been brewing separately on different sides of the world became a single, worldwide war. By September 27, 1940, France had surrendered to Germany and German troops were in occupation of Paris. The new world order that this treaty celebrates would have wedged the United States between two extremely militarized, brutal, and aggressive empires.

The governments of Germany, Italy and Japan, considering it as a condition precedent of any lasting peace that all nations of the world be given each its own proper place, have decided to stand by and co-operate with one another in regard to their efforts in greater East Asia and regions of Europe respectively wherein it is their prime purpose to establish and maintain a new order of things calculated to promote the mutual prosperity and welfare of the peoples concerned.

Furthermore, it is the desire of the three governments to extend co-operation to such nations in other spheres of the world as may be inclined to put forth endeavours along lines similar to their own, in order that their ultimate aspirations for world peace may thus be realized.

Accordingly, the governments of Germany, Italy and Japan have agreed as follows:

ARTICLE ONE

Japan recognizes and respects the leadership of Germany and Italy in establishment of a new order in Europe.

ARTICLE TWO

Germany and Italy recognize and respect the leadership of Japan in the establishment of a new order in greater East Asia.

ARTICLE THREE

Germany, Italy and Japan agree to co-operate in their efforts on aforesaid lines. They further undertake to assist one another with all political, economic and military means when one of the three contracting powers is attacked by a power at present not involved in the European war or in the Chinese-Japanese conflict.

ARTICLE FOUR

With the view to implementing the present pact, joint technical commissions, members which are to be appointed by the respective governments of Germany, Italy and Japan will meet without delay.

ARTICLE FIVE

Germany, Italy and Japan affirm that the aforesaid terms do not in any way affect the political status which exists at present as between each of the three contracting powers and Soviet Russia.(1)

ARTICLE SIX

The present pact shall come into effect immediately upon signature and shall remain in force 10 years from the date of its coming into force. At the proper time before expiration of said term, the high contracting parties shall at the request of any of them enter into negotiations for its renewal.

In faith whereof, the undersigned duly authorized by their respective governments have signed this pact and have affixed hereto their signatures.

Done in triplicate at Berlin, the 27th day of September, 1940, in the 19th year of the fascist era, corresponding to the 27th day of the ninth month of the 15th year of Showa (the reign of Emperor Hirohito).

Source: The Avalon Project at Yale Law School. Available online. URL: http://www.yale.edu/lawweb/avalon/wwii/triparti.htm. Accessed September 8, 2008.

Winston Churchill, The Most Unsordid Act in the Whole of Recorded History (1940) (excerpt)

By the 1930s the United States, though staggering from the effects of the Great Depression, was already the most powerful industrial nation in the world. While its policy of neutrality and isolation made Hitler's bid for power possible, its existence probably doomed Hitler's ambitions. In this speech given by British prime minister Winston Churchill a little less than a month before the Japanese attack on Pearl Harbor and the German declaration of war on the United States, Churchill acknowledges the help the United States was giving Britain through the Lend-Lease program and discusses the situation in the Pacific that would soon make the United States a combatant on the side of the Allies.

Alike in times of peace and war the annual civic festival we have observed to-day has been, by long custom, the occasion for a speech at Guildhall by the Prime Minister upon foreign affairs. This year our ancient Guildhall lies in ruins. Our foreign affairs are shrunken, and almost the whole of Europe is prostrate under the Nazi tyranny. . . .

The condition of Europe is terrible in the last degree. Hitler's firing parties are busy every day in a dozen countries-Norwegians, Belgians, Frenchmen, Dutch, Poles, Czechs, Serbs, Croats, Slovenes, Greeks, and above all, in scale, Russians are being butchered by thousands and by tens of thousands after they have surrendered, while individual and mass executions in all the countries I have mentioned have become part of the regular German routine. . . .

I would say generally that we must regard all these victims of the Nazi executioners in so many lands, who are labelled Communists and Jews—we must regard them just as if they were brave soldiers who died for their country on the field of battle. Aye, in a way their sacrifice may be more fruitful than that of the soldier who falls with his arms in his hands. A river of blood has flowed and is flowing between the German race and the peoples of nearly all Europe. It is not the hot blood of war, where good blows are given and returned. It is the cold blood of the execution yard and the scaffold, which leaves a stain indelible for generations and for centuries. . . .

Here, then, are the foundations upon which the "new order" of Europe is to be inaugurated. Here, then, is the house-warming festival of the *Herrenvolk*. Here, then, is the system of terrorism by which the Nazi criminals and their quisling accomplices seek to rule a dozen ancient, famous cities of Europe, and if possible all the free nations of the world. In no more effective manner could they have frustrated the accomplishment of their own designs. The future and its mysteries are inscrutable, but one thing is plain—never, to those bloodstained, accursed hands, will the future of Europe be confided. . . .

The United States' time-honoured interests in the Far East are well known. They are doing their utmost to find a way of preserving peace in the Pacific. We do not know whether their efforts will be successful, but if they fail, I take this occasion to say—and it is my duty to say—that should the United States become involved in war with Japan the British declaration will follow within the hour.

Viewing the vast, sombre scene as dispassionately as possible, it would seem a very hazardous adventure for the Japanese people to plunge, quite needlessly, into a world struggle in which they may well find themselves opposed in the Pacific by States whose populations comprise nearly three-quarters of the human race.

If steel is a nation's foundation of modern war it would be rather dangerous for a Power like Japan, whose steel production is only about 7,000,000 tons a year, to provoke quite gratuitously a struggle with the United States, whose steel production is now about 90,000,000 tons a year. And I take no account of the powerful contribution which the British Empire can make in many ways. I hope devoutly that the peace of the Pacific will be preserved in accordance with the known wishes of the wisest statesmen of Japan, but every preparation to defend British interests in the Far East and to defend the common cause now at stake has been, and is being, made.

Meanwhile, how can we watch without emotion the wonderful defence of their native soil, and of their freedom and independence, which has been maintained single-handed for five long years by the Chinese people under the leadership of that great Asiatic hero and commander, General Chiang Kai-shek. It would be a disaster of the first magnitude to world civilization if the noble resistance to invasion and exploitation which has been made by the whole Chinese race were not to result in the liberation of their hearths and homes. That, I feel, is a sentiment which is deep in our hearts.

To return for a moment to the contrast between our position now and a year ago. I do not need to remind you here in the City that this time last year we did not know where to turn for a dollar across the American Exchange. By very severe measures we had been able to gather together and to spend in America about £500,000,000 sterling. But the end of our financial resources was in sight; nay, had actually been reached. All we could do at that time—a year ago—was to place orders in the United States without being able to see our way through, but on a tide of hope, and not without important encouragement.

Then came the majestic policy of the President and Congress of the United States in passing the Lease-Lend Bill, under which, in two successive enactments, about £3,000,000,000 was dedicated to the cause of world freedom, without—mark this, because it is unique—without the setting up of any account in money. Never again let us hear the taunt that money is the ruling power in the hearts and thoughts of the American democracy. The Lease-Lend Bill must be regarded without question as the most unsordid act in the whole of recorded history. . . .

Source: British Library of information. Available online. URL: http://www.ibiblio.org/pha/timeline/411110awp.html. Accessed September 8, 2008.

The North Atlantic Treaty (April 1949) (excerpt)

World War II radically changed the balance of power in Eurasia. It made the Soviet Union the greatest power, enlarged in territory, with effective control over eastern Europe and half of Germany. Europe's need for American help had been proven by the war itself, during which France had been easily conquered by the Nazis while the Soviet Union had resisted the onslaught. As the cold war intensified, the United States accepted a long-term commitment as western Europe's protector by joining a defense pact, the North Atlantic Treaty Organization.

The North Atlantic Treaty Organization (NATO) was preceded by a smaller western European alliance, the Treaty of Brussels (March 17, 1949) signed by the United Kingdom, Belgium, the Netherlands, Luxembourg, and France, which is considered the precursor to both NATO and the European Union. Talks of a larger alliance including the United States began almost immediately and the resulting treaty was signed in Washington, D.C., on April 4, 1949. This treaty included the five Treaty of Brussels states, as well as the United States, Canada, Portugal, Italy, Norway, Denmark, and Iceland. Three years later Greece and Turkey also joined. After the fall of the Soviet Union, NATO expanded its membership to include former Soviet allies. This excerpt contains the first seven of the treaty's 14 articles.

The Parties to this Treaty reaffirm their faith in the purposes and principles of the *Charter of the United Nations* and their desire to live in peace with all peoples and all governments.

They are determined to safeguard the freedom, common heritage and civilisation of their peoples, founded on the principles of democracy, individual liberty and the rule of law. They seek to promote stability and well-being in the North Atlantic area.

They are resolved to unite their efforts for collective defence and for the preservation of peace and security. They therefore agree to this North Atlantic Treaty:

ARTICLE 1

The Parties undertake, as set forth in the *Charter of the United Nations*, to settle any international dispute in which they may be involved by peaceful means in such a manner that international peace and security and justice are not endangered, and to refrain in their international relations from the threat or use of force in any manner inconsistent with the purposes of the United Nations.

ARTICLE 2

The Parties will contribute toward the further development of peaceful and friendly international relations by strengthening their free institutions, by bringing about a better understanding of the principles upon which these institutions are founded, and by promoting conditions of stability and well-being. They will seek to eliminate conflict in their international economic policies and will encourage economic collaboration between any or all of them.

ARTICLE 3

In order more effectively to achieve the objectives of this Treaty, the Parties, separately and jointly, by means of continuous and effective self-help and mutual aid, will maintain and develop their individual and collective capacity to resist armed attack.

ARTICLE 4

The Parties will consult together whenever, in the opinion of any of them, the territorial integrity, political independence or security of any of the Parties is threatened.

ARTICLE 5

The Parties agree that an armed attack against one or more of them in Europe or North America shall be considered an attack against them all, and consequently they agree that, if such an armed attack occurs, each of them, in exercise of the right of individual or collective self-defence recognised by *Article 51 of the Charter of the United Nations,* will assist the Party or Parties so attacked by taking forthwith, individually, and in concert with the other Parties, such action as it deems necessary, including the use of armed force, to restore and maintain the security of the North Atlantic area.

Any such armed attack and all measures taken as a result thereof shall immediately be reported to the Security Council. Such measures shall be terminated when the Security Council has taken the measures necessary to restore and maintain international peace and security.

ARTICLE 6 ([1])

For the purpose of Article 5, an armed attack on one or more of the Parties is deemed to include an armed attack:

- on the territory of any of the Parties in Europe or North America, on the Algerian Departments of France ([2]), on the territory of or on the islands under the jurisdiction of any of the Parties in the North Atlantic area north of the Tropic of Cancer;
- on the forces, vessels, or aircraft of any of the Parties, when in or over these territories or any other area in Europe in which occupation forces of any of the Parties were stationed on the date when the Treaty entered into force or the Mediterranean Sea or the North Atlantic area north of the Tropic of Cancer.

Source: The Avalon Project at Yale Law School. Available online. URL: http://www.yale.edu/lawweb/avalon/nato.htm. Accessed September 8, 2008.

Harold Pinter's Nobel Prize Lecture (2005) (excerpt)

The British playwright, director, actor, poet, and political activist, Harold Pinter is a fierce critic of American foreign policy, and since the early 1980s he had made his views known frequently in essays, interviews, and award speeches. Pinter opposed the 1991 Gulf War, the 1999 NATO bombing campaign in Yugoslavia during the fighting in Kosovo, the 2001 war in Afghanistan, and the 2003 invasion of Iraq. In 2005, he received the Nobel Prize in literature and used the occasion to protest U.S. foreign policy. Though Pinter is a highly respected playwright who might have been considered for the Nobel Prize in any case, the decision to give him the prize came at a high point of anti-American feeling in Europe, and may have been motivated by his well-known political views.

> As every single person here knows, the justification for the invasion of Iraq was that Saddam Hussein possessed a highly dangerous body of weapons of mass destruction, some of which could be fired in 45 minutes, bringing about appalling devastation. We were assured that was true. It was not true. We were told that Iraq had a relationship with Al Quaeda and shared responsibility for the atrocity in New York of September 11th 2001. We were assured that this was true. It was not true. We were told that Iraq threatened the security of the world. We were assured it was true. It was not true.
>
> The truth is something entirely different. The truth is to do with how the United States understands its role in the world and how it chooses to embody it. . . .
>
> Everyone knows what happened in the Soviet Union and throughout Eastern Europe during the post-war period: the systematic brutality, the widespread atrocities, the ruthless suppression of independent thought. All this has been fully documented and verified.
>
> But my contention here is that the US crimes in the same period have only been superficially recorded, let alone documented, let alone acknowledged, let alone recognised as crimes at all. I believe this must be addressed and that the truth has considerable bearing on where the world stands now. Although constrained, to a certain extent, by the existence of the Soviet Union, the United States' actions throughout the world made it clear that it had concluded it had carte blanche to do what it liked. . . .
>
> The tragedy of Nicaragua was a highly significant case. I choose to offer it here as a potent example of America's view of its role in the world, both then and now.
>
> I was present at a meeting at the US embassy in London in the late 1980s.
>
> The United States Congress was about to decide whether to give more money to the Contras in their campaign against the state of Nicaragua. I was a member of a delegation speaking on behalf of Nicaragua but the most important member of this delegation was a Father John Metcalf. The leader

of the US body was Raymond Seitz (then number two to the ambassador, later ambassador himself). Father Metcalf said: 'Sir, I am in charge of a parish in the north of Nicaragua. My parishioners built a school, a health centre, a cultural centre. We have lived in peace. A few months ago a Contra force attacked the parish. They destroyed everything: the school, the health centre, the cultural centre. They raped nurses and teachers, slaughtered doctors, in the most brutal manner. They behaved like savages. Please demand that the US government withdraw its support from this shocking terrorist activity.'

Raymond Seitz had a very good reputation as a rational, responsible and highly sophisticated man. He was greatly respected in diplomatic circles. He listened, paused and then spoke with some gravity. 'Father,' he said, 'let me tell you something. In war, innocent people always suffer.' There was a frozen silence. We stared at him. He did not flinch.

Innocent people, indeed, always suffer.

Finally somebody said: 'But in this case "innocent people" were the victims of a gruesome atrocity subsidised by your government, one among many. If Congress allows the Contras more money further atrocities of this kind will take place. Is this not the case? Is your government not therefore guilty of supporting acts of murder and destruction upon the citizens of a sovereign state?'

Seitz was imperturbable. 'I don't agree that the facts as presented support your assertions,' he said.

As we were leaving the Embassy a US aide told me that he enjoyed my plays. I did not reply.

I should remind you that at the time President Reagan made the following statement: 'The Contras are the moral equivalent of our Founding Fathers.'

The United States supported the brutal Somoza dictatorship in Nicaragua for over 40 years. The Nicaraguan people, led by the Sandinistas, overthrew this regime in 1979, a breathtaking popular revolution.

The Sandinistas weren't perfect. They possessed their fair share of arrogance and their political philosophy contained a number of contradictory elements. But they were intelligent, rational and civilised. They set out to establish a stable, decent, pluralistic society. The death penalty was abolished. Hundreds of thousands of poverty-stricken peasants were brought back from the dead. Over 100,000 families were given title to land. Two thousand schools were built. A quite remarkable literacy campaign reduced illiteracy in the country to less than one seventh. Free education was established and a free health service. Infant mortality was reduced by a third. Polio was eradicated.

The United States denounced these achievements as Marxist/Leninist subversion. In the view of the US government, a dangerous example was being set. If Nicaragua was allowed to establish basic norms of social and economic justice, if it was allowed to raise the standards of health care and education and achieve social unity and national self respect, neighbouring countries would ask the same questions and do the same things. There was of course at the time fierce resistance to the status quo in El Salvador.

I spoke earlier about 'a tapestry of lies' which surrounds us. President Reagan commonly described Nicaragua as a 'totalitarian dungeon'. This was taken generally by the media, and certainly by the British government, as accurate and fair comment. But there was in fact no record of death squads under the Sandinista government. There was no record of torture. There was no record of systematic or official military brutality. No priests were ever murdered in Nicaragua. There were in fact three priests in the government, two Jesuits and a Maryknoll missionary. The totalitarian dungeons were actually next door, in El Salvador and Guatemala. The United States had brought down the democratically elected government of Guatemala in 1954 and it is estimated that over 200,000 people had been victims of successive military dictatorships. . . .

The United States finally brought down the Sandinista government. It took some years and considerable resistance but relentless economic persecution and 30,000 dead finally undermined the spirit of the Nicaraguan people. They were exhausted and poverty stricken once again. The casinos moved back into the country. Free health and free education were over. Big business returned with a vengeance. 'Democracy' had prevailed.

But this 'policy' was by no means restricted to Central America. It was conducted throughout the world. It was never-ending. And it is as if it never happened.

The United States supported and in many cases engendered every right wing military dictatorship in the world after the end of the Second World War. I refer to Indonesia, Greece, Uruguay, Brazil, Paraguay, Haiti, Turkey, the Philippines, Guatemala, El Salvador, and, of course, Chile. The horror the United States inflicted upon Chile in 1973 can never be purged and can never be forgiven.

Hundreds of thousands of deaths took place throughout these countries. Did they take place? And are they in all cases attributable to US foreign policy? The answer is yes they did take place and they are attributable to American foreign policy. But you wouldn't know it.

It never happened. Nothing ever happened. Even while it was happening it wasn't happening. It didn't matter. It was of no interest. The crimes of the United States have been systematic, constant, vicious, remorseless, but very few people have actually talked about them. You have to hand it to America. It has exercised a quite clinical manipulation of power worldwide while masquerading as a force for universal good. It's a brilliant, even witty, highly successful act of hypnosis. . . .

The United States no longer bothers about low intensity conflict. It no longer sees any point in being reticent or even devious. It puts its cards on the table without fear or favour. It quite simply doesn't give a damn about the United Nations, international law or critical dissent, which it regards as impotent and irrelevant. . . .

Source: Nobel Lecture—Literature, 2005. Available online. URL: http://nobelprize.org/nobel_prizes/literature/laureates/2005/pinter-lecture-e.html. Accessed August 12, 2008.

LATIN AMERICA

Cuba Leases Guantánamo Bay to the United States (1903) (excerpt)

The U.S. Guantánamo Bay Naval Base, sometimes called GTMO or Gitmo, is the oldest U.S. overseas military base and the only one located in a communist country. It was established in 1898, when the United States took control of Cuba from Spain at the end of the Spanish-American War. The U.S. government obtained a 99-year lease that began on February 23, 1903, from the first president of Cuba. The Platt Amendment—an amendment to an American army appropriations bill—was incorporated into the Cuban constitution, in effect making Cuba an American protectorate rather than an independent country, including the Platt Amendment's provisions establishing the Guantánamo Bay base, which were further strengthened by the terms of this treaty signed July 2, 1903. For the past several years the base has hosted a detainment camp for suspected militant combatants from both Afghanistan and Iraq.

Signed at Habana, July 2, 1903;
Approved by the President, October 2, 1903;
Ratified by the President of Cuba, August 17, 1903;
Ratifications exchanged at Washington, October 6, 1903

The United States of America and the Republic of Cuba, being desirous to conclude the conditions of the lease of areas of land and water for the establishment of naval or coaling stations in Guantanamo and Bahia Honda the Republic of Cuba made to the United States by the Agreement of February 16/23, 1903, in fulfillment of the provisions of Article Seven of the Constitutional Appendix of the Republic of Cuba, have appointed their Plenipotentiaries to that end.-

The President of the United States of America, Herbert G. Squiers, Envoy Extraordinary and Minister Plenipotentiary in Havana.

And the President of the Republic of Cuba, Jose M. Garcia Montes, Secretary of Finance, and acting Secretary of State and Justice, who, after communicating to each other their respective full powers, found to be in due form, have agreed upon the following Articles;—

ARTICLE I

The United States of America agrees and covenants to pay to the Republic of Cuba the annual sum of two thousand dollars, in gold coin of the United States, as long as the former shall occupy and use said areas of land by virtue of said agreement.

All private lands and other real property within said areas shall be acquired forthwith by the Republic of Cuba.

The United States of America agrees to furnish to the Republic of Cuba the sums necessary for the purchase of said private lands and properties and such sums shall be accepted by the Republic of Cuba as advance payment on account of rental due by virtue of said Agreement.

ARTICLE II

The said areas shall be surveyed and their boundaries distinctly marked by permanent fences or inclosures.

The expenses of construction and maintenance of such fences or inclosures shall be borne by the United States.

ARTICLE III

The United States of America agrees that no person, partnership, or corporation shall be permitted to establish or maintain a commercial, industrial or other enterprise within said areas.

ARTICLE IV

Fugitives from justice charged with crimes or misdemeanors amenable to Cuban Law, taking refuge within said areas, shall be delivered up by the United States authorities on demand by duly authorized Cuban authorities.

On the other hand the Republic of Cuba agrees that fugitives from justice charged with crimes or misdemeanors amenable to United States law, committed within said areas, taking refuge in Cuban territory, shall on demand, be delivered up to duly authorized United States authorities.

ARTICLE V

Materials of all kinds, merchandise, stores and munitions of war imported into said areas for exclusive use and consumption therein, shall not be subject to payment of customs duties nor any other fees or charges and the vessels which may carry same shall not be subject to payment of port, tonnage, anchorage or other fees, except in case said vessels shall be discharged without the limits of said areas; and said vessels shall not be discharged without the limits of said areas otherwise than through a regular port of entry of the Republic of Cuba when both cargo and vessel shall be subject to all Cuban Customs laws and regulations and payment of corresponding duties and fees.

It is further agreed that such materials, merchandise, stores and munitions of war shall not be transported from said areas into Cuban territory.

ARTICLE VI

Except as provided in the preceding Article, vessels entering into or departing from the Bays of Guantanamo and Bahia Honda within the limits of Cuban territory shall be subject exclusively to Cuban laws and authorities and orders emanating from the latter in all that respects port police, Customs or Health, and authorities of the United States shall place no obstacle in the way of entrance and departure of said vessels except in case of a state of war.

ARTICLE VII

This lease shall be ratified and the ratifications shall be exchanged in the City of Washington within seven months from this date.

In witness whereof, We, the respective Plenipotentiaries, have signed this lease and hereunto affixed our Seals.

Done at Havana, in duplicate in English and Spanish this second day of July nineteen hundred and three. . . .

Source: The Avalon Project at Yale Law School. Available online. URL: http://www.yale.edu/lawweb/avalon/diplomacy/cuba/cuba003.htm. Accessed September 8, 2008.

Americas Watch Report on Nicaragua (1989) (excerpt)

Human Rights Watch is an independent, nongovernmental organization whose mission is to investigate and expose human rights abuses wherever they occur. It has a reputation for evenhandedness, generally drawing accusations of bias or inaccuracy only from the government of whatever country it is accusing of violating human rights. Americas Watch, an organization that has been folded into Human Rights Watch, has the same reputation. As this excerpt indicates, it reported on human rights abuses both by forces of the Sandinista government of Nicaragua and by the American-supported contras fighting the Sandinista government in the 1980s. In the judgment of Americas Watch, the abuses of the contras were much more serious and systematic.

Under the Reagan administration, U.S. policy toward Nicaragua's Sandinista government was marked by constant hostility. This hostility yielded, among other things, an inordinate amount of publicity about human rights issues. Almost invariably, U.S. pronouncements on human rights exaggerated and distorted the real human rights violations of the Sandinista regime, and exculpated those of the U.S.-supported insurgents, known as the *contras.* In 1989, under the Bush administration, U.S. policy toward Nicaragua has experienced one major change, in that it appears that the *contras* have ceased to be regarded as a viable military and political option. The White House has managed to keep the *contras* alive—against the wishes of the Central American presidents as repeatedly expressed in the agreements that are part of the peace process—but the *contras* have not been a significant fighting force, and they are unlikely to be turned into one after the Nicaraguan elections scheduled for February 1990.

This is an important change from a human rights perspective, because the *contras* were major and systematic violators of the most basic standards of the laws of armed conflict, including by launching indiscriminate attacks on civilians, selectively murdering non-combatants, and mistreating prisoners. In 1989 the number of *contra* abuses has been greatly reduced in comparison to the beginning of the peace process, largely because, at least through September, they were entering Nicaragua less frequently. To the extent that the *contras* have continued to operate, however, they have continued to commit these violations, and toward the end of 1989, abuses by the *contras* appeared to be on the increase. The Bush administration is responsible for these abuses, not only because the *contras* are, for all practical purposes, a U.S. force, but also because the Bush administration has continued to minimize and deny these violations, and has refused to investigate them seriously. As in the Reagan years, the Bush State Department has continued to make too much of monitoring mechanisms within the *contra* movement that have been wholly unsuccessful in prosecuting those responsible for abuses.

In all other respects, U.S. policy toward Nicaragua under the Bush administration is no different than it was throughout the Reagan years. The peace process in Central America has taken hold in Nicaragua, albeit with difficulties, but largely because the Central American presidents who devised it have been able to overcome U.S. objections. The process initiated in Esquipulas, Guatemala in August 1987 has resulted in 1989 in an electoral process in Nicaragua that is well under way. The Sandinista government has offered several concessions to the opposition, whose candidates are openly supported by the United States. There is extensive ongoing international observation of the election campaign by large, independent teams sent to live in the country on behalf of the United Nations and the Organization of American States. By all accounts, this international presence is helping to reduce frictions that might arise during a highly polarized and emotional campaign.

In contrast, the Bush administration has found only negative remarks to make about the electoral process. It has echoed *contra* complaints about the composition of the electoral tribunal, chaired by an independent person appointed by the government, and including two members of the Sandinista party and two members of different factions of the opposition in proportion to their results in the 1984 elections. By contrast, the Bush administration complimented the government of Paraguay for its 1989 elections, even though all members of the electoral council were appointed in accordance with their parties' showings in the elections held under the Stroessner dictatorship. The Sandinista government agreed to allow Nicaraguans living abroad to register, but did not yield to the demand that they be allowed to vote in Miami and Honduras. The State Department considered that a blatant flaw in the elections, although most Latin American countries do not offer polling places abroad and, most notably, the Salvadoran elections, hailed by the State Department as models of fairness, were closed to Salvadorans residing abroad.

In November 1989, the State Department circulated a "Nicaraguan Human and Civil Rights Update," in which it quoted selectively from a report of the Inter-American Commission on Human Rights. It cited the Commission's comments on the need for full freedom of expressions, as well as mechanisms to guarantee it, and on the problems posed by the fact that the Ministry of Interior was responsible for enforcing the newly amended Media Law. The State Department omitted the Commission's acknowledgment that, under the August 1989 agreement between President Daniel Ortega and the opposition, jurisdiction to enforce the Media Law during the electoral campaign had been transferred to the Supreme Electoral Council.

This posturing by the Bush administration leaves the impression that it will find the elections to have been clean and fair only if the U.S.-supported opposition candidates win. If the Sandinistas prevail, the groundwork has been laid for the State Department to claim that the elections were illegitimate.

In a related matter, the Bush administration has continued to press its predecessors' long-standing but indefensible position that the number of prisoners held in Nicaragua for security-related offenses is much larger than it really is. The November "Update" mentions 6,000 such prisoners, when in fact there were no more than about 1,300. This insistence on unsupportable figures is bad enough as an exaggeration, since effective human rights advocacy depends on accuracy, but as the peace process slowly progresses, the U.S. figures may also become an obstacle to peace. The Sandinista government has agreed to release all political prisoners once the *contras* are completely demobilized. The State Department's figures thus may become a tool to impugn the completeness of an eventual prisoner release.

In 1989, for the first time in many years, the State Department spoke about Americas Watch with words of praise. Assistant Secretary of State for Inter-American Affairs Bernard Aronson, appearing on national television, called Americas Watch "an independent human rights organization." Even *contra* leader Adolfo Calero quoted approvingly from an Americas Watch report, released in April 1989, which he waved in front of the cameras. The reason for this praise was that Americas Watch had taken the lead in documenting and publicizing killings in remote, war-torn areas of Nicaragua, where Sandinista military and state-security agents had summarily executed peasants whom they considered *contra* supporters. In an October 1989 report, Americas Watch added to the murders documented in the April report and also analyzed the Nicaraguan government's actions in response to complaints by Americas Watch about the killings. Those actions included investigation, prosecutions and, in some cases, punishment of government agents for the abuses described. The State Department has not commented on the October report. The State Department's November "Update" mentioned references by the Inter-American Commission on Human Rights to the pattern of summary executions, but did not mention, as the Commission did, that the Nicaraguan government had investigated and prosecuted some of those responsible for these killings. . . .

Source: Human Rights Watch. Available online. URL: http://www.hrw.org/reports/1989/WR89/Nicaragu.htm. Accessed August 12, 2008.

Che Guevara Calls for Many Vietnams (1967) (excerpt)

Ernesto Guevara de la Serna (1928–67), popularly known as Che Guevara, was an Argentinian revolutionary with a vision of a united, communist Latin America. As a young man, Guevara studied medicine and traveled throughout Latin America, activities that brought him into direct contact with the poverty in which many lived. Convinced that only revolution could remedy the region's economic inequalities, he became a confirmed Marxist. He was involved in Guatemala's socialist revolution under President Jacobo Árbenz Guzmán and was in Guatemala when Árbenz was overthrown in a CIA–sponsored coup. In the 1950s, he was a major participant in Fidel Castro's ultimately successful insurgency against the unpopular Cuban government of Fulgencio Batista, winning respect for his courage, military prowess, and ruthlessness. He later became a minister in the new Cuban government, an author, a theorist of Cuba's revolution, and a charismatic world celebrity thanks to his irresistible combination of literary gifts, leadership, war experience, and martyrdom—for he died in Bolivia during an effort to spread the revolution and did not live to share the blame for the many disappointments of communist Cuba as Fidel Castro's regime stretched on into the 1970, 1980s, 1990s, and 2000s. Guevara was instrumental in bringing to Cuba the Soviet missiles that precipitated the Cuban missile crisis in 1962 and said shortly afterward that if the missiles were under Cuban control he would have fired them at American cities. The statement excerpted here was made public in Havana by the news service Prensa Latina on April 16, 1967, while Guevara's whereabouts were unknown.

Message to the Tricontinental

Twenty-one years have already elapsed since the end of the last world conflagration; numerous publications, in every possible language, celebrate this event, symbolized by the defeat of Japan. There is a climate of apparent optimism in many areas of the different camps into which the world is divided.

Twenty-one years without a world war, in these times of maximum confrontations, of violent clashes and sudden changes, appears to be a very high figure. However, without analyzing the practical results of this peace (poverty, degradation, increasingly larger exploitation of enormous sectors of humanity) for which all of us have stated that we are willing to fight, we would do well to inquire if this peace is real.

It is not the purpose of these notes to detail the different conflicts of a local character that have been occurring since the surrender of Japan, neither do we intend to recount the numerous and increasing instances of civilian strife which have taken place during these years of apparent peace. It will be enough just to name, as an example against undue optimism, the wars of Korea and Vietnam.

In the first one, after years of savage warfare, the Northern part of the country was submerged in the most terrible devastation known in the annals of modern warfare: riddled with bombs; without factories, schools or hospitals; with absolutely no shelter for housing ten million inhabitants.

Under the discredited flag of the United Nations, dozens of countries under the military leadership of the United States participated in this war with the massive intervention of U.S. soldiers and the use, as cannon fodder, of the South Korean population that was enrolled. On the other side, the army and the people of Korea and the volunteers from the People's Republic of China were furnished with supplies and advice by the Soviet military apparatus. The U.S. tested all sort of weapons of destruction, excluding the thermo-nuclear type, but including, on a limited scale, bacteriological and chemical warfare.

In Vietnam, the patriotic forces of that country have carried on an almost uninterrupted war against three imperialist powers: Japan, whose might suffered an almost vertical collapse after the bombs of Hiroshima and Nagasaki; France, who recovered from that defeated country its Indo-China colonies and ignored the promises it had made in harder times; and the United States, in this last phase of the struggle.

There were limited confrontations in every continent although in our America, for a long time, there were only incipient liberation struggles and military coups d'etat until the Cuban revolution resounded the alert, signaling the importance of this region. This action attracted the wrath of the imperialists, and Cuba was finally obliged to defend its coasts, first in Playa Giron, and again during the Missile Crisis.

This last incident could have unleashed a war of incalculable proportions if a U.S.-Soviet clash had occurred over the Cuban question.

But, evidently, the focal point of all contradictions is at present the territory of the peninsula of Indo-China and the adjacent areas. Laos and Vietnam are torn by a civil war which has ceased being such by the entry into the conflict of U.S. imperialism with all its might, thus transforming the whole zone into a dangerous detonator ready at any moment to explode.

In Vietnam, the confrontation has assumed extremely acute characteristics. It is not our intention, either, to chronicle this war. We shall simply remember and point out some milestones. In 1954, after the annihilating defeat of Dien-Bien-Phu, an agreement was signed at Geneva dividing the country into two separate zones; elections were to be held within a term of 18 months to determine who should govern Vietnam and how the country should be reunified. The U.S. did not sign this document and started maneuvering to substitute the emperor Bao-Dai, who was a French puppet, for a man more amiable to its purposes. This happened to be Ngo-Din-Diem, whose tragic end—that of an orange squeezed dry by imperialism—is well known by all.

During the months following the agreement, optimism reigned supreme in the camp of the popular forces. The last pockets of the anti-French resistance were dismantled in the South of the country, and they awaited the fulfillment of the Geneva agreements. But the patriots soon realized there would be no elections—unless the United States felt itself capable of imposing its will in the polls, which was practically impossible even resorting to all its fraudulent methods. Once again the fighting broke out in the South and gradually acquired full intensity. At present the U.S. army has increased to over half a million invaders, while the puppet forces decrease in number and, above all, have totally lost their combativeness.

Almost two years ago the United States started bombing systematically the Democratic Republic of Vietnam, in yet another attempt to overcome the belligerance [sic] of the South and impose, from a position of strength, a meeting at the conference table. At first, the bombardments were more or less isolated occurrences and were adorned with the mask of reprisals for alleged provocations from the North. Later on, as they increased in intensity and regularity, they became one gigantic attack carried out by the air force of the United States, day after day, for the purpose of destroying all vestiges of civilization in the Northern zone of the country. This is an episode of the infamously notorious "escalation."

The material aspirations of the Yankee world have been fulfilled to a great extent, regardless of the unflinching defense of the Vietnamese anti-aircraft artillery, of the numerous planes shot down (over 1,700) and of the socialist countries' aid in war supplies.

There is a sad reality: Vietnam—a nation representing the aspirations, the hopes of a whole world of forgotten peoples—is tragically alone. This nation must endure the furious attacks of U.S. technology, with practically no possibility of reprisals in the South and only some of defense in the North—but always alone.

The solidarity of all progressive forces of the world towards the people of Vietnam today is similar to the bitter irony of the plebeians coaxing on the gladiators in the Roman arena. It is not a matter of wishing success to the victim of aggression, but of sharing his fate; one must accompany him to his death or to victory.

When we analyze the lonely situation of the Vietnamese people, we are overcome by anguish at this illogical moment of humanity.

U.S. imperialism is guilty of aggression—its crimes are enormous and cover the whole world. We already know all that, gentlemen! But this guilt also applies to those who, when the time came for a definition, hesitated to make Vietnam an inviolable part of the socialist world; running, of course, the risks of a war on a global scale—but also forcing a decision upon imperialism. And the guilt also applies to those who maintain a war of abuse and snares—started quite some time ago by the representatives of the two greatest powers of the socialist camp.

We must ask ourselves, seeking an honest answer: is Vietnam isolated, or is it not? Is it not maintaining a dangerous equilibrium between the two quarrelling powers?

And what great people these are! What stoicism and courage! And what a lesson for the world is contained in this struggle! Not for a long time shall we be able to know if President Johnson ever seriously thought of bringing about some of the reforms needed by his people—to iron out the barbed class contradictions that grow each day with explosive power. The truth is that the improvements announced under the pompous title of the "Great Society" have dropped into the cesspool of Vietnam.

The largest of all imperialist powers feels in its own guts the bleeding inflicted by a poor and underdeveloped country; its fabulous economy feels the strain of the war effort. . . .

We must not underrate our adversary; the U.S. soldier has technical capacity and is backed by weapons and resources of such magnitude that render him frightful. He lacks the essential ideologic motivation which his bitterest enemies of today—the Vietnamese soldiers—have in the highest degree. We will only be able to overcome that army by undermining their morale—and this is accomplished by defeating it and causing it repeated sufferings. . . .

They are pushing us into this struggle; there is no alternative: we must prepare it and we must decide to undertake it.

The beginnings will not be easy; they shall be extremely difficult. All the oligarchies' powers of repression, all their capacity for brutality and demagoguery will be placed at the service of their cause. . . . Hatred is an element of the struggle; a relentless hatred of the enemy, impelling us over and beyond the natural limitations that man is heir to and transforming him into an effective, violent, selective and cold killing machine. Our soldiers must be thus; a people without hatred cannot vanquish a brutal enemy. . . .

Let us sum up our hopes for victory: total destruction of imperialism by eliminating its firmest bulwark: the oppression exercized by the United States of America. To carry out, as a tactical method, the peoples gradual liberation, one by one or in groups: driving the enemy into a difficult fight away from its own territory; dismantling all its sustenance bases, that is, its dependent territories.

This means a long war. And, once more we repeat it, a cruel war. . . . Vietnam is pointing it out with its endless lesson of heroism, its tragic and everyday lesson of struggle and death for the attainment of final victory.

There, the imperialist soldiers endure the discomforts [sic] of those who, used to enjoying the U.S. standard of living, have to live in a hostile land with the insecurity of being unable to move without being aware of walking on enemy territory: death to those who dare take a step out of their fortified encampment. The permanent hostility of the entire population. All this has internal repercussion in the United States; propitiates the resurgence of an element which is being minimized in spite of its vigor by all imperialist forces: class struggle even within its own territory.

How close we could look into a bright future should two, three or many Vietnams flourish throughout the world with their share of deaths and their immense tragedies, their everyday heroism and their repeated blows against imperialism, impelled to disperse its forces under the sudden attack and the increasing hatred of all peoples of the world! . . .

Source: Che-Lives.com. Available online. URL: http://www.che-lives.com/home/modules.php?name=Content&pa= showpage&pid=8. Accessed September 8, 2008.

THE ISLAMIC WORLD

Osama bin Laden on American Foreign Policy (January 6, 2004) (excerpt)

Osama bin Laden, who helped found the terrorist organization al-Qaeda and is considered its leader, has claimed responsibility for the September 11, 2001, attacks on the United States. Together with other militant Islamic authorities, bin Laden issued two fatwas stating that it is a religious duty for all Muslims to kill U.S. citizens, both civilian and military, until they withdraw military forces from Islamic countries and withdraw support for Israel. His views are given in interviews to Western media (prior to 9/11) and in interviews taped in secret locations and broadcast by the Arab-language news network al-Jazeera since 9/11. The speech excerpted here was transmitted by al-Jazeera, translated by the BBC Monitoring Service, and printed in the British newspaper Guardian *on January 6, 2004.*

My message is to urge jihad to repulse the grand plots hatched against our nation, such as the occupation of Baghdad, under the guise of the search for weapons of mass destruction, and the fierce attempt to destroy the jihad in beloved Palestine by employing the trick of the road map and the Geneva peace initiative.

The Americans' intentions have also become clear in statements about the need to change the beliefs and morals of Muslims to become more tolerant, as they put it.

In truth, this is a religious-economic war. The occupation of Iraq is a link in the Zionist-crusader chain of evil. Then comes the full occupation of the rest of the Gulf states to set the stage for controlling and dominating the whole world.

For the big powers believe that the Gulf and the Gulf states are the key to global control due to the presence of the largest oil reserves there. The situation is serious and the misfortune momentous.

The West's occupation of our countries is old, but takes new forms. The struggle between us and them began centuries ago, and will continue. There can be no dialogue with occupiers except through arms. Throughout the past century, Islamic countries have not been liberated from occupation except through jihad. But, under the pretext of fighting terrorism, the west today is doing its utmost to besmirch this jihad, supported by hypocrites.

Jihad is the path, so seek it. If we seek to deter them with any means other than Islam, we would be like our forefathers, the Ghassanids [Arab tribes living under the Byzantine empire]. Their leaders' concern was to be appointed kings and officers for the Romans in order to safeguard the interests of the Romans by killing their brothers, the peninsula's Arabs.

Such is the case of the new Ghassanids, the Arab rulers. Muslims, if you do not punish them for their sins in Jerusalem and Iraq, they will defeat you. They will also rob you of the land of the two holy places [Saudi Arabia].

Today they have robbed you of Baghdad and tomorrow they will rob you of Riyadh unless God deems otherwise. What is the means to stop this tremendous onslaught? Some reformers maintain that all popular and government forces should unite to ward off this crusader-Zionist onslaught.

But the question strongly raised is: are the governments in the Islamic world capable of pursuing their duty to defend the faith and nation and renouncing all allegiance to the United States?

The calls by some reformers are strange. They say that the path to defending the homeland and people passes though the doors of those western rulers. I tell those reformers: if you have an excuse for not pursuing jihad, it does not give you the right to depend on the unjust. God does not need your flattery of dictators.

The Gulf states proved their total inability to resist the Iraqi forces [in 1990–91]. They sought help from the crusaders, led by the United States. These states then came to America's help and backed it in its attack against an Arab state [Iraq in 2003].

These regimes submitted to US pressure and opened their air, land and sea bases to contribute towards the US campaign, despite the immense repercussions of this move. They feared that the door would be open for bringing down dictatorial regimes by armed forces from abroad, especially after they had seen the arrest of their former comrade in treason and agentry to the United States [Saddam Hussein] when it ordered him to ignite the first Gulf war against Iran, which rebelled against it.

The war plunged the area into a maze from which they have not emerged to this day. They are aware that their turn will come. They do not have the will to make the decision to confront the aggression. In short, the ruler who believes in the above-mentioned deeds cannot defend the country. Those who support the infidels over Muslims, and leave the blood, honour and property of their brothers to their enemy in order to remain safe, can be expected to take the same course against one another in the Gulf states.

Indeed, this principle is liable to be embraced within the state itself. And in fact the rulers have started to sell out the sons of the land by pursuing, imprisoning and killing them. This campaign has been part of a drive to carry out US orders.

Honest people concerned about this situation should meet away from the shadow of these oppressive regimes and declare a general mobilisation to prepare for repulsing the raids of the Romans, which started in Iraq and no one knows where they will end.

Source: Osama bin Laden. "Resist the New Rome." *Guardian,* Tuesday, January 6, 2004. Available online. URL: http://www.guardian.co.uk/world/2004/jan/06/terrorism.comment. Accessed September 8, 2008.

ASIA

Chinese Leader Mao Zedong Calls the United States a Paper Tiger (1956) (excerpt)

After the defeat of Japan, which had occupied parts of China during World War II, communists led by Mao Zedong fought a civil war against the Chinese Nationalists led by Chiang Kai-shek. The United States supported Chiang Kai-shek and was shocked when, in 1949, his forces collapsed and fled to the island of Formosa (now Taiwan). Until the early 1970s, the United States maintained that the government in Taiwan was the only legitimate China and insisted that it occupy China's permanent seat on the United Nations Security Council.

The China Mao took charge of in the name of communist revolution was a backward country that—as his speech declares—had undergone many years of foreign domination. During the Korean War, Chinese fighting on the North Korean side had fought Americans fighting on the South Korean side to a standoff despite disproportionately high Chinese casualties. The United States and Mao's China came close to clashing in territorial disputes between China and Taiwan. U.S. and Chinese disdain was mutual during this period, but the tension was less serious than U.S.-Soviet tension because the United States did not fear a Chinese attack. This typical Maoist screed against U.S. imperialism was delivered at a meeting with Latin American public figures.

The United States is flaunting the anti-communist banner everywhere in order to perpetrate aggression against other countries

The United States owes debts everywhere. It owes debts not only to the countries of Latin America, Asia and Africa, but also to the countries of

Europe and Oceania. The whole world, Britain included dislikes the United States. The masses of the people dislike it. Japan dislikes the United States because it oppresses her. None of the countries in the East is free from U.S. aggression. The United States has invaded our Taiwan Province. Japan, Korea, the Philippines, Vietnam and Pakistan all suffer from U.S. aggression, although some of them are allies of the United States. The people are dissatisfied and in some countries so are the authorities.

All oppressed nations want independence.

Everything is subject to change. The big decadent forces will give way to the small new-born forces. The small forces will change into big forces because the majority of the people demand this change. The U.S. imperialist forces will change from big to small because the American people, too, are dissatisfied with their government.

In my own lifetime I myself have witnessed such changes. Some of us present were born in the Ching Dynasty and others after the 1911 Revolution.

The Ching Dynasty was overthrown long ago. By whom? By the party led by Sun Yat-sen, together with the people. Sun Yat-sen's forces were so small that the Ching officials didn't take him seriously. He led many uprisings which failed each time. In the end, however, it was Sun Yat-sen who brought down the Ching Dynasty. Bigness is nothing to be afraid of. The big will be overthrown by the small. The small will become big. After overthrowing the Ching Dynasty, Sun Yat-sen met with defeat. For he failed to satisfy the demands of the people, such as their demands for land and for opposition to imperialism. Nor did he understand the necessity of suppressing the counter-revolutionaries who were then moving about freely. Later, he suffered defeat at the hands of Yuan Shih-kai, the chieftain of the Northern warlords. Yuan Shih-kai's forces were larger than Sun Yat-sen's. But here again this law operated: small forces linked with the people become strong, while big forces opposed to the people become weak. Subsequently Sun Yat-sen's bourgeois-democratic revolutionaries co-operated with us Communists and together we defeated the warlord set-up left behind by Yuan Shih-kai.

Chiang Kai-shek's rule in China was recognized by the governments of all countries and lasted twenty-two years, and his forces were the biggest. Our forces were small, fifty thousand Party members at first but only a few thousand after counter-revolutionary suppressions. The enemy made trouble everywhere. Again this law operated: the big and strong end up in defeat because they are divorced from the people, whereas the small and weak emerge victorious because they are linked with the people and work in their interest. That's how things turned out in the end.

During the anti-Japanese war, Japan was very powerful, the Kuomintang troops were driven to the hinterland, and the armed forces led by the Communist Party could only conduct guerrilla warfare in the rural areas behind the enemy lines. Japan occupied large Chinese cities such as Peking, Tientsin, Shanghai, Nanking, Wuhan and Canton. Nevertheless, like Germany's Hitler the Japanese militarists collapsed in a few years, in accordance with the same law.

We underwent innumerable difficulties and were driven from the south to the north, while our forces fell from several hundred thousand strong to a few tens of thousands. At the end of the *25,000-li* Long March we had only 25,000 men left. . . .

During the War of Resistance, our troops grew and became 900,000 strong through fighting against Japan. Then came the War of Liberation. Our arms were inferior to those of the Kuomintang. The Kuomintang troops then numbered four million, but in three years of fighting we wiped out eight million of them all told. The Kuomintang, though aided by U.S. imperialism, could not defeat us. The big and strong cannot win, it is always the small and weak who win out.

Now U.S. imperialism is quite powerful, but in reality it isn't. It is very weak politically because it is divorced from the masses of the people and is disliked by everybody and by the American people too. In appearance it is very powerful but in reality it is nothing to be afraid of, it is a paper tiger. Outwardly a tiger, it is made of paper, unable to withstand the wind and the rain. I believe the United States is nothing but a paper tiger.

History as a whole, the history of class society for thousands of years, has proved this point: the strong must give way to the weak. This holds true for the Americas as well.

Only when imperialism is eliminated can peace prevail. The day will come when the paper tigers will be wiped out. But they won't become extinct of their own accord, they need to be battered by the wind and the rain.

When we say U.S. imperialism is a paper tiger, we are speaking in terms of strategy. Regarding it as a whole, we must despise it. But regarding each part, we must take it seriously. It has claws and fangs. We have to destroy it piecemeal. For instance, if it has ten fangs, knock off one the first time, and there will be nine left, knock off another, and there will be eight left. When all the fangs are gone, it will still have claws. If we deal with it step by step and in earnest, we will certainly succeed in the end. . . .

Source: Selected Works of Mao Tse Tung. Available online. URL: http://www.marxists.org/reference/archive/mao/selected-works/volume-5/mswv5_52.htm. Accessed September 8, 2008.

RUSSIA AND THE FORMER SOVIET SPHERE

Nikita Khrushchev, "We Will Bury You" (1956) (excerpt)

Nikita Khrushchev, who rose to the leadership of the Soviet oligarchy in the early 1950s, was a moderate in comparison to his predecessors. He tried to create a more humane Soviet Union and a less despotic Soviet sphere of influence. In a famous secret speech made soon after he rose to supreme power, Khrushchev acknowledged the crimes of Joseph Stalin. Before long, however, communist ideology and Soviet insecurity led Khrushchev to fall back on coercive methods of conducting foreign policy.

On November 4, 1956, Soviet tanks rolled into Hungary to reverse the will of its people, whose new leader was liberalizing the country and planning to withdraw from the Warsaw Pact. Thus, although Khrushchev's speech predicts the collapse of the West, he gave it at a time when Russia's own empire was fraying at the edges and had to be maintained by force. The phrase "We Will Bury You" probably means "we will outlive you" not "we will destroy you," but its use did nothing to ease tensions between the United States and the Soviet Union.

At the final reception for Poland's visiting Gomulka, stubby Nikita Khrushchev planted himself firmly with the Kremlin's whole hierarchy at his back, and faced the diplomats of the West, and the satellites, with an intemperate speech that betrayed as much as it threatened.

"We are Bolsheviks!" he declared pugnaciously. "We stick firmly to the Lenin precept—don't be stubborn if you see you are wrong, but don't give in if you are right." "When are you right?" interjected First Deputy Premier Mikoyan—and the crowd laughed. Nikita plunged on, turning to the Western diplomats. "About the capitalist states, it doesn't depend on you whether or not we exist. If you don't like us. don't accept our invitations, and don't invite us to come to see you. Whether you like it or not, history is on our side. We will bury you!"

Just the day before, ambassadors of twelve NATO nations had walked out on a Khrushchev tirade that lumped Britain, France and Israel as bandits. Now Khrushchev was off again.

The Kremlin men cheered. Gomulka laughed. Red-faced and gesticulating, Nikita rolled on: "The situation is favorable to us. If God existed, we would thank him for this. On Hungary—we had Hungary thrust upon us. We are very sorry that such a situation exists there, but the most important thing is that the counterrevolution must be shattered. They accuse us of interfering in Hungary's internal affairs. They find the most fearful words to accuse us. But when the

British, French and Israelis cut the throats of the Egyptians, that is only a police action aimed at restoring order! The Western powers are trying to denigrate Nasser, although Nasser is not a Communist. Politically, he is closer to those who are waging war on him, and he has even put Communists in jail."

"He had to," offered Soviet President Kliment Voroshilov. Khrushchev turned on him and said: "Don't try to help me."

"Nasser is the hero of his nation, and our sympathies are on his side. We sent sharp letters to Britain, France and Israel—well, Israel, that was just for form, because, as you know, Israel carries no weight in the world, and if it plays any role, it was just to start a fight. If Israel hadn't felt the support of Britain, France and others, the Arabs would have been able to box her ears and she would have remained at peace. I think the British and French will be wise enough to withdraw their forces, and then Egypt will emerge stronger than ever."

Turning again to the Westerners, Khrushchev declared: "You say we want war, but you have now got yourselves into a position I would call idiotic" ("Let's say delicate," offered Mikoyan) "but we don't want to profit by it. If you withdraw your troops from Germany, France and Britain—I'm speaking of American troops—we will not stay one day in Poland, Hungary and Rumania." His voice was scornful as he added: "But we, Mister Capitalists, we are beginning to understand your methods."

By this time, the diplomats—who, in turn, have come to understand Mister Khrushchev's methods—had already left the room.

Source: TIME, Monday, November 26, 1956. Available online. URL: http://www.time.com/time/magazine/article/0,9171,867329,00.html. Accessed September 8, 2008.

Brezhnev Doctrine (1968) (excerpt)

The year 1968 was a time of protest, liberation movements, and worldwide fatigue with the rigid lines that had been drawn in the early years of the cold war. In Czechoslovakia student demonstrations led to the resignation of the Stalinist president Antonín Novotný and his replacement by Alexander Dubček, who initiated a program of reforms and liberalization popularly known as the Prague Spring. Like the Hungarian uprising of 1956, the Prague Spring was suppressed by the Soviet armed forces. Soviet leader Leonid Brezhnev justified the intervention in a speech to a congress of Polish workers on November 13, 1968. "When forces that are hostile to socialism try to turn the development of some socialist country toward capitalism, it becomes not only a problem of the country concerned, but a common problem and the concern of all socialist countries," said Brezhnev, leaving it to be understood that the Soviet Union claimed the right to decide when a socialist country was going too far in the direction of capitalism so that armed intervention was necessary. Widely publicized, the principle became known in the West as the Brezhnev doctrine, a mirror of the U.S. determination to contain the spread of communism.

In connection with the events in Czechoslovakia the question of the correlation and interdependence of the national interests of the socialist countries and their international duties acquire particular topical and acute importance. The measures taken by the Soviet Union, jointly with other socialist countries, in defending the socialist gains of the Czechoslovak people are of great significance for strengthening the socialist community, which is the main achievement of the international working class.

We cannot ignore the assertions, held in some places, that the actions of the five socialist countries run counter to the Marxist-Leninist principle of sovereignty and the rights of nations to self determination. The groundlessness of such reasoning consists primarily in that it is based on an abstract, nonclass approach to the question of sovereignty and the rights of nations to self determination.

The peoples of the socialist countries and Communist parties certainly do have and should have freedom for determining the ways of advance of their respective countries.

However, none of their decisions should damage either socialism in their country or the fundamental interests of other socialist countries, and the whole working class movement, which is working for socialism.

This means that each Communist Party is responsible not only to its own people, but also to all the socialist countries, to the entire Communist movement. Whoever forget this, in stressing only the independence of the Communist Party, becomes one-sided. He deviates from his international duty.

Marxist dialectics are opposed to one-sidedness. They demand that each phenomenon be examined concretely, in general connection with other phenomena, with other processes.

Just as, in Lenin's words, a man living in a society cannot be free from the society, one or another socialist state, staying in a system of other states composing the socialist community, cannot be free from the common interests of that community. . . .

It is from these same positions that they reject the leftist, adventurist conception of "exporting revolution," of "bringing happiness" to other peoples.

However, from a Marxist point of view, the norms of law, including the norms of mutual relations of the socialist countries, cannot be interpreted narrowly, formally, and in isolation from the general context of class struggle in the modern world. The socialist countries resolutely come out against the exporting and importing of counterrevolution. . . .

In other words, Czechoslovakia's detachment from the socialist community, would have come into conflict with its own vital interests and would have been detrimental to the other socialist states.

Such "self-determination," as a result of which NATO troops would have been able to come up to the Soviet border, while the community of European socialist countries would have been split, in effect encroaches upon the vital interests of the peoples of these countries and conflicts, as the very root of it, with the right of these people to socialist self-determination.

Discharging their internationalist duty toward the fraternal peoples of Czechoslovakia and defending their own socialist gains, the U.S.S.R. and the other socialist states had to act decisively and they did act against the antisocialist forces in Czechoslovakia.

Source: CNN Cold War—Historical Documents: Speech by Leonid Brezhnev. Available online. URL: http://www.cnn.com/SPECIALS/cold.war/episodes/14/documents/doctrine/. Accessed September 8, 2008.

Mikhail Gorbachev Repudiates the Brezhnev Doctrine (1988) (excerpt)

In 1985 the Communist Party's Politburo—the ruling body of the Soviet Union—selected Mikhail Gorbachev to be the party's general secretary. Under Gorbachev's leadership, the Soviet Union embarked on a comprehensive program of political, economic, and social liberalization under the slogans of glasnost (openness) and perestroika (restructuring). Gorbachev was eager to reduce the Soviet Union's military commitments, which its stagnant economy was no longer able to support. In 1987, he signed a major arms limitation treaty with U.S. president Ronald Reagan, pulling intermediate-range nuclear missiles out of Europe. On December 7, 1988, as new U.S. president George H. W. Bush prepared to take office, Gorbachev repudiated the Brezhnev doctrine in a speech to the United Nations General Assembly.

Our country is undergoing a truly revolutionary upsurge. . . .

We have gone substantially and deeply into the business of constructing a socialist state based on the rule of law. A whole series of new laws has been prepared or is at a completion stage. Many of them come into force as early as 1989, and we trust that they will correspond to the highest standards from the point of view of ensuring the rights of the individual. Soviet democracy is to acquire a firm, normative base. This means such acts as the Law on Freedom of Conscience, on glasnost, on public associations and organizations, and on much else. There are now no people in places of imprisonment in the country who have been sentenced for their political or religious convictions. It is proposed to include in the drafts of the new laws additional guarantees ruling out any form or persecution on these bases. Of course, this does not apply to those who have committed real criminal or state offenses: espionage, sabotage, terrorism, and so on, whatever political or philosophical views they may hold.

The draft amendments to the criminal code are ready and waiting their turn. In particular, those articles relating to the use of the supreme measure of punishment are being reviewed. The problem of exit and entry is also being resolved in a humane spirit, including the case of leaving the country in order to be reunited with relatives. As you know, one of the reasons for refusal of visas is citizens' possession of secrets. Strictly substantiated terms for the length of time for possessing secrets are being introduced in advance. On starting work at a relevant institution or enterprise, everyone will be made aware of this regulation. Disputes that arise can be appealed under the law. Thus the problem of the so-called "refuseniks" is being removed.

We intend to expand the Soviet Union's participation in the monitoring mechanism on human rights in the United Nations and within the framework of the pan-European process. We consider that the jurisdiction of the International Court in The Hague with respect to interpreting and applying agreements in the field of human rights should be obligatory for all states.

Within the Helsinki process, we are also examining an end to jamming of all the foreign radio broadcasts to the Soviet Union. On the whole, our credo is as follows: Political problems should be solved only by political means, and human problems only in a humane way. [. . .]

Now about the most important topic, without which no problem of the coming century can be resolved: disarmament. [. . .]

Today I can inform you of the following: The Soviet Union has made a decision on reducing its armed forces. In the next two years, their numerical strength will be reduced by 500,000 persons, and the volume of conventional arms will also be cut considerably. These reductions will be made on a unilateral basis, unconnected with negotiations on the mandate for the Vienna meeting. By agreement with our allies in the Warsaw Pact, we have made the decision to withdraw six tank divisions from the GDR, Czechoslovakia, and Hungary, and to disband them by 1991. Assault landing formations and units, and a number of others, including assault river-crossing forces, with their armaments and combat equipment, will also be withdrawn from the groups of Soviet forces situated in those countries. The Soviet forces situated in those countries will be cut by 50,000 persons, and their arms by 5,000 tanks. All remaining Soviet divisions on the territory of our allies will be reorganized. They will be given a different structure from today's which will become unambiguously defensive, after the removal of a large number of their tanks. [. . .]

Source: CNN Cold War—Gorbachev's Speech to the United Nations. Available online. URL: http://www.cnn.com/SPECIALS/cold.war/episodes/23/documents/gorbachev/. Accessed September 8, 2008.

PART III

Research Tools

6

How to Research America's Role in the World

GETTING STARTED

The subject of this book, America's role in the world, is an enormous topic: It embraces U.S. history, foreign policy, economy, ideology and the intended and unintended impacts of all these on the rest of the world. Deciding how to begin researching a subject so broad and complex may seem a daunting prospect. It is a maze and a forest; fortunately there are many guides, offering an overview of the subject and suggesting subsequent lines of research. Since this book is one of them, this chapter will begin by discussing the purpose of this book and how to use it.

What is America's role in the world? The discussion in Part I is intended not as a definitive answer to the question, but as an introduction to the terms of ongoing debate about America's impact—what it has been, what it is, what it ought to be. The debate is not a dry one, at least not for the people who are involved in it. It is a debate about power and about good and evil. People express their feelings about it not just by writing books and articles, but by joining the marines or marching in street demonstrations or flying planes into buildings, as 19 fanatics did on September 11, 2001.

America's role in the world is the subject of heated argument. The great failing of many American history textbooks, which are designed to be palatable to everyone—to liberals and conservatives, to school boards in the states of Texas or California or Massachusetts—is the avoidance of controversy. All too often the result is not only rather dull but inaccurate, since the books tend to imply that all disagreements among Americans and all questions of justice and injustice occurred in the past and have been solved. Yet anyone who watches the news or talk show or listens to talk radio knows that this is an age of contention, that experts disagree and that pundits are constantly trying to convince others of their own opinions. The discussion in this book attempts to acknowledge this reality by letting the opinion-makers talk, summarizing their arguments as fairly as possible, permitting them to contradict each other and to make their cases.

In our time, perhaps more than in any other period in American history, the differences in our society are rooted in ideology. Barry Goldwater, a Republican U.S. senator from Arizona who is often credited with pioneering a revolution that brought conservatives to power in the United States, said in 1964 that there was not a dime's worth of difference between the Democratic and Republican parties. This was a considerable exaggeration even then, but it is certainly much less true now. The United States is much more sharply divided by ideology than it was a few decades ago. Presidential candidates have a way of becoming blander and sounding more similar to each other in their attempt to appeal to everybody at once as Election Day approaches, yet today the two parties represent two distinct perspectives on domestic and foreign policy, with different positions on a wide range of issues from global warming to Iran's nuclear program. Their disagreements are rooted in basic philosophical differences as well as in the self-interest and culture of the natural constituencies of each party.

It is often said that labels don't matter. This is a serious error. The truth is rather that labels are insufficient, that people are more than their labels, and that some people fall under multiple labels or require new ones. However, labels—political labels like liberal, progressive, conservative, neoconservative—are indispensable when discussing policy makers in a world where politics counts. As readers who have gotten this far will have noticed, this book does not label. American foreign policy has been made by liberals, progressives, libertarians, conservatives, and neoconservatives, as well as by realists, idealists, protectionists, free traders, internationalists, and isolationists, and this book uses the labels, with the understanding that a label does not complete the explanation but only begins it.

Part II, the documents section, provides relatively long excerpts from primary sources that have a bearing on America's role in the world, chosen in an attempt to tell a story and to complement the narrative of part I. Readers can see for themselves what Jefferson actually said about "entangling alliances," what James Monroe actually said about European recolonization of the Americas, with a little more context than usually is provided when these statements are quoted in American history books. There is not space to give the complete document here; almost all are available in full online and readers are encouraged to find them either through the Internet addresses provided with the excerpts or by googling key words from the documents. The links will lead to other collections of primary sources that are well worth browsing.

The documents section is divided into United States and international documents. The international documents include more than one virulently anti-American screed. The one by the British playwright Harold Pinter actually sounds angrier than the one by Osama bin Laden—perhaps because Pinter is closer to us, expects more of us, and is more shocked by the terrorism he accuses the United States of practicing in El Salvador and Nicaragua. Neither of them is a mindless rant: They make a reasoned case that the United States abuses its power, in much the same way that American neoconservative intellectuals like William Kristol and Paul Wolfowitz make the case that America uses its power for good. Since most people act as both citizens and individuals, to see things from a personal point of view, and to have a better memory for praise than blame, reading these hate letters to America can provide a salutary shock to Americans. Then, it would be educational to check out each of the accusations leveled against the United States, evaluate them for factual accuracy, logic, and learn more about the context in which the events the accusations rest on occurred. Some—like Osama bin Laden's complaint that by asking Saudi Arabia to act against anti-American jihadists the United States is forcing Muslims to act against their religion—will not seem criminal to Americans; we have a right to defend ourselves after all. Others, like Pinter's accusations regarding the contras in Nicaragua, may be harder to answer.

Part III with its long annotated bibliography, short biographies ("Key Players A to Z") of those mentioned in the book, chronology and lists of sources, is a sort of traffic circle from which roads point in various direction to the destinations of specialized subtopics. Sources have been selected for their relevance to each topic and divided into areas of interest for those who want to investigate specifically the U.S. role in Latin America or the U.S. role in nuclear nonproliferation, and so on. Any nonexpert who reads just a few of these books or browses through a few articles in several Web sites will come away knowing a great deal more about America's role in the world. Very few will be so obsessive as to read all of them, and probably very few will limit themselves to the sources provided here—nor should they, since new books and articles come out every day.

The bibliography includes others books that have the same purpose that this one attempts to serve, general introductions to the subject of America's role in the world. If time permits, some of these should be read to provide a corrective to this one, since all books have some bias, even if it is just an unconscious bias of selection.

The amount of information available even in this annotated selected bibliography is overwhelming, and some words about organizing the search may be helpful. Since America's role in the world is a topic fraught with controversy, the question of objectivity will be examined here in detail: what objectivity is and what it is not.

OBJECTIVE IS NOT INHUMAN

Objectivity is not a chilly robotic indifference. It is not the removal of all value judgments from international behavior. Doing that is not only immoral in its own way, it is a handicap to understanding, since history is made by people who act on their beliefs about good and evil.

In 2001, the 19 suicide hijackers of the 9/11 attacks were expressing their opinion of America's role in the world in their particular way. To them, America was an evil so great that God would approve of the murder of thousands of innocent civilians if the net effect was to weaken the United States.

To other people—in particular the administration of George W. Bush, which faced the challenge of responding to the attacks, America was good, good almost by definition, so good that the United States could assert as a foreign policy doctrine (the Bush doctrine) the implication that the rules of international law that applied to all other countries did not apply to the United States. The United States could make war on a country that was not about to attack the United States In their view, the United States had proved by its past actions that it would not abuse power: After all, Japan and Germany had lain prostrate under American might and the United States had lifted them up and helped them, making them strong and free. In the name of freedom, the United States had done the world a great favor in defeating, one after the other, the two great evil powers of the 20th century, Nazi Germany and the Soviet Union. The world ought to be looking forward to what the United States would do next.

Absolute evil and absolute good, the view of America taught to the schoolchildren in Iran versus the view taught in American elementary school classrooms—those are two possible polar opposite opinions of the United States. By high school or the first year of college, most students will have realized that nothing on Earth is that simple. Still, it is not a bad idea to keep in mind, while pursuing a more subtle picture of global realities, that there are moral dimensions to everything a country does. Acting through its governments and armies, the United States wields enormous influence in the world. Its actions enrich some people and impoverish others. Its armies may increase bloodshed or reduce it, protect or destroy. If leaders sometimes use moral language to justify war when the motive is really profit or a cold pursuit of long-term international strategic advantage, that itself is a moral issue. Good and evil are at stake in all human behavior, including the conduct of American foreign policy. When we move away from simplemindedness we do not move away from decisions about good and evil—we just try to see them in a subtler and more complex way.

The reason for mentioning this is to make the case that the effort to make value judgments is a tool of research. Students should seek to be objective without leaving value judgments behind. The questions of whether America is a net force for good or evil in the world or whether a given American policy is a net force for good or evil in the world should not be shunned: They are good goals for research; they are questions which the makers of American policy continually grapple with. Students who concern themselves with these questions are less likely to be bored with their research than students who attempt to avoid them.

SEEK ANSWERS TO PARTICULAR QUESTIONS

What is true about the questions of value is true as well about the controversies of fact and principle that swirl around America's role in the world. Did Ronald Reagan's decision to step up U.S. defense spending contribute to the fall of the Soviet Union? Was Saddam Hussein a menace to world peace, and is the world better or worse after the 2003 American invasion of Iraq? Does the United States have a mission to "drain the swamps" of terrorism by bringing democracy to the Middle East? Have U.S. economic policies—the Washington consensus policies of economic shock therapy—brought greater prosperity to Latin America and eastern Europe? Is the Democratic Peace Theory, which holds that democracies do not make war on each other and thus spreading democracy means spreading peace, valid, and is it a good guide to foreign policy? Does missile defense work or will it work in the future? The debates that swirl around these questions and thousands of others are intense, partisan, ideological, and fierce—and they give the subject interest and focus.

From a researcher's point of view, controversy is good. It may be a little frustrating to realize that there is no settled, undisputed answer to many of these questions, which cannot be answered as easily and definitively as the date of the invention of the telephone or the signing of the Treaty of Versailles. On some large historical question the debate will never end. But controversial questions do something better than providing certainty: they link facts, they give them a point and a story. The quest to settle an argument or at least to support a viewpoint with well-documented facts and authoritative expert opinions, to acknowledge and answer opposing arguments, brings a better overall understanding of the topic. Information acquired in this way lasts longer than information amassed by cramming for standardized tests.

BIAS VERSUS BAD FAITH

Bias comes in two forms, honest and dishonest. There is no such thing as complete objectivity. Every writer comes to a subject with a set of assumptions and prejudices and some kind of point to make. In general, the more interesting and insightful writers are those who care about the subject, which often means that their biases are more pronounced. Even a book that attempts to present many points of view has to make a selection and decide which opinions are too bizarre to be worthy of representation. By giving a range of opinions, it tends to imply a middle where the truth may lie. The search for an absolutely objective source is therefore futile—at best it turns up a bland book or essay that is unaware of its own prejudices. Books with a strong point of view actually have a better chance to free themselves from the unquestioned everyday errors of their time. They should not be avoided, but rather sought out; however, they should be read with the understanding that we are listening to one voice among many—and books written by equally able writers exist on the other side of the debate. Read the works of neoconservatives like Robert Kagan or William Kristol and traditional conservatives like Niall Ferguson. Read the work of liberals like Naomi Klein and Paul Krugman and leftists like Noam Chomsky. The truth does not necessarily lie in the middle: It may lie quite firmly on one side or the other—and the right-left axis implied in this selection may itself be insufficient. But anyone who carefully attends proponents of a variety of viewpoints will emerge with a much greater and deeper understanding of the issues than someone who has only heard one side.

Though sources with strong opinions should not be avoided, those with bad faith and intellectual dishonesty should be treated very warily. In an intensely political world, many writers with excellent credentials do act in bad faith. A great many media personalities act in bad faith—whether because they are cynical or because they cannot help themselves, they suppress evidence that tends to contradict their point of view. Honest writers acknowledge the contradicting fact and explain why it has not changed their minds. Writers who act in bad faith attempt to take advantage of ignorance. They usually do not lie outright, but they choose facts selectively in the belief that much of their audience will accept their word.

Some kinds of bad faith are subtle, and only experts will escape being fooled. Many times, however, the instances are more obvious. They are read mainly by people who enjoy a polemic and prefer propaganda to analysis on certain subjects. One walks away from these instances not better informed, but armed with talking points. Propaganda of this kind does not usually consist of bald lies, but it has low standards of verification, it accepts rumors as truth. When it has a range of estimates to choose from, it chooses the highest or lowest as demanded by the argument of the moment. It not only presents one side of the story, it suppresses the other side. The propaganda of an extremist group or of a foreign government is usually fairly easy to detect; the propaganda of one's own government is harder but not impossible to recognize. Except in times of national emergency, when people tend to have more faith in the government, most assume that the official line is not the whole story.

An article about a military conflict that details the war crimes committed by the soldiers on one side is not just biased, it is acting in bad faith: Even if the facts are true it is propaganda. A book that presents a case against a country, citing every evil thing that it is has done, and leaves out the context, is propaganda. The best protection against bad faith and propaganda is to read more and be exposed to other viewpoints.

INTERPRETING STATISTICAL INFORMATION

How has the North American Free Trade Agreement (NAFTA) affected the lives of workers in the United States and Mexico? Did it make employment go up or down? Did it raise or lower local standards of living? How has it affected immigration? Asking questions like these—in fact evaluating the success of almost any government policy—brings answers that bristle with statistics. Since most of us are not expert in the use of raw data, but rely on the statistics presented in news articles, books, speeches, and government reports, we need to see statistics as a function of bias.

An old saying states that, "Figures don't lie but liars figure." One should not avoid using figures; after all some things must be quantified, so figures are necessary. But they must be used with common sense, and they must be carefully questioned. If a country's GDP grew 5 percent the year a certain policy was put into place, might that be because the country was in a recession the year before and the GDP had fallen by 10 percent? The selection of a time frame is a very common way to massage numbers to make things look better or worse than they really are without actually lying. Defining terms a little differently than others do is another way of making numbers make your point. When discussing U.S. defense spending in proportion to the GDP, has spending on nuclear weapons been included in the statistic? Often it is not included, because the nuclear weapons are part of the budget of the harmless-sounding Department of Energy, not the Department of Defense.

The best way to learn how to use figures like these is to listen to strongly held opposing views that make use of the statistics. It is better to question their validity rather than accept them at face value and to compare how various sources interpret the data. One should understand how the figures were derived, and what particular motive the source might have. It will become apparent fairly rapidly how numbers are being selected and manipulated and which ones can be trusted.

CONSPIRACY THEORIES

Government affairs are full of conspiracies. People do, in fact, conspire. Sometimes governments conspire, especially agencies like the CIA, whose primary business is to conduct affairs covertly. We learn about conspiracies many years after they have succeeded or failed—the overthrow of Iranian prime minister Mohammed Mossadeq or the plans to kill Fidel Castro by means of an exploding cigar. So labeling an account of secret events a "conspiracy theory" should not immediately discredit it. Lately proponents of conspiracy theories have begun to be assertive. When you tell them that it is a conspiracy theory to hold that the Bush administration orchestrated the 9/11 attacks, that the planes flying into the World Trade Center were empty, and that the buildings were brought down with explosive charges, they say, "That doesn't mean it isn't true: see the film."

Conspiracy theories can be true, but the overwhelming majority of them are not true. Thus, they pose an immense and subtle problem for the judgment of fair-minded people who know that strange things sometimes happen—but who cannot spare the lifetimes that would be needed to fairly evaluate the thousands of conspiracy theories that grow and multiply like viruses around significant historical events. Conspiracy theories represent an even greater snare to young people who do not have the experience that older generations do and who have only recently discovered that presidents of the United States sometimes lie and not everything their country does is noble and well meant. It is fortunate that most people who believe in conspiracy theories also maintain a certain amount of rationality—to them conspiracy theories are an interest that does not significantly affect other parts of their lives. To accept what certain conspiracy theories imply about the world is to accept a warped and despairing view of the universe.

Conspiracy theories assert directly or indirectly that the main conduits of information coming to us are giving false information—the vast majority of journalists, historians, and other experts are either dupes or liars, and only a tiny minority are telling the truth. If that is true, society is in a great deal of trouble. Almost all information is known from secondary or tertiary sources, through the testimony of trusted experts. Even molecular biologists take the theories of astrophysicists on trust. The molecular biologists, at least some of them, have seen DNA under the electron microscope, but they do not have that kind of first-hand information about quasars and blacks holes; on those things they trust the experts. Similarly, many people have a similar trust in news sources—they appreciate the information, with reservations. News sources may give a distorted picture of the world—its commentators were wrong, for example, about Iraq's weapons of mass destruction, just as today's astrophysicists may be wrong about the big bang. We think they can be fooled and mistaken; but most of us do not think they're conscious participants in a big hoax.

To complicate matters, conspiracy theories come with a small group of experts who assert their truth. However, advocates for these theories are basically choosing to believe that this small minority of experts is truthful and accurate, while the majority of experts are dupes and liars.

Conspiracy theories tempt us with the promise of being a secret knower; they promise to lift the lid off the world and show us the moving parts with a single swift gesture. They point out reasonably enough that sometimes the majority is wrong. Whole societies have been wrong. Once all educated Europeans believed the Sun went around Earth and the stars were stuck on transparent spheres. Most of us today believe they are not—because of what textbooks say, not because of our personal observations.

Despite these attractions, most of us do not believe in conspiracies. It is not necessarily because we are more rational than the believers. It is rather because most of us are reluctant to live permanently in the paranoid universe they require us to inhabit.

We cannot examine everything in detail. Not one of us has the expertise needed for such an evaluation. We go by widely accepted rules and beliefs. The more moving parts a conspiracy requires for its execution, the more unlikely it is. For example, accepting that the United States planned the 9/11 attacks requires the participation of thousands of people, any of whom might talk and reveal the conspiracy—other thousands who might find out and have to be killed to keep them from talking—people working at the Pentagon, the FBI, the Federal Aviation Administration, the entire American media establishment, not to mention the police forces of the many foreign governments tracking the actual 9/11 conspiracy of suicide bombers who had ample motive, means, and opportunity to commit this very well-studied crime.

AUTHORITATIVE SOURCES AND HOW TO USE THEM

Anyone with access to the Internet has access to an abundance of information on America's role in the world. Here is an overview of the basic types of resources available and their virtues for the researcher.

Books

Well-written and well-researched books stay with a subject long enough to offer comprehensive analysis, context, deep historical background, answers to opposing arguments, and an explanation of difficult points. The Internet is very fast, but it is also shallow and does not have a long memory—and so it will remain until all the books are one day put on the Internet.

Students researching America's role in the world should read one or two general books on the topic and then move on to whatever special topics interest them. The annotated bibliography in part III of this book offers guidance in this search. If the arguments quoted or paraphrased in this volume seem interesting, readers might like looking at the books from which they were quoted. Books can be surfed as surely as the Web can; it just takes a little longer. Instead of going from link to link to Web page to link, scholars go from book to footnote to book. Computerized library catalogs have made the process much easier than it used to be.

Web Sites of Governments and International Institutions

Web sites of the president, the Department of State, the Department of Defense, the Central Intelligence Agency, and many other government Web sites provide the latest press releases of the institution, links to treaties and other important primary source documents, and summaries and analyses. Some U.S. government agencies, such as the Congressional Research Service and the General Office of Accountability, employ expert to write up-to-date reports analyzing internationally problems. These reports, created for the use of lawmakers, are then made available to the public. These clear, generally surprisingly frank and objective writings can be very useful to students and other researchers.

Nongovernmental agencies like Amnesty International and Human Rights Watch also maintain Web sites where their reports can be accessed. Some examples are given in the Organizations and Agencies chapter of this book; more can be found at the site NGOwatch, the Web address of which is also given in the Organizations chapter.

Web Sites of Research Institutes (Think Tanks)

Research institutes are designed to formulate and influence policy in the United States and elsewhere. Virtually every foreign policy issue and every international economic issue the United States contends with are discussed and analyzed on the Web pages of research institutes like the Carnegie Endowment for International Peace, the Brookings Institution, and the American Enterprise Institute. Think tanks tend to represent a definite political point of view. Some announce it frankly on their home pages; some do not. A very valuable Web resource called SourceWatch (www.sourcewatch.org/index.php?title=Think_tanks) lists a great many think tanks and assesses their political bent. SourceWatch, like the popular Wikipedia, is user written—which means that anyone on the Internet can edit it, add to it, or temporarily wreck it. Like Wikipedia, which is discussed later in this chapter, it can be very informative but cannot be taken as authoritative. Its statements must be double-checked, and most teachers will frown on its use in a bibliography or footnotes.

If their biases are taken into account, think tanks can be a good source of quick information on specific subjects and deep background and analysis of foreign policy and globalization issues. Neoconservative think tanks like the American Enterprise Institute tend to employ neoconservative policy makers and officials when the tides of politics have shifted against them. They are a good place to go to get the neoconservative take on current events. Comparing analysis of one think tank with another gives a sense of the controversies that beset any field.

Web Sites of Academic Institutions

Similar to think tanks, but affiliated with a university, academic Web sites are also a useful source of key documents, histories, and analysis.

Mass Market Magazines and Newspapers

Magazines aimed at the general reader, like *Time, Newsweek,* the *Economist,* and national newspapers like the *New York Times,* the *Wall Street Journal,* and the *Washington Post* are indispensable as sources of breaking news as well as for clear well-explained background pieces. Back issues have articles that can be used to compile a quick rough history of the recent past. Many schools and libraries have access to online catalogues such as *Proquest Direct,* by means of which these magazines can by searched using key words. The back issues of the most popular mass market newspapers and magazines are available online.

Scholarly Journals

Some scholarly journals are affiliated with think tanks, some with universities, and some are independent. They produce peer-reviewed articles—articles that must pass the scrutiny of experts in the field. Peer review is no guarantee of truth, especially in subjects such as political science and international relations, but it does help catch factual errors and exerts a steady pressure for high quality.

THE NONAUTHORITATIVE WEB

The Web is a realm of free speech, and some of the most popular and influential things on it are authored by amateurs. They can be useful for serious research if their limitations are well understood.

Wikipedia

In search engines based on popularity, like Google, a Wikipedia article is likely to be among the first articles that show up on the screen. Wikipedia is a user-written encyclopedia. Anyone can write or edit most Wikipedia articles, and that is why there are Wikipedia articles on collectible dolls, computer games, and television shows, subjects a regular encyclopedia would not have room for. These articles are alongside traditional articles on topics such as the Monroe Doctrine, John L. O'Sullivan, and Manifest Destiny (an excellent one, the last time this author looked—the problem is, it may have changed). Wikipedia articles by and large offer a useful introduction to the subjects they cover. They tend to work their way toward accuracy through the actions of the Internet community of interested users who watch for errors and correct them as they appear. But they can never have the authority of a regular encyclopedia article because there is no way of being certain of the expertise of the contributors and because practical jokers can and frequently do vandalize Wikipedia articles by deliberately adding mistakes they find amusing. For this reason teachers tend to be hard on students who cite Wikipedia as a source. They may warn students away from Wikipedia entirely. That is a pity. Wikipedia articles are an excellent start to research, and they can quickly lead to more authoritative sources, which are offered in the bibliographies and footnotes that contributors are encouraged to provide. Many of the footnotes have hyperlinks. Each Wikipedia article also links to a discussion page which can put a student instantly in touch with an assortment of people with disparate views, strong opinions, and a great deal of knowledge. Try the discussion page of Wikipedia articles on such fraught topics as Sunnis, Shiis, or Islam to see how interesting and broadening it can be.

Blogs

Anyone can maintain a blog, or Web log, an ongoing journal of opinion, fact, and interesting lies, with links to and from sundry other sites and places for strings of comment by random contributors. Most blogs are trivial, but there are many written by people with impressive credentials as well as by people with no credentials who nevertheless do excellent work and have interesting viewpoints. Since anyone can link to a blog and some of them appeal to a very select audience, people with scandal to disseminate can do it by going to a blog (as they might in earlier years have contacted a newspaper columnist) and linking a hot story, a report, or a piece of video. By this means in recent years blogs have broken news stories that 24-hour news networks have missed. Thus accessing the right blogs can be a way of staying current. But be aware that blogs are just people talking, and they do not necessarily know what they are talking about. They should be consulted after other sources have provided a context, and everything they say has to be checked.

7

Facts and Figures

INTRODUCTION

Top 25 Countries Ranked by Population

RANK	COUNTRY	POPULATION	DATE OF INFORMATION
1	*World*	6,602,224,175	July 2007 est.
2	*China*	1,321,851,888	July 2007 est.
3	*India*	1,129,866,154	July 2007 est.
4	*European Union*	490,426,060	July 2007 est.
5	*United States*	301,139,947	July 2007 est.
6	*Indonesia*	234,693,997	July 2007 est.
7	*Brazil*	190,010,647	July 2007 est.
8	*Pakistan*	164,741,924	July 2007 est.
9	*Bangladesh*	150,448,339	July 2007 est.
10	*Russia*	141,377,752	July 2007 est.
11	*Nigeria*	135,031,164	July 2007 est.
12	*Japan*	127,433,494	July 2007 est.
13	*Mexico*	108,700,891	July 2007 est.
14	*Philippines*	91,077,287	July 2007 est.
15	*Vietnam*	85,262,356	July 2007 est.
16	*Germany*	82,400,996	July 2007 est.
17	*Egypt*	80,335,036	July 2007 est.
18	*Ethiopia*	76,511,887	July 2007 est.
19	*Turkey*	71,158,647	July 2007 est.

RANK	COUNTRY	POPULATION	DATE OF INFORMATION
20	*Congo, Democratic Republic of the*	65,751,512	July 2007 est.
21	*Iran*	65,397,521	July 2007 est.
22	*Thailand*	65,068,149	July 2007 est.
23	*France*	64,057,790	July 2007 est.
24	*United Kingdom*	60,776,238	July 2007 est.
25	*Italy*	58,147,733	July 2007 est.
26	*Korea, South*	49,044,790	July 2007 est.

Source: CIA World Factbook

Top 25 Countries Ranked by Country GDP

RANK	COUNTRY	GDP (PURCHASING POWER PARITY)	DATE OF INFORMATION
1	*World*	$ 65,820,000,000,000	2007 est.
2	*European Union*	$ 14,450,000,000,000	2007 est.
3	*United States*	$ 13,860,000,000,000	2007 est.
4	*China*	$ 7,043,000,000,000	2007 est.
5	*Japan*	$ 4,346,000,000,000	2007 est.
6	*India*	$ 2,965,000,000,000	2007 est.
7	*Germany*	$ 2,833,000,000,000	2007 est.
8	*United Kingdom*	$ 2,147,000,000,000	2007 est.
9	*Russia*	$ 2,076,000,000,000	2007 est.
10	*France*	$ 2,067,000,000,000	2007 est.
11	*Brazil*	$ 1,838,000,000,000	2007 est.
12	*Italy*	$ 1,800,000,000,000	2007 est.
13	*Spain*	$ 1,362,000,000,000	2007 est.
14	*Mexico*	$ 1,353,000,000,000	2007 est.
15	*Canada*	$ 1,274,000,000,000	2007 est.
16	*Korea, South*	$ 1,206,000,000,000	2007 est.
17	*Iran*	$ 852,600,000,000	2007 est.
18	*Indonesia*	$ 845,600,000,000	2007 est.
19	*Australia*	$ 766,800,000,000	2007 est.

(continues)

(continued)

RANK	COUNTRY	GDP (PURCHASING POWER PARITY)	DATE OF INFORMATION
20	*Taiwan*	$ 690,100,000,000	2007 est.
21	*Turkey*	$ 667,700,000,000	2007 est.
22	*Netherlands*	$ 638,900,000,000	2007 est.
23	*Poland*	$ 624,600,000,000	2007 est.
24	*Saudi Arabia*	$ 572,200,000,000	2007 est.
25	*Argentina*	$ 523,700,000,000	2007 est.
26	*Thailand*	$ 519,900,000,000	2007 est.

Source: CIA World Factbook

Top 25 Countries Ranked by per Capita GDP

RANK	COUNTRY	GDP–PER CAPITA (PPP)	DATE OF INFORMATION
1	*Luxembourg*	$ 80,800	2007 est.
2	*Qatar*	$ 75,900	2007 est.
3	*Bermuda*	$ 69,900	2004 est.
4	*Jersey*	$ 57,000	2005 est.
5	*Norway*	$ 55,600	2007 est.
6	*Kuwait*	$ 55,300	2007 est.
7	*United Arab Emirates*	$ 55,200	2007 est.
8	*Singapore*	$ 48,900	2007 est.
9	*United States*	$ 46,000	2007 est.
10	*Ireland*	$ 45,600	2007 est.
11	*Guernsey*	$ 44,600	2005
12	*Equatorial Guinea*	$ 44,100	2007 est.
13	*Cayman Islands*	$ 43,800	2004 est.
14	*Hong Kong*	$ 42,000	2007 est.
15	*Switzerland*	$ 39,800	2007 est.
16	*Iceland*	$ 39,400	2007 est.
17	*Austria*	$ 39,000	2007 est.
18	*Andorra*	$ 38,800	2005
19	*Netherlands*	$ 38,600	2007 est.
20	*British Virgin Islands*	$ 38,500	2004 est.

RANK	COUNTRY	GDP–PER CAPITA (PPP)	DATE OF INFORMATION
21	*Canada*	$ 38,200	2007 est.
22	*Gibraltar*	$ 38,200	2005 est.
23	*Australia*	$ 37,500	2007 est.
24	*Denmark*	$ 37,400	2007 est.
25	*Sweden*	$ 36,900	2007 est.

Source: CIA World Factbook

Top 25 Countries Ranked by Oil Consumption

RANK	COUNTRY	OIL-CONSUMPTION (BBL/DAY)	DATE OF INFORMATION
1	*World*	80,290,000	2005 est.
2	*United States*	20,800,000	2005 est.
3	*European Union*	14,570,000	2004
4	*China*	6,930,000	2007 est.
5	*Japan*	5,353,000	2005
6	*Russia*	2,916,000	2006
7	*Germany*	2,618,000	2005
8	*India*	2,438,000	2005 est.
9	*Canada*	2,290,000	2005
10	*Korea, South*	2,130,000	2006
11	*Brazil*	2,100,000	2006 est.
12	*Mexico*	2,078,000	2005 est.
13	*Saudi Arabia*	2,000,000	2005
14	*France*	1,999,000	2005 est.
15	*United Kingdom*	1,820,000	2005 est.
16	*Italy*	1,732,000	2005 est.
17	*Iran*	1,630,000	2006 est.
18	*Spain*	1,600,000	2005 est.
19	*Indonesia*	1,100,000	2006 est.
20	*Netherlands*	1,024,000	2005 est.
21	*Thailand*	929,000	2005 est.
22	*Australia*	903,200	2005 est.

(continues)

(continued)

RANK	COUNTRY	OIL-CONSUMPTION (BBL/DAY)	DATE OF INFORMATION
23	*Taiwan*	816,700	2006 est.
24	*Singapore*	802,000	2005 est.
25	*Turkey*	660,800	2005 est.
26	*Egypt*	635,000	2005 est.

Source: CIA World Factbook

Top 25 Countries Ranked by Proven Oil Reserves

RANK	COUNTRY	OIL-PROVED RESERVES (BBL)	DATE OF INFORMATION
1	*World*	1,295,000,000,000	1 January 2006 est.
2	*Saudi Arabia*	266,800,000,000	1 January 2006 est.
3	*Canada*	178,800,000,000	1 January 2006 est.
4	*Iran*	132,500,000,000	1 January 2006 est.
5	*Iraq*	115,000,000,000	1 January 2007 est.
6	*Kuwait*	104,000,000,000	1 January 2006 est.
7	*United Arab Emirates*	97,800,000,000	1 January 2006 est.
8	*Venezuela*	79,730,000,000	1 January 2006 est.
9	*Russia*	60,000,000,000	1 January 2006 est.
10	*Libya*	39,130,000,000	1 January 2006 est.
11	*Nigeria*	35,880,000,000	1 January 2006 est.
12	*United States*	21,760,000,000	1 January 2006 est.
13	*Qatar*	15,210,000,000	1 January 2006 est.
14	*Mexico*	12,880,000,000	1 January 2006 est.
15	*China*	12,800,000,000	2007 est.
16	*Algeria*	11,350,000,000	1 January 2006 est.
17	*Brazil*	11,240,000,000	1 January 2006 est.
18	*Kazakhstan*	9,000,000,000	1 January 2006 est.
19	*Norway*	7,705,000,000	1 January 2006 est.
20	*European Union*	7,072,000,000	1 January 2005
21	*Azerbaijan*	7,000,000,000	17 April 2007 est.
22	*Sudan*	6,400,000,000	1 January 2006 est.
23	*India*	5,848,000,000	1 January 2006 est.

RANK	COUNTRY	OIL-PROVED RESERVES (BBL)	DATE OF INFORMATION
24	*Oman*	5,506,000,000	1 January 2006 est.
25	*Angola*	5,412,000,000	1 January 2006 est.
26	*Ecuador*	4,630,000,000	1 January 2006 est.

Source: CIA World Factbook

Top 25 Countries Ranked by Reserves of Foreign Exchange and Gold

RANK	COUNTRY	RESERVES OF FOREIGN EXCHANGE AND GOLD	DATE OF INFORMATION
1	*China*	$ 1,493,000,000,000	31 December 2007 est.
2	*Japan*	$ 881,000,000,000	2006 est.
3	*Russia*	$ 470,000,000,000	31 December 2007 est.
4	*Taiwan*	$ 274,700,000,000	31 December 2007
5	*Korea, South*	$ 262,200,000,000	31 December 2007
6	*India*	$ 239,400,000,000	31 December 2007 est.
7	*Brazil*	$ 178,000,000,000	24 December 2007
8	*Singapore*	$ 157,000,000,000	31 December 2007 est.
9	*Hong Kong*	$ 152,700,000,000	31 December 2007 est.
10	*Germany*	$ 111,600,000,000	2006 est.
11	*Malaysia*	$ 104,800,000,000	31 December 2007 est.
12	*Thailand*	$ 100,000,000,000	31 December 2007 est.
13	*Algeria*	$ 99,330,000,000	31 December 2007 est.
14	*France*	$ 98,240,000,000	2006 est.
15	*Mexico*	$ 85,110,000,000	31 December 2007 est.
16	*Turkey*	$ 74,390,000,000	31 December 2007 est.
17	*Australia*	$ 71,150,000,000	31 December 2007 est.
18	*Libya*	$ 69,510,000,000	31 December 2007 est.
19	*Iran*	$ 69,200,000,000	2007 est.
20	*Italy*	$ 69,000,000,000	31 December 2007 est.
21	*United States*	$ 65,890,000,000	2006 est.
22	*Switzerland*	$ 64,500,000,000	2006 est.
23	*Poland*	$ 61,460,000,000	31 December 2007 est.

(continues)

(continued)

RANK	COUNTRY	RESERVES OF FOREIGN EXCHANGE AND GOLD	DATE OF INFORMATION
24	*Norway*	$ 56,840,000,000	2006 est.
25	*Indonesia*	$ 53,270,000,000	31 December 2007 est.

Source: CIA World Factbook

Top Ten Countries Ranked by Account Balance

RANK	COUNTRY	CURRENT ACCOUNT BALANCE	DATE OF INFORMATION
1	*China*	$ 363,300,000,000	2007 est.
2	*Japan*	$ 195,900,000,000	2007 est.
3	*Germany*	$ 185,100,000,000	2007 est.
4	*Saudi Arabia*	$ 88,890,000,000	2007 est.
5	*Russia*	$ 74,000,000,000	2007 est.
6	*Switzerland*	$ 67,890,000,000	2007 est.
7	*Netherlands*	$ 59,280,000,000	2007 est.
8	*Norway*	$ 55,820,000,000	2007 est.
9	*Kuwait*	$ 51,490,000,000	2007 est.
10	*Singapore*	$ 41,390,000,000	2007 est.

Source: CIA World Factbook

Bottom Ten Countries Ranked by Account Balance

RANK	COUNTRY	CURRENT ACCOUNT BALANCE	DATE OF INFORMATION
154	*South Africa*	$ –20,060,000,000	2007 est.
155	*Romania*	$ –20,950,000,000	2007 est.
156	*France*	$ –35,940,000,000	2007 est.
157	*Turkey*	$ –36,270,000,000	2007 est.
158	*Greece*	$ –36,400,000,000	2007 est.
159	*Australia*	$ –50,960,000,000	2007 est.
160	*Italy*	$ –57,940,000,000	2007 est.
161	*United Kingdom*	$ –111,000,000,000	2007 est.
162	*Spain*	$ –126,300,000,000	2007 est.
163	*United States*	$ –747,100,000,000	2007 est.

Source: CIA World Factbook

FOCUS ON THE UNITED STATES

U.S. Military Spending v. the World, 2008

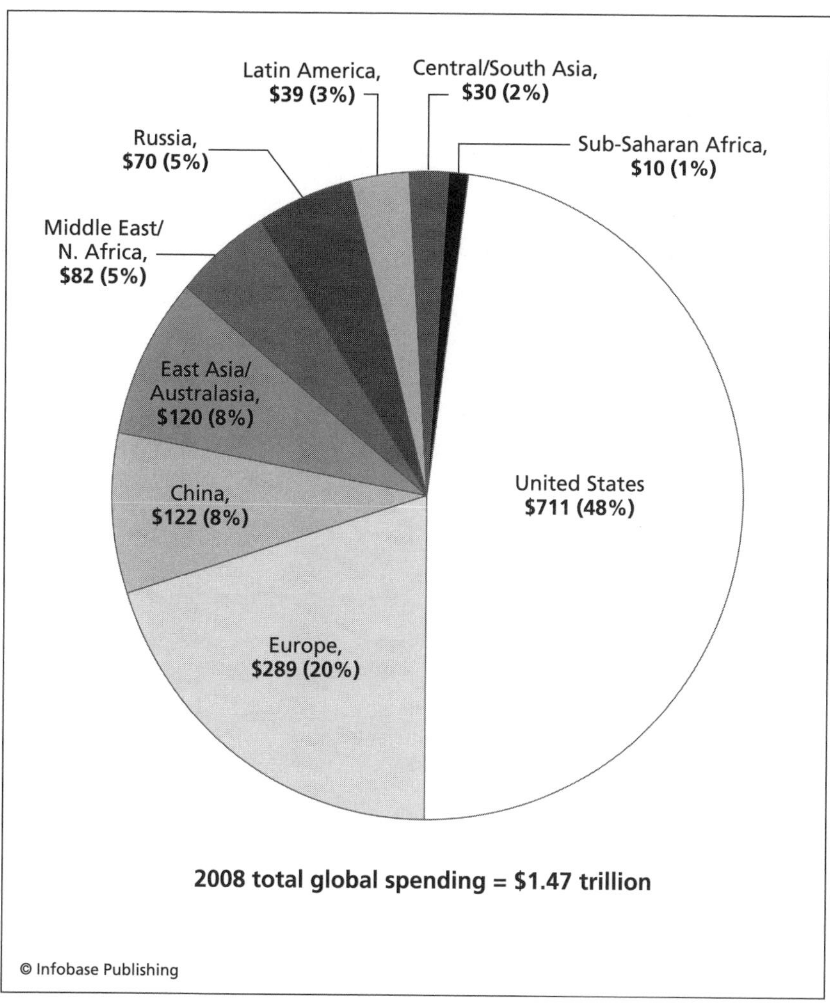

As this pie chart illustrates, in 2008 the U.S. military expenditure was nearly equal to the combined military expenditure of the rest of the world. Numbers are in billions of U.S. dollars, with percentage of total global. The total for the United States is the FY 2009 request and includes $170 billion for military operations in Iraq and Afghanistan, as well as funding for DOE nuclear weapons activities. All other figures are projections based on 2006, the last year for which accurate data is available.

Source: International Institute for Strategic Studies, *The Military Balance 2008,* and Department of Defense.

Military Expenditure Increase, 1996–2005

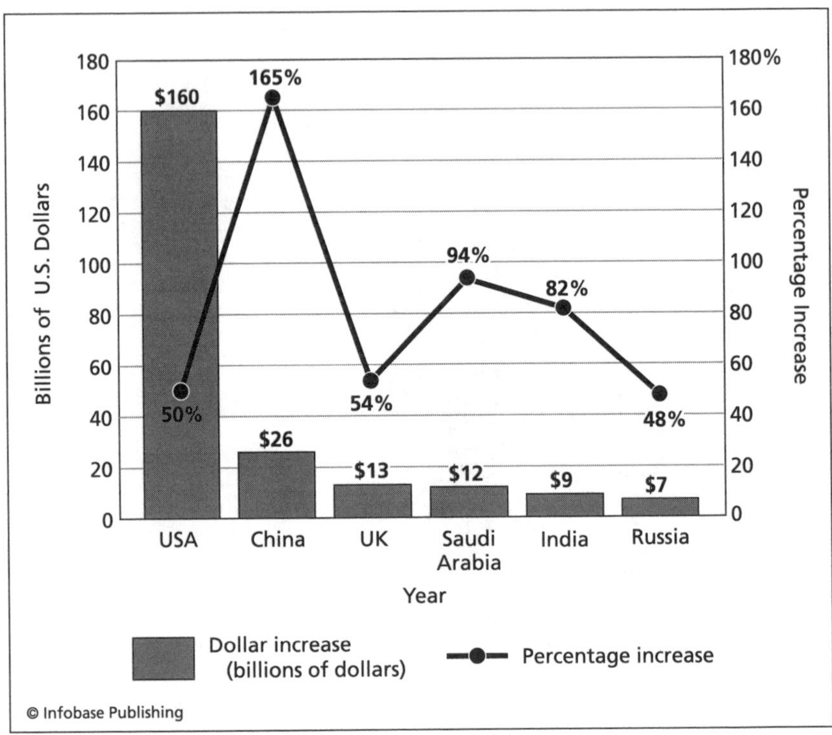

Already the world's largest, U.S. military expenditures rose by $160 billion between 1996 and 2005, in part due to the costs of wars in Afghanistan and Iraq. China's military spending increase, though smaller, represented a cumulative jump of 165 percent.

Source: Stockholm International Peace Research Institute, 2006

U.S. Troop Deployments (2008)

ACTIVE DUTY MILITARY PERSONNEL STRENGTHS

REGION	TOTAL	ARMY	NAVY	MARINE CORPS	AIR FORCE
Total - United States and Territories	1,083,027	451,757	221,038	141,526	268,706
Total - Foreign Countries	290,178	71,280	111,120	47,819	59,959
NATO Countries	81,709	45,831	4,215	662	31,001
Forward Deployment Pacific Theater	74,016	20,483	15,916	15,066	22,551
Total - Worldwide	**1,373,205**	**523,037**	**332,158**	**189,345**	**328,665**

DEPLOYMENTS (NOT COMPLETE—ROUNDED STRENGTHS)

	TOTAL	ARMY	NAVY	MARINE CORPS	AIR FORCE
Operation Iraqi Freedon (OIF) (Active Component portion of strength included in above)					
Total (in/around Iraq as of March 31, 2008) Includes deployed Reserve/National Guard	195,000	126,000	20,800	27,100	21,100
Operation Enduring Freedom (OEF) (Active Component portion of strength included in above)					
Total (in/around Afghanistan as of March 31, 2008) Includes Deployed Reserve/National Guard	31,100	22,500	1,000	2,700	4,900
* Deployed From Locations for OIF/OEF (other than U.S.) (Active Component portion of strength included in country)					
Germany	14,200	12,300	0	0	1,900
Italy	2,500	2,100	100	0	300
Japan	2,100	200	400	1,100	400
Korea	100	100	0	0	0
United Kingdom	400	0	0	0	400

Source: Department of Defense Personnel & Procurement Statistics. Department of Defense. Available online. URL: http://siadapp.dmdc.osd.mil/personnel/MILITARY/history/hst0803.pdf. Accessed March 9, 2009.

GLOBAL PERSPECTIVES

Top 25 World Companies, 2008

COMPANY	2008 RANK	2007 RANK	BUSINESS	COUNTRY	2006 REVENUES ($MILLIONS)
Wal-Mart	1	1	Retailing	United States	378,799
Exxon Mobil	2	2	Oil	United States	372,824
Royal Dutch Shell	3	3	Oil	Netherlands	355,782
BP	4	4	Oil	UK	291,438
Toyota	5	6	Carmaker	Japan	230,201
Chevron	6	6	Oil	United States	210,783
ING Group	7	13	Financial Conglomerate	Netherlands	201,516
Total	8	10	Oil	France	187,280
General Motors	9	5	Carmaker	United States	182,347
Conoco-Phillips	10	9	Oil	United States	178,558
Daimler	11	8	Carmaker	Germany	177,167
General Electric	12	11	Energy/ Manufacturing	United States	176,656
Ford Motor	13	12	Carmaker	United States	172,468
Fortis	14	20	Banking	Netherlands	164,877
AXA	15	15	Insurance	France	162,762
Sinopec	16	14	Oil	China	159,620
Citigroup	17	14	Banking	United States	159,229
Volkswagen	18	16	Carmaker	Germany	149,054
Dexla Group	19	36	Banking	Belgium	147,648
HSB Holdings	20	22	Banking	UK	146,500
BNP Paribas	21	25	Banking	France	140,726
Allianz	22	19	Insurance	Germany	140,618
Credit Agricole	23	18	Banking	France	138,155
State Grid	24	29	Energy	China	132,885
China National Petroleum	25	24	Oil	China	129,798

Source: Fortune http://money.cnn.com/magazines/fortune/global500/2008/

World's Top Brands and their Countries

BRAND	VALUE (BILLIONS OF DOLLARS)	COUNTRY
Coca Cola	67.5	United States
Microsoft	59.9	United States
IBM	53.4	United States
General Electric	50	United States
Intel	35.6	United States
Nokia	26.5	Finland
Disney	26.4	United States
McDonald's	26	United States
Toyota	24.8	Japan
Marlboro	21.1	United States

According to a five-year survey by the consultancy firm Interbrand, U.S. firms made up more than half of the top 10 and the top 100 most valuable world brands. Interbrand's survey showed little changed in the top five since 2001. Japan's Toyota increased its brand value by 10 percent to $24.8 billion. US carmaker Ford only managed to be 22 on the list, slipping two places from last year—and in 2001 it had been number eight.

New companies in the top 100 included the delivery group UPS, Internet search engine Google, drug firm Novartis (all U.S. companies) Spanish chain Zara, vehicle maker Hyundai, luxury goods company Bulgari, and electronics group LG.

Source: Interbrand, via BBC News

Widening Deficit

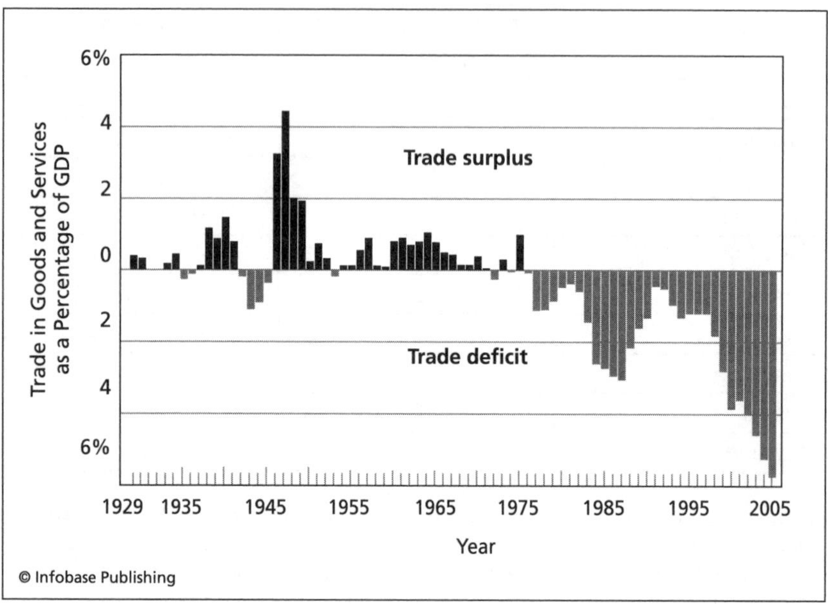

Starting in the 1970s, the total value of imports to the United States began to exceed the value of its exports.

Source: Bureau of Economic Analysis

Status of Nuclear Weapons and Their Nuclear Capabilities

		United States	Russia	United Kingdom	France	China	Israel	India	Pakistan	North Korea	Total
Weapons	Stockpile	5,400	14,000	~185	348+	~240	~100	~60-70	~60	<19	~20,400
	Deliverable	4,075	5,549	<160	348	~193	~80	~60	~60	?	~10,540
ICBM	Number	488	453			26					~970
	Warheads	764	1,743			26				?	~2,530
SRBM, IRBM, MRBM	Number					~100	50	<58	<150		<350
	Warheads					~100	~50	~20	~35	?	~200
SLBM	Number	288	176	50	48	(12)					~570
	Warheads	1,728	624	<144	288	(12)					~2,796
Strategic Bombers	Number	114	78			~100					~192
	Warheads	1,083	872			Bombs DH-10 LACM	~20 ~15				~1,990
Theater Weapons	Number				?	?					
	Warheads	500	2,330		ASMP 60	Bombs ~20	~30	Bombs	~25	?	~3,000

ABM: Anti-Ballistic Missile; ALCM: Air-Launched Cruise Missile; DF: Dong-Feng; ICBM: Intercontinental Ballistic Missile; IRBM; Intermediate-Range Ballistic Missile; JL: Julang; LACM: Land-Attack Cruise Missile; MRBM: Medium-Range Ballistic Missile; SLBM: Sea-Launched Ballistic Missile; SLCM: Sea-Launched Cruise Missile; SRBM: Short-Range Ballistic; SSBN: Nuclear-Powered Ballistic Missile Submarine: TD: Taepo Dong.

Source: Federation of American Scientists

8

Key Players A to Z

JOHN ADAMS (1735–1826) Founding father and second president of the United States from 1797 to 1801. He was an influential delegate from Massachusetts to the First and Second Continental Congresses and signed the Declaration of Independence in 1776. He served as the first U.S. vice president from 1789 to 1796 and succeeded GEORGE WASHINGTON as president in 1797.

JOHN QUINCY ADAMS (1767–1848) Son of JOHN ADAMS and the sixth president of the United States, serving from 1825 to 1829. Before assuming the presidency, Adams was secretary of state in the Monroe administration (1817–25), during which time he engineered the acquisition of Florida from Spain and arranged with England for the joint occupation of Oregon. His most notable accomplishment was the formulation of the Monroe Doctrine, which declared U.S. opposition to European nations meddling in the affairs of the Western Hemisphere. Adams is also famous for his vigorous post-presidency. As a congressman from the district of Plymouth, Massachusetts, from 1830 until his death, Adams opposed slavery, Andrew Jackson's forced removal of American Indian tribes, and the invasion of Mexico.

ETHAN ALLEN (1738–89) Hero of the American Revolution, leader of a militia group known as the Green Mountain Boys. At the outbreak of the American Revolution, Allen and Colonel Benedict Arnold captured Fort Ticonderoga in the first colonial victory of the war. Allen was an outspoken religious freethinker, publishing his views in a 1784 pamphlet entitled *Reason, the Only Oracle of Man.* "I have generally been denominated a Deist, the reality of which I never disputed, being conscious I am no Christian, except mere infant baptism makes me one; and as to being a Deist, I know not strictly speaking, whether I am one or not."

Key Players A to Z

SALVADOR ALLENDE (1908–73) Leftist Chilean politician. In 1933 he helped to found the Chilean Socialist Party, a Marxist organization that opposed the Soviet-influenced Communist Party. In 1970, in a time of economic turmoil for Chile, he became Chile's president in a free democratic election. Allende initiated a comprehensive program of land reform, nationalization, and price fixing, and restored Chile's diplomatic relations with Cuba, China, and East Germany. In 1973, his government was overthrown and Allende himself died—allegedly a suicide—during a violent coup that was encouraged, if not directed, by the United States. The military regime that took power after the coup wiped out the leftist opposition by means of systematic kidnappings and assassinations, while receiving support from the United States.

ALBERT J. BEVERIDGE (1862–1927) U.S. senator from Indiana from 1899 to 1911. He was a powerful orator and a staunch advocate of expanded federal power and U.S. overseas expansion. After the completion of his second Senate term he retired from elective politics and became an acclaimed historian. He was awarded a Pulitzer Prize for his *Life of John Marshall,* published in four volumes from 1916 to 1919.

JAMES G. BLAINE (1830–93) American politician. He served in the U.S. Congress and was secretary of state from 1889 to 1892. He was an ardent supporter of U.S. expansionism and increased investment in Latin America.

LEONID BREZHNEV (1906–82) Leader of the Soviet Union from the mid-1960s until his death in 1982. A lifelong Communist Party politician, in 1964 he was one of a small group appointed to the leadership by the Politburo after NIKITA KHRUSHCHEV was ousted from office. Brezhnev gradually rose to unchallenged power, and since he had been appointed as part of a conservative reaction against Khrushchev's attempts at reform, he resisted reform and presided over an economically and politically stagnant Soviet Union.

WILLIAM JENNINGS BRYAN (1860–1925) Secretary of state and three-time Democratic Party nominee for president of the United States. Nicknamed the Great Commoner, Bryan was a prominent leader of populism in the United States during the late 19th and early 20th centuries. Among the issues he supported were free silver, anti-imperialism, and trust-busting. Bryan was appointed secretary of state in 1913, an office he resigned in 1916 in protest against what he viewed as provocative statements by President Woodrow Wilson toward Germany prior to U.S. entry in World War I. A devout Christian, Bryan was a strong supporter of Prohibition and a passionate crusader against

Darwinism, which culminated in the Scopes Trial in 1925. He died five days after the case was decided.

AARON BURR (1756–1836) The third vice president of the United States from 1801 to 1805. He is best remembered today for his tie vote with THOMAS JEFFERSON in the 1800 election, for killing Alexander Hamilton in a duel in 1804, and for his 1807 treason trial that resulted from his mysterious plan to invade Mexico. He was accused of conspiring to steal Louisiana Purchase lands away from the United States and crown himself a king or emperor and attempting to declare an illegal war against Spanish possessions in Mexico. Burr was arrested in 1807 and brought to trial on charges of treason, for which he was acquitted. After several years in self-imposed exile in Europe, Burr returned to practicing law in New York City.

GEORGE H. W. BUSH (1924–) President of the United States from 1989 to 1993. Born on June 12, 1924, George H. W. Bush became the 41st president of the United States. After the dissolution of the Soviet Union in 1991, President Bush and Soviet president MIKHAIL GORBACHEV declared a U.S.-Soviet partnership, acknowledging the end of the cold war. While Bush's foreign policy toward the new nations that resulted from the breakup of the Soviet Union was restrained, he was very active in the use of American military force in other parts of the world. In 1991, in response to Iraqi president SADDAM HUSSEIN's invasion and annexation of Kuwait and threat to move into Saudi Arabia, Bush launched the Gulf War and led the United Nations coalition in an invasion of Iraq. The U.S. military operations, dubbed Desert Shield and Desert Storm, succeeded in driving Saddam out of Kuwait. In a decision that would later be thrown into question, Bush chose to leave Saddam Hussein in power. Later, he would explain that his reason for not overthrowing the Iraqi government was that it would have "incurred incalculable human and political costs . . . We would have been forced to occupy Baghdad and, in effect, rule Iraq." President Bush sent American troops into Panama to overthrow the corrupt regime of General MANUEL NORIEGA, who had formerly held power with American support. The popularity that Bush earned as a result of his military triumph in the Gulf War was not sufficient to overcome voters' dissatisfaction with his domestic policies and he was defeated in his bid to earn reelection by BILL CLINTON.

GEORGE WALKER BUSH (1946–) Governor of Texas from 1995 to 2000 and president of the United States from 2001 to 2009. The eldest son of former president GEORGE HERBERT WALKER BUSH, George W. Bush became president in an intensely controversial election only after the Supreme Court—in a move that itself was widely regarded as controversial and partisan—ordered a halt to the recount of votes in the state of Florida. In response to the September 11, 2001, attacks on the United States, Bush announced a global war on terrorism. He proceeded to order an invasion of Afghanistan to overthrow the Taliban, destroy al-Qaeda, and capture OSAMA BIN LADEN. In March 2003, Bush ordered the invasion of Iraq, asserting that Iraq was in violation of UN Security Council Resolution 1441 and that the war was necessary for the protection of the United States. During his first term as president Bush announced a foreign policy principle that became known as the Bush doctrine, stating that because of the existence of rogue states and terrorist organizations the United States must be prepared to wage preventive war against emerging threats. Bush surrounded himself with advisers who believed in a stronger executive power with a great deal of independence from the influence of the other branches of government.

ANDREW CARNEGIE (1835–1919) American steel tycoon and philanthropist. The son of a radical Scottish handloom weaver who emigrated to the United States in 1848, Carnegie became one of the richest men in the world, while continuing to hold egalitarian political views that put him at odds with his fellow plutocrats. He opposed the United States's annexation of the Philippines.

JIMMY CARTER (1924–) President of the United States from 1977 to 1981. Taking office soon after the traumatic U.S. defeat in the Vietnam War, the forced resignation of President Richard Nixon, and the caretaker government of President Gerald Ford (the only president not elected to national office), Carter announced that the United States would pursue a foreign policy based on support for human rights around the world. A peacemaker, Carter helped negotiate a treaty between Egypt and Israel and obtained ratification in the United States for controversial treaties that ceded control of the Panama Canal to Panama. Building on the work of his predecessors, he established full diplomatic relations with China and completed negotiation of the SALT II nuclear limitation treaty with the Soviet Union. Before the end of Carter's term his gentle foreign policy seemed unrewarding for the United States or Carter's own political prospects. The Soviet invasion of Afghanistan caused the suspension of plans for the ratification of the SALT II pact. After an Islamic fundamentalist revolution in Iran in 1979, radical Iranian students seized over 50 hostages at the American embassy—for 14 months their captivity dominated the headlines, contributing to Carter's defeat after one term in office.

FIDEL CASTRO (1926–) Marxist revolutionary and premier of Cuba. He overthrew the U.S.-supported government of Fulgencio Batista in 1959 and ruled Cuba from then until 2006 when he announced that he was transferring his political responsibilities to his brother Raúl. During Castro's long term of office, Cuba was economically isolated by the United States. It was given economic and diplomatic support by the Soviet Union, and Cuban troops fought with Soviet-leaning groups around the world. In 1961, soon after President John F. Kennedy took office in the United States, Cuba foiled the Bay of Pigs invasion, an attempt to overthrow Castro by Cuban exiles with the help of the Central Intelligence Agency. The following year Castro permitted the Soviet Union to install medium-range nuclear missiles in Cuba, leading to a tense 13-day standoff between the United States and the Soviet Union.

GEORGE CATLIN (1796–1872) American painter. Catlin produced two major collections of paintings recording the life of Native Americans in the Old West and published a series of books about his travels among the native peoples of North, Central, and South America. He considered U.S. expansion inevitable, but regretted its destructiveness toward Native Americans and their way of life.

NICOLAE CEAUŞESCU (1918–89) Communist party leader and the unchallenged dictator of Romania. He remained in the role of dictator from 1965 until his death by firing squad in the most violent of the transitions that occurred when the Soviet Union relaxed its hold on eastern Europe in the late 1980s. While he charted a relatively independent foreign policy for Romania, often defying Soviet Russia with impunity, Ceauşescu was a totalitarian leader in the Stalinist mold.

DICK CHENEY (1941–) U.S. vice president in the George W. Bush administration. He is widely regarded as the most powerful man ever to occupy that office, with influence exceeding that of most if not all of Bush's cabinet members. An extremely partisan and controversial figure, he repeatedly asserted in the run-up to the 2003 Iraq invasion that there was a connection between al-Qaeda and Iraq, despite contrary claims from the Pentagon. Cheney served in several positions in the Nixon administration, was White House chief of staff in the Ford administration, and secretary of defense in the administration of George H. W. Bush. From 1995 to 2000, without prior business experience, he was chairman and chief executive officer of Halliburton, a Fortune 500 company with interests in the energy and defense industries. This connection, which made Cheney wealthy, became controversial when Halliburton won lucrative multibillion-dollar contracts to work in Iraq following the 2003 Iraq invasion.

CHIANG KAI-SHEK (1887–1975) Leader of the Kuomintang, the Chinese Nationalist Party. He assumed the role soon after the death of its founder and first leader, Sun Yat-sen, and fought to unify China in the 1920s and 1930s, sometimes in opposition to Mao Zedong's communist army and sometimes in temporary alliance with it. After the bombing of Pearl Harbor, Chiang and his government began to receive significant amounts of financial support from the United States, against the advice of an American commander, General Joseph Stillwell, who maintained that Chiang was an inept military leader. In the civil war that followed the defeat of Japan, the communists led by Mao Zedong defeated Chiang's Nationalists. The People's Republic of China was established on the Chinese mainland, while Chiang and the remainder of his forces fled to the island of Taiwan (then called Formosa). Until the early 1970s, the United States maintained that Chiang's small island state was the only true China, and Taiwan occupied the permanent Chinese seat on the United Nations Security Council.

GENERAL WESLEY CLARK (1944–) Four-star general of the U.S. Army. Clark commanded Operation Allied Force in the Kosovo War during his term as Supreme Allied Commander Europe of NATO from 1997 to 2000. He retired from the army in May 2000.

WILLIAM JEFFERSON CLINTON (1946–) President of the United States from 1993 to 2001. Early in his presidency a U.S. humanitarian mission in Somalia came to grief when photos of a U.S. soldier being dragged through the streets of Mogadishu were flashed around the world. Fearing for his domestic agenda, Clinton pulled U.S. troops out hastily and shied away from future U.S. military interventions that involved the use of ground forces. Though apparently reluctant to expand the United States's long-term military commitments, Clinton used the military several times during his two-term presidency, intervening in Haiti to restore its president, Jean-Bertrand Aristide, to office, bombing Iraq when its dictator Saddam Hussein expelled UN weapons inspectors, launching a cruise missile strike against al-Qaeda camps in Afghanistan, and, working with NATO, sending U.S. troops into the former Yugoslavia to stop the ethnic cleansing perpetrated by Serbs against Muslims in Bosnia and Kosovo.

CALVIN COOLIDGE (1872–1933) President of the United States from 1923 to 1929. Vice president under Warren G. Harding, Coolidge became president following Harding's death on August 2, 1923. He served until 1929, having announced without explanation, "I do not choose to run for president in 1928." Coolidge was an extremely uninvolved and inactive president and the country seemed to like it: the U.S. economy boomed, and the boom was referred to as Coolidge prosperity. However, hidden weaknesses in the U.S. economic structure led to the depression that began soon after his successor, Herbert Hoover, took office.

MILTON FRIEDMAN (1912–2006) Influential economist of the 20th century. Friedman was an advocate of free-market economics and an opponent of the economic policies that were prevalent in Europe and the United States in the mid-20th century. Much of Friedman's technical thinking centers on the relationship between money supply and prices. His views are often summed up in the term *monetarism,* the theory that price levels are directly related to the money supply. In the 1960s, while most economists believed that a certain amount of inflation had the beneficial effect of tending to increase employment, Friedman maintained that while permitting or encouraging inflation in the short term increased employment, an accelerating (and therefore, dangerous) inflation was necessary to sustain that effect. To achieve sustained high employment and productivity he recommended that the U.S. government follow the money supply rule—requiring that the Federal Reserve increase the money supply at the same rate as the real GNP increased: Inflation would then disappear. Freidman's medicine seemed right for the economic woes of the 1970s, when the United States and other countries faced both runaway inflation and low employment. His name became familiar to noneconomists in the 1980s when Ronald Reagan and Margaret Thatcher adopted many of his recommendations. In addition to his monetarist views, Friedman was a modern advocate of laissez-faire capitalism, vigorously promoting his conviction that the unrestricted free market could bring universal prosperity. He provided the intellectual underpinnings for the neoliberal policies that the United States and the International Monetary Fund have promoted around the world over the last 25 years and receives credit and blame for the effects of economic shock therapy in Latin America, Russia, and eastern Europe.

DAVID FRUM (1960–) Neoconservative journalist and scholar. Frum was a speechwriter for George W. Bush and is widely credited with having come up with the phrase axis of evil (in Frum's original suggestion axis of hatred) for Bush's 2002 State of the Union address. In *An End to Evil,* cowritten with Richard Perle, Frum provides a defense of the 2003 invasion of Iraq and advocates regime change in Iran and Syria.

FRANCIS FUKUYAMA (1952–) American philosopher and political economist. Fukuyama specializes in the study of political and economic development. He is best known for his 1992 book, *The End of History.* In the 1990s he was identified with neoconservatives, sharing their view of the benign influence of American military power. Following the 2003 Iraq invasion he began to criticize neoconservative influence on U.S. policy.

JOHN KENNETH GALBRAITH (1908–2006) Influential American economist. Galbraith was a Keynesian who served in the presidential administrations of Franklin Roosevelt, Harry Truman, and John F. Kennedy. In a best-selling book *The Affluent Society* (1958), Galbraith argues that economics functions differently in the present age of affluence than it did in previous eras of poverty. According to Galbraith, the affluent society is one in which companies create new needs through advertising, private goods are overprovided, while public goods—such as clean air and good public education—are underprovided.

MIKHAIL GORBACHEV (1931–) Leader of the Soviet Union from 1985 to 1991. The last Soviet leader, Gorbachev was instrumental in bringing about the end of the cold war. Taking an active role in relaxing the tensions between the United States and the Soviet Union, Gorbachev met with President Reagan and President Bush nine times over the years between 1985 and 1991. In 1987 he signed the INF treaty (intermediate nuclear forces arms limitation treaty) with President Reagan, and in 1991 he signed the START I (Strategic Arms Reduction Treaty) treaty with President Bush (Sr.). Gorbachev reached out to many other world leaders, withdrawing Soviet troops from Afghanistan in 1989 and removing Soviet support of communist governments around the globe, actions that resulted in the collapse of the Berlin Wall in 1989 and the slow breakup of the Soviet Union. In 1990 Gorbachev was awarded the Nobel Peace Prize. In 1991 Gorbachev's power was significantly diminished after what turned out to be an unsuccessful communist coup in Russia, and he resigned as Soviet president on December 25 of that year, thus marking the end of the Soviet Union.

HORACE GREELEY (1811–72) American journalist, founder and editor of the *New York Tribune*. Within its pages Greeley vigorously promoted a wide assortment of views, including utopian socialism, opposition to slavery and capital punishment, and support for the distribution of free government land to settlers. He is remembered for the phrase, "Go west young man, and grow with the country."

WARREN G. HARDING (1865–1923) President of the United States from 1921 to 1923. A handsome, personable man but an undistinguished politician, Harding staffed his administration with a group of home-town cronies historians have dubbed the "Ohio gang." He is remembered for the isolationist views he pronounced in his inaugural speech and for the rampant corruption of his administration, which became known after his death.

CORDELL HULL (1871–1955) American politician, U.S. secretary of state from 1933 to 1944, a 12-year period that was the longest time anyone has yet held that office. Like FRANKLIN ROOSEVELT, in whose administration he served, Hull was an internationalist. In the 1930s he advocated American rearmament to prepare for the coming war, and he was later deeply involved in the creation of the United Nations.

SAMUEL P. HUNTINGTON (1927–) Conservative political scientist. He is best known for his suggestion, put forward in a 1993 essay "The Clash of Civilizations?" that in the 21st century conflicts will result from cultural rather than ideological differences. In *Who Are We? The Challenges to America's National Identity,* Huntington argues that large-scale immigration from Latin America could "divide the United States into two peoples, two cultures, and two languages."

SADDAM HUSSEIN (1937–2006) Dictator of Iraq from 1979 until 2003. His regime was overthrown in 2003 by a United States–led invasion. Under his rule, Iraq was engaged in a decade-long war with Iran and in August 1990 his forces invaded Kuwait. GEORGE H. W. BUSH, with the help of a broad alliance, succeeded in running Hussein's forces out of Kuwait in the Gulf War. The war ended in 1991 with Hussein still in power. In March of 2003, under the leadership of the second president George Bush, U.S. and British forces succeeded in overthrowing Hussein's regime. Hussein, who went into hiding after the invasion, was captured by U.S. forces on December 13, 2001. On December 30, he was executed by hanging in Baghdad.

THOMAS JEFFERSON (1743–1826) Principal author of the Declaration of Independence (1776) and the third president of the United States (1801–09). Prior to assuming the presidency he was the first secretary of state and the second vice president. Jefferson's greatest success as president was in the area of foreign affairs. Most significant among his accomplishments was the Louisiana Purchase (1803), in which he doubled the size of America by purchasing 800,000 square miles of uncharted territory from Spain for $11.25 million. Even before the treaty was signed, Jefferson planned an expedition to explore this country. The legendary Lewis and Clark expedition (led by Meriwether Lewis [1774–1809] and William Clark [1770–1838]) explored the land gained in the Louisiana Purchase, and the expedition became a spectacular product of Jefferson's vision of westward expansion.

LYNDON JOHNSON (1908–73) President of the United States, serving from the death of John F. Kennedy in November 1963 to 1969. A long career in the House of Representatives and the Senate made Johnson a skillful legislator, an ability he used to his advantage as president in promoting progressive social programs such as the Civil Rights Act of 1964, Medicare, and a comprehensive antipoverty program he called the Great Society. Johnson's popularity and his hopes for the Great Society foundered due to his decision to increase America's involvement in the war in Vietnam. In March 1968, when protests against the war were at their height, Johnson shocked the nation with his decision not to seek another term as president.

ROBERT KAGAN (1958–) Influential neoconservative scholar and political commentator. In 1997 he cofounded the Project for a New American Century with fellow neoconservative William Kristol; former secretary of defense and future vice president DICK CHENEY was also a founding member. Kagan is best known for his 2003 book, *Paradise and Power,* which analyzes America's relationship with Europe and maintains that it is America's guarantee of European security that gives Europeans the luxury to take an antiwar stance.

GEORGE KENNAN (1904–2005) American diplomat and historian. Kennan was considered a leading authority on the cold war. His writings inspired the Truman Doctrine and the West's policy of containment toward Soviet communism, which he articulated in his article "The Sources of Soviet Conduct," published in *Foreign Affairs* in 1947. He took a number of controversial positions, including opposing the division of Germany after World War II and American participation in the Korean and Vietnam Wars and the 2003 invasion of Iraq. An early opponent of nuclear weapons, he opposed the development of the hydrogen bomb.

PAUL KENNEDY (1945–) British historian specializing in international relations. He has written books about the history of the Royal Navy, the Great Power struggles, and the Pacific War. His most famous book, *The Rise and Fall of the Great Powers,* concerns the interaction between great powers' relative economic strength (relative to other countries) and their military and diplomatic commitments. Kennedy's book makes its case by following the rise and fall of several imperial powers since 1500. His most recent book, *The Parliament of Man,* is about the history of the United Nations.

JOHN MAYNARD KEYNES (1883–1946) British economist. Keynes's theories became the orthodoxy of his field for four decades and profoundly influenced government behavior in the wake of the Great Depression and

World War II. A founder of modern theoretical macroeconomics, Keynes recommended that governments use fiscal and monetary measures to mitigate the adverse effects of economic recessions, depressions, and booms. In his most influential work, *The General Theory of Employment, Interest, and Money,* Keynes argued that macroeconomic relationships differ from their microeconomic counterparts, and he disagreed with the theory—accepted in classical economics—that the market ultimately and automatically settles on a state of full employment. Instead, he held that many self-sustaining states of economic equilibrium were possible, including the equilibrium of low employment that evidently prevailed during the depression, when Keynes was writing.

ROUHOLLAH MOUSAVI KHOMEINI (1902–89) Shii Muslim cleric and the political leader of the 1979 Iranian Revolution. The revolution overthrew SHAH REZA PAHLAVI and established Iran as an Islamic fundamentalist state under the government of God, as Khomeini put it. Khomeini's personal popularity and political skills helped him suppress secular-minded allies once the shah had been driven from the country, and he established a theocracy of Islamic clerics as the ultimate rulers of the nation, able to veto the actions of the democratically elected leaders below them. Khomeini's rule was further solidified during a desperate war with Iraq, which solidified national unity. Fiercely anti-American, anti-British, and anti-Israeli, he supported terrorism against U.S. and Israeli targets around the world and remained Iran's supreme leader until his death.

MARTIN LUTHER KING, JR. (1929–68) Prominent leader of the American civil rights movement of the 1950s and 1960s. A Baptist minister, King began his career as a civil rights activist when he led black residents in the boycott of Montgomery, Alabama, buses. In December 1956, the U.S. Supreme Court declared Alabama's segregation laws unconstitutional. Building on the national prominence he had gained for his success in the boycott, King was elected leader of the Southern Christian Leadership Conference (SCLC), an organization of black churches and ministers he helped found. SCLC was created to provide leadership for the now-burgeoning civil rights movement and in the ensuing years it led protests against racial segregation through marches, demonstrations, and boycotts. Influenced by Mahatma Gandhi, a believer in peaceful civil disobedience, King advocated that the African-American protests against segregation and racial discrimination be nonviolent. King was assassinated in 1968.

RUDYARD KIPLING (1865–1936) English journalist, poet, short story writer, and novelist. He was born in Bombay (today, Mumbai) and educated in England. Kipling's writings depicted and sometimes glorified British imperialism. His poem "The White Man's Burden" (1899) written when the United States was involved in a war suppressing native independence in the Philippines, appears to invite Americans to join the British in the imperialist enterprise of governing and (supposedly) civilizing non-European peoples.

HENRY KISSINGER (1923–) German-born American political scientist. Kissinger served as national security advisor and secretary of state in Richard Nixon and Gerald Ford's administrations. A controversial figure, Kissinger has been credited with the successful cold war strategy of establishing closer U.S. relations with the People's Republic of China, thereby exploiting the Sino-Soviet split, and he has been accused of war crimes for his policies in Vietnam, Cambodia, and East Timor, and the U.S.–supported coup that deposed Chile's elected leader Salvador Allende.

WILLIAM KRISTOL (1952–) Neoconservative writer, journalist, Republican strategist, and media pundit. As chairman of the Project for a Republican Future in 1993, Kristol argued that Republicans should "kill," not amend or compromise, the Clinton health care plan, because the success of the Clinton program would "revive . . . the Democrats, as the generous protectors of middle-class interests." In 1994, Kristol cofounded *The Weekly Standard,* an influential conservative magazine. Kristol was a strong advocate of the 2003 invasion of Iraq, in the run-up to which he dismissed the "pop sociology," of those who suggested "that the Shia can't get along with the Sunni," a statement that invited criticism later when Iraq descended into sectarian violence. Since January 2008, he has written a weekly column for the op-ed page of the *New York Times.*

PAUL KRUGMAN (1953–) American economist, author, professor at Princeton University, and political pundit. Krugman is highly critical of the domestic and foreign policies of the George W. Bush administration. Since January 2000, he has contributed a twice-weekly column to the op-ed page of the *New York Times.*

ABRAHAM LINCOLN (1809–65) President of the United States from 1861 to 1865. Shortly after his election, the Civil War broke out. Initially, Lincoln declared that the war was being fought over secession rather than slavery, but later, in 1863, Lincoln, redefined the war as a crusade against slavery with the Emancipation Proclamation. In 1865, he oversaw the passage of the Thirteenth Amendment, which legally ended slavery. In his Gettysburg Address, delivered in 1863, Lincoln further defined his conception of the war as a struggle for preservation of the democratic idea of "government of the people, by the people, for the people." Lincoln was assassinated by John Wilkes Booth in Ford's Theatre in 1865.

GONZALO SANCHEZ LOZADO (1930–) Bolivian businessman, politician, and former president. He is known for using economic shock therapy to combat runaway inflation in Bolivia and for moving Bolivia from a state-planned to a free-market economy. He served two separate terms as Bolivian president, 1993–97 and 2002–03. In 2003, amid widespread social and political unrest, Lozado resigned, passing the presidency to his vice president.

ALFRED THAYER MAHAN (1840–1914) American naval historian. He argued that the strength of a country's navy was the key to a strong foreign policy. His views were expressed in his 1890 work, *The Influence of Sea Power Upon History, 1660–1783.* Appearing at the time of an international arms race and a scramble for empire, Mahan's analysis had a profound influence on the naval policies of Japan, France, Germany, and the United States.

MAO ZEDONG (1893–1976) Chinese military and political leader. He led the Communist Party of China to victory over the Kuomintang, or Nationalist Party, and was the absolute ruler of the People's Republic of China from its establishment in 1949 until his death. The center of a Stalin-style personality cult in his lifetime, Mao is still revered in China as the man who unified the country, rid it of foreign domination, and enabled it to become, once again, a world power. Mao Zedong was in fact as responsible as any one man can be for these accomplishments. He was also a totalitarian ruler who suppressed freedom of thought and action. He used his unquestioned power to impose drastic and ill-advised programs like the Great Leap Forward and the Cultural Revolution, which caused immediate human suffering and long-lasting damage to Chinese society.

WILLIAM MCKINLEY (1843–1901) President of the United States from 1897 to 1901. He was president during the Spanish-American War. A reluctant imperialist, McKinley gave into popular sentiment when the U.S. Congress voted a series of resolutions that in effect declared war on Spain. He permitted subordinates to push him into the conquest of the Philippines, a Spanish possession that the United States later annexed and where it suppressed a native independence movement. McKinley was assassinated early in his second term in 1901.

LUDWIG VON MISES (1881–1973) Austrian economist and social philosopher. His theories of classic liberalism—which echo Adam Smith's praise of the free market and are even more hostile to government intervention—are frequently cited as an influence by modern conservatives.

JAMES MONROE (1758–1831) President of the United States from 1817 to 1825. The major accomplishments of his presidency were the acquisition of Florida in 1819; the Missouri Compromise (1820), which declared Missouri a slave state, and, with then-secretary of state John Quincy Adams, the statement of the Monroe Doctrine (1823), in which the United States declared its opposition to European interference in the Americas.

MOHAMMED MOSADDEQ (1882–1967) Prime minister of Iran from 1951 to 1953. He was deposed by a coup d'état supported and funded by the British and American governments. He was appointed to the post of prime minister by the young SHAH REZA PAHLAVI. Though very popular in Iran, where he was admired for his fiery speeches opposing British control of Iran's oil industry, Mosaddeq had authoritarian tendencies, conducting a national referendum to win approval for the dissolution of Parliament. Not a communist himself, he was supported by the communists, which helped turn the United States against him. In 1953, an attempt by the shah to dismiss Mosaddeq led to angry street demonstrations and the shah fled the country. Possibly believing that Iran under Mosaddeq would align itself with the Soviet Union, the United States helped engineer a coup in which Mosaddeq was arrested and the shah restored to the throne. Mosaddeq served three years in prison and for the rest of his life was confined to his estate near Tehran.

PERVEZ MUSHARRAF (1943–) President of Pakistan (2001–08) and the chief of staff of the Pakistani army (1991–2007). He assumed power in 1999 by means of a military coup d'état, ousting Nawaz Sharif, the elected prime minister and dismissing the national and provincial legislative assemblies. Musharraf was the fourth army chief to assume executive control since the country's founding in 1947. He appointed himself president in 2001. Although prior to 2001, Pakistan had been one of the few countries in the world to support the extreme Islamic fundamentalist Taliban regime in Afghanistan, after 9/11 Musharraf decided that it would be wise to join the United States in its war on terror and he provided assistance in the U.S. invasion of Afghanistan. For Musharraf, ruling a country 97 percent of whose inhabitants are Muslims, many of whom support the Taliban, the last several years have been a difficult balancing act. There are tribal regions in Pakistan where the government has little control and it is widely believed that al-Qaeda's leader, OSAMA BIN LADEN, lives there. Bin Laden, who may have received funding from Musharraf in the past, has called for a holy war against Musharraf and his government. In 2007, rather than face an election as required by the Pakistani constitution, Musharraf declared a state of emergency, bringing his popularity in Pakistan to an all-time low. Many opinion makers around the world and in Pakistan have suggested that he leave gracefully and allow Pakistan's next leader to be chosen democratically, but there were just as many who feared the chaos of a nuclear-armed, possibly Islamic fundamentalist Pakistan. In August 2008, facing impeachment by a newly elected coalition government, Musharraf resigned.

RICHARD NIXON (1913–94) President of the United States from 1969 to 1973. During his terms as president, Nixon accomplished goals that are still widely admired, such as the establishment of relations with the People's Republic of China and the founding of the Environmental Protection Agency. His presidency has a dark legacy, however, in the futile bombing of North Vietnam and Cambodia—which killed many innocent people in both countries and destabilized Cambodia, helping the mass murderer Pol Pot to come to power—and in his systematic abuse of federal power for partisan political purposes. He resigned from office in 1974 after his efforts to conceal his role in the Watergate scandal were revealed.

MANUEL NORIEGA (1934–) Panamanian general and dictator of Panama from 1983 to 1989. At first an ally of the United States, Noriega was on the payroll of the Central Intelligence Agency from the late 1950s to the 1980s. Eventually, however, Noriega's human rights violations and drug-trafficking activities forced the United States to end the already uneasy alliance. In 1989 the United States invaded Panama for the express purpose of capturing Noriega, who was detained as a prisoner of war and taken to the United States. In 1992 he was convicted under federal charges of cocaine trafficking, racketeering, and money laundering in Miami, Florida, and sentenced to 40 years in prison. In 2007, after spending 18 years at Miami's Federal Correctional Institution, he was extradited to France to be tried for money laundering.

JOHN L. O'SULLIVAN (1813–95) American journalist. O'Sullivan favored westward expansion of the United States, especially annexation of Texas and the Oregon Territory. In 1845 he coined the term *Manifest Destiny,* believing that the United States had a God-given responsibility to spread democracy and Christianity across all of North America.

SHAH REZA PAHLAVI (1919–80) King of Iran from 1941 to 1979. He became shah in 1941 when the Soviet Union and Great Britain, concerned with Iran's overtures to Nazi Germany, forced his father to abdicate. The young shah cooperated with the allied war effort, making Iran a major avenue of supply to the USSR. After the war he became involved in a power struggle with his prime minister, Mohammed Mosaddeq, a popular leader who nationalized Iran's oil industry. When Shah Reza Pahlavi attempted to dismiss Mosaddeq in 1953, angry street demonstrations forced the shah to flee the country. Soon afterward, Mosaddeq was deposed and arrested in a coup d'état planned and funded by the United States and Great Britain and the shah was restored to the throne. For the remainder of his rule, the shah was a loyal ally of the United States, combining Western-style modernization and liberal reforms with political repression of his opponents. In the final years of his reign, his rule became increasingly despotic, and opposition to it grew. In 1979, as unrest in the country threatened to grow out of control, he left the country at the request of his prime minister, Shahpur Bakhtiar. Within a month, Ayatollah Khomeini, whom Bakhtiar had permitted to return from exile, had taken over the country in the name of the revolution. The shah, unpopular in the West, moved from country to country in the last year of his life, before President JIMMY CARTER reluctantly permitted him to visit the United States for treatment of cancer. In the last year of his life, the shah maintained that human rights advocates in the U.S. State Department were responsible for his ouster. "It is clear to me now that the United States wanted me out."

THOMAS PAINE (1737–1809) American revolutionary and political writer. Paine is best known as the author of the pamphlet *Common Sense* (1776), which urged the American colonies to declare their independence from Great Britain, and *The American Crisis,* a pamphlet supporting the Revolution. Later, Paine would be a great influence on the French Revolution. His pamphlet *The Rights of Man* (1791) promulgated the ideas of the Enlightenment. He became notorious with his book, *The Age of Reason* (1793–94), which advocated Deism and took issue with Christian doctrines.

RICHARD PERLE (1941–) Neoconservative analyst, author, and adviser, assistant secretary of defense during the Reagan administration, member of the Defense Policy Board Advisory Committee from 1987 to 2004. Within the Bush administration Perle was one of the most determined and influential voices arguing for an invasion of Iraq, for which he began to lobby immediately after the 9/11 attacks. On March 9, 2003, a *New Yorker* article by Seymour Hersh alleged that Perle had a conflict of interest: Due to his business connections with intelligence- and defense-related firms, he stood to profit from a war in Iraq. Perle, interviewed on CNN, said: "Sy Hersh is the closest thing American journalism has to a terrorist, frankly." In 2003 Perle and DAVID FRUM co-authored *An End to Evil,* a justification of the Iraq invasion.

AUGUSTO PINOCHET (1915–2006) Chilean army general, president, and military dictator from 1974 to 1990. In 1973, with U.S. backing, he overthrew the elected government of SALVADOR ALLENDE, who had naively appointed him commander in chief of the army. Pinochet initiated a systematic program of kidnappings, executions, and assassinations in which approximately 3,000 people were killed and 27,000 imprisoned without trials and tortured. Meanwhile, advised by a group of American-trained economists who adhered to the theories of MILTON FRIEDMAN and other leading monetarists, Pinochet embarked on a program of deregulation and privatization, rescinding the rights of trade unions, abolishing the minimum wage, privatizing the pension system, and lowering income taxes. The effects of these neoliberal economic policies continue to be widely contested, with some acclaiming them as a great success, since they brought rapid overall economic growth, and others decrying the sharp decreases in wages and increases in poverty and inequality that occurred during Pinochet's rule. In 1987, Pinochet permitted himself to be voted out of office. However, he remained commander in chief of the army until 1998, at which point he had himself declared senator for life, a post that made him immune from prosecution. On October 17, 1998, while visiting the United Kingdom, Pinochet was arrested on a warrant from the Spanish government for the murder of Spanish citizens in Chile while he was president. In a controversial move, he was released on medical grounds by the British home secretary. After his return to Chile, the Chilean Supreme Court acted indecisively, sometimes moving to allow Pinochet to be prosecuted for human rights abuses, sometimes protecting him. In October 2006, when Pinochet was 90 years old, he was charged with 36 counts of kidnapping, 23 counts of torture, and one of murder. A month later, just after turning 91, he died.

VLADIMIR PUTIN (1952–) Leader of Russia since 1999, when Boris Yeltsin made him acting president. Though, as of 2008, he is officially the prime minister of the country and his handpicked successor, Dmitry Medvedev, has been elected president, many believe that Putin will continue to hold ultimate authority. Arriving in Moscow in the late 1990s after a career in the Soviet spy agency the KGB and its successor the FSB, Putin rose rapidly and mysteriously to power in the last years of Yeltsin, who was Russia's first post-Soviet president. In 1996, he became deputy head of the president's administrative directorate. In 1998, he was appointed head of the FSB; in 1999, he was appointed prime minister and soon afterward acting president, and he was elected president in 2000. His eight years as president coincided with rising world energy prices that benefited the Russian economy. A rising standard of living combined with a more orderly society helped make people grateful for his firm hand after the chaos of the 1990s, when Russia's transition to capitalism was badly mismanaged. Meanwhile, Putin moved to centralize authority, bring Russia's lucrative energy business under government control, squelch freedom of the press, and manage elections to assure that his party continues in office. His legacy—if indeed he is actually finished—is a more stable but much less democratic Russia.

RONALD WILSON REAGAN (1911–2004) President of the United States from 1981 to 1989. Reagan's aggressive stance against communism, which included supporting anticommunist movements across the world, is often given credit for hastening the end of the cold war. He has also been held responsible for the human rights abuses—death squads, rapes, and murders—perpetrated by the governments and insurgencies that the Untied States supported and encouraged while he was in office. He rejected the strategy of détente that had been pursued by his predecessors and instead ordered a military buildup in the arms race with the Soviet Union, which he portrayed as an evil empire. Despite his rejection of détente, he managed to negotiate with Gorbachev to shrink both countries' nuclear arsenals.

WHITELAW REID (1837–1912) American journalist and diplomat. Reid favored U.S. annexation of the Philippines. He served as U.S. ambassador to France and Great Britain in the Harrison and McKinley administrations, respectively.

CONDOLEEZZA RICE (1954–) National Security Advisor from 2001 to 2005 and the secretary of state from 2005 to 2008 in the administration of President George W. Bush. As National security advisor, Rice was a vocal advocate for the 2003 invasion of Iraq and appeared frequently on television news shows making the administration's case for war and defending the decision afterward.

FRANKLIN DELANO ROOSEVELT (1882–1945) President of the United States, serving from 1933 to his death in 1945. He was the only president to be elected to four terms. Assuming office during the worst period of the Great Depression of the 1930s, Roosevelt found the American people in a cooperative frame of mind and launched a series of social and economic experiments and reforms collectively known as the New Deal. Among the lasting accomplishments of the New Deal were the Social Security program, stronger unions, a more closely regulated financial sector, and a redistributive tax code. Historians and economists disagree as to the New Deal's success in ending the depression—many, if not most, maintain that only World War II accomplished that—but certainly Roosevelt's policies made most of the American people feel that they were sharing its burdens more fairly. The New Deal programs laid the groundwork for a more stable and egalitarian society. In foreign policy, Roosevelt was a Wilsonian internationalist, believing that America should have a leadership role in the world and that it should work through international institutions. His legacy in foreign relations includes the defeat of Nazi Germany and militarist Japan, the formation of the United Nations, and the Bretton Woods Agreement, which developed new international economic and trade agreements.

THEODORE ROOSEVELT (1858–1919) President of the United States from 1901 to 1909. Theodore Roosevelt was the youngest and perhaps the most dynamic and talented person to hold this office. He is remembered for his progressive social legislation and his ardent imperialism. In order to further the goal of building the Panama Canal, he assisted a revolution which split off Panama from Colombia. In 1904, in response to a debt crisis in the Dominican Republic, he voiced an opinion that became known as the Roosevelt corollary to the Monroe Doctrine: The United States had a direct interest and obligation to impose order on the affairs of Latin American countries. Roosevelt was an internationalist as well as an imperialist: In 1904 he acted as a mediator between the warring parties at the conclusion of the Russo-Japanese war. When World War I (1914–18) began in Europe, he was an early advocate of American involvement.

DONALD RUMSFELD (1932–) Secretary of defense in two administrations, under Gerald Ford (1975–77) and GEORGE W. BUSH (2001–06). One of the key architects and promoters of the war in Iraq, Rumsfeld enjoyed unusual visibility and confidence after the attacks of 9/11 and the U.S. invasion of Afghanistan that followed. He came under increasing criticism for his apparent mismanagement of the occupation of Iraq. In particular, he was criticized for drastically underestimating the number of troops that would be needed to stabilize Iraq following the fall of its government; for ignoring State Department plans for the occupation; and for creating within his command the climate of indifference to prisoner's rights that led to the torture of suspected terrorists and insurgents and the detainee abuse scandal of Abu Ghraib. He resigned as secretary of defense a day after the November 2006 mid-term elections, in which the Democrats gained control of both houses of Congress.

ARTHUR SCHLESINGER JR. (1917–2007) American historian, social critic, and Democratic Party activist. He is known for his best-selling studies of presidents and their administrations, as well as for his work as a speechwriter for the presidential campaigns of John F. Kennedy, Robert Kennedy, and George McGovern. He coined the term *imperial presidency* in a book of that title describing the Nixon administration.

HELMUT SCHMIDT (1918–) Chancellor of the Federal Republic of Germany (West Germany) from 1974 to 1982. In November 2007, Schmidt wrote in the German weekly *Der Zeit* that the United States was a greater threat to world peace than Russia. He called the 2003 U.S. invasion of Iraq "a war of choice, not a war of necessity."

BRENT SCOWCROFT (1925–) National security advisor to both presidents Gerald Ford and GEORGE H. W. BUSH. He served as a military assistant to President Nixon and as deputy assistant to the president for national security affairs to presidents Ford and NIXON. It was Brent Scowcroft who coined the term *New World Order.* Currently, he is president and founder of the Scowcroft Group, a consulting group on international policy. In August 2002, Scowcroft said "that U.S. action against Iraq, without resolving tensions between Israel and the Palestinians, could turn the whole region into a cauldron and thus destroy the war on terrorism."

ADAM SMITH (1723–90) Philosopher and political economist. Smith founded the discipline of classical economics and authored the book *The Wealth of Nations* (1776). An opponent of mercantilism, the economic theory that guided European foreign policy in his time, Smith coined the term *the invisible hand* to describe the self-regulating processes of free markets and drew attention to the economic advantages of the division of labor.

JOSEPH STALIN (1879–1953) Soviet communist dictator. Stalin acquired total control of the Communist Party and the Soviet state in a power struggle after the death of Vladimir Lenin in 1924. After playing his opponents against each other to achieve a monopoly of power in the one-party state, Stalin systematically killed off virtually every major figure of the revolution and embarked on a series of purges of whole categories of citizens that continued until his death. Under his rule the Soviet Union became a totalitarian state riddled with informers, plastered over with statues and posters of Stalin, and dotted with vast prisons camps—the Gulag archipelago in the words of the recently deceased, Nobel-Prize–winning, dissident writer Alexander Solzhenitsyn. Though Stalin's domestic policies were responsible for millions of deaths, the people of the Soviet Union endured their greatest hardships during World War II, with an estimated 25 million deaths, more than any other country endured during this conflict. After Hitler's rise to power in 1933, Stalin had the Soviet Union join the League of Nations and attempted to win the cooperation of Britain and France in a common front against Nazi Germany. When this failed, Stalin signed a non-aggression pact with Hitler, which gave Russia territorial concessions at the expense of other eastern European nations. The pact protected Germany's eastern front and gave

Hitler the confidence to invade Poland, the act that brought France and Britain into the war. In 1941, with his western flank secured, Hitler invaded the Soviet Union. The attack apparently took Stalin by surprise. At a cost higher than that paid by any other country, the Russians stopped Hitler's advance, emerging from the war the second greatest power in the world, controlling eastern Europe, and, by 1949, possessing the atomic bomb.

JOSEPH E. STIGLITZ (1943–) Nobel Prize–winning American economist. He was chief economist for the World Bank during the Clinton administration and has been a frequent critic of the shock therapy development policies advocated by the International Monetary Fund. He is the author of several books on economic policy for the general reader, including *Globalization and Its Discontents* (2002) and *The Three Trillion Dollar War* (2008), a book on the real costs of the Iraq war, coauthored with Linda J. Bilmes.

MARGARET THATCHER (1925–) Prime minister of the United Kingdom from 1979 to 1990. Serving three consecutive terms, she held the position longer than any other British prime minister in the 20th century. She considered that her missions as prime minister and Conservative Party leader were to revamp the British economy, reducing the power of labor unions, combating inflation, privatizing industry, and improving productivity by means of free-market reforms and monetarist financial policies recommended by economists like MILTON FRIEDMAN. Like her U.S. counterpart and contemporary RONALD REAGAN, she succeeded in rolling back many state welfare programs.

HENRY DAVID THOREAU (1817–62) American author, naturalist, and philosopher, best known for *Walden,* a collection of essays about living in harmony with nature, and "Civil Disobedience," an essay concerning the rights of the individual to self-government. Thoreau's essay was based on his refusal to pay taxes in protest against the Mexican-American War. Thoreau's writings had a strong influence on political leaders and reformers such as Mahatma Gandhi, President John F. Kennedy, and MARTIN LUTHER KING JR.

EMMANUEL TODD (1951–) French historian, sociologist, and political scientist. In 1976, in *La Chute Finale: Essai sur la Décomposition de la Sphère Soviétique* (*The Final Fall: An Essay on the Decomposition of the Soviet Sphere*), he predicted the collapse of the Soviet Union. In *After the Empire: The Breakdown of the American Order* (2001), he predicted the decline of American power.

FRANCES TROLLOPE (1780–1863) Prolific British writer. Trollope is best known today for *Domestic Manners of the Americans,* a hostile but highly readable account of her sojourn among the rude, ill-washed Americans of the 1820s. She is also the mother of the Victorian novelist Anthony Trollope.

FREDERICK JACKSON TURNER (1861–1932) American historian and scholar. Turner developed the influential frontier thesis of American society, the theory that "The existence of an area of free land, its continuous recession, and the advance of American settlement westward explain American development."

GEORGE WASHINGTON (1732–99) The first president of the United States, serving from 1789 to 1797. As the commander in chief of the American revolutionary forces, Washington led the Continental army to victory over Great Britain. When France and England went to war, in response to the French Revolution, Washington insisted that the United States remain neutral, despite the recommendations of his secretary of state THOMAS JEFFERSON, who was pro-French, and his secretary of the treasury Alexander Hamilton, who was pro-British. In so doing, Washington established a pattern of nonintervention in European affairs, which the United States pursued until World War I.

WOODROW WILSON (1856–1924) President of the United States from 1913 to 1924. On domestic issues he was a progressive in the mold of THEODORE ROOSEVELT, pushing programs to regulate labor conditions and limit the power of monopolies. He also pursued Roosevelt-like policies in Latin America, sending U.S. troops to Mexico, Cuba, Haiti, and the Dominican Republic. When German submarine warfare drew the United States into World War I, Wilson showed himself an internationalist committed to a role of world leadership for the United States, with a strong faith in the power of treaties and international bodies, and a missionary conviction that enlightened people everywhere would see the good sense of running the world on democratic, American principles.

JOHN WINTHROP (1588–1649) British lawyer, Puritan leader, and the founder and first governor of the Massachusetts Bay Colony. He gave lasting expression to the American sense of destiny in a lay sermon he gave aboard the *Arbella* in 1630; the speech was later reprinted under the title "A Model of Christian Charity."

PAUL WOLFOWITZ (1953–) Neoconservative strategist and policy maker and former ambassador to Indonesia. While undersecretary of defense in the administration of GEORGE H. W. BUSH, he supervised the preparation of "Defense Planning Guidance for the Fiscal Years 1994–1999," which made the case that the United States should retain an overwhelming superiority of power in the world. In 1997, he was a founding member, with DICK CHENEY and WILLIAM KRISTOL, of Project for a New American Century, a neoconservative pressure group that saw many of its recommendations fulfilled when GEORGE W. BUSH became president, with Dick Cheney as vice president. As deputy secretary of defense under George W. Bush, Wolfowitz was a major architect of the adminstration's Iraq policy. In 2006, Bush appointed him president of the World Bank, from which he resigned amid controversy in 2007. He is currently a visiting scholar at the American Enterprise Institute, a neoconservative think tank.

BORIS YELTSIN (1937–2007) Soviet and Russian politician, president of Russia. Yeltsin was Russia's first elected president, serving from 1991 to 1999. Originally groomed for leadership by MIKHAIL GORBACHEV, he later became Gorbachev's most vocal liberal opponent, insisting that Gorbachev's reforms were too slow. An August 1991 coup against Gorbachev by Communist Party hard-liners, though it failed, effectively shifted power from Gorbachev to Yeltsin, since it discredited the people on whom Gorbachev's authority depended. Without consulting Gorbachev, Yeltsin negotiated with the leaders of Belarus and Ukraine for a new arrangement, a Commonwealth of Independent States, to replace the Soviet Union. In December, Gorbachev resigned; Yeltsin remained the president of the Soviet Union's successor state. He oversaw Russia's changed relations with the United States and the privatization of Soviet industry during the turbulent 1990s. Yeltsin bears some of the responsibility for the mismanagement of the Soviet transition to capitalism, a process plagued by theft and corruption and a lowered standard of living for ordinary Russians. By staying in power past the point when he could be an effective leader, Yeltsin may also have prepared the way for VLADIMIR PUTIN's authoritarian presidency.

9

Organizations and Agencies

A wide range of organizations and agencies provide information and debate on issues related to American foreign policy and American influence. The U.S. government itself studies international affairs, explains its policies, and at times offers surprisingly critical studies of past U.S. diplomacy, through the Department of State, the Department of Defense, the Central Intelligence Agency, and the Congressional Research Service of the Library of Congress. Such international bodies as the United Nations, the International Monetary Fund, and the World Bank are also useful for the study of international relations. Like the United States, all countries maintain public relations bodies, with Web sites, to present a face to the world.

In addition, many nongovernmental organizations, research institutes (think tanks), and advocacy groups are devoted entirely or partly to the study of international affairs, in which American influence and behavior figure prominently.

Think tanks tend to have very pronounced political points of view and are designed to promote and generate policies that are conservative, neoconservative, centrist, or liberal. They commonly label themselves as nonpartisan, but usually this is true only in the sense that they do not endorse every policy of a particular political party—it does not mean they are above politics or without ideology. The descriptions below attempt to give a rough idea of the political slant of the think tanks included here.

The American Enterprise Institute
1150 Seventeenth Street NW
Washington, DC 20036
Phone: (202) 862-5800
Web: http://www.aei.org/

The American Enterprise Institute is a private, not-for-profit institution that conducts research and education on issues of government, politics, economics, and social welfare. Though AEI describes itself as nonpartisan, its mission statement includes a forthright assertion of conservative principles, stating that its purpose is to "defend the principles and improve the institutions of American freedom and democratic capitalism—limited government, private enterprise, individual liberty and responsibility, vigilant and effective defense and foreign policies, political accountability, and open debate." AEI serves as home base for several former George W. Bush administration officials like John Bolton, Paul Wolfowitz, Richard Perle, John Yoo, and David Frum.

The American Enterprise Institute and the Federalist Society jointly maintain a Web resource NGO Watch, which studies the funding of non-governmental organizations, some of which it alleges are biased or overly political.

Amnesty International
1 Easton Street
London
WC1X 0DW, UK
Phone: +44(20-74)135500
Amnesty International USA
5 Penn Plaza—16th floor
New York, NY 10001
Phone: (212) 807-8400
Web: http://www.amnestyusa.org/

Amnesty International (AI) is a worldwide movement of people who campaign for internationally recognized human rights. Amnesty International USA (AIUSA) is the U.S. section of Amnesty International. Initiatives of Amnesty International include human rights in Iraq; justice in Russia; the death penalty; transfer of military, security, and police goods and services; refugees; international justice; economic globalization and human rights; treaties; human rights education; human rights in the Caribbean and Latin America; health; violence against women.

Arms Control Association (ACA)
1313 L St, NW, Suite 130
Washington, DC 20005
Phone: (202) 463-8270
Web: http://www.armscontrol.org/

The Arms Control Association, founded in 1971, is a national organization dedicated to promoting public understanding of and support for effective arms control policies. Through its public education and media programs and its magazine, *Arms Control Today* (ACT), ACA provides policy makers, the press, and the interested public with authoritative information, analysis, and commentary on arms control proposals, negotiations, agreements, and related national security issues.

The Asian Institute at the University of Toronto
1 Devonshire Place
Toronto, Ontario, M5S 3K7
Canada
Phone: (416) 946-8996
Web: http://webapp.mcis.utoronto.ca/ai/

The mission of the Asian Institute is to provide the intellectual core for interdisciplinary research and teaching on Asia. The institute is organized along subregional lines—with centers for South Asian studies, Korean studies, and related groups focusing on Southeast Asia and Central and Inner Asia.

Belfer Center for Science and International Affairs
John F. Kennedy School of Government
Harvard University
Box 53
79 John F. Kennedy Street
Cambridge, MA 02138
Phone: (617) 495-1400
Web: http://bcsia.ksg.harvard.edu/

The Belfer Center for Science and International Affairs is a research institute devoted to international security and other critical issues where science, technology, environmental policy, and international affairs intersect.

The Brookings Institution
1775 Massachusetts Ave. NW
Washington, DC 20036
Phone: (202) 797-6000
Web: http://www.brook.edu/

The Brookings Institution, a think tank whose origins go back to 1916, describes itself as a "nonprofit organization devoted to independent research and innovative policy solutions." Its studies are frequently cited by members of Congress.

Bulletin of the Atomic Scientists
6042 South Kimbark Ave.
Chicago, IL 60637
Phone: (773) 702-2555
Web: http://www.thebulletin.org/

The Bulletin of the Atomic Scientists is both a magazine devoted to the study of nuclear proliferation and a nonprofit organization "dedicated to security, science & survival since 1945." The bulletin was founded specifically to study the problems created by the advent of nuclear weapons. It has since expanded its focus to include other planet-threatening trends such as the degradation of the environment and global warming, but it remains an excellent source of information and opinion on the effort to contain the spread of nuclear weapons.

Bureau of International Security and Nonproliferation (ISN)
U.S. Department of State
2201 C Street NW
Washington, DC 20520
Phone: (202) 647-4000
Web: http://www.state.gov/t/isn/

The Bureau of International Security and Nonproliferation (ISN), a bureau within the State Department, is responsible for managing a broad range of nonproliferation, counterproliferation, and arms control functions. The ISN Bureau's Web page contains links to information concerning nonproliferation regimes and export controls. All of the major nonproliferation and arms control treaties that are in force and that the United States has signed can be accessed through this site.

CAIR
Council on American-Islamic Relations
453 New Jersey Avenue SE
Washington, DC 20003
Phone: (202) 488-8787

CAIR is a moderate advocacy group for American Muslims. Its mission is to enhance understanding of Islam, encourage dialogue, protect civil liberties, empower American Muslims, and build coalitions that promote justice and mutual understanding.

Carnegie Endowment for International Peace
1779 Massachusetts Ave. NW

Washington, DC 20036-2103
Phone: (202) 483-7600
Web: http://www.carnegieendowment.org/

The Carnegie Endowment for International Peace is a private, nonprofit organization dedicated to advancing cooperation between nations and promoting active international engagement by the United States. Founded in 1910, its work is nonpartisan and dedicated to achieving practical results.

The Cato Institute
1000 Massachusetts Avenue NW
Washington, DC 20001-5403
Phone: (202) 842-0200
Web: http://www.cato.org/index.html

The Cato Institute was founded in 1977 by Edward H. Crane. It is a nonprofit public policy research foundation headquartered in Washington, D.C. The Institute is named for Cato's letters, a series of libertarian pamphlets that helped lay the philosophical foundation for the American Revolution.

Center for Strategic and International Studies
1800 K. Street NW
Washington, DC 20006
Phone: (202) 887-0200
Web: http://www.csis.org/

The Center for Strategic and International Studies (CSIS) seeks to advance global security and prosperity in an era of economic and political transformation by providing strategic insights and practical policy solutions to decision makers. CSIS serves as a strategic planning partner for the government by conducting research and analysis and developing policy initiatives that look into the future and anticipate change.

Central Intelligence Agency (CIA)
Office of Public Affairs
Washington, DC 20505
Phone: (703) 482-0623
Web: https://www.cia.gov/

The Central Intelligence Agency is the best known of several U.S. agencies devoted to the collection of foreign intelligence. It was created in 1947 with the signing of the National Security Act, which also created a director of

Central Intelligence (DCI) to serve as head of the United States intelligence community and act as the principal adviser to the president for intelligence matters related to national security and to serve as head of the Central Intelligence Agency. The CIA publishes declassified sections of formerly classified reports as well as a great number of unclassified studies like *Chiefs of State and Cabinet Members of Foreign Governments,* a directory of foreign government officials. The CIA's *World Factbook,* available online through the CIA's Web pages, is a source of quick, authoritative statistics about countries around the world.

Chatham House
Royal Institute of International Affairs
London SW1Y 4LE
Phone: +44 (0)20 7957 5700
Web: http://www.chathamhouse.org.uk/contact/

Founded in 1920 and based in London, Chatham House is one of Europe's leading foreign policy think tanks, an independent membership-based organization that brings together people from government, politics, business, NGOs, the academic world, and the media.

Congressional Research Service
The Library of Congress
101 Independence Avenue SE
Washington, DC 20540-7500
Phone: (202) 707-5627
Web: http://www.loc.gov/crsinfo/whatscrs.html

The Congressional Research Service is the public policy research arm of the U.S. Congress. Created by Congress as a source of nonpartisan, objective analysis and research on all legislative issues, CRS produces reports, many of which are subsequently made available to the public. Currently, the easiest way to access CRS reports is through the following U.S. State Department Web page: Congressional Research Service (CRS) Reports and Issue Briefs http://fpc.state.gov/c4763.htm.

Council on Foreign Relations
New York office:
The Harold Pratt House
58 East 68th Street
New York, NY 10065

Phone: (212) 434-9400
Web: http://www.cfr.org/
Washington office:
1779 Massachusetts Avenue NW
Washington, DC 20036
Phone: (202) 518-3400

Founded in 1921, the Council on Foreign Relations is an independent, national membership organization and a nonpartisan center for scholars dedicated to producing and disseminating ideas so that individual and corporate members, as well as policy makers, journalists, students, and interested citizens in the United States and other countries, can better understand the world and the foreign policy choices facing the United States and other governments.

Department of Defense (DOD)
1000 Defense Pentagon
Washington, DC 20301-1000
Phone: (703) 428-0711
Web: http://www.defenselink.mil/
Web: http://www.usa.gov/Agencies/Federal/Executive/Defense.shtml
DefenseLINK

The mission of the Department of Defense is to provide the military forces needed to deter war and to protect the security of the United States. The Department of Defense Web site directs browsers to many separate addresses and phone numbers for specific requests.

The Defense Department's home page, DefenseLINK, dispenses information about defense policies, organizations, functions, and operations. Through this page researchers can link to press releases promoting the department's views, transcripts of news briefings, and the home pages of other organizations within the Defense Department, including those of all the armed services.

Department of Homeland Security
Washington, DC 20528
Phone: (202) 282-8000
Web: http://www.dhs.gov/index.shtm

The Department of Homeland Security, established as a response to the terrorist attacks of September 11, 2001, is a federal agency whose primary mission is to help prevent, protect against, and respond to acts of terrorism in the United States.

Department of State
2201 C Street NW
Washington, DC 20520
Phone: (202) 647-4000
Web: http://www.state.gov/

The U.S. Department of State is the foreign policy arm of the executive branch of the United States government. It currently defines its mission as being to "Create a more secure, democratic, and prosperous world for the benefit of the American people and the international community."

Its Web sites are a source of information about past and present U.S. diplomatic efforts, including the major arms control treaties to which the United States is a party and the specific sanctions currently being used to deter nuclear proliferation.

Europa
http://europa.eu/abouteuropa/index_en.htm

EUROPA is the portal site of the European Union (http://europa.eu). It provides up-to-date coverage of European Union affairs and essential information on European integration. Users can also consult all legislation currently in force or under discussion, access the Web sites of each of the EU institutions, and find out about the policies administered by the European Union under the powers devolved to it by the treaties.

Freedom House, Inc.
1301 Connecticut Ave. NW, Floor 6
Washington, DC 20036
Phone: (202) 296-5101
Web: http://www.freedomhouse.org/
120 Wall Street, fl. 26
New York, NY 10005
Phone: 212-514-8040

Freedom House is a United States–based international nongovernmental organization that conducts research and advocacy on democracy, political freedom, and human rights. It is best known for its annual assessment of the degree of democratic freedoms in each country, which is widely used in political science research. Freedom House receives most of its funding from the U.S. government, and prominent U.S. government officials reside on its board, and it has been criticized from the left for promoting U.S. government policies and for its ties to conservative institutions.

Geneva Centre for Security Policy
7 bis, Avenue de la Paix
P.O. Box 1295
1211 Geneva 1
Phone: (41) 22 906 1600
Web: http://www.gcsp.ch/e/index.htm

The Geneva Centre for Security Policy (GCSP) is an international foundation that was established in 1995 under Swiss law to promote the building and maintenance of peace, security, and stability.

Global Policy Forum
777 UN Plaza, suite 3D
New York, NY 10017
Phone: (212) 557-3161
Web: http://www.globalpolicy.org/

Global Policy Forum has for many years monitored policy making at the United Nations, promoted accountability of global decisions, educated and mobilized for global citizen participation, and advocated on vital issues of international peace and justice. Since it believes in strengthening international institutions, the Global Policy Forum may be said to have a liberal, internationalist slant.

The Henry L. Stimson Center
1111 19th Street—twelfth floor
Washington, DC 20036
Phone: (202) 223-5956
Email: info@stimson.org
Web: http://www.stimson.org/home.cfm

Founded in 1989, the Henry L. Stimson Center is a nonprofit, nonpartisan institution devoted to enhancing international peace and security through a unique combination of rigorous analysis and outreach.

Human Rights Watch
350 Fifth Avenue, 34th floor
New York, NY 10118-3299
Phone: (212) 290-4700
http://www.hrw.org/

Human Rights Watch is an independent, nongovernmental organization, dedicated to protecting the human rights of people around the world. Human

Rights Watch publishes reports on several topics and compiles annual reports ("World Report") presenting an overview of the worldwide state of human rights. It investigates human rights violations, supporting victims and activists in order to prevent discrimination, uphold political freedom, protect people from inhumane conduct in wartime, and bring offenders to justice. Human Rights Watch's reports enjoy a great deal of credibility, and perhaps for that very reason it has been criticized from both the left and the right, as too pro-Western and too anti-Western. Contributions to the organization come from private individuals and foundations worldwide. It accepts no government funds, directly or indirectly,

Institute for Science and International Security (ISIS)
236 Massachusetts Avenue NE
Suite 500
Washington, DC 20002
Phone: (202) 547-3633
Web: http://www.isis-online.org/

ISIS is a nonprofit, nonpartisan institution dedicated to informing the public about science and policy issues affecting international security. Its efforts focus on stopping the spread of nuclear weapons, bringing about greater transparency of nuclear activities worldwide, and achieving deep reductions in nuclear arsenals.

International Government Information at UC Berkeley
University of California, Berkeley
Berkeley, CA 94720
Phone: (510) 642-6000
Web: http://www.lib.berkeley.edu/doemoff/govinfo/intl/

The UC Berkeley libraries are depositories for documents from the United Nations, the European Union, the Asian Development Bank, and the Organization for Security and Cooperation in Europe. The library also participates in selective depository arrangements, approval plans, and exchange agreements for publications from other international governmental organizations (IGOs). Much, though not all, of the material is available for free to those not affiliated with the University of California at Berkeley.

International Monetary Fund (IMF)
700 19th Street NW
Washington, DC 20431

Phone: 202-623-7000
Web: http://www.imf.org/external/index.htm

The International Monetary Fund (IMF) is an international organization that oversees the global financial system by observing exchange rates and balance of payments, as well as offering financial and technical assistance. Financial research concerning countries around the world and the health of the world economy generally are integral to the IMF's responsibilities, so it produces a great many reports that are available for download through its Web pages.

Iraq Body Count
Web: http://www.iraqbodycount.org/

Iraq Body Count is an ongoing human security project that maintains and updates the world's largest public database of violent civilian deaths during and since the 2003 invasion. The count encompasses noncombatants killed by military or paramilitary action and the breakdown in civil security following the invasion. Though Iraq Body Count is implicitly and explicitly critical of the Iraq War and the U.S. presence in Iraq, it has come under criticism for underestimating the number of civilian deaths.

The Library of Congress
101 Independence Ave SE
Washington, DC 20540
Phone: (202) 707-5000
Web: http://www.loc.gov/index.html

The Library of Congress serves as a research arm of Congress and is also the largest library in the world, with more than 130 million items on approximately 530 miles of bookshelves. There are many ways to search through the Library of Congress collections. For a quick start, enter key words into the search field on the home page.

Library of Congress
Country Studies
Web: http://lcweb2.loc.gov/frd/cs/cshome.html
Federal Research Division
101 Independence Ave. SE
John Adams Building, LA 5281
Washington, DC 20540-4840

Phone: (202) 707-3900
Web: http://lcweb2.loc.gov/pow/powhome.html

The Federal Research Program of the Library of Congress performs research on domestic and international subjects for agencies of the U.S. Government, the District of Columbia, and authorized federal contractors. Some of these studies are available to the public and can be accessed through FRD's Web pages.

A link can be found on the Federal Research Division Web site to the Library of Congress's Country Studies, which can be very useful in the early stages of research and as a source of statistics. Each country study presents a description and analysis of the historical setting and the social, economic, political, and national security systems and institutions of countries throughout the world.

Library of Congress
THOMAS Congressional Service
101 Independence Avenue SE
Washington, DC 20540
Phone: (202) 707-5000
Web: http://thomas.loc.gov/home/abt_thom.html

THOMAS was launched in January of 1995 at the inception of the 104th Congress. The leadership of the 104th Congress directed the Library of Congress to make federal legislative information freely available to the public. Since that time, THOMAS has expanded the scope of its offerings to include bills, resolutions, activity in Congress, the Congressional Record, schedules, calendars, committee information, presidential nominations, treaties, and government resources. On the THOMAS Web site, researchers can search by key word or type, for treaties or bills.

The National Security Archive
George Washington University
Gelman Library, suite 701
21030 H. Street NW
Washington, DC 20037
Phone: (202) 994-7000
Web: http://www.gwu.edu/~nsarchiv/index.html

An independent nongovernmental research institute and library located at George Washington University, the archive collects and publishes declassified documents obtained through the Freedom of Information Act. The archive also serves as a repository of government records on a wide range of topics pertaining to the national security, foreign, intelligence, and economic policies of the United States. The archive won the 1999 George Polk Award, one of U.S. journalism's most prestigious prizes, for—in the words of the citation—"piercing the self-serving veils of government secrecy, guiding journalists in the search for the truth and informing us all."

Oxford Research Group
Development House
56-64 Leonard Street
London EC2A 4LT
Phone: +44 (0)20 7549 0298 (London)
Phone: +44 (0)1865 242 819 (Oxford)
Web: http://www.oxfordresearchgroup.org.uk/

Oxford Research Group (ORG) is an independent nongovernmental organization and registered charity, which works together with others to promote a more sustainable approach to security for Britain and the world. The ORG works to promote disarmament and nonviolent methods for resolving conflict. In April 2005 it was named one of the top 20 think tanks in Britain by the *Independent.*

Partnership for Global Security (PGS)
1025 Connecticut Avenue NW
Suite 1106
Washington, DC 20036
Phone: (202) 332-1412
Web: http://www.partnershipforglobalsecurity.org/

The Partnership for Global Security is an NGO that grew out of the effort to secure the nuclear weapons and fissile materials of the former Soviet Union after the breakup of the USSR. Its goal is to help foster systems and agreements that reduce the risk posed by nuclear arsenals and stockpiles. As the days of close U.S.-Russian cooperation on nuclear issues recede into the past, PGS has begun to turn its attention to nuclear security in other nuclear weapons states, such as Pakistan.

Political Research Associates
1310 Broadway, suite 201
Somerville, MA 02144
Phone: (617) 666-5300
Web: http://www.publiceye.org/about.html; http://rightweb.irc-online.org/

Political Research Associates is described in its mission statement as "a progressive think tank devoted to supporting movements that are building a more just and democratic society," which "seeks to advance progressive thinking and action by providing research-based information, analysis, and referrals." PRA maintains the Web site Right Web, which monitors and criticizes leading neoconservative thinkers and think tanks.

Project for the New American Century (PNAC)
1150 17th St. NW, suite 510
Washington, DC 20036
Phone: (202) 293-4983
Web: http://www.newamericancentury.org/

The Project for the New American Century (PNAC) is an American neoconservative think tank based in Washington, D.C., cofounded as "a nonprofit educational organization" by William Kristol and Robert Kagan in early 1997. The PNAC's stated goal is "to promote American global leadership." It may be of mostly historical interest now, but that interest is enormous, since its many goals were adopted by the George W. Bush administration, and many of its members occupied positions within the administration.

RAND Corporation
National Defense Research Institute
1776 Main Street
Santa Monica, CA 90401-3208
Phone: (310) 393-0411
Web: http://www.rand.org/nsrd/ndri.html

Originally a think tank serving the United States Defense Department, RAND has branched out to study a variety of matters from obesity to international terrorism for a variety of private and government clients. One RAND division, the federally funded National Defense Research Institute (NDRI), continues to do national security research for the Defense Department, the Marine Corps, and other U.S. agencies.

United Nations
First Avenue at 46th Street
New York, NY 10017
Phone: (212) 963-5012
Web: http://www.un.org/; http://www.un.org/english/

The United Nations (UN), which has its headquarters in New York City, is an international organization whose mission is to facilitate cooperation in international law, international security, economic development, social progress, and human rights. Many of the major diplomatic initiatives intended to slow the spread of nuclear weapons, including Atoms for Peace and the Nuclear Nonproliferation Treaty, were negotiated through the United Nations, and the United Nations is an arena of diplomacy and negotiation for the United States, its allies, and such would-be nuclear weapons states as Iraq, Iran, and North Korea. The UN is a prolific creator of reports, analysis, and statistics useful to researchers. Much of this information is available their extensive Web pages.

United Nations Monitoring, Verification and Inspection Commission
First Avenue at 46th Street
New York, NY 10017
Phone: (212) 963-5012
Web: http://www.unmovic.org/

The United Nations Monitoring, Verification and Inspection Commission (UNMOVIC) was created through the adoption of Security Council resolution 1284 of December 17, 1999. UNMOVIC replaced the former UN Special Commission (UNSCOM). Its job was to verify Iraq's compliance with its obligation to be rid of its WMDs. UNMOVIC's Web site is of use to those researching the background of the 2003 U.S.–led invasion of Iraq.

The UN Security Council
First Avenue at 46th Street
New York, NY 10017
Phone: (212) 963-5012
Web: http://www.un.org/Docs/sc/

The UN Security Council is the United Nations' most powerful organ. It makes decisions that member governments must carry out under the United Nations Charter. The decisions of the council are known as United Nations Security Council Resolutions. Of the Security Council's 15 member states, five have permanent seats and five have temporary seats. The five permanent members (China, France, Russia, the United Kingdom, and the United States) have a veto power over Security Council votes. The five states that have permanent seats on the United Nations Security Council are also the five official nuclear weapons states—that is, the five nuclear weapons states who are signatories to the Nuclear Nonproliferation Treaty.

The Security Council's Web pages can be used for quick access to information regarding Security Council debates and resolutions, UN peacekeeping operations, reports of the United Nations's Secretary General, and the progress of other operations directed by the UN Security Council.

United Nations Weapons of Mass Destruction Branch Department for Disarmament Affairs
First Avenue at 46th Street
New York, NY 10017
Phone: (212) 963-5012
Web: http://disarmament.un.org/wmd/

The Weapons of Mass Destruction Branch of the UN's Department for Disarmament supports the activities of the United Nations in the area of weapons of mass destruction by tracking developments and trends affecting the spread of WMDs. The WMD Branch Web page links to information on many disarmament issues, including nuclear weapon and ballistic missiles proliferation, and the international agreements governing them.

US Government Web Portal: http://www.usa.gov/
The U.S. Government Web Portal provides access to the public Web pages of all U.S. government departments and agencies—those described here as well as many more. The page contains a search field. Entering a phrase or word such as "nuclear non-proliferation" or "iraq" will produce articles from various U.S. government Web sites, departments, and agencies. Most other U.S. government Web pages also provide search fields and can be searched by key word.

The Washington Institute for Near East Policy
1828 L Street NW, suite 1050
Washington DC 20036
Phone: (202) 452-0650
Web: http://www.washingtoninstitute.org/templateI01.php

Founded in 1985, the Washington Institute for Near East Policy was established to advance a balanced and realistic understanding of American interests in the Middle East.

The White House
1600 Pennsylvania Avenue NW
Washington, DC 20500

Phone: (202) 456-1111 (comments); (202) 456-1414 (switchboard)
Web: http://www.whitehouse.gov/

The White House is the headquarters of the president of the United States. Its Web pages track the activities of the president and advocate the policies of the president's administration.

The World Bank
1818 H Street NW
Washington, DC 20433
Phone: (202) 473-1000
Web: http://www.worldbank.org/

The World Bank is an international body that has the mission of providing financial and technical assistance to developing countries around the world. It is made up two development institutions owned by 185 member countries—the International Bank for Reconstruction and Development (IBRD) and the International Development Association (IDA). More than 27,000 World Bank publications are available online through its Web site.

10

Annotated Bibliography

This chapter is divided into subjects, with books listed before articles in each subject. Researchers may want to browse other categories after they have searched through their area of specific interest, since some books and articles touch on one subject—and a book listed under globalization may also be relevant to trade policy or foreign policy. So many books have been written in the past decade on the subject of American hegemony that this subject has been given its own heading.

The topics given separate bibliographies in this chapter are:

American Foreign Policy

American Hegemony

The Cold War

The War on Terror

American Trade Policy

Globalization and Development

Economic Theory

Europe

Latin America

The Islamic Word

Asia

Russia and the Former Soviet Sphere

AMERICAN FOREIGN POLICY

Books

Blum, William. *Rogue State: A Guide to the World's Only Superpower.* Monroe, Maine: Common Courage Press, 2000. In *Rogue State,* William Blum, author of *Freeing the World to Death: Essays on the American Empire,* delivers a harsh critique of the United States. Blum maintains that while supposedly acting on behalf of freedom and human rights, the United States has committed criminal acts.

Brown, Michael E., ed. *America's Strategic Choices.* Cambridge, Mass.: MIT Press, 2000. The essays in this volume present opposing perspectives on the future of U.S. strategy for dealing with the post–cold war world. Brown contends that the United States has yet to reach a consensus on a coherent approach to the international use of American power. Included among U.S. policy options are primacy, cooperative security, selective engagement, and retrenchment.

Bucklin, Steven J. *Realism and American Foreign Policy: Wilsonians and the Kennan-Morgenthau Thesis.* Westport, Conn.: Praeger, 2001. Steven Bucklin provides a comparative analysis of the foreign policies of Woodrow Wilson and his disciples and those of George Kennan and Hans Morgenthau, focusing on the debate over whether or not Wilson's policies were in the national interest.

Callinicos, Alex. *New Mandarins of American Power: The Bush Administration's Plans for the World.* Cambridge: Polity Press; distributed in the U.S.: Malden, Mass.: Blackwell Publishing, 2003. Alex Callinicos, author of *An Anti-Capitalist Manifesto,* here examines the neoconservative foreign policies of aggressive unilateralism of the Bush administration and the Project for the New American Century. Criticizing the justifications of the war on terrorism, Callinicos analyses the strategy of the Republican neoconservatives who dominated American foreign policy during the George W. Bush administration.

Carter, Dale, and Robin Clifton, eds. *War and Cold War in America, 1942–62.* Houndmills, Basingstoke, Hampshire; New York: Palgrave, 2002. This collection of original essays on the wartime and postwar United States reevaluates well-known crises and documents many less familiar aspects of the nation's mid-20th-century conflicts. Leading diplomatic historians here offer new evidence about the risks run and the costs incurred in the prosecution of the cold war, from Korea to the Caribbean. And they provide an up-to-date accounting of mid-20th-century American diplomacy's global purposes and consequences.

Glad, Betty, and Chris J. Dolan, eds. *Striking First: The Preventive War Doctrine and the Reshaping of U.S. Foreign Policy.* New York: Palgrave Macmillan, 2004. Leading American scholars here assert that the Bush administration's emphasis on a preemptive first strike doctrine, along with its resort to unilateral decision-making and its commitment to sustaining U.S. hegemony in the world, have challenged the fundamentals of both the world political order and American political institutions. The contributors explore the manner in which these policies have been made, the premises upon which they are based, and their possible consequences for U.S. domestic institutions and the nation's position in the world.

Goff, Stanley. *Full Spectrum Disorder: The Military in the New American Century.* Brooklyn, N.Y.: Soft Skull Press, 2004. Drawing on his Delta Force and Army Ranger experiences, which took him from the invasions of Panama and Haiti to army training grounds in Colombia and South Korea, Goff depicts the new

American empire as overreliant on technology, ignorant of the lessons of history, and backward in the stereotyping of other countries.

Goodman, Melvin, and Craig Eisendrath. *Bush League Diplomacy: How the Neoconservatives Are Putting the World at Risk.* Former CIA official Melvin Goodman and ex-diplomat Craig Eisendrath charge the Bush administration with rolling back over half a century of accomplishments by bullying with military force and rejecting the broad collaborative approach in effect since the founding of the UN. The authors assert that the centralization of power in the presidency characterized by the Bush administration must be stopped in order to restore America's reputation abroad to prevent deterioration of the domestic situation.

Halberstam, David. *War in a Time of Peace: Bush, Clinton, and the Generals.* New York: Simon & Schuster, 2002. Pulitzer Prize–winning journalist David Halberstam describes the influences that the cold war still exerts on American foreign policy and how domestic politics have determined our role as a world power. Halberstam discusses the internecine conflicts among the key figures in the White House, the State Department, and the military, providing portraits of people such as Clinton, Bush, Reagan, Kissinger, James Baker, Dick Cheney, Madeleine Albright, and others.

Harris, Paul G., ed. *Climate Change and American Foreign Policy.* New York: St. Martin's Press, 2000. Paul Harris examines the actors, institutions, and ideas shaping the U.S. policy on global warming. He analyzes the domestic and international politics of U.S. climate change policy, covering such issues as science, the presidency, and Congress, nongovernmental organizations, diplomacy, and the international negotiations leading to the Framework Convention on Climate Change and the Kyoto Protocol. The book concludes by looking at the role of international norms in shaping U.S. climate change policy.

Harvey, Frank P. *Smoke and Mirrors: Globalized Terrorism and the Illusion of Multilateral Security.* Toronto: University of Toronto Press, 2004. Frank P. Harvey here makes a case in favor of American unilateralism, exposing the costs, potential risks, and failures of multilateral alternatives. He addresses the relationship between globalization, terrorism, and unilateralism and provides a systematic explanation for and defense of Washington's response to threats of terrorism and the proliferation of weapons of mass destruction.

Hentz, James J., ed. *The Obligation of Empire: United States' Grand Strategy for a New Century.* Lexington: University Press of Kentucky, 2004. Scholars of international affairs examine the debates over the U.S. strategy for meeting the challenges of international security in light of U.S. security policies and interests in tactical regions around the world. The contributors begin by describing neoisolationism, selective engagement, cooperative security, and primacy. Focusing on regions such as sub-Saharan Africa, the Middle East, and Latin America, the contributors assess the effectiveness of competing strategies in each region.

Hess, Gary R. *Presidential Decisions for War: Korea, Vietnam, and the Persian Gulf.* Baltimore: Johns Hopkins University Press, 2001. Four-time Fulbright scholar Gary Hess re-creates the unfolding crises in Korea, Vietnam, and the Persian

Gulf, explaining why the presidents and their advisers concluded that the use of military power was ultimately necessary to uphold U.S. security. Hess evaluates how effectively the president assessed U.S. interests, explored alternatives to war, adhered to constitutional processes, and built congressional, popular, and international support. After tracing how Truman, Johnson, and Bush responded to unfolding military developments, Hess evaluates the wartime leadership of each president.

Hopgood, Stephen. *American Foreign Environmental Policy and the Power of the State.* New York: Oxford University Press, 1997. Drawing on primary research, the author examines the key role central state officials have played in formulating American foreign environmental policy, concluding that claims for the diminishing domestic-international divide and the erosion of state sovereignty are overstated.

James Joes, Anthony, ed. *Saving Democracies: U.S. Intervention in Threatened Democratic States.* Westport, Conn.: Praeger, 1999. This study written at the end of the last decade brought together experts from the intelligence, military, and academic communities to discuss the role of U.S. forces undertaking peacekeeping missions around the world, a role that raises the prospect of confrontation with guerrilla movements, combat for which troops are largely untrained. This book contains analyses of past and present conflicts involving the American military.

Johnson, Kermit D. *Ethics and Counterrevolution: American Involvement in Internal Wars.* Lanham, Md.: University Press of America, 1997. This book is an ethical critique of U.S. policy and involvement in counterrevolutionary war. It rejects the thesis that the end of the cold war meant the end of revolution, since revolution is grounded in root causes. The book advocates the adoption of a modest political Hippocratic oath of "Do no harm" and argues that civilization, demilitarization, and the root causes for revolution are necessary for the building of true democracy.

Kagan, Donald, and Frederick W. Kagan. *While America Sleeps: Self-delusion, Military Weakness, and the Threat to Peace Today.* New York: St. Martin's Press, 2000. In this 2000 publication, one of many that argued for the policies the second Bush administration would ultimately put into place, historians Donald and Frederick W. Kagan suggest that in the wake of the Vietnam War, the American government was reluctant to commit its forces to the purpose of policing the world, instead pursuing a policy of brief, limited military encounters that involve little risk of incurring casualties, a policy the Kagans believe would lead to disaster, as some other Hitler, such as Saddam Hussein or Kim Jong-il, rises to trouble the world.

Krugman, Paul R. *The Great Unraveling: Losing Our Way in the New Century.* New York: W. W. Norton, 2004. In this collection of op-ed pieces he wrote for the *New York Times* between 2000 and 2003, economist and liberal political commentator Paul Krugman covers the political and social events of the past decade. He chronicles the process by which "the heady optimism of the late 1990s" gave way to gloom as a result of "incredibly bad leadership, in the private sector and in the corridors of power."

Kugler, Richard L. *Changes Ahead: Future Directions for the U.S. Overseas Military Presence.* Santa Monica, Calif.: RAND, 1998. This study prepared for the U.S. Air Force by RAND's Project Air Force offers eight options that can be used to help guide thinking and planning for the coming era of change for U.S. military forces stationed abroad.

Landau, Saul. *The Pre-Emptive Empire: A Guide to Bush's Kingdom.* Sterling, Va.: Pluto Press, 2003. Saul Landau analyzes the 9/11 attacks and the ensuing wars in Afghanistan and Iraq in the context of the historical, political, and economic events that have helped shape the 21st-century United States. Landau makes a case for what he identifies as the transformation of a nation founded on republican fabric to its current manifestation: a preemptive empire.

Macdonald, Scot. *Rolling the Iron Dice: Historical Analogies and Decisions to Use Military Force in Regional Contingencies.* Westport, Conn.: Greenwood Press, 2000. Scot Macdonald analyzes the role of historical information in decision making. He examines the role that historical analogies have played in Anglo-American decision making during crises involving the possible use of force during the 1950s.

Mann, James. *Rise of the Vulcans: The History of Bush's War Cabinet.* New York: Viking, 2004. James Mann here tells the behind-the-scenes story of the role played by George W. Bush's inner circle of advisers—Dick Cheney, Donald Rumsfeld, Colin Powell, Paul Wolfowitz, Richard Armitage, and Condoleezza Rice, who called themselves the Vulcans. Mann examines their early careers and rise to power, the interactions and underlying tensions among them, their visions, and their roles in the administration.

McCrisken, Trevor B. *American Exceptionalism and the Legacy of Vietnam: US Foreign Policy since 1974.* Basingstoke, England; New York: Palgrave Macmillan, 2003. This book examines the influence of the belief in American exceptionalism on the history of the United States since the Vietnam War. Trevor B. McCrisken analyzes attempts by each post-Vietnam U.S. administration to revive the popular belief in exceptionalism. He argues that exceptionalism consistently provided the framework for discussion of foreign affairs but that the conduct of foreign affairs was limited by the American failure in Vietnam.

McDougall, Walter A. *Promised Land, Crusader State: The American Encounter with the World since 1776.* Boston: Houghton Mifflin, 1997. Pulitzer prize–winning historian Walter McDougall here looks at America's place in foreign affairs from 1776 to the present. Looking back over two centuries, he contrasts America as a "Promised Land" and America as a "Crusader State." McDougall explores eight traditions of American foreign policy: exceptionalism, unilateralism, the American System, expansionism, progressive imperialism, Wilsonianism, containment, and global meliorism.

Meernik, James David. *The Political Use of Military Force in U.S. Foreign Policy.* Aldershot, Hampshire, England: Ashgate Publishing, 2004. James Meernik looks at the instances in which the United States, throughout its history, has used military force just short of war. The United States's justifications for the use of military force include security objectives, economic self-interests, promoting democracy and human rights, and domestic political purposes. Meernik assesses the utility of each of these reasons throughout U.S. history through an historical narrative and statistical analysis. His book provides an account of important events, from the Quasi War with France and the opening of Japan to the numerous interventions of the 1990s.

Meho, Lokman I., ed. *The Kurdish Question in U.S. Foreign Policy: A Documentary Sourcebook.* Westport, Conn.: Praeger, 2004. This documentary sourcebook on U.S.-Kurdish relations reproduces the full text of over 325 of the most important U.S. government documents dealing with the Kurdish question, in addition to providing both a guide to U.S. government sources for locating subsequently published materials and an annotated list of over 200 primary and secondary sources.

Mertus, Julie A. *Bait and Switch: Human Rights and U.S. Foreign Policy.* New York: Routledge, 2004. Julie Mertus, a leading human rights expert, argues that talk of human rights has become the political equivalent of a bait and switch. Like the car salesman promoting an amazing but bogus deal in order to get people into the showroom, politicians promise human rights to gain support for their policies, then offer a substitute unreflective of a genuine concern for rights. Based on extensive interviews with leading policy makers, military officials, and human rights advocates, Mertus says that America's attempts to promote human rights abroad have, paradoxically, undermined those rights in other countries.

Randall, Stephen J. *United States Foreign Oil Policy since World War I: For Profits and Security.* Montreal: McGill-Queen's University Press, 2005. Exploring the relationship between the state and the private sector in the development of American foreign oil policy, the author believes that the foreign oil policy has been consistently dependant on maintaining a delicate balance between private and public interests—between profits and security. The result has been an ongoing search for energy security that has taken the United States into regions of the world where its national security interests would not otherwise have been at stake.

Reveron, Derek S., ed. *America's Viceroys: The Military and U.S. Foreign Policy.* New York: Palgrave Macmillan, 2004. In this book, Derek Reveron, an associate professor at the Naval War College, explores the controversial role played by the United States's regional commanders in chief (CINCs) in shaping American foreign policy. Reveron describes the tremendous power wielded by these military commanders, who function as diplomats, advisers, and intermediaries between other countries and Washington in both the military and economic spheres.

Schlesinger, Arthur M. *War and the American Presidency.* Pulitzer Prize–winning historian Arthur M. Schlesinger Jr. discusses the war in Iraq, the presidency, and the future of democracy. Warning of the dangers posed by the changes in the United States from deterrence and containment to preventive war, he criticizes George W. Bush's expansion of presidential power. Assessing Bush's faith-based presidency, he looks at the historical role religion has played in American politics.

Western, Jon. *Selling Intervention and War: The Presidency, the Media, and the American Public.* Baltimore: Johns Hopkins University Press, 2005. This book discusses the role the media plays in the promotion of American foreign policy initiatives. Jon Western shows, in a series of five case studies, how groups in American government try to promote their varying positions for or against intervention. Doris A. Graber of *International History Review* writes: "Western's book is especially timely because the era of active interventionism sponsored by the George W. Bush administration may continue beyond the presidential election of 2008."

Articles

Beinart, Peter. "The Rehabilitation of the Cold-War Liberal." *New York Times Magazine,* April 30, 2006, pp. 40–45. Peter Beinart writes that American voters for the third time since 9/11 will choose between Democrats and Republicans while knowing what only one party believes about national security, noting that although Democrats have no shortage of worthwhile foreign policy proposals, they cannot tell a coherent story about the post-9/11 world because they have not found their usable past.

Foreign Policy. "What America Must Do." *Foreign Policy,* January/February 2008. A compilation of 12 essays from various thinkers, including Newt Gingrich, Dmitri Trenin, and Kenneth Rogoff, all answer the question: "What single policy or gesture can the next president of the United States make to improve America's standing in the world?"

Fukuyama, Francis. "After Neoconservatism." *New York Times Magazine,* February 19, 2006. Available online. URL: http://www.nytimes.com/2006/02/19/magazine/neo.html?_r=1&oref=slogin. Accessed September 8, 2008. Francis Fukuyama, a former neoconservative theorist, argues that with the Iraq conflict, the ideology that won the cold war has come to threaten peace. Fukuyama asserts that the so-called Bush doctrine is in shambles and the idealistic effort to use American power to promote democracy and human rights abroad has suffered a setback because of the perceived failure in Iraq.

Kaplan, Robert D. "America's Elegant Decline." *The Atlantic,* November 2007. In this article, Robert Kaplan questions America's ability to remain the world's top military power, noting that a nation's power has historically mirrored the strength of its navy. Kaplan points out that suggestions that the United States will have to do more with less is not a strategy for maintaining naval superiority, but rather one for "elegantly managing American decline."

Myers, Robert J. "Hans Morgenthau's Realism." *American Foreign Policy,* Vol. 11, 1997. Robert Myers discusses the history of U.S. foreign policy and the ongoing debate over the continued relevance of realist thought in the post–cold war era. By means of his analysis of Hans Morgenthau's *Politics Among Nations,* Myers provides discussion of his theory that despite vast changes in the international system, realism is an accurate description of human nature and hence of the interactions among nations.

AMERICAN HEGEMONY

Books

Boggs, Carl, ed. *Masters of War: Militarism and Blowback in the Era of American Empire.* Foreword by Ted Rall. New York: Routledge, 2003. With contributions from critics of the Iraq war, *Masters of War* cautions that worldwide economic and military dominance have their price, both globally and domestically. The contributors argue that the constantly expanding global U.S. military power is imperialism bent on global domination. The authors argue this has resulted in a growing widespread resistance and opposition that is likely to make the 21st century an era marked by sustained, and generally unanticipated, blowback.

Chomsky, Noam. *Hegemony or Survival: America's Quest for Global Dominance.* New York: Henry Holt, 2004. In this criticism of American foreign policy from the late 1950s to the present, Noam Chomsky redefines many of the terms commonly used in the ongoing American war on terrorism. Surveying U.S. foreign military actions over the past half century, Chomsky asserts that America is just as much a terrorist state as any other government or rogue organization.

Fraser, Matthew. *Weapons of Mass Distraction: Soft Power and American Empire.* New York: Thomas Dunne Books, 2005. Matthew Fraser says that the United States uses its soft power (a term that refers to "the global appeal of American lifestyles, culture, forms of distraction, norms, and values") to assert its global influence. The author accuses American culture of overpowering other cultures' movies, television, music, and fast food.

Guilhot, Nicolas. *Democracy Makers: Human Rights and International Order.* New York: Columbia University Press, 2005. Nicolas Guilhot explores how the international movement for democracy and human rights has gone from being a weapon against power to being part of the arsenal of power itself. He looks at how the U.S. government, the World Bank, political scientists, NGOs, think tanks, and various international organizations have appropriated the movement for democracy and human rights to export neoliberal policies throughout the world.

Johnson, Chalmers A. *Blowback: The Costs and Consequences of American Empire.* New York: Metropolitan Books, 2000. Chalmers Johnson, an authority on Japan and its economy, offers a troubling prognosis of what the repercussions of American global interventionism will be for the United States and the world in the 21st century. Warning that the United States will experience blowback—a CIA neologism describing the unintended consequences of American activity—Chalmers calls on the United States to rethink its position in the world.

Judis, John B. *Folly of Empire: What George W. Bush Could Learn from Theodore Roosevelt and Woodrow Wilson.* New York: Scribner, 2004. John B. Judis writes about how presidents from Franklin Roosevelt to Bill Clinton drew upon what Theodore Roosevelt and Woodrow Wilson learned about the pitfalls of using American power unilaterally to carve out a world in America's image. In examining America's role in the international community—then and now—Judis charges the Bush administration of ignoring the lessons of history and in so doing creating a quagmire of terror and ethnic conflict.

Lodal, Jan. *Price of Dominance: The New Weapons of Mass Destruction and Their Challenge to American Leadership.* New York: Council on Foreign Relations Press, 2001. Jan Lodal, former principal deputy undersecretary of defense for policy, argues here that America's growing military, economic, and cultural preeminence motivate states to oppose American power through whatever means possible.

Mann, Michael. *Incoherent Empire.* London; New York: Verso, 2003. Michael Mann charges that the Bush administration's emphasis on military unilateralism is hurting the reputation of the United States throughout the world. Focusing on military threats, both ongoing and potential, Mann documents what international opinions about this policy are. Mann posits here that new militarism is a product of neoconservatism. He concludes his book by writing that the "political solution" to this situation is to "throw the new militarists out of office."

Serewicz, Lawrence W. *America at the Brink of Empire: Rusk, Kissinger, and the Vietnam War.* Baton Rouge: Louisiana State University Press, 2007. *America at the Brink of Empire* explores the foreign policy leadership of Dean Rusk and Henry Kissinger regarding the United States's mission to ensure a world order. Lawrence Serewicz argues that in the Vietnam conflict, the United States experienced an identity crisis, whereby America stretched to the limits of its identity as a republic.

Soderberg, Nancy. *Superpower Myth: The Use and Misuse of American Might.* Hoboken, N.J.: John Wiley, 2005. Nancy Soderberg argues here that by putting forth the superpower myth of unilateralism the Bush administration is sabotaging its own stated goals of peace and increased democracy. In her book, Soderberg, a former U.S. ambassador to the UN and Clinton foreign policy adviser, argues that unlike his successor, Clinton understood the limits of American power.

Vickers, Rhiannon. *Manipulating Hegemony: State Power, Labour and the Marshall Plan in Britain.* Houndmills, Basingstoke, England: Macmillan, 2000. Drawing on Marxist theories of international political economy, this book explores the impact of the Marshall Plan on labor and government in Britain. Rather than the United States imposing a "politics of productivity" on an unwilling government, the center-right of the Labour Party used the Marshall Plan to achieve its own political ends. *Manipulating Hegemony* shows how the government was able to marginalize the left to create a pattern of state-labor politics that was to endure until the end of the 1970s.

Articles

Greenway, H. D. S. "The Nightmare from the Daydream Believers." *Boston Globe,* February 26, 2008, p. A 13. H. D. S. Greenway writes that contrary to what America's leaders have believed, the shift in global politics that resulted from the end of the cold war and the collapse of the Soviet Union has not made America all-powerful.

Ignatieff, Michael. "The Burden." *New York Times Magazine,* January 5, 2003, pp. 6–22. Michael Ignatieff contends that America is becoming an empire. He explains that the September 11, 2001, terrorist attacks pitched the Islamic world into a struggle to determine how it will be ruled and by whom: the authoritarians, the Islamists, or the democrats. Ignatieff says that America can help repress and contain the struggle, but that it cannot ultimately control it.

Kaplan, Fred. "Downsizing Our Dominance. The Next President Will Have to Deal with a World in Which U.S. Hegemony Is a Thing of the Past." *Los Angeles Times,* February 3, 2008, p. M6. Fred Kaplan writes that America is weaker today than we were a decade or two ago. Pointing out that no ambitious politician is willing to acknowledge this, Kaplan writes we need a new foreign policy that acknowledges and builds on that fact.

Samuelson, Robert J. "Farewell to Pax Americana." *Washington Post,* December 14, 2006, p. A31. Pointing out that ever since World War II the United States has used its military and economic superiority to promote a stable world order, Robert Samuelson writes that the United States increasingly lacks both the power and the will to play this role. According to this article, 2006 might have marked the end of Pax Americana.

THE COLD WAR

Bell, Jonathan. *Liberal State on Trial: The Cold War and American Politics in the Truman Years.* New York: Columbia University Press, 2004. Discussing the role the cold war played in shifting the center of gravity in American politics sharply to the right in the years immediately following World War II, Jonathan Bell says that the United States has developed a much less state-centered orthodoxy than other comparable, powerful liberal states. He explains how this approach shaped the character and direction of American society during the second half of the 20th century.

Freedman, Lawrence. *Kennedy's Wars: Berlin, Cuba, Laos, and Vietnam.* New York: Oxford University Press, 2000. The historian Lawrence Freedman discusses Kennedy's approach to war and his efforts for peace at the height of the cold war when communist advances were being made in Europe and the Third World. Drawing on cold war scholarship and newly released government documents, Freedman describes the political and intellectual milieu of the foreign policy establishment during Kennedy's era.

Gaddis, John Lewis. *Strategies of Containment: A Critical Appraisal of American National Security Policy during the Cold War.* New York: Oxford University Press, 2005. This updated edition of a book that was first published when the Soviet Union was still a superpower, Ronald Reagan was president of the United States, and the Berlin Wall was still standing tells the history of containment through the end of the cold war, starting with Franklin D. Roosevelt's postwar plans through Reagan and Gorbachev.

Gilman, Nils. *Mandarins of the Future: Modernization Theory in Cold War America.* Baltimore: Johns Hopkins University Press, 2003. Nils Gilman studies the American sense of global mission in the post–World War II/cold war period. He charts the development of the so-called modernization theory and explains the background and context for the United States's Third World programs during the period of competition with the Soviet Union.

Latham, Michael E. *Modernization as Ideology: American Social Science and "Nation Building" in the Kennedy Era.* Chapel Hill: University of North Carolina Press, 2000. Michael Latham presents a study of several important U.S. cold war foreign policies. He shows how, in the midst of America's protracted struggle to contain communism in the developing world, the concept of global modernization moved beyond its beginnings in academia to become a motivating ideology behind policy decisions.

Lukacs, John. *George Kennan: A Study of Character.* New Haven: Yale University Press, 2007. John Lukacs describes the development and the essence of George Kennan's thinking; the misinterpretations of his advocacies; his roles as a leading realist critic during the cold war; and the importance of his work as a historian during the second half of his long life.

Magyar, Karl P., ed.; Davis, Bradley S., Charles Tustin Kamps, and Vicki J. Rast, assoc. eds. *United States Post–Cold War Defence Interests: A Review of the First Decade.* New York: Palgrave Macmillan, 2004. Karl P. Magyar, who has served as a senior research associate at the Center for Aerospace Doctrine, Research, and Education has gathered analysts to examine traditional military concerns and responses to the new post–cold war environment. The authors tell how with the end of the cold war, the security concerns of the United States became fragmented and proliferated throughout the world.

Njølstad, Olav, ed. *Last Decade of the Cold War: From Conflict Escalation to Conflict London.* Portland, Ore.: Frank Cass, 2004. This collection of essays by 18 scholars of international relations and history from various countries addresses the role of the United States, the former Soviet Union, and the countries of western and eastern Europe in the last decade of the cold war. The book covers the course of the cold war, discussing how particular events as well as underlying political, ideological, social, and economic factors may have contributed to the transformation that took place.

Ojserkis, Raymond P. *Beginnings of the Cold War Arms Race: The Truman Administration and the U.S. Arms Build-up.* Westport, Conn.: Praeger, 2003. This book presents an account of the strategy and politics behind the Truman administration's decision to engage in a massive arms buildup in 1950, a decision that initiated the cold war arms race and ultimately resulted in the United States assuming a global military presence that lasted for decades.

Preble, Christopher. *John F. Kennedy and the Missile Gap.* DeKalb: Northern Illinois University Press, 2004. Christopher Preble argues that John F. Kennedy owed his victorious bid for the presidency—as well as his success in reversing former president Dwight D. Eisenhower's military and economic policies while in office—largely to his ability to exploit fears of an alleged Soviet strategic superiority, famously known as the "missile gap." According to Preble, the missile gap was a myth that was perpetrated by the Kennedy administration in order to justify a massive military buildup that had profound implications both for the domestic economy and for American foreign relations.

Wenger, Andreas. *Living with Peril: Eisenhower, Kennedy, and Nuclear Weapons.* Lanham, Md.: Rowman & Littlefield Publishers, 1997. This book discusses the ways in which the Eisenhower and Kennedy administrations adapted to the reality of a Soviet nuclear force capable of destroying the United States and against which there was no effective defense. Wenger illuminates the development, implementation, and evolution of U.S. government policies designed to avoid war and to respond to the vulnerability of nuclear destruction.

THE WAR ON TERROR

Ahmed, Nafeez Mosaddeq. *The War on Truth: 9/11, Disinformation, and the Anatomy of Terrorism.* Northampton, Mass.: Olive Branch Press, 2005. In *The War on Truth,* a sequel to *The War on Freedom,* Nafeez Ahmed presents a study of the vested interests and intrigues responsible for the collapse of U.S. national security in the years and months leading to 9/11. Deconstructing the government's official version of what happened on 9/11, Ahmed exposes liaisons between American, British, and European intelligence services and al-Qaeda operatives in the Balkans, the Caucasus, North Africa, the Middle East, Central Asia, and Asia-Pacific—liaisons linked not only to 9/11, but also to prior terrorist attacks.

Allison, Graham, ed. *Confronting the Specter of Nuclear Terrorism.* Thousand Oaks, Calif.: SAGE Publications, 2006. The papers in this volume take a historical look at the development of the threat of nuclear terrorism, and how that threat has changed over time. Some questions explored here are: What role should the United States play in confronting and combating this danger? Is nuclear terrorism preventable? What steps has the United States already taken to prevent a nuclear catastrophe and what future steps should it take?

Allman, T. D. *Rogue State: America at War with the World.* New York: Nation Books, 2004. In this account of the Bush administration's foreign policy, T. D. Allman charges that after September 11 George W. Bush squandered the goodwill of the world, insulted America's allies, lost the respect of developing nations, and unleashed a new era of danger and instability in international affairs.

Bovard, James. *Bush Betrayal.* New York: Palgrave Macmillan, 2004. Focusing on the Bush administration's restrictions on liberty and its expansion of governmental powers after 9/11, James Bovard delivers a harsh critique of the presidency of George W. Bush. Writing from a libertarian perspective, Boyard says that after 9/11"[t]he simple solution was to increase the power of good—i.e., government—to vanquish evil." Bovard charges that the Bush administration's policies on free trade, its No Child Left Behind Act, and AmeriCorps, were other wasteful ways for Bush to invoke virtue.

Brawley, Mark R. *Afterglow or Adjustment?: Domestic Institutions and Responses to Overstretch.* New York: Columbia University Press, 1999. Mark R. Brawley here addresses the issue of the peace dividend and the new world order that was expected to be a bonus of the end of the cold war. *Afterglow or Adjustment* examines differing responses to overstretch in modern history, focusing on military and economic policies in the United States and Britain over the past century. Brawley explains how hegemonic powers respond to overcommitment with "afterglows," maintaining leadership obligations long after such policies have ceased to be rational from a national or domestic perspective.

Carafano, James Jay, and Paul Rosenzweig. *Winning the Long War: Lessons from the Cold War for Defeating Terrorism and Preserving* Freedom. Washington, D.C.: Heritage Foundation, 2005. Experts on homeland security, civil liberties, and economics examine current U.S. policy and map out a long-term national strategy for the war on terrorism, one that balances prudent military and security measures with the need to protect civil liberties and maintain continued economic growth.

Clark, Wesley K. *Winning Modern Wars: Iraq, Terrorism, and the American Empire.* New York: PublicAffairs, 2003. Retired general Wesley Clark (who at the time of this book's publication was a presidential candidate) begins his book by analyzing the United States's successful military invasion of Iraq, a country whose fighting power it had significantly overestimated. Clark then goes on to criticize the Bush administration for having been unprepared for the occupation and reconstruction that followed the war. He criticizes Bush for having failed to build on the world's goodwill toward the United States, following 9/11, bringing it to task for refusing to seek legitimacy from the UN and NATO. Clark charges that the Bush administration had lost focus on what he refers to as the real war against terrorism and had neglected domestic security in the process.

Clarke, Richard A., et al. *Defeating the Jihadists: A Blueprint for Action: The Report of a Task Force.* New York: Century Foundation Press, 2004. *Defeating the Jihadists* discusses the threat of terrorism and accuses the Bush administration of mishandling it. Included is a chapter describing five nations (Saudi Arabia, Egypt, Iran, Pakistan, and Iraq) where terrorists, or jihadists, are seeking to replace existing governments or have already succeeded in installing fundamentalist regimes. Clarke discusses the policy in Iraq. Also included is a chapter about how the United States can partner with Islamic countries to promote ideas like democracy, civil liberties, nonviolence, and the protection of noncombatants.

Foreign Policy, September/October 2007. A report about what leading experts have to say concerning the success of America's actions against terrorism. A majority of the experts believe that the surge in Iraq is not working and dismiss President Bush's claim that troop withdrawal would result in the terrorists "following us home."

Friedman, Norman. *Terrorism, Afghanistan, and America's New Way of War.* Annapolis, Md.: Naval Institute Press, 2003. Norman Friedman, head of the global intelligence company Stratfor (which has been dubbed by *Barron's* as "the shadow CIA"), gives a behind-the-scenes picture of the war on terror, what he calls the "fourth global war." Friedman tells how since 9/11 the CIA has been working in close partnership with the intelligence services of dozens of nations.

Kramer, Paul. "The Water Cure." *The New Yorker,* February 25, 2008. Implicitly drawing parallels to our current waterboarding debate, Kramer tells the story here about how during the Philippine-American War American soldiers used a torture method called the water cure to extract information from Filipino fighters.

Lapham, Lewis. *Theater of War.* New York: New Press, 2002. In this collection of 14 selections from his *Harper's* Notebook column (October 2000–March 2002), *Harper's* editor Lewis Lapham attempts to debunk the war on terror. Railing against incompetence and hypocrisy in the media and government, Lapham observes that "all societies, like most individuals, are always in some kind of trouble," but he suggests that it isn't trouble that kills, but rather "the fear of thought and the paralysis that accompanies the wish to believe that only the wicked perish."

Lifton, Robert Jay. *Superpower Syndrome: America's Apocalyptic Confrontation with the World.* New York: Thunder's Mouth Press/Nations Books, 2003. Speaking here of the creation of something he calls Superpower Syndrome, psychiatrist Robert Jay Lifton, a leading scholar of thought control and mass violence, writes about the United States's experience of itself as a survivor nation, in the wake of 9/11. He discusses the feelings of vulnerability of Americans, citizens and leaders alike, and how the Bush administration's unprecedented use of military power has intensified these feelings of vulnerability and danger.

Piszkiewicz, Dennis. *Terrorism's War with America: A History.* Westport, Conn.: Praeger, 2003. Piszkiewicz discusses the evolution of modern international terrorism from a disorganized activity of individuals and small groups, through its adoption of political warfare by nationalists, insurgents, and the disenfranchised, to its current incarnation as a weapon of political change used by rogue states and radical religious movements.

Rogers, Paul. *War on Terror: Afghanistan and After.* London; Sterling, Va.: Pluto Press, 2004. Paul Rogers, one of the world's leading security experts, presents a radical assessment of Bush's war on terror, the way it has affected world security and the grave implications that it holds for future peace, not only in the Middle East but throughout the world.

AMERICAN TRADE POLICY

Blau, Joel. *Illusions of Prosperity: America's Working Families in an Age of Economic Insecurity.* New York: Oxford University Press, 1999. In *Illusions of Prosperity,* Blau writes that while the share of the national income is held by the bottom four-fifths of the population has continued to decline, the top fifth gained 97 percent of the increase in total household income between 1979 and 1994. Citing recent reforms in NAFTA, education, job training, and welfare, etc., Blau argues that the new social policies have made matters worse, because reforms that rely on the market can't compensate for the market's deficiencies.

Cohen, Stephen D., Joel R. Paul, and Robert A. Blecker. *Fundamentals of U.S. Foreign Trade Policy: Economics, Politics, Laws, and Issues.* Boulder, Colo.: Westview Press, 1996. This book examines the ways in which U.S. trade policy is formulated and implemented, taking into account economics, politics, and law. Aiming to analyze U.S. trade policy as it is and not what it could or should be, the authors discuss the political forces that govern the inner workings of the U.S. trade policy decision-making process.

Collins, Susan M., ed. *Imports, Exports, and the American Worker.* Washington, D.C.: Brookings Institution Press, 1998. Bringing together the diverse perspectives of international economists, labor economists, and policy makers, this volume analyzes how international trade affects the level and distribution of wages and employment in the United States, examines the need for government intervention, and evaluates policy options.

Deardorff, Alan V., and Robert M. Stern, eds. *Social Dimensions of U.S. Trade Policies.* Ann Arbor: University of Michigan Press, 2000. Members of the trade policy community analyze and discuss the salient social dimensions of U.S. trade policies, including the effects of trade on wage inequality; trade and immigration policy; U.S. trade adjustment assistance policies; the effects of NAFTA on environmental quality; the role of labor standards in U.S. trade policies; the economics of labor standards and the GATT; issues of child labor; and the role of interest groups in the design and implementation of U.S. trade policies.

DeSouza, Patrick J., ed. *Economic Strategy and National Security: A Next Generation Approach.* Boulder, Colo.: Westview Press, 2000. In this volume, former senior members of the Clinton and George H. W. Bush administrations and a "next generation" of private sector voices analyze the new intersections between economic strategy and national security. The book takes account of emerging markets, as well as new threats and new opportunities that are changing our conception of American security.

Feenstra, Robert C., ed. *Effects of U.S. Trade Protection and Promotion Policies.* Chicago: University of Chicago Press, 1997. This collection of 12 essays by leading international economists explores crucial issues in U.S. trade policy today, issues such as the markets for automobile and automobile parts in the United States and Japan, the U.S. response to unfair trading practices such as dumping, and the effects of industry- and country-specific policies.

Hody, Cynthia Ann. *Politics of Trade: American Political Development and Foreign Economic Policy.* Hanover, N.H.: Dartmouth College University Press of New England, 1996. Cynthia Hody here examines the link between domestic and international policies shown by exploring the implications of institutional change.

Krueger, Anne O., ed. *Political Economy of Trade Protection.* Chicago: University of Chicago Press, 1996. This summary of the analyses presented in *The Political Economy of American Trade Policy* examines the level, form, and evolution of American trade protection. In case studies of trade barriers imposed during the 1980s, the contributors trace the evolution of efforts to obtain protection, protectionist measures, and their results.

Pattison, Joseph E. *Breaking Boundaries: Public Policy vs. American Business in the World Economy.* Princeton, N.J.: Peterson's/Pacesetter Books, 1996. Joseph Pattison addresses the harm that he believes that the United States's antiglobal bias is doing to American enterprise. He argues that American competitiveness is endangered by outdated elements of public policy that were built around the standards of the industrial age.

Pearson, Charles. *United States Trade Policy: A Work in Progress.* Hoboken, N.J.: John Wiley, 2004. This is an account of U.S. trade policy over the last four decades. It explains how trade policy is practiced and what the roots and evolution of today's trade issues are.

Pletcher, David M. *Diplomacy of Trade and Investment: American Economic Expansion in the Hemisphere, 1865–1900.* Columbia: University of Missouri Press, 1998. David Pletcher begins this study with a survey of U.S. trade following the Civil War. He goes on to outline the problems of building a coherent trade policy with Canada, Mexico, Central America, the Caribbean, and South America.

Prasad, Monica. *Politics of Free Markets: The Rise of Neoliberal Economic Policies in Britain, France, Germany, and the United States.* Chicago: University of Chicago Press, 2006. This book examines why neoliberal policies gained such prominence in the United States under Ronald Reagan and in Britain under Margaret Thatcher, but not in similarly industrialized Western countries such as France and Germany.

Preeg, Ernest H. *From Here to Free Trade: Essays in Post–Uruguay Round Trade Strategy.* Washington, D.C.: Center for Strategic and International Studies; Chicago: University of Chicago Press, 1998. Ernest Preeg analyzes international trade and investment in the 1990s and lays out a U.S. trade strategy for the future. He examines the influence of the World Trade Organization and argues that economic globalization is beneficial to the U.S. economy in the short to medium term, while raising questions about national sovereignty and security over the longer term. Preeg says that the central challenge for U.S. trade strategy is to integrate the now largely separate multilateral and regional tracks of the world trading system.

Rosenberg, Emily S. *Financial Missionaries to the World: The Politics and Culture of Dollar Diplomacy, 1900–1930.* Cambridge, Mass.: Harvard University Press, 1999. This book discusses the broad scope and significance of dollar diplomacy to early 20th-century U.S. foreign policy. Drawing on diplomatic, economic, and cultural history, historian Emily S. Rosenberg explains how private bank loans were extended to leverage the acceptance of American financial advisers by foreign governments. Revealing how the practice became embroiled in controversy, Rosenberg tells how by the mid-1920s early supporters of dollar diplomacy worried that facilitating excessive borrowing might induce the instability and default that it supposedly worked against.

Rothgeb, John M. Jr. *U.S. Trade Policy: Balancing Economic Dreams and Political Realities.* Washington, D.C.: CQ Press, 2001. John Rothgeb discusses the enormous changes spurred by the Reciprocal Trade Agreements Act, the Bretton Woods system, and the GATT, to the controversy surrounding trade relations with the European Union and China. The book covers international trade, the political tensions it arouses, and its historical roots, tracing the forces that affect U.S. trade policy's development and implementation, including the strategic and competitive international arena, policy makers' views on the value of trade, the influence of special interest groups, and the impact of institutional rivalries.

Schoppa, Leonard J. *Bargaining with Japan: What American Pressure Can and Cannot Do.* New York: Columbia University Press, 1997. This is a critical examination of the outcome of recent U.S.-Japan trade talks, focusing on the Bush administration's Structural Impediments Initiative and the Clinton Framework talks. Schoppa provides a comprehensive account of the political climate on both sides of the Pacific, drawing lessons about which tactics are most likely to work best for the United States. He says that before new policies can be established, it must be understood why neither administration was able to compel Japan to end anticompetitive practices that inhibit the access of U.S. firms to Japanese consumers.

Stokes, Bruce. *New Beginning: Recasting the U.S.-Japan Economic Relationship.* New York: Council on Foreign Relations Press, 2000. This book lays out a road map for U.S.-Japan economic relations in the 21st century. Bruce Stokes asserts that the time is ripe to recast the U.S.-Japan economic relationship for the 21st century. Pointing to the rise of foreign investment in Japan, Tokyo's deregulation and restructuring of its economy, Stokes examines the emergence of a new generation of entrepreneurs and venture capitalists.

Van Hook, James C. *Rebuilding Germany: The Creation of the Social Market Economy, 1945–1957.* Cambridge: Cambridge University Press, 2004. James Van Hook evaluates the American role in West German recovery and the debates about economic policy within West Germany. He examines the 1948 West German economic reforms that dismantled the Nazi command economy and ushered in the fabled economic miracle of the 1950s.

GLOBALIZATION AND DEVELOPMENT

Books

Appelbaum, Richard P., and William I. Robinson, eds. *Anti-Globalization Movement. Critical Globalization Studies.* New York: Routledge, 2005. This book contains new theoretical perspectives on globalization. The contributors address the issue of global justice.

Bhagwati, Jagdish N. *Anti-Globalization Movement: In Defense of Globalization.* New York: Oxford University Press, 2007. Responding to charges that globalization has harmed poorer nations by being responsible for everything from child labor to environmental degradation and cultural homogenization, renowned economist Jagdish Bhagwati asserts that globalization, when properly controlled, is in fact the most powerful force for social good in the world today.

———. *Wind of the Hundred Days: How Washington Mismanaged Globalization.* Cambridge, Mass.: MIT Press, 2000. In this collection of public policy essays, Jagdish Bhagwati writes about the Clinton administration's mismanagement of globalization—resulting in the paradox of immense domestic policy success combined with dramatic failure on the external front. Bhagwati assigns the bulk of the blame for the East Asian financial and economic crisis to the administration's hasty push for financial liberalization in the region.

Binns, Jack R. *United States in Honduras, 1980–1981: An Ambassador's Memoir.* Jefferson, N.C.: McFarland & Co., 2000. A former ambassador to Honduras, Jack R. Binns, writes about developments as the country moved from a relatively benign military dictatorship to a democratic constitutional leadership in the period from 1980 through 1981. Binns writes about the consequences of an inadequate U.S. policy formulation in Central America, charging that the U.S. effort to overthrow the Sandinista regime was a costly failure, that U.S. support of the Salvadoran military enlarged rather than reduced the conflict, and that U.S. activity in Honduras encouraged human rights abuses.

Burtless, Gary, Robert Z. Lawrence, Robert E. Litan, et al. *Globaphobia: Confronting Fears about Open Trade.* Washington, D.C.: Brookings Institution; Washington, D.C.: Progressive Policy Institute; New York: Twentieth Century Fund, 1998. Responding to the widely growing complaints against globalization, the authors of this book contend that globalization has not reduced the availability of jobs nor has it reduced the average wage. According to *Globaphobia,* globalization has played only a small part in the deteriorating situation of America's least skilled workers. The authors assert that the challenge is for all Americans to embrace globalization and the benefits it brings, while adopting targeted policies to ease the pain of those few Americans whom globalization may harm.

Curran, Giorel. *21st Century Dissent: Anarchism, Anti-globalization and Environmentalism.* Basingstoke, England; New York: Palgrave Macmillan, 2006. *21st Century Dissent* contends that anarchism has had a considerable influence on the modern political landscape. Giorel Curran explores the contemporary face of anarchism as expressed in environmental protests and the antiglobalization movement.

Eichengreen, Barry, ed. *Transatlantic Economic Relations in the Post–Cold War Era.* New York: Council on Foreign Relations, 1998. This collection of essays considers the relationship between the American and European economies that has come about as a result of globalization and economic integration. The book considers whether the trend will be toward increased conflict or collaboration. According to the authors, the changes that will take place in this transatlantic relationship will be incremental rather than revolutionary.

Eschle, Catherine, and Bice Maiguashca. eds. *Critical Theories, International Relations and 'the Anti-globalisation Movement': The Politics of Global Resistance.* New York: Routledge, 2005. This textbook introduces students to the main theories in international relations. It explains and analyzes each theory and the myths and assumptions behind them. The theories discussed include realism and neorealism, idealism and neoidealism, liberalism, constructivism, postmodernism, gender and globalization.

Etzioni, Amitai. *From Empire to Community: A New Approach to International Relations.* New York: Palgrave Macmillan, 2004. In this book, Etzioni offers what he terms "a new approach to international relations," what he calls a "global normative synthesis," that would involve the creation of a transnational community of shared values and mores. He discusses what he perceives to be the tendency within the world community toward a "chemical fusion" of Western individualism and Eastern social authoritarianism.

Gould, Erica R. *Money Talks: The International Monetary Fund, Conditionality, and Supplementary Financiers.* Stanford, Calif.: Stanford University Press, 2006. *Money Talks* argues that the changes in the terms of IMF conditionality agreements are best explained by shifts in the sources for borrowing state financing.

Kiely, Ray. *Clash of Globalisations: Neo-Liberalism, the Third Way and Anti-globalisation.* Leiden, Netherlands: Brill Academic Publisher, 2005. This work is a critique of the politics of globalization through an examination of neoliberalism, the third way, and anticapitalist responses and alternatives. Using a Marxist approach, it challenges the claims made by apologists for "actually existing globalization" and explains the rise of antiglobalization politics. It examines the role of the state as an agent of globalization, particularly the United States.

Klein, Naomi. *Shock Doctrine: The Rise of Disaster Capitalism.* New York: Metropolitan Books/Henry Holt, 2007. Naomi Klein, creator of the term *disaster capitalism,* asserts that the global free market has exploited crises and shock for three decades, from Chile to Iraq. *Shock Doctrine* tells the dark side of Milton Friedman's free-market economic revolution. Klein posits here that, contrary to the popular opinion that this movement was a peaceful global victory, it has exploited disasters—both natural and manmade—in order to implement its economic policies throughout the world.

Macesich, George. *United States in the Changing Global Economy: Policy Implications and Issues.* Westport, Conn.: Praeger, 1997. This book takes account of the accelerating globalization of world markets and increasing interdependence of the economies of the world. Macesich addresses the question of whether the United States is capable of simultaneously dealing with serious domestic challenges and economic challenges from the rest of the world.

Navarro, Vicente, ed. *Neoliberalism, Globalization, and Inequalities: Consequences for Health and Quality of Life.* Amityville, N.Y.: Baywood Publishing, 2007. This collection of essays presents analyses of neoliberal globalization. According to Noam Chomsky, the essays show the "human consequences of the dominant intellectual and policy paradigms of the past several decades."

Paloni, Alberto, and Maurizio Zanardi, eds. *IMF, World Bank and Policy Reform.* New York: Routledge, 2006. This book centers around the debate of whether or not the International Monetary Fund and World Bank and their intervention strategies are a positive force for change in the developing world. It brings together an international team of contributors who address three broad themes: the ideology of the IMF and World Bank, poverty reduction, and conditionality.

Reitan, Ruth. *Anti-globalization Movement. Global Activism.* New York: Routledge, 2007. This study traces the transnationalization of activist networks such as the World Bank, the IMF, and the World Trade Organization. It analyzes the changing compositions and characters in these entities and examines the roles played by the World Social Forum. Reitan points out that in spite of their diversity, these networks follow a similar globalizing path.

Sachs, Wolfgang, and Tilman Santarius, eds. *Fair Future: Resource Conflicts, Security and Global Justice: A Report of the Wuppertal Institute for Climate, Environment and Energy.* New York: Zed Books, 2007. In this analysis the authors, who are senior research fellows at the Wuppertal Institute for Climate, Environment and Energy, address the problems of social justice and environmental sustainability, focusing on questions such as how poor countries can raise their standards of living on a planet with limited resources without putting it under additional environmental stress.

Skidelsky, Robert. *John Maynard Keynes: 1883–1946: Economist, Philosopher, Statesman.* London: Macmillan, 2003. In this biography of John Maynard Keynes, Skidelsky has abridged his original three-volume opus into one definitive book, which examines in its entirety the intellectual and ideological journey that led an extraordinarily gifted young man to concern himself with the practical problems of an age overshadowed by war.

Vreeland, James Raymond, and Stephen Kosack. *Globalization and the Nation State: The Impact of the IMF and the World Bank.* New York: Routledge, 2006. This book brings together an international team of contributors to discuss whether or not the International Monetary Fund and World Bank and their intervention strategies are a positive force for change in the developing world. This book focuses on three broad themes: the ideology of the IMF and World Bank, poverty reduction, and conditionality.

Wiefek, Nancy. *Impact of Economic Anxiety in Postindustrial America.* Westport, Conn.: Praeger, 2003. Nancy Wiefek addresses the political consequences of the strains that have been created over the last 30 years by the United States's transition to a postindustrial, globalized economy, focusing on the emotional anxiety accompanying this transition. Wiefek analyzes the anxiety citizens experience in their daily lives as a consequence of these changes, taking into account psychological, sociological, economic, and political science theories and findings. Using data from a mail survey, the author estimates what the impact of economic anxiety is and presents evidence of how it affects political opinion. She concludes with a discussion of the political implications of these findings.

Woods, Ngaire. *Globalizers: The IMF, the World Bank, and Their Borrowers.* Ithaca, N.Y.: Cornell University Press, 2006. This book explains the political context of IMF and World Bank actions and their impact on the countries in which they intervene. It traces the impact of the bank and the fund in the recent economic history of Mexico, of post-Soviet Russia, and in the independent states of Africa, concluding with proposals for a range of reforms that would make the World Bank and the IMF more effective, equitable, and just.

Zweifel, Thomas D. *International Organizations and Democracy: Accountability, Politics, and Power.* Boulder, Colo.: L. Rienner Publishers, 2005. Thomas Zweifel explores the issue of whether international organizations represent the interests of the global citizenry or are instead merely vehicles for the agendas of powerful nations and special interests. Zweifel covers regional organizations such as the EU, NAFTA, NATO, and the AU, and global institutions such as the United Nations, the World Bank, and the World Trade Organization.

Articles

Brooks, David. "Follow the Fundamentals." *New York Times,* November 27, 2007. Disputing people's fears about the ill effects of globalization, such as job outsourcing and tainted imports, David Brooks points out that America still boasts "the most potent economy on earth." He also points out that while the trade deficit has increased, unemployment has dipped, and job losses are mostly influenced by domestic forces.

Chang, Jeff. "It's a Hip-Hop World." *Foreign Policy,* November/December 2007. Jeff Chang explores the world of hip-hop through the eyes of rap-loving youth around the globe, from France to Ghana to China. Chang looks at how hip-hop has become an international phenomenon and is being accepted and adapted by people all over the world.

Collier, Paul. "Will the Bottom Billion Ever Catch Up?" *Washington Post,* October 21, 2007. According to Paul Collier, the widening gap between the rich and the poor is not just an American phenomenon. He points out how once poverty-stricken countries like China and India are on the fast-track to prosperity, while income and living standards have stagnated for the poorest billion people, many of them from Africa. Collier argues that the World Bank should devise a comprehensive strategy to help the bottom billion.

The Economist. "Keep the Borders Open." January 5, 2008. *The Economist* argues that migration, both legal and illegal, offers more benefits than costs by providing an influx of new ideas, talent, and human capital. The editors recommend that Congress establish a worker-permit program and give amnesty to "long-standing, law-abiding workers already in the country." Objections such as wage-depression, xenophobia, and national security concerns are misplaced, they contend.

———. "Wind of Change." January 10, 2008. *The Economist* points out there is a great deal more to globalization than an opportunity for Western multinational corporations to colonize developing nations economically. This is exemplified by the rise of emerging-market multinationals. *The Economist* suggests that it is time for emerging-market multinationals to speak up for the fact that trade liberalization is in their best interests, as well.

Fox, Justin. "Why Denmark Loves Globalization." *Time,* November 26, 2007. Justin Fox reports about a recent survey in Denmark that found that 76 percent of Danes support globalization. Discussing Denmark's economy, he points out that the country has both the world's second highest tax rate and the third most competitive economy, which seems to contradict the claim that small government is good for big business.

Geoghegan, Thomas. "What Worker Rights Can Do." *American Prospect,* August 13, 2007. In this discussion of labor rights and trade bills, Thomas Geoghegan argues that corporations should be held accountable for disparities in workers' rights. He says workers' rights should be protected on a global scale by allowing workers the opportunity to sue over unfair labor practices by American companies who go overseas to find their workers.

Annotated Bibliography

Ghemawat, Pankaj. "The World's Biggest Myth." *Foreign Policy,* November/December 2007. Pankaj Ghemawat, a professor at Harvard Business School, here endeavors to debunk the idea that globalization puts more power in the hands of the few. Instead, Ghemawat writes that globalization has resulted in more competition and diversity.

Greenspan, Alan. "The World in 2030." *Newsweek,* September 24, 2007. In an excerpt from his new book, *The Age of Turbulence,* Greenspan predicts a "positive outcome" for the U.S. economy in 2030. Anchoring his analysis in demographics and trends in productivity growth, he ultimately projects steady GDP growth at around 2.5 percent annually. However, he writes that his forecast depends on the triumph of prudence over politics.

Harrison, Lawrence E. "The End of Multiculturalism." *Christian Science Monitor,* February 26, 2008. p. 9 Lawrence Harrison writes here that efforts to perpetuate "old country" values in a multicultural salad bowl undermine acculturation to the mainstream and are likely to result in continuing underachievement.

Herbst, Jeffrey. "Africa Trades Down." *Foreign Policy,* November/December 2007. Jeffrey Herbst criticizes the editors of *From the Slave Trade to "Free" Trade: How Trade Undermines Democracy and Justice in Africa* for ignoring the benefits of international trade in Africa. Defending globalization, which he calls "a revolution in attitude that forces leaders to confront and overcome a brutal past," Herbst rails against "breezy assertions about a complicated world."

Kagan, Robert. "Free Elections Come First." *Washington Post,* October 28, 2007. Robert Kagan dismisses the theory that post–cold war autocracies like China and Russia represent a phase on a linear path toward liberalization. According to him, despotic nations have managed to monopolize state power to achieve economic growth without democratization and it therefore doesn't make sense to respond to a globalized economy by gradually pursuing political reforms.

Kearney, A. T. "The Globalization Index 2007." *Foreign Policy,* November/December 2007. In this, *Foreign Policy*'s seventh annual Globalization Index, the magazine points out that "globalization" is a concept that is often bandied about without any real precision. The magazine here ranks the world's 72 largest economies according to their integration with the rest of the global community. According to *Foreign Policy,* while globalization continues to "flatten" our world, it is by no means an irresistible force.

Mills, Nicolaus. "A Globalism for Our Time." *American Prospect,* July/August 2007. Nicolaus Mills argues that the Marshall Plan, used to organize recovery efforts in Europe after World War II, is as relevant today as it was 60 years ago. He says that key points from the plan, such as bipartisanship and multilateralism and participating in international affairs and "acceptance of the limits of American power" are constructive in a post-9/11 world.

Naim, Moises. "Can the World Afford a Middle Class?" *Foreign Policy,* March/April 2008. Moises Naim looks at the repercussions of a growing global middle class on the world economy. While commending the efforts to lift the world's population out of poverty, he also warns that this "fastest-growing segment of the world's population" will create unprecedented pressure on food prices, medicine, textiles, and raw materials as inhabitants of developing countries adopt a less frugal lifestyle.

———. "The Free-Trade Paradox." *Foreign Policy,* September/October 2007. Moses Naim explains the apparent paradox concerning whys, while free-trade negotiations are stalling, free trade between nations is booming. A confluence of factors has accounted for this unexpected situation, including advancements in technology and unilateral tariff reductions. Naim goes on to warn against complacency and abandoning negotiations, citing quality controls and continued alleviation of poverty as reasons for nations to continue to seek agreements. A straightforward and useful article on a controversial subject.

Popkin, Barry M. "The World Is Fat." *Scientific American,* September 2007. Barry Popkin reports here about the worldwide rise in obesity rates. Popkin blames this phenomenon on globalization, which has resulted in the spread of the Western diet with its sugary beverages, cheap snacks, vegetable oils, and animal products, along with the export of the sedentary, TV-watching, Western lifestyle. Popkin examines various solutions being considered by national governments and international aid organizations.

Roubini, Nouriel. "The Coming Financial Pandemic." *Foreign Policy,* March/April 2008. Nouriel Roubini predicts here that the U.S. financial crisis will spread globally. He says that the flatlining of American consumer spending will cripple the world's export economies, especially China, and that this, in turn, will cause commodity prices to collapse, spreading pain through Latin America and Africa. He also says that the tightening of global credit markets, caused by the subprime meltdown, will set off property busts in Europe and Asia.

Samuelson, Robert J. "Globalization to the Rescue?" *Newsweek,* October 29, 2007. Robert Samuelson discusses America's falling trade deficit, pointing out that globalization is what is currently keeping the economy afloat and that trade balance has little overall effect on employment. While expressing some concern about the depreciating dollar and possible negative effects of the shrinking trade deficit, he maintains that taking an isolationist trade stance will only exacerbate any problems.

Sasseen, Jane. "Economists Rethink Free Trade." *BusinessWeek,* February 11, 2008. Jane Sasseen writes about how some American economists are starting to have doubts about free trade. Sasseen notes the benefits of free trade appear to be very unequally distributed, with only 4 percent of American workers, professionals, or Ph.D.s having had their incomes rise in the past few years, while the vast majority of workers have lost ground, as a result of jobs moving overseas.

Scheve, Kenneth F., and Matthew J. Slaughter. "A New Deal for Globalization." *Foreign Affairs,* July/August 2007. Kenneth Scheve and Matthew J. Slaughter point out that the globalization of the marketplace has done very little to benefit average Americans, who are losing wages as a result of the rise in free trade. The inequality in the global economy has resulted in a protectionist attitude among Americans, and the authors suggest one way of combating the growing protectionism among the American worker might be to redistribute global income.

Schwartz, Nelson D. "One World, Taking Risks Together." *New York Times,* October 21, 2007. Pointing to the recent subprime crisis, Nelson Schwartz argues that the increasing globalization of the stock and credit markets has made investment riskier than ever before. He contends that as international markets grow more inextricably linked, diversification has become nearly impossible.

Steil, Benn. "The End of National Currency." *Foreign Affairs,* May/June 2007. Arguing that globalization is a fact of life, Benn Steil says that developing countries should replace their weak national currencies with dollars or euros to end currency crises and improve the world economy. To the globalization critics, Steil contends that states have never had complete sovereignty over their monetary policy anyway.

Stoll, Steven. "Fear of Fallowing: The Specter of a No-Growth World." *Harper's,* March 2008. Stoll here examines three authors' views on the Earth's biophysical capacities and the future of the global economy. Reviewed here are Brink Lindsay's, *The Age of Abundance,* Benjamin Friedman's, *The Moral Consequences of Economic Growth,* and Bill McKibben's, *Deep Economy.*

Yang, Jia Lynn. "Indian Call Center Lands in Ohio." *Foreign Affairs,* August 6, 2007. Jia Lynn Yang writes here that some of the same foreign companies that took American jobs overseas are bringing them back. For example, the Indian conglomerate the Tata Group recently opened a customer service center in Reno, Ohio, to answer Expedia's phones.

Zakaria, Fareed. "What People Will Die For." *Newsweek,* January 14, 2008. Zakaria writes about the rise of subnational identity in politics around the globe. Advocating the importance of subnationalism, he points the finger at democratization and globalization in exacerbating subnational politics, noting the foolishness of imposing an ideological narrative (like Western democracy versus islamic extremism) on conflicts that have much older and deeper roots.

———. "The World Bails Us Out." *Newsweek,* February 4, 2008. Zakaria writes that if the United States slides into recession, emerging markets will continue to expand, which will likely serve as a prop for the U.S. economy. Another boon to the United States will be sovereign wealth funds. All these foreign investments signal a radical change in the financial world order: American economic power is waning, and emerging markets are strengthening.

ECONOMIC THEORY

Friedman, Milton. *Capitalism and Freedom.* Chicago: University of Chicago Press, 2002. Milton Friedman lays out his economic philosophy—one in which competitive capitalism serves as both a device for achieving economic freedom and a necessary condition for political freedom.

———. *The Optimum Quantity of Money.* New Brunswick, N.J.: Aldine Transaction, 2006. This set of essays concerns the role of money, focusing on specific topics related to the empirical analysis of monetary phenomena and policy.

———. *Milton Friedman on Economics: Selected Papers.* Chicago: University of Chicago Press, 2007. This volume collects a variety of Friedman's papers on topics in economics that were originally published in the *Journal of Political Economy.* Opening with Friedman's 1977 Nobel Lecture, the volume spans nearly the whole of his career, incorporating papers from as early as 1948 and as late as 1990.

Keynes, John Maynard. *General Theory of Employment, Interest, and Money.* Amherst, N.Y.: Prometheus Books, 1997. This new edition of John Maynard Keynes's 1936 *General Theory* features a new introduction by Paul Krugman discussing the significance and continued relevance of the general theory.

———. *Economic Consequences of the Peace.* New Brunswick, N.J.: Transaction Publishers, 2003. This volume (first published in 1919) is considered the most influential social science treatise of the 20th century. Here, the legendary economist John Maynard Keynes argued that the Treaty of Versailles that ended World War I was destined to create tension and conflict ahead.

Lawlor, Michael S. *Economics of Keynes in Historical Context: An Intellectual History of the General Theory.* Michael Lawlor here analyzes how economist John Maynard Keynes's general theory can be understood in the context of the social thought, policy questions, and economics literature that shaped his outlook on theoretical questions.

Tily, Geoff. *Keynes's General Theory, the Rate of Interest and 'Keynesian' Economics.* London: Palgrave Macmillan, 2007. According to Tily, Keynesian economists have betrayed Keynes's theory and policy conclusions. Tily argues that Keynesians have focused attention exclusively on policies for dealing with the effects of economic failure as they arise, whereas in contrast, Keynes was concerned with the cause and then the prevention of economic failure.

EUROPE

Books

Ash, Timothy Garton. *History of the Present: Essays, Sketches, and Dispatches from Europe in the 1990s.* New York: Random House, 2000. Timothy Garton Ash chronicles the formative decade of the 1990s in this collection of essays, sketches, and dispatches that he wrote while the old order collapsed along with the Berlin Wall and everyone looked forward to the emergence of a brave new Europe.

Engelbrekt, Kjell, and Jan Hallenberg, eds. *The European Union and Strategy: An Emerging Actor.* New York: Routledge, 2007. This book examines the character of the European Union and its ability to act and otherwise influence both its periphery and the wider world. The final section includes personal assessments by a group of contributors regarding the character of the union as a strategic actor in the present and future.

Grantham, Bill. *Some Big Bourgeois Brothel: Contexts for France's Culture Wars with Hollywood.* Luton, Bedfordshire, England: University of Luton Press, 2000. Examining Franco-American cinema relations, Bill Grantham, a reporter who has covered the international entertainment industry for various publications, details France's periodic attempts to curb Hollywood's access to the European market.

Hitchcock, William I. *Struggle for Europe: The Turbulent History of a Divided Continent, 1945–2002.* New York: Doubleday, 2003. William Hitchcock examines the transformation of Europe from a deeply fractured land to a continent striving for stability, tolerance, democracy, and prosperity. Exploring the role of cold war politics in Europe's peace settlement and the half century that followed, Hitchcock reveals how leaders such as Charles de Gaulle, Willy Brandt, and Margaret Thatcher balanced their nations' interests against the demands of the reigning superpowers.

Jolly, Mette. *The European Union and the People.* Oxford: Oxford University Press, 2007. Addressing the charge that the European Union has a "democratic deficit," the author argues that the most severe dimension of the democracy problem is not procedural, but sociopsychological, and that it cannot be remedied by increasing the powers of the European Parliament relative to those of the Council and the Commission. He suggests that policies that require high levels of solidarity or a common identity should either remain fully within the nation-states or be subject to intergovernmental rather than supranational decision-making at EU-level.

Nugent, Neill. *The Government and Politics of the European Union.* Durham, N.C.: Duke University Press, 2006. Nugent offers an explanation of the historical development and ongoing evolution of the EU. It presents an account and analysis of the origins of the union, the key treaties, the main institutions and political actors, and the EU's policies and policy processes.

Pommerin, Reinder, ed. *American Impact on Postwar Germany.* Providence, R.I.: Berghahn Books, 1995. This collection of scholarly papers presented at the Goethe Institute–sponsored colloquium in 1993 (with two additional articles) addresses the impact the United States had on German society after 1945 and the German responses to it.

Pond, Elizabeth. *Friendly Fire: The Near-Death of the Transatlantic Alliance.* Pittsburgh, Pa.: European Union Studies Association, 2004. In *Friendly Fire,* a veteran reporter examines the decline in relations between the United States and Europe, which she asserts are worse today than they have been at any time since the 1960s. Addressing the widening gulf and worsening acrimony between the United States and its traditional allies on the European continent, Elizabeth Pond here examines a number of disputes—chronic trade quarrels, the International Criminal Court, the Kyoto Protocol, Israeli-Palestinian violence, and Iraq—and identifies the ways in which they reinforce and exacerbate one another.

Wapshott, Nicholas. *Ronald Reagan and Margaret Thatcher: A Political Marriage.* New York: Sentinel, 2007. This is a study of the complex personal and political friendship of Ronald Reagan and Margaret Thatcher, who during their eight overlapping years in office worked together to promote lower taxes, deregulation, free trade, and an aggressive stance against the Soviet Union.

Articles

Eberstadt, Nicholas, and Hans Groth. "Healthy Old Europe." *Foreign Affairs,* May/June 2007. The authors suggests that the dramatic increase in the proportion of elderly people in western Europe will seriously damage European economic productivity unless governments implement structural changes in their economies to give the healthy elderly population incentives to work. Most Europeans retire much earlier than Americans, at least partly due to monetary disincentives to work.

The Economist. "Winners and Losers." February 28, 2008. Referring to a new study by American academics that says the European Union has increased its share of world exports, while most of the economic proceeds from Chinese-made goods wind up in the country they are actually sold in, this editorial says that a shift in Europe from manufacturing to service jobs is not inherently a bad thing.

Kuttner, Robert. "The Copenhagen Consensus." *Foreign Affairs,* March/April 2008. Robert Kuttner explains why Denmark has the world's second highest tax rate and also the world's third most competitive economy. He also writes about the challenges posed to Denmark's system by factors such as immigration.

Theil, Stefan. "Europe's Philosophy of Failure." *Foreign Policy,* January/February 2008. Stefan Theil writes that the "highly biased" economics textbooks used in schools in France and Germany does much to explain those countries' policies. Two examples he uses to illustrate this point are a French textbook that describes capitalism as "savage" and "American" and a German text that recommends antireform protests to combat unemployment. Theil argues that this explains why the French and Germans think the way they do—and what might be done to temper their views.

LATIN AMERICA

Books

Burns, Bradford E., and Julie A. Charlip. *Latin America: A Concise Interpretive History.* New York: Prentice Hall, 2006. This textbook weaves together the story of Latin America, including coverage of broad themes and regional differences. An example of one of the themes covered here is the idea that poor people inhabit rich lands, which the authors point out as being paradoxical since this results in a tiny group of elites confusing the nation's well-being with their own.

Chasteen, John Charles. *Born in Blood and Fire: A Concise History of Latin America.* New York: W. W. Norton, 2005. This text presents a survey of history of Latin America. Drawing on the most current scholarship, the book spans six centuries and 20 countries. Revised in light of recent Latin American history, this second edition introduces new maps, chapter time lines, and a new student Web site.

Goodwin, Paul B. *Global Studies: Latin America.* New York: McGraw-Hill/Dushkin, 2006. This textbook provides comprehensive background information on Latin America. It includes introductory essays on Mexico, Central America, South America, and the Caribbean region, with concise reports and current statistics for each of the countries within these regions. This background information is complemented by a selection of articles from the world press.

Reid, Michael. *Forgotten Continent: The Battle for Latin America's Soul.* New Haven: Yale University Press, 2008. Michael Reid, editor of the Americas section of the *Economist,* argues here that Latin America's efforts to build fairer and more prosperous societies make it one of the world's most vigorous laboratories for capitalist democracy. Reid points to countries like Brazil, Chile, and Mexico, where democratic leaders are laying the foundations for faster economic growth and more inclusive politics.

Skidmore, Thomas E., and Peter H. Smith. *Modern Latin America.* New York: Oxford University Press, 2004. This textbook presents an interpretive history of Latin America, examining topics such as the impact of 9/11 on U.S.–Latin American relations, globalization, drug trafficking, women's roles in society and politics, and the fragility and uncertainty of democracy in Latin America. This updated version includes a new chapter on the history of Colombia from the wars of independence to the violent conflicts of the present day.

Articles

Dickerson, Marla. "Location, Raw Materials Are Draws. Indian Firms Look to Latin America." *Houston Chronicle,* June 20, 2007, p. 6. Marla Dickerson writes that the relatively small $7 billion India now invests in Latin America is figured to double in the next five years. Indian manufacturing firms, accustomed to catering to low-income consumers at home, are finding Latin America a natural market.

———. "Latin America Lures Investors from India; Similarities in Consumer Bases Help Make the Region a Natural Market." *Los Angeles Times,* June 9, 2007, p. C1. This article tells how Indian companies are helping to develop Latin America's human resources by sharing technology and employing chemists, engineers, and programmers. This is boosting the nation's standing among the region's leaders.

Fukuyama, Francis. "A Quiet Revolution." *Foreign Affairs,* November/December 2007. In his review of Michael Reid's *Forgotten Continent,* Fukuyama writes about the ideological battle brewing in Latin America between reformist and revolutionary governments and how democratic institutions, free markets, and social programs are beginning to thrive in parts of Brazil, Colombia, Chile, and Mexico.

Gray, Kevin. "The Banana War." *Portfolio.com.* (October 2007). Available online. URL: http://www.portfolio.com/news.markets/international-news/portfolio/2007/09/17/Chiquita-Deat h-Squads. Accessed September 8, 2008.

———. "The Banana War in Portfolio." October 2007 Kevin Gray here asserts that there is a connection between bananas and terrorism in this story about fruit giant Chiquita, which has allegedly funded Colombian terrorists thought to be responsible for thousands of deaths. His investigation also links company executives to the American government, who indirectly paid guerrilla fighters, ostensibly out of fear.

Klein, Naomi. "Latin America's Shock Resistance." *Nation,* November 26, 2007. In this survey of Latin American politics, Naomi Klein describes how many nations have been distancing themselves from the United States—from the closing down of U.S. military bases to the nationalization of major industries.

Padgett, Tim. "Latin America's Peculiar New Strength." *Time,* November 26, 2007. Tim Padgett looks at the growing regions of Argentina, Brazil, and Chile, each of which is run by a socialist president. Padgett describes the recent economic successes of each country, which he attributes to following prudent fiscal policies.

Portes, Alejandro. "The Fence to Nowhere." *American Prospect,* October 2007. Alejandro Portes makes a case for migrant workers to be able to make a legal living in the United States. Denouncing the immigration position of the cultural Right, he says that the border fence promotes crime and will force workers from Mexico to return and face the poverty of their homelands.

THE ISLAMIC WORLD

Books

Abraham, A. J. *Islamic Fundamentalism and the Doctrine of Jihad.* Lima, Ohio: Wyndham Hall Press, 2002. This study is a sympathetic discussion of the theory of Islamic fundamentalism and the doctrine of jihad and its place in both Sunni and Shii Islam.

Byman, Daniel L., and Matthew C. Waxman. *Confronting Iraq: U.S. Policy and the Use of Force since the Gulf War.* Santa Monica, Calif.: RAND, 2000. Daniel Byman and Matthew Waxman here analyze the United States's attempts to coerce Iraq, dating back to Desert Storm. The authors point out that, at the time the book was written, although Iraq remained hostile to the United States, Baghdad repeatedly compromised, and at times caved, in response to U.S. pressure and threats.

Davidson, Lawrence. *Islamic Fundamentalism: An Introduction.* Westport, Conn.: Greenwood Press, 2002. In this collection of essays, biographical portraits, and primary documents, Lawrence Davidson explains the history of Islamic fundamentalism, identifying its adherents throughout history, and analyzing what the fundamentalists believe and what they want.

Everest, Larry. *Oil, Power and Empire: Iraq and the U.S. Global Agenda.* Monroe, Maine: Common Courage Press, 2004. Larry Everest, a correspondent for the *Revolutionary Worker* newspaper who has reported from Iran, the West Bank, Gaza, India, and Iraq, examines George W. Bush's agenda behind his desire to topple Saddam Hussein—whether it was motivated by Saddam's acquisition of biological and other weapons of mass destruction or if it was George Jr.'s desire for revenge for the attempted assassination of his father.

Hollis, Rosemary, ed. *Managing New Developments in the Gulf.* London: Royal Institute of International Affairs, 2001. This book depicts how regional political dynamics are determining the energy scene in the Persian Gulf. Hollis explains the difficulties of market management in unstable regions such as the Middle East. She asserts that the United States, in the name of protecting the free flow of oil, is now so entrenched in the security arrangements of the Persian Gulf that it has become as much a local as an external actor, and is likely to remain so as long as Iraq is considered a threat.

Milton-Edwards, Beverley. *Islamic Fundamentalism since 1945.* London: Routledge, 2005. This book provides a historical overview of Islamic fundamentalism, putting it in a global context, with debates about issues such as the effects of colonialism on Islam, secularism, and the Islamic reaction.

Mohaddessin, Mohammad. *Islamic Fundamentalism: The New Global Threat.* Washington, D.C.: Seven Locks Press, 2001. Tracing the history of Islamic fundamentalism throughout history, Mohammad Mohaddessin argues that Iran's version of the religion distorts the basic tenets of Islam. The author also writes about specific terrorist acts carried out by Iran and the devastating effects Iran's leaders have had on their nation's social order and how they have spread their radical philosophy into Asia, North Africa, and the eastern Mediterranean.

Sidahmed, Abdel Salam, and Anoushiravan Ehteshami, eds. *Islamic Fundamentalism.* Boulder, Colo.: Westview Press, 1996. This book analyzes the rise of Islamic and fundamentalist movements, examining the various manifestations they take and evaluating their influence in the emerging post–cold war order.

Spencer, William. *Islamic Fundamentalism in the Modern World.* Rookfield, Conn.: Millbrook Press, 1995. This is an overview of the influence of militant Islam on our global society. Covered here are the tenets of Islam and the general nature of religious fundamentalism. Additional topics include the relationship of Islam with the West; Islamic influences in the societies and governments of Egypt and Iran; Islamic fundamentalism in other countries, including Algeria and the Sudan; and speculations on the role of Islamic fundamentalism in the future of these nations and the world at large.

Thomas, Michael Tracy. *American Policy toward Israel: The Power and Limits of Beliefs.* London: Routledge, 2007. Michael Thomas here explains American support of Israel during the Reagan administration and its persistence in the first Bush administration in terms of the competition of belief systems in American society and politics. Explaining policy changes over time, Thomas provides insights into what circumstances might lead to lasting changes in this policy.

Articles

Boot, Max. "How Not to Get Out of Iraq." *Commentary,* September 2007. Max Boot examines the numerous plans offered up by politicians and pundits for how, if, and when to end the U.S. presence in Iraq. Options covered here are partition and federalism, diplomacy, and brute force.

Feldman, Noah. "Vanishing Act." *New York Times Magazine,* January 13, 2008, pp. 11–12. Feldman discusses the significance of changing American public opinion on the Iraqi situation, including the *Foreign Policy* considerations of further improving the conditions of the Islamic country.

Fuller, Graham E. "A World without Islam." *Foreign Policy,* January/February 2008. Presenting his thoughts on political Islam, Graham Fuller asks a series of rhetorical questions such as: What if Islam had never arisen in the Middle East? Would there still be violent clashes between the West and that part of the world? Answering that yes there would be, Fuller points out that history demonstrates that the conflict between East and West was driven by greed and conquest—and that religion was a subtext or pretext for invasion. He repudiates here the idea that Islam is the root of all conflict.

Gimbel, Barney. "Mission Impossible." *Foreign Affairs,* September 17, 2007. This is a profile of Paul Brinkley, a one-time Silicon Valley executive, who has spent the past year trying to put Iraqis back to work, in the belief that a person with a job is less likely to plant roadside bombs. To date he has reopened 16 factories, which employ 5,000 people.

Gorenberg, Gershom. "And the Land Was Troubled for 40 Years." *American Prospect,* 2007. Writing that Israel's occupation of the West Bank has become akin to "a chronic degenerative disease," Gershom Gorenberg says that the only cure is a negotiated peace settlement and withdrawal. Presenting his research into the immediate aftermath of the war, Gorenberg says that the present situation was nothing less than "a tragedy foretold" by the victors themselves.

Langewiesche, William. "The Mega-Bunker of Baghdadin." *Vanity Fair,* November 2007. William Langewiesche analyzes the construction project of the U.S. embassy in Baghdad, the only such project in the region that is progressing as planned. Langewiesche also looks at the design of U.S. embassies around the world, concluding that diplomats' "need for protection has limited their views at the very same time when globalization has diminished their roles."

Mandelbaum, Michael. "Democracy without America." *Foreign Affairs,* September/October 2007. Criticizing the Bush administration for its attempts to establish democracy in the Middle East, Michael Mandelbaum contends that military interventions rarely result in the establishment of democracy. He says that it is a voluntary adoption of the free-market system that tends to predict a switch toward democracy.

Mann, James. "A Shining Model of Wealth without Liberty." *Washington Post,* May 20, 2007. Mann begins this article about China's place in the world today with the lead sentence: "The Iraq war isn't over, but one thing's already clear: China won." Writing that China has a booming economy and an equally healthy dictatorship, Mann argues that this does not bode well for the spread of democracy. He suggests that the United States stop concerning itself with liberating China and start thinking of itself.

Massing, Michael. "As Iraqis See It." *New York Review of Books,* January 17, 2008. Massing presents excerpts from a blog written by Iraqi journalists that describes how the war affects Iraqis. He adds his own commentary and follow-up reporting to these excerpts, including a story about a contributor's father, who was wrongly arrested and released only after an editor petitioned General David Petraeus in person.

Packer, George. "Planning for Defeat." *New Yorker,* September 17, 2007. Packer looks at various proposals for salvaging some kind of victory—moral, military, or otherwise—from the war in Iraq. Packer writes that a hasty and complete withdrawal is likely to increase the bloodshed, but the current situation is also completely untenable. He provides a realistic overview of both the current situation and the long-term prospects for Iraq.

Riedel, Bruce. "Al Qaeda Strikes Back." *Foreign Affairs,* May/June 2007. Riedel recommends that the United States implement a phased withdrawal from Iraq and focus on eliminating al-Qaeda's leadership by strengthening Afghanistan, bringing real democracy to Pakistan, improving America's image, and addressing the Arab-Israeli conflict and India-Pakistan relations. Pointing to Al Qaeda's recent expansion, Riedel says that U.S. policy to counter terrorism needs to be reworked.

Rosen, Nir. "The Myth of the Surge." *Rolling Stone,* March 6, 2008. Rosen describes the divisive U.S. efforts to arm and train (primarily Sunni) insurgents into cooperative militias called Iraqi Security Volunteers. He addresses how American soldiers struggle with the "moral ambiguity" of essentially recruiting militants who recently were attacking U.S. troops.

Wright, Robin. "Major Powers Discuss Iran Strategy; Hope Is to Lure Nation to Talks without Overdoing Incentives." *Washington Post,* February 26, 2008, p. A12. Robin Wright describes a meeting among representatives of Britain, China, France, Germany, Russia, and the United States focused on possible new overtures, such as international help with Iran's growing narcotics crisis, deals on energy field exploitation, and support for security talks among the oil-rich Persian Gulf nations.

ASIA

Books

Brazinsky, Gregg. *Nation Building in South Korea: Koreans, Americans, and the Making of a Democracy.* Chapel Hill: University of North Carolina Press, 2007. This study of U.S.-Korean relations explains rapid economic development and democratization of South Korea. Brazinsky also examines the social and cultural interactions between Americans and South Koreans.

Brookings Northeast Asia survey. Washington, D.C.: Center for Northeast Asian Policy Studies, Brookings Institution, 2001. This collection of essays reviews the developments in northeast Asia during 2003. The book provides perspectives on the crisis on the Korean Peninsula, U.S.-China relations, Japan's international security role, Russia's role in northeast Asia, the rise of a new generation in South Korean politics, state-society relations in China, military reform in Taiwan, and politics in Indonesia.

Cronin, Patrick M., ed. *Double Trouble: Iran and North Korea as Challenges to International Security.* Westport, Conn.: Praeger Security International, 2008. The contributors to this volume examine how and why attempts to curb the nuclear programs and broader political ambitions of Iran and North Korea have failed. It also explains how both nations have managed to defy the United States, as well as other major powers and the United Nations.

DiFilippo, Anthony. *Japan's Nuclear Disarmament Policy and the U.S. Security Umbrella.* New York: Palgrave Macmillian, 2006. Anthony DiFilippo maintains that Japan's desire for nuclear abolition has been compromised by its U.S.-centered security policy. The author discusses the "struggles between cultural pacifism, emergent nationalism, and ongoing pressure from Washington" in Japan's position on nuclear disarmament.

Frieman, Wendy. *China, Arms Control and Non-Proliferation.* London: Routledge Curzon, 2004. Wendy Frieman explores the nature of Chinese military power and the regimes that have attempted to constrain it. Documented here is China's participation in international arms control in the late 20th and early 21st centuries. Distinguishing between the United States's expectations of the Chinese, Frieman suggests how to gain China's commitment and compliance in the future.

Ikenberry, John, and Chung-in Moon, eds. *United States and Northeast Asia: Debates, Issues, and New Order.* Lanham, Md.: Rowman & Littlefield, 2007. This compilation of scholarly essays provides an analysis of the emerging security terrain in northeast Asia. Explored here are the shifting power configurations represented by China's rise, Japan's quest for a normal state, North Korea's nuclear ambitions, South Korea's projection into a middle power, and U.S. strategic realignments. Also examined are anti-Americanism, the North Korean crisis, and the clash of parochial nationalisms among China, Japan, and Korea.

Kent, A. E. *Beyond Compliance: China, International Organizations, and Global Security.* Stanford, Calif.: Stanford University Press, 2007. This study of Chinese participation in international organizations argues that the record of China's international behavior since the 1970s indicates the long-term effectiveness of the multilateral system, concluding that engagement with the multilateral system is the key to the gradual socialization of rogue states.

Lasater, Martin L. *The Taiwan Issue in Sino-American Strategic Relations.* Boulder, Colo.: Westview Press, 2000. This book explains the complex policy interaction between Washington, Taipei, and Beijing in the context of their respective values, politics, strategies, and interests.

Preeg, Ernest H. *The Emerging Chinese Advanced Technology Superstate.* New York: Manufacturers Alliance and Hudson Institute, 2005. Ernest Preeg assesses the rapid development of Chinese advanced technology investment, production, and trade to emerge as a major competitor in the new global playing field in which the United States had a $36 billion trade deficit in 2004, compared to the balanced trade relationship that existed between the two countries in 1998.

Weber, Maria, ed. *Welfare, Environment, and Changing US-Chinese Relations: 21st Century Challenges in China.* Cheltenham, England: Edward Elgar Publishing, 2005. This book explains the political, economic, domestic, and foreign issues facing the United States and China over the next decades. It addresses issues such as sustainable growth, the imbalances in society deriving from growing inequalities, and environmental threats.

Wei, C. X. *Sino-American Economic Relations, 1944–1949.* Westport, Conn.: Greenwood Press, 1997. This book explores postwar U.S.-China economic relations. Based on both Chinese and English archival material, C.X. Wei looks into the reconstruction of China with American involvement during the late 1940s and the problems that led to the Nationalists' failure and the impact of American economic policy toward China during that time.

Annotated Bibliography

Articles

Bradsher, Keith, and Jad Mouawad. "China to Pass U.S. in 2009 in Emissions." *New York Times,* November 7, 2006, p. C1. This article discusses how unregulated emissions from China, India, and other developing countries are likely to account for most of the global increase in carbon dioxide emissions over the next quarter-century.

Burns, R. Nicholas. "America's Strategic Opportunity with India." *Foreign Affairs,* November/December 2007. While lauding India as an indispensable strategic partner and a responsible international stakeholder, Burns challenges the country's positions on trade barriers, global warming, military issues, and intelligence cooperation, as well as its support of Burma and Iran.

Chan, Thomas, Noel Tracy, and Zhu Wenhui. *China's Export Miracle: Origins, Results, and Prospects.* Basingstoke, England: Macmillan, 1999. The article analyzes China's transformation from a minor player to the world's 10th largest trader in the period 1978 through 1997. In particular, it examines the role played in China's economic transformation by entrepreneurs in Hong Kong, Taiwan, and Southeast Asia. The book also examines the dynamics behind Japan's increasing role in China's foreign trade in the late 1990s and the growing trade friction between China and the United States.

Chandler, Clay. "India's Firms Build Global Empires." *Foreign Affairs,* October 29, 2007. Chandler looks at the Indian conglomerates that are going global. Following the IT sector, where this evolution has already been happening, companies in the manufacturing and pharmaceutical sectors are also looking to capture overseas markets like Indonesia, Egypt, and Brazil.

The Economist. "Howling at the Moon." November 10, 2007. Discussed are the high-tech ambitions of China and India. Responding to the anxiety stemming from their rise, *The Economist* argues that these two countries lack the institutions necessary for a successful technology industry.

Goodman, Peter. "In China, Paulson's Currency Is Patience; with Expectations High, Treasury Chief Plans Go-Slow Approach in Trade Talks." *Washington Post,* September 20, 2006, p. D01. In this article, Treasury Secretary Henry M. Paulson Jr. says he will be able to persuade China's leaders to significantly raise the value of their currency, the yuan. In the American view, China's exports and its resulting trade surplus with the United States are the result of an undervalued yuan, which makes Chinese goods unfairly cheap on world markets. China's response to this charge is that it has been made a scapegoat for the decline of U.S. manufacturing.

Steinfeld, Edward S. "The Rogue That Plays by the Rules." *Washington Post,* September 2, 2007. Steinfield argues that while China does not always operate by international standards, when prompted by outside pressure, it tends to readily adopt foreign norms. Steinfeld concludes by urging America to lead the way in combating the threat of climate change and to have confidence that, while China may not lead, it's very likely to follow.

Tschang, Chi-Chu. "China Rushes Upmarket." *BusinessWeek,* September 17, 2007. Chi-Chu Tschang writes here that China's response to the problems with quality control it has experienced lately is to go upscale, with the government implementing policies designed to encourage more sophisticated manufacturing and phasing out subsidies for high-pollution industries.

Yardley, Jim. "Indian Leader in China Urges Closer Ties." *New York Times,* January 16, 2008, p. A8. According to this article, Indian leader Manmohan Singh has no ambitions to try to contain China's rise, but thinks both countries should cooperate for mutual benefit. "There is enough space for both India and China to grow and prosper while strengthening our cooperative engagement," he said.

RUSSIA AND THE FORMER SOVIET SPHERE

Books

Andrew, Jack. *Inside Putin's Russia.* Oxford: Oxford University Press, 2006. Andrew, the Moscow bureau chief of the *Financial Times,* writes about the rise of Vladimir Putin and his first term as president of Russia. Drawing on interviews with Putin himself, and with a number of the country's leading figures, as well as many ordinary Russians, Jack describes how, defying domestic and foreign expectations, the former KGB official became the most powerful man in Russia.

Bacon, Edwin, and Bettina Renz. *Securitising Russia: The Domestic Politics of Putin.* Manchester, England: Manchester University Press, 2006. The book focuses on the internal security issues common to many states in the early 21st century and places them in the particular context of Russia. It demonstrates how Putin has wrestled with terrorism, immigration, media freedom, religious pluralism, and economic globalism and argues that fears of a return to old-style authoritarianism oversimplify the complex context of contemporary Russia.

Barner-Barry, Carol, and Cynthia A. Hody. *The Politics of Change: The Transformation of the Former Soviet Union.* New York: St. Martin's Press, 1995. This book explores the political, economic, and cultural issues involved in the disintegration of the former Soviet Union and the emergence of newly independent states. It examines Russia and other post-Soviet states as they try to develop their own identities as 15 separate countries, as they try to develop their own market economies, and as they try to integrate themselves into an international system that is itself in flux.

Evangelista, Matthew. *Chechen Wars: Will Russia Go the Way of the Soviet Union?* Washington, D.C.: Brookings Institution Press, 2002. Evangelista examines the causes of the Chechen wars of 1994 and 1999 and challenges Moscow's claims that the Russian Federation was too fragile to withstand the potential loss of one rebellious republic.

Hedenskog, Jakob, ed. *Russia as a Great Power: Dimensions of Security under Putin.* New York: Routledge, 2005. This book provides a comprehensive assessment of Russia's current security situation, addressing such topics as the type of player the new Russia will be in the field of security, the essence of Russian security policy, the sources, capabilities, and priorities of the country's security policy, and its prospects for the future.

Annotated Bibliography

Herspring, Dale R., ed. *Putin's Russia: Past, Imperfect, Future Uncertain.* Lanham, Md.: Rowman & Littlefield, 2007. Distinguished scholars offer a full-scale assessment of Putin's leadership.

Hesli, Vicki L., and William M. Reisinger, eds. *1999–2000 Elections in Russia: Their Impact and Legacy.* Cambridge: Cambridge University Press, 2003. This is an analysis of Russia's 1999–2000 elections, during which the Boris Yeltsin era in Russia gave way to the leadership of Vladimir Putin.

McFaul, Michael. *Russia's Unfinished Revolution: Political Change from Gorbachev to Putin.* Ithaca, N.Y.: Cornell University Press, 2002. Michael McFaul traces Russia's tumultuous political history from Gorbachev's rise in 1985 through the 1999 resignation of Boris Yeltsin in favor of Vladimir Putin. McFaul divides his account of the post-Soviet country into three periods: the Gorbachev era (1985–91), the first Russian Republic (1991–93), and the second Russian Republic (1993–present).

Nygren, Bertil. *Rebuilding of Greater Russia: Putin's Foreign Policy towards the CIS Countries.* London: Routledge, 2008. This book describes the strategies used by Putin from 2000 onward to re-create Greater Russia, that is, a Russia that controls most of the territory of the former Soviet Union.

Politkovskaya, Anna. *A Russian Diary.* London: Harvil Secker, 2007. This is the diary of Anna Politkovskaya, the courageous Russian journalist who was gunned down in a contract killing in Moscow in fall 2006. Completed just before her death, Politkovskaya tells the story of a devastated Russia, from the parliamentary elections of December 2003 to the summer of 2005, in the aftermath of the Beslan school siege.

Pravda, Alex, ed. *Leading Russia—Putin in Perspective: Essays in Honour of Archie Brown.* Oxford: Oxford University Press, 2005. *Leading Russia* looks at Putin's rule from four perspectives. The volume considers his leadership in the context of Russia's revolutionary transformation, breakdown, consolidation, and stagnation; analyzes how normative and institutional components of democracy have fared under Putin's regime; examines the strengths and weaknesses of presidential power; and concludes with assessments of the strategic direction in which Putin is taking Russia.

Schmidtke, Oliver, and Serhy Yekelchyk. *Europe's Last Frontier?: Belarus, Moldova, and Ukraine between Russia and the European Union.* London: Palgrave Macmillan, 2007. This volume examines the foreign and domestic policies of the three former western Soviet republics of Ukraine, Belarus, and Moldova.

Shiraev, Eric, and Vladislav Zubok. *Anti-Americanism in Russia: From Stalin to Putin.* New York: Palgrave, 2000. Eric Shiraev and Vladislav Zubok analyze growing anti-Americanism in Russia. The authors investigate to what extent Russian anti-Americanism is a phenomenon of a democratic polity.

Velychenko, Stephen, ed. *Ukraine, the EU and Russia: History, Culture and International Relations (Studies in Central and Eastern Europe).* New York: Palgrave Macmillan, 2007. This book surveys the Ukrainian-EU relationship in light of the legacies of Russian rule.

Yekelchyk, Serhy. *Ukraine: Birth of a Modern Nation.* New York: Oxford University Press, 2007. This survey of Ukrainian history includes coverage of the Orange Revolution and its aftermath. It describes the construction of a modern Ukrainian nation, incorporating new Ukrainian scholarship and archival revelations of the post-communist period.

Articles

Aron, Leon. "We'll Always Have Putin." *New York Times,* October 25, 2007. Russian scholar Aron here urges the United States to reconsider its supposition that President Vladimir Putin will be content to lead the government as prime minister after the March 2008 elections.

The Economist. "The West and Russia: Speak Truth to Power." June 2, 2007. *The Economist* argues that Russia is behaving badly and that the West must develop a new policy toward Putin's government, walking the line between naïve generosity and dangerous provocation.

———. "Democracy, Soviet-style." October 4, 2007. *The Economist* writes that during his term, Putin has "crushed opposition, stripped regional governments of their autonomy, reasserted state control of Russia's energy resources and eliminated most independent media." *The Economist* suspects that—once out of office—Putin will find someone to run for president whom he can control.

———. "Leaders—Russia and the West: No Divide, No Rule." May 19, 2007. Criticizing Russia's attempts to route oil supplies to western Europe through its mainland, *The Economist* argues that it is time for EU countries to work together to regain a more powerful position in negotiations.

———. "Putin's People." August 25, 2007. Noting that three-fourths of senior Russian officials are former KGB or have ties to other security or military organizations, *The Economist* argues that Putin's government is the culmination of a quiet resurgence by the KGB.

Ignatius, Agni. "A Tsar Is Born." *Time,* December 31, 2007. Ignatius profiles *Time*'s person of the year, former Russian president Vladimir Putin, tracing his rise from St. Petersburg's slums to Russia's top office.

Matthews, Owen, and Anna Nemtsova. "War Inside the Kremlin." *Newsweek,* December 10, 2007. Following Vladimir Putin's disturbing rollback of democracy in Russia, the authors investigate the Kremlin's internal power struggle.

Meier, Andrew. "Putin's Pariah." *New York Times Magazine,* March 2, 2008. As Vladimir Putin installs Dmitry Medvedev as president of Russia and retains power behind the scenes, Edward Limonov leads the National Bolshevik Party in resistance. Limonov is a writer, populist, and nationalist who embraces all things underground and heads a coalition of mostly youths in "internecine warfare," such as hanging a 40-foot anti-Putin banner from a hotel and egging Putin's first prime minister (that's right, as in pelting with eggs). Meier's profile of this behind-the-scenes force in Russian politics is a detailed portrait of a man who symbolizes both hope for democracy and the instability of Russia.

Remnick, David. "The Tsar's Opponent." *New Yorker,* October 2007. Remnick profiles Russian chess master Garry Kasparov, who led a prominent opposition movement against former Russian president Vladimir Putin.

Sheff, David. "Garry Kasparov." *Playboy,* March 2008. Sheff interviews chess champion and Russian opposition leader, Garry Kasparov, after his release from his stint in a Russian prison for leading a protest. Kasparov recounts what he says was a crooked trial that led to his conviction and condemns Putin for degrading the Russian democracy. Kasparov also has his say about the global political landscape.

Stengel, Richard, and Adi Ignatius. "A Bible, but No Email." *Time,* December 31, 2007. In this conversation with Vladimir Putin, the Russian leader discusses geopolitics, his view of U.S. failures in Iraq, his KGB training, and American misconceptions about Russians. As for his view of gas pricing for former Soviet bloc countries, he asks "Could you come to a store in the U.S. and ask, 'Well, I'm from Canada. We Canadians are close neighbors. Give me that Chrysler at half price?'" he asks.

Thornburgh, Nathan. "In Search of Russia's Big Idea." *Time,* December 31, 2007. Thornburgh writes that Russia lost its sense of purpose after the collapse of communism and says that now it has a clear goal: to become an economic superpower.

Verini, James. "Putin's Power Grab." *Portfolio,* December 2007. This article explores how Russia's economy and prominence are tied to its energy exports and explores the implications for the country's future.

Chronology

1607

- **May 14** (O.S.[1]): Jamestown, the first permanent English settlement in America, is established by the London Company in southeast Virginia.

1620

- **December 11** (O.S.): The Plymouth Colony in Massachusetts is established by Pilgrims, a group of Puritan separatists, from England. Before disembarking from their ship, the *Mayflower,* 41 male passengers sign the Mayflower Compact, an agreement that forms the basis of the colony's government.

1630

- **March:** John Winthrop leads a Puritan migration of 900 colonists to Massachusetts Bay, where he will serve as the first governor.

1754–1763

- French and Indian War, a major European conflict (the "Seven Years' War") spreads to the French and the British possessions in North America. Each side is assisted by Native American allies.

1763

- France gave up all its territories in mainland North America, ending any foreign military threat to the British colonies there.

[1] Julian calendar date indicated by O.S. (Old Style); the Gregorian calendar in use today would place the date 10 or 11 days later.

Chronology

1774

- Continental Congress meets in Philadelphia with delegates from every one of the 13 colonies except Georgia, to demand repeal of the Intolerable Acts, a series of British punitive measures that were among causes of the American Revolution.

1776

- **July 4:** The Continental Congress endorses Thomas Jefferson's Declaration of Independence, severing the colonies' political connections to Great Britain.

1778

- The French sign a treaty of alliance with the United States that commits the French to the war on the condition that the Americans do not seek a separate peace with Britain.

1781

- **September 28–October 19:** American and French forces defeat the British at the Battle of Yorktown.

1783

- Treaty of Paris grants full independence and recognizes the borders of the new United States of America.

1787–1789

- Constitutional Convention and ratification. Federalists support the development of strong international commerce and a navy capable of protecting U.S. merchant vessels. Jeffersonians favor expansion across the vast continent that the new republic occupies.

1789

- The French Revolution begins. In the United States, Federalists distrust revolutionary France and encourage closer commercial ties to England, while Jeffersonians favor the new French republic.

1791–1801

- The Haitian Revolution creates the second independent country in the Americas. U.S. political leaders, many of them slave-owners, react to the emergence of a state borne out of a slave revolt with suspicion.

AMERICA'S ROLE IN THE WORLD

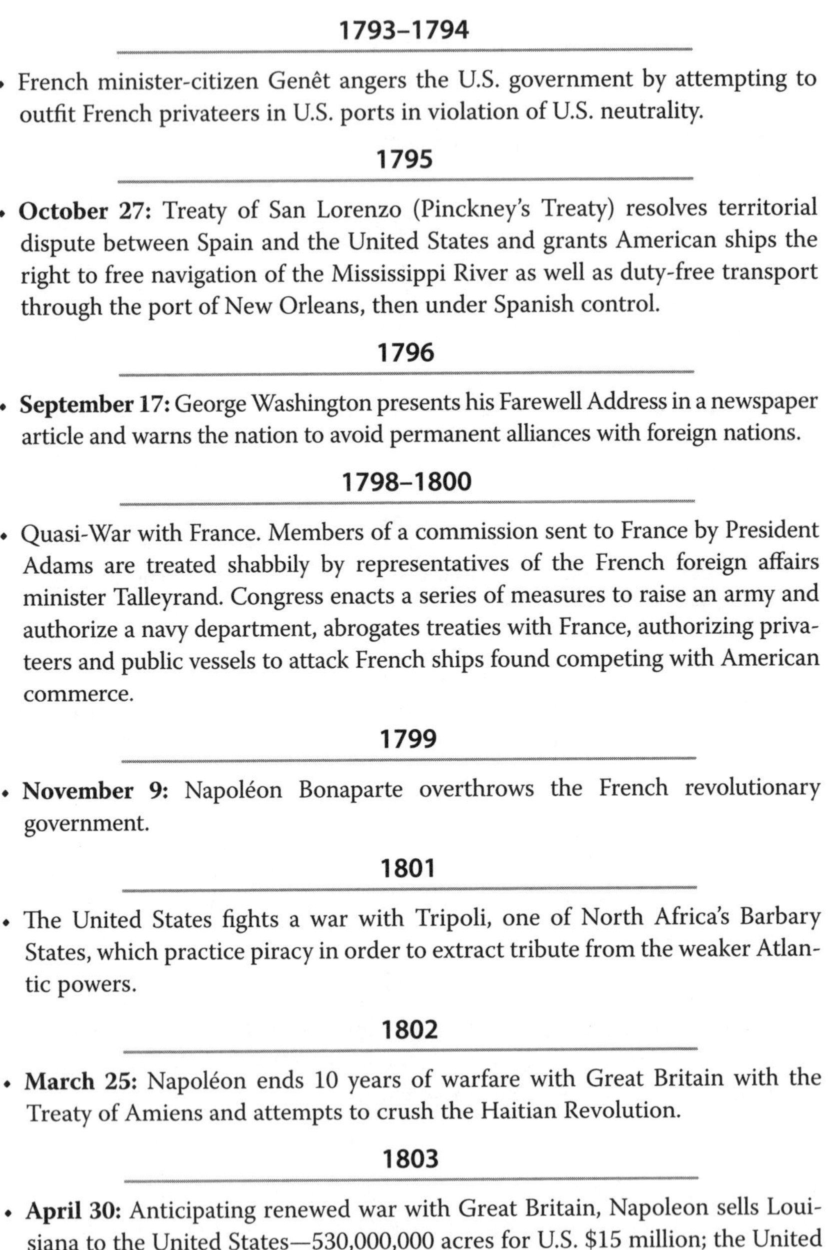

1793–1794

- French minister-citizen Genêt angers the U.S. government by attempting to outfit French privateers in U.S. ports in violation of U.S. neutrality.

1795

- **October 27:** Treaty of San Lorenzo (Pinckney's Treaty) resolves territorial dispute between Spain and the United States and grants American ships the right to free navigation of the Mississippi River as well as duty-free transport through the port of New Orleans, then under Spanish control.

1796

- **September 17:** George Washington presents his Farewell Address in a newspaper article and warns the nation to avoid permanent alliances with foreign nations.

1798–1800

- Quasi-War with France. Members of a commission sent to France by President Adams are treated shabbily by representatives of the French foreign affairs minister Talleyrand. Congress enacts a series of measures to raise an army and authorize a navy department, abrogates treaties with France, authorizing privateers and public vessels to attack French ships found competing with American commerce.

1799

- **November 9:** Napoléon Bonaparte overthrows the French revolutionary government.

1801

- The United States fights a war with Tripoli, one of North Africa's Barbary States, which practice piracy in order to extract tribute from the weaker Atlantic powers.

1802

- **March 25:** Napoléon ends 10 years of warfare with Great Britain with the Treaty of Amiens and attempts to crush the Haitian Revolution.

1803

- **April 30:** Anticipating renewed war with Great Britain, Napoleon sells Louisiana to the United States—530,000,000 acres for U.S. $15 million; the United States doubles in size.
- **May 18:** Great Britain declares war on France, marking the beginning of the Napoleonic Wars which will continue until 1815.

Chronology

1810

- American settlers in western Florida, under Spanish control, rebel, declaring independence from Spain.

1812

- The United States goes to war with Great Britain over British violations of American neutrality.

1817

- The United States and Great Britain agree to eliminate their fleets from the Great Lakes.

1818

- Convention of 1818 sets the western boundary between the United States and British North America at the 49th parallel up to the Rocky Mountains.

1819

- Spain cedes eastern Florida to the United States and renounces claims to western Florida.

1823

- **December 2:** President James Monroe's seventh annual message to Congress announces: "The American continents . . . are henceforth not to be considered as subjects for future colonization by any European powers." The statement is little noted by the Great Powers of Europe, but eventually became known as the Monroe Doctrine.

1830

- Indian Treaties and the Removal Act. U.S president Andrew Jackson persuades Congress to support a process whereby Native American tribes in the Southeast are persuaded, bribed, and threatened into agreeing to move to lands west of the Mississippi River.

1836

- American settlers in Texas fight successful war of independence from Mexico.

1842

- Anglo-Chinese Treaty of Nanjing ends the First Opium War; China, defeated in a series of naval conflicts, agrees to trade on favorable terms (including legal importation of opium by British of Indian-grown opium).

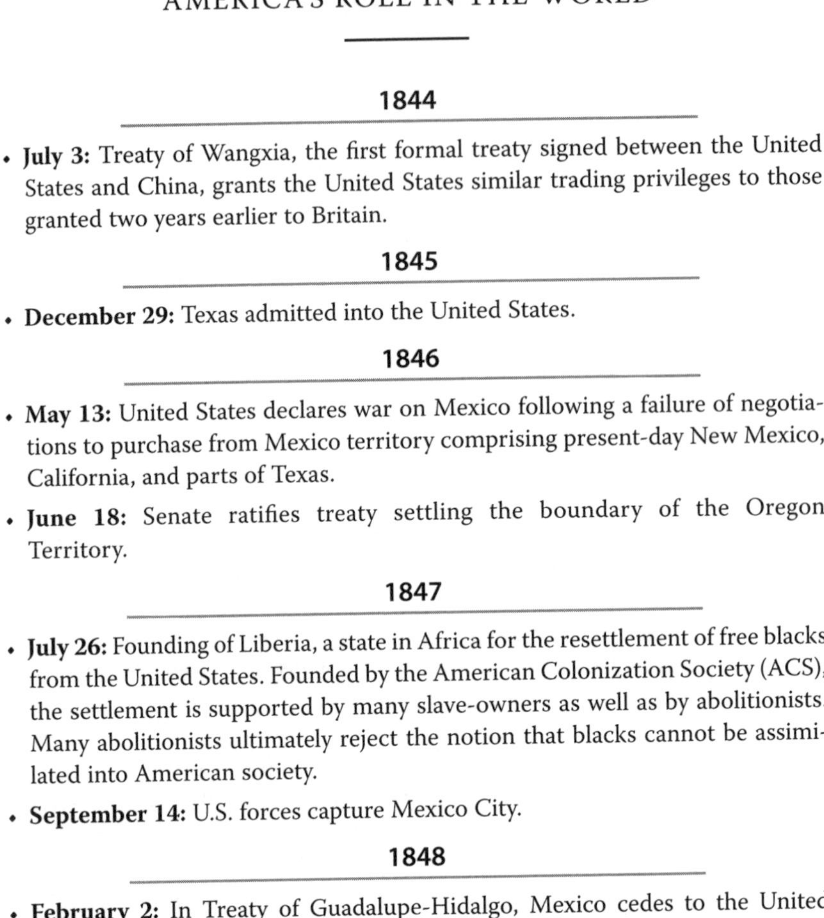

1844

- **July 3:** Treaty of Wangxia, the first formal treaty signed between the United States and China, grants the United States similar trading privileges to those granted two years earlier to Britain.

1845

- **December 29:** Texas admitted into the United States.

1846

- **May 13:** United States declares war on Mexico following a failure of negotiations to purchase from Mexico territory comprising present-day New Mexico, California, and parts of Texas.
- **June 18:** Senate ratifies treaty settling the boundary of the Oregon Territory.

1847

- **July 26:** Founding of Liberia, a state in Africa for the resettlement of free blacks from the United States. Founded by the American Colonization Society (ACS), the settlement is supported by many slave-owners as well as by abolitionists. Many abolitionists ultimately reject the notion that blacks cannot be assimilated into American society.
- **September 14:** U.S. forces capture Mexico City.

1848

- **February 2:** In Treaty of Guadalupe-Hidalgo, Mexico cedes to the United States approximately 525,000 square miles (55 percent of its prewar territory) in exchange for $15 million and the assumption by the U.S. government of all debts owed by Mexico to U.S. citizens.

1853

- **July 8:** American commodore Matthew Perry leads his four ships into the harbor at Tokyo Bay, seeking to reestablish for the first time in over 200 years regular trade and discourse between Japan and the Western world. The ships are armed, and the gifts Perry brings to show the Japanese include a working model of a steam locomotive, a telescope, and a telegraph.

1854

- Finalization of Gadsden Purchase. The United States agrees to pay Mexico $10 million for a 29,670-square-mile portion of Mexico that later becomes part of Arizona and New Mexico.

Chronology

1861

- Eleven states secede from the United States to form the Confederate States of America. Over the next four years, the Confederacy seeks international support for its cause. The Union strives to prevent other nations from recognizing the Confederacy and from getting involved in the Civil War.

1862

- The United States officially recognizes the independence of Haiti.

1866

- **July 27:** Completion of the first successful transatlantic cable revolutionizes diplomacy by putting capitals in direct electric telegraph contact with their foreign ministers.

1867

- **March 30:** United States reaches agreement with Russia to purchase Alaska for $7.2 million. This marks the end of Russian efforts to expand trade and settlements on the Pacific coast of North America and is an important step in the United States's rise as a great power in the Asia-Pacific region.

1882

- **May 6:** Chinese Exclusion Act limits future Chinese immigration to the United States. Starting in the 1850s, Chinese workers had migrated to the United States, first to work in the gold mines, later to take agricultural jobs, work in factories, and build railroads.

1890

- Captain Alfred Thayer Mahan, a lecturer in naval history and the president of the United States Naval War College, publishes *The Influence of Sea Power Upon History, 1660–1783,* a revolutionary analysis of the importance of naval power as a factor in the rise of the British Empire. Two years later, he completed a supplementary volume, *The Influence of Sea Power Upon the French Revolution and Empire, 1793–1812.* Mahan influences the imperialist policies of Japan, Germany, England, and the United States at the turn of the 20th century.

1898

- **July 7:** Spurred by the nationalism aroused by the Spanish-American War, the United States annexes Hawaii, an action that extends U.S. territory into the Pacific.

- **February 15:** Explosion sinks the battleship *Maine* in Havana harbor, and American newspapers use the occasion to demand war with Spain.
- **April 23:** War is formally declared between Spain and the United States.
- **May 1:** U.S. commodore George Dewey defeats the Spanish squadron in Manila Bay, the Philippines Islands.

1899

- **February 4:** Two days after ratification of the treaty in which Spain cedes the Philippines to the United States, fighting breaks out between American forces and Filipino nationalists led by Emilio Aguinaldo. The ensuing war lasts three years and results in the death of over 4,200 American and over 20,000 Filipino combatants. As many as 200,000 Filipino civilians die from violence, famine, and disease.

1899–1900

- Secretary of State John Hay articulates the concept of the Open Door in China in a series of notes. Hay seeks to secure international agreement to the U.S. policy of promoting equal opportunity for international trade and commerce in China and respect for China's administrative and territorial integrity.

1901

- **March 2:** U.S. Congress approves the Platt Amendment, laying down conditions to which Cuba must agree before the U.S. military occupation will end. The United States reserves the right to intervene in Cuban affairs. The Cuban government must agree to sell or lease territory for coaling and naval stations to the United States. (This clause ultimately leads to the perpetual lease by the United States of Guantánamo Bay.) The United States pressures the Cubans to incorporate the terms of the Platt Amendment into the Cuban constitution. The Platt Amendment will remain in force until 1934 when both sides agree to cancel the treaties that enforced it.

1903

- **November 3:** Panama, the part of Colombia that includes the Isthmus of Panama, declares its independence. The move had been encouraged by the United States and supported with U.S. gunboats, after Colombia rejected the terms of an American proposal for the building of the Panama Canal.

1904

- **December 6:** In his annual message, U.S. president Theodore Roosevelt asserts what becomes known as the Roosevelt Corollary to the Monroe Doctrine. He states that the United States would intervene as a last resort to ensure that other nations in the Western Hemisphere fulfil their obligations to international creditors, do not violate the rights of the United States, or invite foreign aggression. The United States might "exercise international police power in flagrant cases of such wrongdoing or impotence." As the corollary worked out in practice, the United States frequently used military force in the region.

1905

- **September 5:** The Treaty of Portsmouth formally ends the Russo-Japanese War. At the request of the Japanese, Theodore Roosevelt mediates a peace agreement. The Japanese public is dissatisfied with the terms of the treaty and protests with street demonstrations.

1909

- **December 7:** U.S. president William Howard Taft in his first annual message to Congress says, "Today, more than ever, American capital is seeking investment in foreign countries." Taft and his secretary of state Philander C. Knox follow a foreign policy that would be characterized later as "dollar diplomacy." In their view, the goal of diplomacy was to create stability and order abroad that would best promote American commercial interests. However, dollar diplomacy fails to prevent economic instability or stem the tide of revolution in Mexico, the Dominican Republic, Nicaragua, and China.

1911

- **June 6:** Adolfo Diaz, a former employee of U.S. Steel who has come to power in Nicaragua, signs the Knox-Castrillo Convention that gives the United States the right to intervene in Nicaragua to maintain order and protect American interests. The marines are sent to Nicaragua and remain there, though sometimes as a small token force, until 1933.
- **October:** A group of revolutionaries in southern China lead a successful revolt against the Qing dynasty, establishing in its place the Republic of China.

1914

- **June 28:** Archduke Franz Ferdinand of Austria-Hungary is assassinated in Sarajevo by a Bosnian member of the Black Hand, a Serbian separatist group. The assassination begins the chain of events that will lead to World War I.
- **August 15:** Panama Canal officially opened.

1915

- President Woodrow Wilson sends the U.S. Marines into Haiti, following the assassination of seven Haitian presidents in five years. The United States forces the election of a new pro-American president. A long occupation begins, during which the United States will dissolve the Haitian legislature when it refuses to accept a new constitution allowing foreign ownership of Haitian land. The occupation, characterized by racial segregation, press censorship, and forced labor, will last until 1934.

- **May 7:** German submarine sinks the British ocean liner *Lusitania*. Though the *Lusitania* carries munitions, it is primarily a passenger ship, and among the 1,201 drowned in the attack were many women and children, including 128 Americans. The Germans' strategy of unrestricted submarine warfare will eventually bring the United States into the war.

1916

- **March 9:** After the Mexican bandit and guerrilla leader Pancho Villa kills U.S. citizens in Mexico and on U.S. soil, U.S. brigadier general John J. Pershing, on President Wilson's order, crosses the Mexican border in pursuit of Villa.

1916

- **May 15:** U.S. Marines land in Santo Domingo. U.S. occupation of the Dominican Republic continues until 1924.

1917

- **January:** British cryptographers decipher a telegram from German foreign minister Arthur Zimmerman to the German minister to Mexico, von Eckardt, offering U.S. territory to Mexico in return for joining the German cause. When revealed to the United States, the message will help draw the United States into the war.
- **March 1** (O.S.) Czar Nicholas II abdicates the throne amid a spontaneous revolutionary uprising against his rule. By the time it is over, 1,300,000 Russians have been killed in battle, 4,200,000 have been wounded, and 2,417,000 have been captured.
- **April 2:** President Wilson appears before a joint session of Congress and asks for a declaration of war to make the world "safe for democracy."
- **November 6:** (October 24, in the Julian calendar used in Russia) The Bolsheviks stage a nearly bloodless coup, helped by workers and sailors. They capture the government buildings and the Winter Palace in St. Petersburg.
- **December 6:** The U.S. government breaks off diplomatic relations with Russia, where the new Bolshevik government has refused to honor debts to the United States incurred by the czarist government, ignored preexisting treaty agreements, and seized American property. The Bolsheviks also concluded a separate peace with Germany at Brest-Litovsk in March 1918, ending Russian involvement in World War I. Despite extensive commercial links between the United States and the Soviet Union throughout the 1920s, Wilson's successors will uphold his policy of not recognizing the Soviet Union.

Chronology

1918

- **January 8:** In a speech to a joint session of the U.S. Congress, Woodrow Wilson proposes the Fourteen Points, an idealistic list of U.S. war aims.

1919

- **June 28:** Germany signs the Treaty of Versailles, which imposes reparations payments on them. Though most Americans favor the treaty, it is never ratified in the United States due to opposition in the U.S. Senate, which does not want the United States to join the League of Nations.

1921

- **November–February:** The world's largest naval powers gathered in Washington for a conference to discuss naval disarmament and ways to relieve growing tensions in East Asia.

1922

- **February 9:** Congress creates the United States War Debt Commission to negotiate repayment of loans with 17 countries that borrowed money from the United States during World War I. The European debtors say the war debt forces them to demand that Germany pay its reparations though the German economy is in crisis.

1923

- **January:** A committee of the International Reparations Commission meets in Chicago to arrive at a new plan for German reparations, reducing annual payments, and to reorganize the German economy under foreign supervision. Over the next four years U.S. banks lend Germany enough money to pay the reparations and stabilize its economy.

1924

- **May 26:** Immigration Act limits the number of immigrants allowed entry into the United States through a national origins quota. The quota provides immigration visas to 2 percent of the total number of people of each nationality in the United States as of the 1890 national census. It completely excludes immigrants from Asia.

1927

- **June 20–August 4:** The United States, Great Britain, and Japan meet in Geneva to discuss making joint limitations to their naval capacities. The parties do not reach an agreement, and the naval arms race will continue unabated.

AMERICA'S ROLE IN THE WORLD

1928

- **August 27:** United States signs Kellogg-Briand Pact, an international agreement to outlaw war.
- **July 31:** Several American, British, and French oil companies strike a deal ("The Red Line Agreement") concerning the oil resources within territories that formerly comprised the Ottoman Empire in the Middle East.

1929

- **October 24:** Black Thursday is the beginning of the weeklong crash of the New York Stock Exchange that signaled the onset of the Great Depression of the 1930s. The depression becomes international in scope and will contribute to the rise of fascism in Europe.

1930

- **April 22:** The London Naval Treaty is signed after Great Britain, the United States, Japan, France, and Italy gather in London for the third in a series of five meetings that place limits on the naval capacity of the world's largest naval powers.
- **June 17:** Congress passes the Smoot-Hawley Tariff Act, a protectionist measure that, in the view of some historians, led to retaliatory tariffs by U.S. trading partners and a drastic contraction of international trade, worsening the depression.

1931

- **September 18:** A dispute near the Chinese city of Mukden (Shenyang) precipitates events that lead to the Japanese conquest of Manchuria.

1933

- **January 30:** Adolf Hitler becomes chancellor of Germany.
- **March 4:** In his inaugural address, U.S. president Franklin Delano Roosevelt announces the Good Neighbor Policy. The United States will emphasize cooperation and trade rather than military force to maintain stability in the hemisphere.
- **November 16:** The United States officially recognizes the Soviet Union.

1934

- **December 1:** In the Soviet Union, the assassination of the Leningrad Communist Party boss, Sergey Kirov, is used by Joseph Stalin as the pretext for the first of the Great Purges that will lead to the death or imprisonment of millions of Soviet citizens as the Stalinist regime liquidates any potential critics of the government.

Chronology

1935

- **August 31:** Congress passes the Neutrality Act prohibiting the export of "arms, ammunition, and implements of war" from the United States to foreign nations at war. American citizens traveling in war zones were also advised that they did so at their own risk. President Franklin D. Roosevelt originally opposed the legislation, but relented in the face of strong congressional and public opinion.

1936

- **February 29:** Congress renews the Neutrality Act until May of 1937 and prohibits Americans from extending any loans to belligerent nations.
- **July:** After the electoral victory in Spain of a government including liberals, socialists, and communists, right-wing army officers rebel, beginning the Spanish civil war.
- Congress expands on the Neutrality Act. U.S. citizens are forbidden from traveling on belligerent ships, and American merchant ships are prevented from transporting arms to belligerents. Civil wars fall under the terms of the act.

1937

- **July 7:** Chinese and Japanese forces clash on the Marco Polo Bridge near Beijing, throwing the two nations into a full-scale war. Japanese atrocities in Nanking swing U.S. popular opinion in favor of the Chinese. After the Japanese army bombs the USS *Panay* as it evacuates American citizens, killing three, the United States accepts an apology and indemnity from the Japanese. An uneasy truce will hold between the two nations until 1940.

1938

- **March 12:** German troops march into Austria to annex the German-speaking nation to the Third Reich.
- **March 18:** Mexico nationalizes the oil industry. The United States will support efforts by American companies to obtain payment for their expropriated properties but admit Mexico's right to expropriate foreign assets as long as prompt and effective compensation is provided.
- **September 30:** Germany, France, Britain, and Italy sign an agreement (the Munich Agreement) that permits German annexation of Czechoslovakia's Sudetenland. The agreement, which stripped Czechoslovakia of territory important to its defense, has become a byword for ill-advised and cowardly diplomacy, or appeasement.

1939

- **March 15:** After Slovakia, under pressure from Hitler, secedes from Czechoslovakia, Germany annexes the remainder of the country.

- **May 22:** Germany and the Soviet Union sign non-aggression pact.
- **September 1:** Germany invades Poland.
- **September 3:** Britain, France, Australia, and New Zealand declare war on Germany.
- **November 4:** The U.S. Congress passes a final Neutrality Act. The act permits limited aid under a loophole that Roosevelt has worked hard to put in the bill.

1940

- **September 2:** President Roosevelt signs a "Destroyers for Bases" agreement under which the United States gives the British more than 50 obsolete destroyers, in exchange for 99-year leases to territory in Newfoundland and the Caribbean, which will be used as U.S. air and naval bases. It is the beginning of the program known as Lend-Lease.
- **June 14:** Germans enter Paris, beginning a four-year occupation.
- **June 22:** Germany invades the Soviet Union.

1941

- **August 13:** The Atlantic Charter, a joint declaration, is released by Roosevelt and British prime minister Winston Churchill and provides a broad statement of U.S. and British war aims, though the United States is not yet officially in the war.
- **December 7:** The Japanese attacks the U.S. naval installation at Pearl Harbor, and the United States formally enters World War II.

1943

- U.S. Congress repeals the Chinese Exclusion Act.
- **November:** At a meeting in Cairo, Egypt, with Chinese leader Chiang Kai-shek, Roosevelt and Churchill agreed to a preeminent role for China in postwar Asia.
- **November–December:** Roosevelt, Churchill, and Stalin meet in Teheran (Tehran), Iran. Churchill and Roosevelt promise a cross-channel invasion of German-occupied France, and Stalin promises that the Soviets will eventually enter the war against Japan.
- **July 1–22:** Delegates from 44 nations meet in Bretton Woods, New Hampshire, to agree upon a series of new rules for the post–World War II international monetary system. The conference creates the International Monetary Fund (IMF) and the International Bank for Reconstruction and Development (IBRD).

1944

- **August–September:** U.S., British, Soviet, and Chinese representatives meet at Dumbarton Oaks in Washington to draft the charter of a postwar international organization based on the principle of collective security.

Chronology

1945

- **February:** Roosevelt, Churchill, and Stalin meet in Yalta, in the Soviet Union. Recognizing the Soviet army's strong position on the ground, Churchill and an ailing Roosevelt agree to a number of compromises with Stalin that lead to Soviet hegemony in Poland and other eastern European countries, granted territorial concessions to the Soviet Union, and outlined punitive measures against Germany.
- **April–June:** Representatives of 50 nations meet in San Francisco to complete the Charter of the United Nations.
- **July 1, 1945:** U.S., British, and French troops move into Berlin. Allied occupation of Germany will continue until 1952.
- **July:** The new U.S. president Harry Truman meets for a final "big three" wartime conference in Potsdam, Germany.
- **September 2:** General Douglas MacArthur accepts Japanese surrender on board USS *Missouri.* The Japanese constitution will be rewritten under U.S. direction and the U.S. occupation of Japan will continue until 1952.

1946

- **February 22:** George Kennan, an American diplomat at the U.S. embassy in Moscow, answers a State Department request for analysis with his Long Telegram outlining the cold war strategy of containment.
- **July 14:** United States presents Baruch Plan for control of atomic energy to the United Nations.

1947

- **March 12:** U.S. president Harry Truman asks Congress for $400 million in military assistance for Turkey and Greece. "It must be the policy of the United States to support free peoples who are resisting attempted subjugation by armed minorities or by outside pressures." The statement becomes known as the Truman Doctrine.
- **July 12:** The European Recovery Program, better known as the Marshall Plan, is established.
- **August 14:** Pakistan gets its independence when British India is dissolved. India is given its independence on the same day.

1948

- **June 24:** The Soviets cut off all surface traffic to Berlin (a city in the Soviet-zone whose occupation the four wartime allies share) and the United States responds by supplying Berlin by air. Crisis lasts till May 12, 1949.

- **May 14:** The Jewish Agency in the former British Mandate of Palestine declares the creation of the state of Israel. Truman recognizes Israel on the same day, and forces from surrounding Arab countries promptly invade Israel.

1949

- **April 4:** The North Atlantic Treaty Organization (NATO) is established, formally committing the United States to the protection of western Europe.
- **August 29:** The Soviet Union explodes an atomic bomb.
- **October 1:** Mao Zedong proclaims the founding of the People's Republic of China.
- **December 7:** Chiang Kai-shek proclaims Taipei, Taiwan, the capital of the Republic of China.

1950

- **January 11:** President Truman announces a program to develop the hydrogen bomb.
- **June 28:** Seoul, the South Korean capital, falls to the forces of North Korea. The United States is involved in a war that will last until 1953 and leave a long-term U.S. presence in South Korea.

1953

- **August 19:** Iranian prime minister Mohammed Mosaddeq is ousted in a coup directed by the CIA and British intelligence. Shah Reza Pahlavi, who had fled the country earlier that month, is restored to the throne.

1954

- **June 27:** Guatemalan president Jacobo Arbenz Guzmán resigns in the face of a CIA–supported coup d'état. Guatemala is destabilized and between 140,000 and 250,000 Guatemalans die in counterinsurgency warfare over the next four decades.
- **May 7:** Dien Bien Phu falls to the Viet Minh, bringing an end to France's attempt to hold onto Indochina. Vietnam is divided into a communist North and noncommunist South, setting the stage for U.S. involvement.
- **September 8:** South-East Asian Treaty Organization, a collective anticommunist alliance intended to resemble NATO, is founded.
- **December 2:** United States signs Mutual Defense Treaty with the Republic of China (Taiwan).

1955

- **March 14:** Soviet Union and several eastern European countries form the Warsaw Treaty Organization (Warsaw Pact).

- **February 24:** The Baghdad Pact, also known as the Central Treaty Organization (CENTO), is formed by Turkey, Iraq, Pakistan, and Great Britain, with the United States as an unofficial partner.

1956

- **February 24–25:** Khrushchev delivers secret speech to Twentieth Communist Party Congress, denouncing the late Soviet leader Joseph Stalin.
- **June 26:** Egyptian president Gamal Abdel Nasser nationalizes the Suez Canal.
- **October:** Acting on a secret agreement with Britain and France, Israel attacks Egypt as part of a plan to regain British control of the Suez Canal. Under pressure from the United States, Great Britain backs down.
- **November 3:** After Hungarian Prime Minister Imre Nagy's decision to withdraw from the Warsaw Pact, the Soviet Union invades Hungary and deposes him. Over the next five years about 2,000 Hungarians involved in the anti-Soviet movement are executed and 25,000 imprisoned.

1957

- **January 5:** In a message to Congress, U.S. president Dwight D. Eisenhower proclaims the Eisenhower doctrine: The United States promises military or economic aid to any Middle Eastern country needing help in resisting communist aggression.
- **March 25:** Formation of the European Economic Community.

1958

- **July 15:** At request of pro-Western Lebanese president Camille Chamoun, Eisenhower sends around 14,000 U.S. troops to Lebanon to quell opposition.

1959

- **January 1:** Rebels led by Fidel Castro overthrow Cuban president Fulgencio Batista.

1961

- **August 13:** The border between East and West Berlin is closed and the Berlin Wall is built.
- **April 17:** Hoping to depose Fidel Castro, 1,400 Cuban exiles launch an invasion at the Bay of Pigs on the south coast of Cuba, with U.S. air support. Everything that can go wrong goes wrong, and the invasion fails.
- **September 14:** Patrice Lumumba, Congo's first elected prime minister, is overthrown and soon afterward assassinated in prison under mysterious circumstances. The United States had suspected him of communist sympathies.

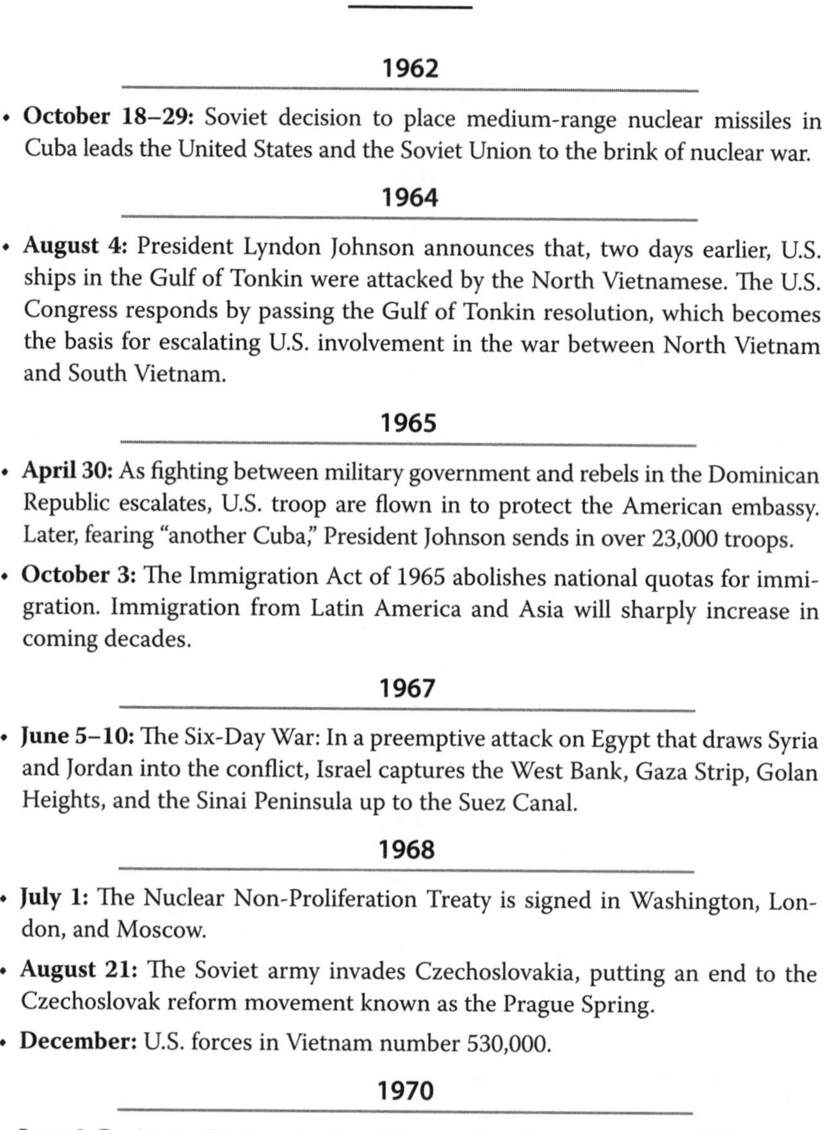

1962

- **October 18–29:** Soviet decision to place medium-range nuclear missiles in Cuba leads the United States and the Soviet Union to the brink of nuclear war.

1964

- **August 4:** President Lyndon Johnson announces that, two days earlier, U.S. ships in the Gulf of Tonkin were attacked by the North Vietnamese. The U.S. Congress responds by passing the Gulf of Tonkin resolution, which becomes the basis for escalating U.S. involvement in the war between North Vietnam and South Vietnam.

1965

- **April 30:** As fighting between military government and rebels in the Dominican Republic escalates, U.S. troop are flown in to protect the American embassy. Later, fearing "another Cuba," President Johnson sends in over 23,000 troops.
- **October 3:** The Immigration Act of 1965 abolishes national quotas for immigration. Immigration from Latin America and Asia will sharply increase in coming decades.

1967

- **June 5–10:** The Six-Day War: In a preemptive attack on Egypt that draws Syria and Jordan into the conflict, Israel captures the West Bank, Gaza Strip, Golan Heights, and the Sinai Peninsula up to the Suez Canal.

1968

- **July 1:** The Nuclear Non-Proliferation Treaty is signed in Washington, London, and Moscow.
- **August 21:** The Soviet army invades Czechoslovakia, putting an end to the Czechoslovak reform movement known as the Prague Spring.
- **December:** U.S. forces in Vietnam number 530,000.

1970

- **June 8:** Beginning Vietnamization, Nixon orders first troops out of Vietnam.
- **April 29:** U.S. troops invade Cambodia to obstruct passage of troops and supplies from North Vietnam to South Vietnam.

1971

- **July 15:** In a nationally televised surprise announcement, U.S. president Richard Nixon reveals that he will visit China in early 1972.

Chronology

1973

- **October 6:** Egypt and Syria launch a coordinated surprise attack against Israel in an attempt to regain territories Israel has occupied since the 1967 Six-Day War. Both sides suffer heavy losses, but Israel retains control of the territories. After nearly three weeks, a cease-fire is declared under pressure from the Soviets and the United States.
- **October 16-17:** Members of the Organization of Petroleum Exporting Countries announce that they will no longer ship oil to countries that support Israel in its conflict with Syria and Egypt. The OPEC oil embargo ensues and lasts until March 1974.
- **September 11:** President Salvador Allende of Chile is overthrown and dies during a military coup led by General Augusto Pinochet and supported by the United States.

1975

- **April 30:** Saigon, capital of South Vietnam, falls to North Vietnamese troops as Americans evacuate.

1979

- **February 1:** Nicaraguan dictator Anastasio Somoza Debayle, who has lost U.S. support due to his many human rights abuses, is deposed by the National Patriotic Front, a coalition of lefist insurgents and business leaders.
- **March 26:** Egyptian president Anwar Sadat, U.S. president Jimmy Carter, and Israeli prime minister Menachem Begin sign the Camp David Accords, a peace treaty between Israel and Egypt. It leaves the disposition of several important matters unsettled.
- **April 1:** Iran becomes an Islamic republic after a national referendum. Ayatollah Khomeini becomes the country's supreme spiritual leader and effectively its political leader as well.
- **May 4:** Margaret Thatcher becomes prime minister of the United Kingdom.
- **July** U.S. president Jimmy Carter secretly authorizes funding for anticommunist guerrillas in Afghanistan.
- **July 3:** President Jimmy Carter signs a directive authorizing secret aid to the opponents of the pro-Soviet regime in Afghanistan.
- **November 4:** Iranian students storm the U.S. embassy, taking 66 people hostages. They will be held until January 1981.
- **September 22:** Iraq invades Iran, beginning a long war in which over 300,000 die.

- **December 24:** Soviet Union invades Afghanistan to help prop up a Marxist government.

1981

- Claiming that Nicaragua, with help from Cuba and the Soviet Union, is providing arms to guerrillas in El Salvador, the administration of U.S. president Ronald Reagan suspends aid to the country and begins funding and training the right-wing contras.
- **February 19:** The U.S. government releases a report calling the insurgency in El Salvador "a text book case of indirect armed aggression by communist powers." Although the government of El Salvador is extremely brutal, the United States will personally direct its war against the rebels throughout the 1980s.

1982

- **June 6:** Israel invades Lebanon.
- **August 25:** U.S. Marines arrive in Lebanon as part of a "peacekeeping force" between warring Christian and Muslim factions.

1983

- **March 23:** Reagan proposes a ballistic missile defense system, which will be called the Strategic Defense Initiative. The Soviets fear the system is intended to give the United States an edge that would enable it to survive (and therefore be willing to start) a nuclear war.
- **October 23:** A suicide truck bomber kills 241 members of the U.S. peacekeeping force stationed in Beirut, Lebanon, when he crashes into the marine barracks.
- **October 25:** 5,000 U.S. troops invade the island nation of Grenada, to protect against a perceived communist threat and to protect U.S. medical students from growing unrest.

1985

- **February:** Sheik Ibrahim al-Amin issues the manifesto of Hizballah, a militant Islamic fundamentalist group based in Lebanon.
- **March 11:** The Soviet Communist Party's Politburo elects Mikhail Gorbachev general secretary of the Communist Party of the Soviet Union. Gorbachev soon embarks on a program of sweeping reforms to make Soviet society more open.

1987

- **December 8:** Reagan and Gorbachev sign the Intermediate-Range Nuclear Forces (INF) treaty, a major arms reduction treaty that prefigures the end of the cold war.

Chronology

1988

- **December:** Mikhail Gorbachev addresses the UN and declares that force "neither can nor should be the instruments of foreign policy."

1989

- **November 9:** The Berlin Wall falls.
- **December 20:** United States invades Panama to overthrow its corrupt military dictator, Manuel Noriega.

1990

- **August 2:** Iraq invades Kuwait and is condemned by United Nations Security Council Resolution 660, calling for Iraq's full withdrawal from Kuwait.
- **November 29:** United Nations Security Council Resolution 678 authorizes the states cooperating with Kuwait to use "all necessary means" to uphold UNC Resolution 660.

1991

- **January 16–17:** Operation Desert Storm, the invasion of Iraq by U.S.-led coalition forces, begins with the aerial bombing of Iraq.
- **April 3:** Soon after Iraq is pushed out of Kuwait, the United Nations Security Council passes Resolution 687, which states that Iraq must destroy its stockpile of weapons of mass destruction, its ability to produce them, and undertake not to produce WMDs in the future. International inspection teams from the UN and the International Atomic Energy Agency are assigned to documenting the destruction of Iraq's WMDs.
- **December 25:** Mikhail Gorbachev resigns as president of the USSR, declaring the office extinct and ceding all powers still vested in it to the president of Russia, Boris Yeltsin.

1992

- **March 1:** Bosnia and Herzegovina declares independence from the former Yugoslavia.
- **April 6:** War breaks out in the Bosnian city of Sarajevo; in three years of war, as Serbs massacre ethnic Bosnians in an effort to drive them from the country, the world learns of a new term, *ethnic cleansing.*
- **December:** U.S. Marines land in Somalia as part of a multinational UN mission to help people who are starving due to the country's civil war. Though lives are saved, publicity given to American casualties leads to the withdrawal of the multinational forces in October of the following year.

1993

- **February 1–8:** North Korea bars IAEA inspectors access to several facilities that are suspected to be part of the North Korean nuclear program.
- **March 12:** North Korea announces that it is withdrawing from the Nuclear Non-Proliferation Treaty (NPT).
- **January 3:** U.S. president George H. W. Bush and Russian president Boris Yeltsin sign the Strategic Arms Reduction Treaty (START II), which reduces their nations' arsenals of long-range nuclear weapons to 3,000–3,500 and eliminates all MIRV land-based missiles over the next 10 years.
- The Somalian civil war and UN Intervention, 1992–93.
- **September 13:** President Clinton, PLO chairman Yasser Arafat, and Israeli prime minister Yitzhak Rabin sign the Oslo Accords, an agreement in which each side recognizes the other's existence, which, it is hoped, will lead to peace between Palestinians and Israelis.

1994

- **January 1:** The North American Free Trade Agreement (NAFTA), a pact that calls for the gradual removal of tariffs and other trade barriers on most goods produced and sold in North America, becomes effective in Canada, Mexico, and the United States.
- **January 14:** U.S. president Bill Clinton and Russian president Boris Yeltsin announce that, by the end of May, no country will be targeted by the missiles of the United States or Russia.
- **May 10:** Nelson Mandela becomes the first black president of South Africa after three centuries of white rule.
- **October 21:** North Korea and the United States sign the "agreed framework," whereby North Korea pledges to freeze and eventually dismantle its nuclear weapons program in exchange for international aid to build two power-producing nuclear reactors.

1996

- **September 24:** China, France, the United Kingdom, Russia, and the United States all sign the Comprehensive Test Ban Treaty. India says it will not sign the treaty until the five declared nuclear weapons states commit themselves to the elimination of their nuclear weapons.

1997

- **November:** President Clinton signs Presidential Decision Directive 60 (PDD 60) on U.S. nuclear warfare policy. Under this directive, the military will no longer prepare to win a protracted nuclear war.

Chronology

1998

- UNSCOM (United Nations Special Commission) and IAEA (International Atomic Energy Agency) weapons inspectors leave Iraq, due to a lack of cooperation by Saddam Hussein's government.
- **April 6:** Pakistan announces that it has successfully test-fired a medium-range, 1,000-mile surface-to-surface missile, which is believed to be capable of carrying a nuclear warhead.
- **April 10:** The Northern Ireland and Belfast Agreement ends 30 years of fighting between Protestants and Catholics in Northern Ireland, as an outcome of talks chaired by former U.S. senator George Mitchell.
- **May 11:** India conducts three underground nuclear tests. One of the tests is a thermonuclear weapon.
- **May 13:** India conducts two more nuclear tests.
- **May 28:** Pakistan conducts five nuclear tests. Pakistan's prime minister Nawaz Sharif says, "Today we have settled the score with India."
- **August 7:** Terrorists simultaneously bomb U.S. embassies in Nairobi, Kenya, and Dar es Salaam, Tanzania, killing 258 people and wounding more than 5,000.
- **August 20:** In response to embassy bombings, the United States launches cruise missiles on an al-Qaeda training camp in Afghanistan and a pharmaceutical manufacturing facility in Khartoum, Sudan, that reportedly produced nerve gas.

1999

- **October 18:** The U.S. Senate rejects the Comprehensive Test Ban Treaty (CTBT).
- **March 24–June 10:** A U.S.-led NATO bombing campaign attacks Yugoslav targets in an effort to stop the Kosovo war.

2000

- **October 12:** A small boat explodes alongside the USS *Cole,* which is refueling in the port city of Aden, Yemen. The attack, which kills 17 sailors and wounds 39 others, is later linked to al-Qaeda.

2001

- **March 29:** On the grounds that it will hurt the U.S. economy, President George Bush renounces the Kyoto Protocol, an international agreement to halt global warming.
- **September 11:** Nineteen members of the jihadist group al-Qaeda hijack four large passenger planes simultaneously and fly them into the World Trade

Center and the Pentagon, two symbols of American power, killing nearly 3,000 people.

- **October 7:** Start of Operation Enduring Freedom, the overthrow of the Taliban regime in Afghanistan.

2002

- **January 29:** Bush labels North Korea, Iran, and Iraq an axis of evil in his State of the Union address. By seeking weapons of mass destruction, these regimes pose a grave and growing danger," he says.
- **May 6, 2002:** United States withdraws from a treaty to establish an International Criminal Court (ICC).
- **June 1:** In a speech at West Point, George W. Bush proclaims the Bush doctrine. Due to the elusive nature of terrorism, the United States must "confront the worst threats before they emerge."

2003

- **February 5:** U.S. secretary of state Colin Powell addresses the UN Security Council and presents evidence that Iraq is seeking to manufacture nuclear weapons.
- **March 7:** U.S. secretary of defense Donald Rumsfeld foresees a swift end to the Iraq War. "It could last, you know, six days, six weeks. I doubt six months."
- **March 19:** U.S.-led coalition invades Iraq.
- **May 1:** President Bush, aboard the aircraft carrier USS *Abraham Lincoln,* announces the end of major combat operations in Iraq.

2004

- **January 28:** David Kay, leader of the Iraq Survey group charged with finding weapons of mass destruction in Iraq after the invasion, reports to the Senate Arms Services Committee. "We were almost all wrong," says Kay—Iraq did not have a viable weapons program at the time of the invasion.

2005

- **March 16:** The White House releases its National Security Strategy, which reaffirms President Bush's doctrine of preemptive war.
- **May 30:** On the TV show *Larry King Live,* Vice President Dick Cheney predicts the end of fighting in Iraq: "I think they're in the last throes, if you will, of the insurgency."

2006

- **July 31:** At urging of the United States, the UN Security Council passes Resolution 1696, calling upon Iran to suspend uranium enrichment by August 31, 2006, or face sanctions.

- **December 23:** The UN Security Council passes Resolution 1737 imposing sanctions on Iran.
- **September 26:** A U.S. National Intelligence Estimate determines that the Iraq War has increased the terrorist threat to the United States.

2007

- **February 13:** U.S. secretary of state Condoleezza Rice announces that North Korea has agreed to take steps to dismantle its nuclear program, in return for an aid package from the United States.

2008

- **January 1:** Iraq Body Count, which maintains an ongoing database of documented Iraqi civilian deaths resulting from violence in Iraq, puts the number at between 81,174 and 88,585 by the end of 2007.
- **June 1:** The U.S. military announces that fatalities in Iraq in May dropped to 19, the lowest level since the war began in 2003.
- **August 7:** Outbreak of war in South Ossetia, involving Georgia, the Russian Federation, South Ossetia, and Abkhazia.
- **September 17:** The U.S. Federal Reserve lends $85 billion to American International Group (AIG) to avoid bankruptcy, amid signs of an international credit crisis and a deepening global economic recession.
- **October 17:** Iraq and the U.S. complete a draft of a security agreement that calls for all U.S. troops to be withdrawn from Iraq by the end of 2011, depending on the conditions in Iraq.

2009

- **January 20:** Barack Obama sworn in as 44th president of the United States.
- **February 10:** U.S. Secretary of State Hillary Clinton suggests that the United States might rethink plans for a missile defense shield in Europe if Iran decides against pursuing nuclear weapons.
- **February 17:** President Obama orders the deployment of an additional 12,000 U.S. troops and 5,000 support personnel to Afghanistan.

Glossary

Allies in World War I, the military alliance of Britain, France, Italy, Russia, and the United States; in World War II, the military alliance of Britain, the Soviet Union, and the United States.

American exceptionalism the view that the United States is in a special class among nations because of its dedication to freedom and democracy; it has lately been used—especially by critics of American foreign policy—to refer to the supposed view that the United States need not comply with accepted rules of international conduct.

appeasement giving into the demands of an aggressor in order to avoid war—i.e., France and Great Britain's appeasement of Germany before World War II.

Baghdad Pact (CENTO) the Central Treaty Organization, a defensive, anti-communist military alliance created in 1955 by Iraq, Pakistan, Turkey, and the United Kingdom. Within the Middle East, the Baghdad Pact was widely viewed as an attempt by the United Kingdom to regain the power it had once wielded in the region. Egyptian president Gamal Abdel Nasser, an Arab nationalist who often sought Soviet assistance, was extremely hostile to CENTO; in part through Nasser's influence, Syria and Jordan refused to join. The monarchy that the United Kingdom had installed in Iraq was overthrown in 1958 in a violent coup.

behaviorism a science that studies and analyzes human behavior without reference to mental events.

Bretton Woods System an international system of monetary management decided upon by 730 delegates from the 44 allied nations meeting at the Mount Washington Hotel in Bretton Woods, New Hampshire, during the first three weeks of July 1944. While the war was still going on in Europe, the delegates established the rules for commercial and financial relations among the world's major industrial states. The International Bank for Reconstruction and Development (IBRD) (now one of five institutions in the World

Bank Group) and the International Monetary Fund (IMF) were two institutions to emerge from the Bretton Woods conference; a third decision was to make the U.S. dollar the official international reserve currency. Though the IMF and the World Bank still exist, the Bretton Woods monetary system is usually said to have ended with the unilateral decision by the United States in 1971 to devalue the dollar, ending its direct convertability into gold.

Bush doctrine the American political doctrine, proposed by U.S. president George W. Bush in 2002 that states that, due to the possibility that rogue states may give weapons of mass destruction to terrorists, the United States cannot wait for attacks to be imminent, but must respond preemptively to emerging threats. The Bush doctrine is usually held to be a justification for preventive war, though statements of it avoid using that term.

caliph the leader of the entire Islamic community in direct succession to the prophet Mohammed. The office of the caliph was abolished by the Turkish Grand National Assembly in 1924.

CENTO *see* BAGHDAD PACT.

Central Powers the World War I military alliance of Germany, Austria-Hungary, the Ottoman Empire, and Bulgaria.

Comecon an economic organization or trading bloc of eastern European communist states similar to the European Economic Community. Comecon existed between 1949 and 1991.

communism an economic theory and political ideology that holds that all history is the history of class struggle and that promotes the establishment of a classless society based on common ownership of the means of production.

conservatism in politics, the desire to maintain, or conserve, the existing order. Conservatives value the wisdom of the past and are generally opposed to widespread reform.

containment an American foreign policy strategy aimed at stopping the spread of Soviet influence, while avoiding direct military confrontation with the Soviet Union.

cruise missile a guided missile that travels at moderate speed and low altitude.

Cultural Revolution a campaign launched in 1966 by Chinese leader Mao Zedong ostensibly in an effort to rid China of its counterrevolutionary elements and revive the class struggle; it is widely seen today as an attempt by Mao to regain control of the party from his rivals, Liu Shaoqi and Den Xiaoping, after the Great Leap Forward led to disaster. Between 1966 and 1968 Mao incited a youth militia called the Red Guards to seize control of the state and party apparatus. In the chaos and violence that ensued, many revolutionary elders, authors, artists, and religious figures were purged and killed, millions of people were persecuted, and as many as half a million people died.

Deist a person who believes in a supreme being but denies revealed religion and thus denies the divine inspiration and infallibility of the Bible.

democratic peace theory the theory in international relations that democracies do not make war upon each other. The philosopher Immanuel Kant proposed the theory in an essay "Perpetual Peace," written in 1775. Kant reasoned that the majority of people would never vote to go to war unless in self-defense. Therefore if all nations were republics, it would end war. In modern times there have been enough democracies to provide a track record for the theory, and it seems to be empirically true that democracies never, or at least very rarely, go to war with each other. The democratic peace theory was evoked by U.S. president Woodrow Wilson in an April 2, 1917, message to Congress, as he explained his reasons for asking for a declaration of war against Germany, an authoritarian state: "Cunningly contrived plans of deception or aggression, carried, it may be, from generation to generation, can be worked out and kept from the light only within the privacy of courts or behind the carefully guarded confidences of a narrow and privileged class. They are happily impossible where public opinion commands and insists upon full information concerning all the nation's affairs."

ethnic cleansing the effort to terrorize a certain ethnic or religious group to force them to leave a country by committing rape, murder, and other atrocities against its members.

euro the basic unit of the official currency of the European Union. It was established by provisions of the 1992 Maastricht Treaty on European Union drafted to further economic and monetary union, put into circulation in 2002, and by 2008 was the official currency of the European Union and 13 of its members. It is the second largest reserve currency in the world after the United States dollar and economists widely debate the possibility that it may become the first reserve currency in the near future. In September 2007, former Federal Reserve chairman Alan Greenspan said that it is "absolutely conceivable that the euro will replace the dollar as reserve currency, or will be traded as an equally important reserve currency."[1]

European Economic Community a western European trading bloc, founded in 1957 by the Treaty of Rome. From its inception it was meant not merely to stimulate trade within western Europe by knocking down trade barriers, but also as a step toward closer integration of the countries of Europe, as its preamble states, to "preserve peace and liberty and to lay the foundations of an ever closer union among the peoples of Europe." The European Economic Community is due to be completely absorbed by the European Union in 2009.

[1] "Euro could replace dollar as top currency-Greenspan," *Reuters, March 17, 2007.* Available online at http://www.reuters.com/article/bondsNews/idUSL1771147920070917.

Glossary

European Enlightenment an 18th-century western European intellectual movement committed to secular views based on reason or human understanding only.

European Union (EU) the European Union is a union of 27 independent states founded to enhance political, economic, and social cooperation.

fatwa a ruling based on Islamic scripture by a scholar of Islamic law.

Federal Reserve short for Federal Reserve Board, a group of 7 Federal Reserve Board of Governers appointed to 14-year terms by the president of the United States and approved by the Senate. The Federal Reserve Board is a part of the Federal Reserve System, established in 1913 to maintain a sound and stable banking system throughout the United States and to promote a strong economy. The Federal Reserve System, which also includes 12 Federal Reserve banks, and national and state member banks, is the central bank of the United States: it serves as a bank for other banks and for the government itself. By setting the rate at which banks will loan money to their borrowers, it affects all other rates of interest and thus restricts or loosens the amount of credit generally available in the U.S. economy.

freethinker person who forms opinions about religion on the basis of reason, independently of tradition, authority, or established belief. Freethinkers include atheists, agnostics, and rationalists.

Freudianism the psychological theories of Sigmund Freud that view human behavior and mental life as dominated by unconscious drives and desires.

Friedmanism economic theories and policies based on the ideas of the economist Milton Friedman, especially monetarism, the theory that price levels are directly related to the money supply. In recent years, thanks to Milton Friedman's own vigorious advocacy, Friedmanism has become identified with a general admiration for free-market principles and a suspicion of government intervention in the economy.

FSB the Federal Security Service of the Russian Federation, the main domestic security service of the Russian Federation, and the main successor agency of the KGB.

GDP (Gross Domestic Product) the total market value of all the final goods and services produced within a given country in a given period of time—usually a year, and when a country's GDP is given without a time period mentioned, a year is generally assumed.

globalization the ongoing integration of world culture and economy, impelled by advances in communication and transport and hastened by the lowering of government-imposed trade barriers.

Great Leap Forward a sweeping economic program by means of which the government of the People's Republic of China attempted to transform China very rapidly from an agrarian country to a modern, industrialized, communist society. The Great Leap Forward lasted from 1958 and 1960 and is acknowledged within China to have been a catastrophe. It resulted in the deaths by famine of between 14 and 43 million people.

hegemony the predominant influence, as of a state, region, or group, over another or others.

Hutu a Central African ethnic group, living mainly in Rwanda and Burundi.

ideology systematic body of concepts especially about human life or culture, especially one that constitutes a sociopolitical program.

imperialism the policy or practice of extending the power and dominion of one nation over others, whether by direct territorial acquisitions or by gaining indirect control over political or economic life.

intermediate range nuclear missiles ballistic missiles with ranges between 300 and 3,400 miles (500 and 5,500 km).

International Monetary Fund (IMF) an international organization that oversees the global financial system by observing exchange rates and balance of payments, as well as offering financial and technical assistance.

isolationism a noninterventionist foreign policy that avoids what Jefferson termed "entangling alliances" with other countries.

junta a group of persons controlling a government especially after a revolutionary seizure of power.

Keynesianism the economic theory of British economist John Maynard Keynes, which argues that a fall in national income, lack of demand for goods, and rising unemployment should be countered by increased government expenditure to stimulate the economy.

League of Nations a world organization established in 1920 to promote international cooperation and peace. It was first proposed in 1918 by President Woodrow Wilson, although the United States never joined the league. Essentially powerless, it was officially dissolved in 1946.

legitimacy in political science, the popular acceptance of a governing regime or law as an authority.

liberalism a philosophy or movement that has as its aim the development of individual freedom. Modern liberalism favors government action to redistribute wealth, reduce inequality, and enforce social justice. Classical liberalism favors limited government and jealously guards private property rights, in common with modern conservatives. The apparent confusion may derive from the success of liberalism: both modern liberals and many modern conservatives insist that their ultimate goal is to maximize human freedom.

madrassa an Islamic religious school.

Manifest Destiny the belief, current during the 19th century, that it was the destiny of the United States to expand to include the breadth of the American continent from the Atlantic to the Pacific.

Marxists those who follow the theories of 19th-century political economist Karl Marx or advocate policies based on those theories.

nationalist someone devoted to the interests of a culture or nation; someone hostile to foreign domination who wishes their country to achieve independence.

nationalization the confiscation by a government of private and especially of foreign private assets, sometimes with payment and sometimes without. Industries that are nationalized are usually major industries that involve the use of natural resources, especially energy resources.

National Security Advisor the assistant to the president for national security affairs, who serves as the chief adviser to the president of the United States on national security issues. The National Security Advisor serves on the National Security Council.

neoconservative a group of influential American political thinkers who are highly critical of modern liberalism and advocate small government in the United States and an aggressive foreign policy. Neoconservatives' ambitious plans to democratize the world distinguish them from traditional conservatives.

Neutrality Acts a series of acts passed between 1935 and 1939 by the U.S. Congress in an effort to keep the United States out of another world war.

New Europe the formerly communist nations of eastern Europe.

nuclear proliferation the spread of nuclear weapons, the increase in the number of countries that possess nuclear weapons.

Organization of American States organization formed to promote economic, military, and cultural cooperation among its members, which include almost all of the independent states of the Western Hemisphere.

Ottoman Empire a dynastic state centered in what is now Turkey, founded in the late 13th century and dismantled after World War I. At its height in the mid-1500s, the Ottoman Empire controlled a vast area extending from the Balkan Peninsula to the Middle East and North Africa.

privatization the act of removing an industry or business from governmental or public ownership or control and putting it under the control of private enterprise.

protectionism policy of protecting domestic industries against foreign competition by means of tariffs, subsidies, import quotas, or other restrictions or handicaps placed on the imports of foreign competitors.

Puritans a group of English Protestants who in the 16th and 17th centuries advocated strict religious discipline along with simplification of the ceremonies and creeds of the Church of England.

realism (in international relations) a theory that states are primarily motivated by the desire for military and economic power or security, rather than ideals or ethics; the foreign policy based on that theory.

Second Great Awakening An early 19th-century American Christian movement, which used revival meetings to help people achieve a personal experience of religious grace and salvation.

secular not overtly religious, without reference to religion.

self-determination a principle that all peoples have the right to freely determine their political status and freely pursue their economic, social, and cultural developments.

Shiism a political movement supporting Ali (cousin and son-in-law of Mohammed, the Prophet of Islam) as the rightful leader of the Islamic state. A special body of beliefs and rituals have grown up among the partisans of Ali, who are themselves divided into factions and account for between 10 and 15 percent of Muslims. Most Shiites are Twelfth-Imam Shiites, adhering to the doctrine that the Twelfth Imam, who has disappeared from view, is the only legitimate and just ruler, and therefore no political action taken in his absence can be fruitful. This belief has not prevented Twelfth-Imam Shiites from establishing an Islamic republic in Iran.

Six-Day War the war in June 1967 between Israel and the Arab states of Egypt, Jordan, and Syria. In six days, Israel conquered the Sinai Peninsula, Gaza Strip, West Bank, and Golan Heights, which became collectively known as the Occupied Territories.

Smoot-Hawley tariff U.S. legislation (June 17, 1930) that raised import duties to protect American businesses and farmers. Many historians believe that the Smoot-Hawley tariff led to retaliatory tariffs by U.S. trading partners, thus diminishing world trade and worsening the international depression.

socialism any or all of many ideologies and political movements that wish to bring about a socioeconomic system in which the community as a whole controls property and the distribution of wealth. As an economic system, socialism is often characterized by state, worker, or community ownership of the means of production. Many parties calling themselves socialist make relatively modest demands, and when in power move rather slowly in the direction of this long-term goal.

South-East Asia Treaty Organization (SEATO) an organization formed in 1954 by the United States, France, Great Britain, New Zealand, Australia, the Philippines, Thailand, and Pakistan, intended to prevent communism from gaining ground in the region.

Spanish-American War a military conflict between Spain and the United States, lasting from April 1898 until August of that same year, and culuminating in a treaty signed between the belligerents in December.

Sunni the largest denomination of Islam, representing between 85 and 90 percent of Muslims; Sunnis recognize the heirs of the first four caliphs as legitimate religious leaders of Islam; they therefore reject the body of doctrine and ritual that has sprung up around the martyred fourth caliph, Ali, and his heirs.

Taliban a Sunni fundamentalist movement that ruled most of Afghanistan from 1996 until 2001, when their leaders were overthrown by the United States in cooperation with the forces of NATO and an Afghan rebel group called the Northern Alliance.

tariff a schedule of duties or taxes imposed by a government on imported goods, usually to protect the industries and workers of the home country from foreign competition; tariffs are often imposed to implement a policy of PROTECTIONISM.

Third World the large group of nations generally considered to be underdeveloped economically during the 20th century. The word came into use during the cold war and implies a world divided into three parts—countries that belong to the West, countries that belong to the communist bloc, and countries that are part of neither, most of which also happened to be lagging in economic development. The terms *underdeveloped world* and *nonaligned nations* were also used to describe essentially the same group of countries.

trade deficit a negative balance of trade consisting of the difference between the monetary value of a country's exports and imports within a given period of time. A country that exports more than it imports has a trade surplus. A country that imports more than it exports has a trade deficit.

Treasury securities government bonds issued by the United States Department of the Treasury, available in four marketable forms—Treasury bills (T-bills), Treasury notes, Treasury bonds, and Treasury Inflation Protected Securities (TIPS). They are said to be highly liquids—it is easy to buy and sell them and many people, banks, and governments buy them from sources other than the Department of the Treasury. Treasury bills are a valued investment in countries like China and Japan, which have a large trade imbalance with the United States.

U-boat German submarine.

United Nations an international organization composed of most of the countries of the world, founded in 1945 to promote peace, security, and economic development.

Wahhabism a strict, puritanical variation of Sunni Islam that originated in Saudi Arabia.

Washington Consensus a range of economic policy prescriptions widely advocated by economists in the United States, the International Monetary Fund, and the World Bank; in the view of these institutions (all based in Washington), these policies would help stabilize crisis-wracked countries and put them on the road to rapid growth and high employment. Detractors use the term to describe a variety of free-market, antigovernment policies that are also labeled pejoratively as neoliberalism or free-market fundamentalism. In the 1990s, the Washington Consensus came under criticism by groups who argue that it is a way to open up less developed corporations for investment from large multinational corporations, without the promised benefits of steady growth and high employment.

Wilsonianism an approach to foreign policy associated with U.S. president Woodrow Wilson, combining a zeal to spread democracy, an advocacy of the principle of self-determination (that national groups should, if possible and if they choose, be self-governing), and a faith in multilateral action through representative international bodies (i.e., the League of Nations, the United Nations).

World Bank an international organization providing financing, advice, and research to developing nations to assist their economic advancement. It was founded in the late 1940s to help the countries of Europe recover from the devastation of World War II.

World Trade Organization (WTO) an international agency that encourages trade between member nations, administers global trade agreements, and resolves disputes when they arise. Established in 1995, the WTO is the only global international organization dealing with the rules of trade between nations. At its heart are the WTO agreements, negotiated and signed by the bulk of the world's trading nations and ratified in their parliaments. The goal is to help producers of goods and services, exporters, and importers conduct their business.

Index

Note: page numbers in **boldface** indicate major treatment of a subject. Page numbers followed by *f* indicate figures. Page numbers followed by *b* indicate biographical entries. Page numbers followed by *c* indicate chronology entries. Page numbers followed by *g* indicate glossary entries.

Index

Index

Index

Index